Remains of the Jews

Divinations: Rereading Late Ancient Religion

SERIES EDITORS

Daniel Boyarin, University of California, Berkeley
Virginia Burrus, Drew University
Charlotte Fonrobert, Stanford University
Robert Gregg, Stanford University

Remains of the Jews

THE HOLY LAND AND CHRISTIAN EMPIRE
IN LATE ANTIQUITY

Andrew S. Jacobs

STANFORD UNIVERSITY PRESS
STANFORD, CALIFORNIA

Stanford University Press
Stanford, California

© 2004 by the Board of Trustees of the
Leland Stanford Junior University

Printed in the United States of America
on acid-free, archival-quality paper.

Library of Congress Cataloging-in-Publication Data

Jacobs, Andrew S., 1973–
    Remains of the Jews : the holy land and Christian empire in late
antiquity / Andrew S. Jacobs.
        p.   cm. — (Divinations)
    Includes bibliographical references and index.
    ISBN 0-8047-4705-9
    1. Christianity and other religions—Judaism.
2. Judaism—Relations—Christianity. 3. Palestine—History—
Religious aspects—Judaism. 4. Palestine—History—Religious
aspects—Christianity. 5. Jews—Palestine—History—To 1500.
6. Christians—Palestine—History—To 1500. 7. Palestine—
History—70–638. 8. Palestine—Ethnic relations. 9. Rome—
History—Empire, 284-476. I. Title. II. Series.
BM535 .J26 2003
261.2'6'095694—DC21

                                                2003010165

Original printing 2004

Last figure below indicates year of this printing:
13   12   11   10   09   08   07   06   05   04

Typeset at Stanford University Press in 11/14 Adobe Garamond

for my family

.

Contents

ᗺ Abbreviations

Abbreviations of biblical books follow the standards of the *Journal of Biblical Literature*; translations from the Bible are from the New Revised Standard Version unless otherwise noted. The following abbreviations are used for citations of critical texts in the notes and bibliography (followed by volume and page numbers):

CCL Corpus Christianorum, series Latina. Turnhout: Brepols, 1954– .

CSEL Corpus scriptorum ecclesiasticorum latinorum. Vienna: Akademie Verlag, etc., 1866– .

CSCO Corpus scriptorum christianorum orientalium. Louvain: Secretariat du Corpus SCO, 1903– .

ep(p). *Epistula(e)*, Letters

FC *The Fathers of the Church: A New Translation.* Washington, D.C.: Catholic University Press, 1947– .

GCS (n.f.) Griechischen christlichen Schriftsteller (neue folge). Leipzig: J. C. Hinrichs, etc., 1899– .

LCL Loeb Classical Library. Cambridge, Mass.: Harvard University Press, 1912– .

LXX Septuagint, the Seventy

PG Patrologia Graeca. Ed. J.-P. Migne. Paris: Migne, 1857–66.

PL Patrologia Latina. Ed. J.-P. Migne. Paris: Migne, 1844–65.

SC Sources Chrétiennes. Paris: Editions du Cerf, 1943– .

TU Texte und Untersuchungen zur Geschichte der altchristlichen Literatur. Berlin: Akademie Verlag, 1883– .

⌒ Acknowledgments

This book is a revised version of my 2001 Duke University doctoral dissertation. I owe a great debt of gratitude to friends and colleagues on both coasts of North America for their invaluable assistance in transforming this project into a book. At Duke University I benefited from the guidance of my dissertation readers: Mary T. Boatwright, Dale B. Martin, Eric M. Meyers, and Annabel Wharton. My adviser, Elizabeth A. Clark, remains for me an incomparable model of scholarly diligence and generosity. I cannot begin to express how much I have learned from her and how much I continue to learn. Several colleagues at Duke University and the University of North Carolina, Chapel Hill, were tireless readers and advisers as well: Catherine M. Chin, L. Stephanie Cobb, George Demacopoulos, Gil Renberg, Tina Shepardson, and Caroline T. Schroeder. I express deep thanks to additional readers over the years who have allowed me to subject them to various permutations of the pages herein: Kalman Bland, Daniel Boyarin, Virginia Burrus, Averil Cameron, Jan Willem Drijvers, Paula Fredriksen, Christopher Frilingos, Blake Leyerle, Mark Vessey, and Susan Weingarten. I especially thank the editorial board of Divinations for their encouragement in bringing this project to light. Some parts of this book were presented to patient audiences at the American Academy of Religion/Society of Biblical Literature; the North American Patristics Society; the International Oxford Conference on Patristic Studies; the University of California, Riverside; the University of British Columbia; and Drew University. Two interinstitutional groups also read parts of the manuscript and provided helpful suggestions: the Christianity in Antiquity group (University of North Carolina–Duke University) and the joint meeting of Penates and Lares, the Southern and Northern California working groups on late ancient religion and culture.

The University of California, Riverside, provided invaluable resource assistance. I owe special thanks to Laura Nasrallah and Kim Peterson for reading through the entire manuscript and helping me tame it at last into its final shape and to Kim Lewis Brown at Stanford University Press for her tireless efforts to bring this project to light. Any remaining mistakes and infelicities are my own.

Earlier versions of some portions of this book have appeared previously in print. Part of Chapter 3 was originally published as "The Place of the Biblical Jew in the Early Christian Holy Land" in *Studia Patristica* 38 (2001): 417–42, and appears here by permission of Peeters Press (Leuven). Chapter 4 appears in revised form, reprinted from *Religion* 32, no. 3, "'The Most Beautiful Jewesses in the Land': Imperial Travel in the Early Christian Holy Land," 225–45, copyright (2002), with permission from Elsevier Science. A version of one section of Chapter 5 was published as "The Remains of the Jew: Imperial Christian Identity in the Late Ancient Holy Land" in the *Journal of Medieval and Early Modern Studies* 33, no. 1 (2003): 23–45, and appears here with the permission of Duke University Press. Finally, some of the conclusions discussed in Chapter 6 appear in a much expanded form as "The Lion and the Lamb: Reconsidering Jewish-Christian Relations in Antiquity," in *The Ways that Never Parted: Jews and Christians in Late Antiquity and the Early Middle Ages*, ed. A.H. Becker and A.Y. Reed, Texts and Studies in Ancient Judaism, 95 (Tübingen: Mohr Siebeck, 2003), 95–118.

1 ∝ Introduction: Holy Land, Empire, and Jews

> All that I desire to point out is the general principle that Life imi-
> tates Art far more than Art imitates Life. . . . Life holds the mirror
> up to Art, and either reproduces some strange type imagined by the
> painter or sculptor, or realizes in fact what has been dreamed in fic-
> tion. . . . Think of what we owe to the imitation of Christ, of what
> we owe to the imitation of Caesar.
>
> Oscar Wilde, "The Decay of Lying"

When Emperor Constantine lay dying in Nicomedia (according to his worshipful biographer, Eusebius of Caesarea), he called at last for the "seal of immortality," Christian baptism. He noted, with perhaps a twinge of regret, "I had in mind to partake of this [baptism] on the banks of the river Jordan, at one time; at that place where also the Savior is re-membered as having partaken of it, as our model [*eis hēmeteron tupon*]."[1] We can only imagine what a spectacle this baptism would have been: the first Christian emperor, who had reversed the fortunes of a minority sect actively persecuted by his imperial predecessors,[2] dressed as a catechu-men, wading into the waters of the Jordan to be baptized. Surely crowds of locals and visitors would have filed out from the holy places to watch, mindful at once of Jesus' example (*tupos*) and Constantine's fulfillment. Unprecedented prestige would have attached to the bishop fortunate enough to be entrusted with this rite of passage (perhaps Eusebius, met-ropolitan bishop of the province, spun out his own wistful fantasy here).

---

[1] Eusebius, *Vita Constantini* 4.62.2 (GCS 7:146).

[2] T. D. Barnes, *The New Empire of Diocletian and Constantine* (Cambridge, Mass.: Harvard University Press, 1982), has also noted Constantine's administrative similarities to his predeces-sors.

Not only would such an event put the seal on Constantine's membership in the Christian community, but the spectacle of Constantine imbuing the holy places with his magisterial approval and simultaneously incorporating that special sanctity into his imperial person would have emblematized the particular manner in which Christianity had begun to be implicated in the glory and majesty of the Roman Empire during Constantine's reign. This evocative intersection of imperial power, Christian piety, and the revered sites of the holy land, whether coming from Constantine himself or Eusebius's imagination, signifies more than merely deathbed fancy. It is itself the imaginative setting of Christian Empire.[3]

Before Constantine's reign the *loca sancta* of the province of Palestine had received only cursory notice from Christians of a particularly scriptural frame of mind.[4] By the time of Constantine's death, Jerusalem had been rebuilt by imperial munificence into a shining Christian center, and the first trickle of pilgrims from across the Mediterranean had started to build up into the floods of the fifth and sixth centuries.[5] The elevation of the holy land in the imagination and reverence of late ancient Christianity was not just a by-product of the intertwining of Christian religion and imperial power. The holy land itself was a prime locus for the elaboration of new modes of imperial Christianity in which a new Christian self could be fashioned and manipulated. In this book I explore how the early Christian holy land functioned as a site of the formation of explicitly Christian imperial power. Before I explain my own focus on the inscription of identity and alterity in the landscape of the Christian holy land, however, I want to consider the ways in which the holy land has been studied in modernity and the academic and religious contexts within which such studies have been conducted. My own analysis, as much as

[3]See Benedict Anderson, *Imagined Communities: Reflections on the Origin and Spread of Nationalism,* rev. ed. (London: Verso, 1991).

[4]Eusebius makes reference to individuals who visited the holy land for the explicit purpose of biblical exegesis: Melito of Sardis and Alexander, a Cappadocian bishop and friend of Origen (*Historia ecclesiastica* 4.26.14, 6.11.2 [GCS n.f. 6:368–88, 540]).

[5]For debates on when Christian pilgrimage to and veneration of the holy land "started" see E. D. Hunt, "Were There Christian Pilgrims Before Constantine?" in *Pilgrimage Explored,* ed. J. Stopford (Suffolk: York Medieval Press, 1999), 25–40; the *religionsgeschichtliche* account of Bernhard Kötting, *Peregrinatio Religiosa: Wallfahrten in der Antike und das Pilgerwesen in der alten Kirche* (Münster: Regensberg, 1950); and Robert Wilken, *The Land Called Holy: Palestine in Christian History and Thought* (New Haven, Conn.: Yale University Press, 1992), esp. 82–125.

those of my scholarly predecessors, necessarily emerges from a particular social and intellectual context.

The earliest critical historical examinations of holy land pilgrimage as a religious phenomenon emerged during the Protestant Reformation, as the critical divide between theologies of "flesh" and "spirit" took on a new urgency.[6] Protestant polemic against Catholic materialism and worldliness was honed using the scholarly tools of humanist philology and historical criticism.[7] This early apologetic historiography crystallized into the field of *Dogmengeschichte*. Such a study of the filiations of ideas and doctrines by definition set aside more material practices, such as asceticism, relic veneration, or pilgrimage, as deformations of authentic religiosity.[8] In many ways the heir to this idealist historiographic mentality, contemporary historical theological studies of the holy land and pilgrimage (when executed) tend to seek out the dogmatic motives behind such practices.[9] Central doctrinal conflicts are discerned—between flesh and spirit, mind and body, "Jerusalem above" and "Jerusalem below"—that are seen to be representative of broader theological conflicts operative in the early church. Certainly less overtly confessional and polemic than their sixteenth-century predecessors, theologically oriented approaches to holy spaces and pilgrimage often significantly nuance our understanding of doctrinal formation in early Christianity, dispelling some simplistic views of Christian spirituality in the ancient world.[10]

[6]Sabine MacCormack, "Loca Santa: The Organization of Sacred Topography in Late Antiquity," in *The Blessings of Pilgrimage,* ed. Robert Ousterhout (Urbana: University of Illinois Press, 1990), 8–31.

[7]See Pierre Maraval, "Une querelle sur les pèlerinages autour d'un texte patristique (Grégoire de Nysse, *Lettre* 2)," *Revue d'Histoire et de Philosophie Religieuse* 66 (1982): 131–46.

[8]Glen Chesnut, "A Century of Patristic Studies, 1888–1988," in *A Century of Church History: The Legacy of Philip Schaff,* ed. Henry W. Bowden (Carbondale: Southern Illinois University Press, 1988), 36–77; and Elizabeth A. Clark, "The State and Future of Historical Theology: Patristic Studies," in Clark, *Ascetic Piety and Women's Faith: Essays on Late Ancient Christianity* (Lewiston, N.Y.: Edwin Mellen Press, 1986), 3–19.

[9]Recent significant examples include Francine Cardman, "The Rhetoric of Holy Places: Palestine in the Fourth Century," *Studia Patristica* 17, no. 1 (1982): 18–25; idem, "Fourth-Century Jerusalem: Religious Geography and Christian Tradition," in *Schools of Thought in the Christian Tradition,* ed. Patrick Henry (Philadelphia, Pa.: Fortress Press, 1984), 49–64; and Peter Walker, *Holy City, Holy Places? Christian Attitudes to Jerusalem and the Holy Land in the Fourth Century* (Oxford: Clarendon Press, 1990).

[10]See, e.g., David Brakke, " 'Outside the Places, Within the Truth': Athanasius of Alexandria and the Localization of the Holy," in *Pilgrimage and Holy Space in Late Antique Egypt,* ed. David Frankfurter (Leiden: Brill, 1998), 445–81; Susanna Elm, "Perceptions of Jerusalem Pil-

Shifts in the academic study of early Christianity in the twentieth century encouraged historians outside the discipline of religious studies to investigate the holy land as well. As classicists developed an appreciation for the later Roman Empire (traditionally the period following the "high Empire," inaugurated by the reforms of Diocletian in the late third century, later dubbed "late antiquity"), the third and fourth centuries no longer seemed quite so culturally murky and uninteresting. Edward Gibbon's pronouncement that "Ausonius' poetical fame condemns the taste of his age"[11] began to give way, especially in postwar Europe and the United States, to meticulous studies of the social and economic history of the later empire.[12] This interest in the later Roman Empire led classicists to view the Christianity of fourth- and fifth-century emperors with fresh eyes, divested of Gibbonian distaste.[13] Military, political, economic, and literary history (staples of classical studies in Europe and the United States) were now seen to be fully operative in the formerly suspect arena of "late ancient Christianity." Classicists could therefore safely produce solid, reliable history from a geographical and intellectual space that had previously been the purview of beliefs. Romanists and Byzantinists of the 1970s and 1980s could mine the florid and fantastic literature of the early Christian holy land (saints' lives, monastic treatises, pilgrimage texts) for historical *realia,* details of travel conditions, or architectural innovation. Even theological debates could be studied, not in the interests of *Dogmengeschichte* but rather in order to trace out social networks and lines of imperial benefaction.[14]

grimage as Reflected in Two Early Sources on Female Pilgrimage (3rd and 4th Centuries A.D.)," *Studia Patristica* 20 (1987): 219–23.

[11] Edward Gibbon, *The History of the Decline and Fall of the Roman Empire,* bk.3, chap. 27n1 (1781; ed. David Womersley [London: Penguin, 1994], 2:19–20n1). Gibbon's legacy on the study of the late Roman Empire is eloquently portrayed in the opening essays of Peter Brown, *Society and the Holy in Late Antiquity* (Berkeley: University of California Press, 1982): "Learning and Imagination," "Gibbon's Views on Culture and Society in the Fifth and Sixth Centuries," and "In Gibbon's Shade."

[12] See Mark Vessey's historiographic overview, "The Demise of the Christian Writer and the Remaking of 'Late Antiquity': From H.-I. Marrou's Saint Augustine (1938) to Peter Brown's Holy Man (1983)," *Journal of Early Christian Studies* 6 (1998): 377–411.

[13] So a relatively large section of John F. Matthews, *Western Aristocracies and Imperial Court, A.D. 364–425* (1975; repr., Oxford: Clarendon Press, 1990), treats "Christianity and the Court" in Constantinople and Milan.

[14] The signal work is E. D. Hunt, *Holy Land Pilgrimage in the Late Roman Empire, A.D. 312–460* (Oxford: Oxford University Press, 1982).

The interest of classicists in the Christian holy land accompanies another shift in historical studies that impacted the study of early Christianity profoundly in the last decades of the twentieth century: the rise of "social historical" studies. Scholars once trained in the methods of historical theology began to study the literature of early Christianity from a decidedly untheological (although not always antitheological) perspective. When social historians turned to the holy land, they sought the interactions of real persons on the ground, not of ideas.[15] Social historians self-consciously departed from the model of historical theology and sought out new historiographic methods. The interest in the people "behind" the ideas led many scholars to turn to anthropology and the social sciences in the hopes that social scientific models could be used to spin sometimes sparse or recalcitrant historical data into rich and fruitful narratives of real lives.[16] Diverse sociological methods were applied to the phenomenon of early Christian holy land pilgrimage, as in Blake Leyerle's recent and ongoing work on the sociology of tourism and pilgrimage texts.[17]

In tandem with the interests of classicists and social historians of early Christianity, the rise of mainstream studies of Jews and Judaism in the Roman Empire added a new texture to studies of the holy land.[18] Often this Jewish historical focus resulted in explicit juxtaposition or contrast of

[15]Here the studies of Robert Wilken stand out: "Heiliges Land," in *Theologische Realenzyklopädie* (Berlin: Walter de Gruyter, 1985), 14:684–94; and *Land Called Holy*, which, despite the subtitle, *Palestine in Christian History and Thought,* is grounded as much in Christian "thinkers" as in Christian "thought."

[16]Victor Turner and Edith Turner, *Image and Pilgrimage in Christian Culture: Anthropological Perspectives* (New York: Columbia University Press, 1978). I have found only the Duke University dissertation of Joseph T. Rivers III, "Pattern and Process in Early Christian Pilgrimage" (1983), as a study that carries out an explicit, full-length application of Turner's "ritual process" anthropological method to the materials of early Christian pilgrimage to the holy land.

[17]Blake Leyerle, "Landscape as Cartography in Early Christian Pilgrimage Narrative," *Journal of the American Academy of Religion* 64 (1996): 119–43; idem, "Pilgrims to the Land: Early Christian Perceptions of the Galilee," in *Galilee Through the Centuries: Confluence of Cultures,* ed. Eric M. Meyers (Winona Lake, Ind.: Eisenbrauns, 1999), 348–53. Dr. Leyerle has informed me of her intentions to expand this work into a book-length study (personal communication).

[18]See, among others, Michael Avi-Yonah, *The Jews of Palestine* (New York: Schocken, 1976); Ze'ev Safrai, *The Missing Century: Palestine in the Fifth Century: Growth and Decline* (Leuven: Peeters, 1998); and Seth Schwartz, *Imperialism and Jewish Society, 200 B.C.E. to 640 C.E.* (Princeton, N.J.: Princeton University Press, 2001), which focuses primarily on Palestinian Jews.

Jews and Christians.[19] These new comparative studies set a great variety of source materials—literary and archaeological; Christian, Jewish, and "pagan"—on a level playing field, emphasizing the diverse nature of cultural, political, and religious interactions in late ancient Palestine. This method of social-historical comparativism, mixed in with the occasional insight from sociology or anthropology, frames most current studies of the early Christian holy land. The presence of Jews, the social and economic networking of elites, and the practice of material forms of piety have all become standard rubrics for understanding what was going on, and why, in late Roman Palestine. The holy land, once the academic jousting ground for "faith" and "works," has become a showpiece of ancient diversity and multiculturalism, not always pleasant or without difficulties but a notable space in which Jews, Christians, Samaritans, Romans, Greeks, and others existed and interacted for several centuries.[20]

My own approach is somewhat different. Although I believe the desire to find exemplary periods of multicultural détente is laudable, I fear it is not always as politically expedient as some scholars may believe. It is necessary also to take the inscription of social and political difference and inequity seriously. The holy land in which Jews and Christians interacted was, first and foremost, part of an empire.[21] The period during which this interaction occurred was the period of imperial Christianity, that is, the time during which the operations and interests of the Roman Empire dovetailed with those of the Christian church. Far from being a facile instance of Caesaropapism (the marionette-like control of state by church) or Erastianism (that is, the unscrupulous takeover of church by state), the Christian world from the reign of Constantine to Justinian was a world in which power was under constant negotiation and contention. The creation of imperial Christianity (a term to which I will return below) was a delicate and variable process, permeated and structured by language about power and dominion. Students of late antiquity have become increasingly sensitive to notions of discourse and power analysis. The im-

[19]Günter Stemberger, *Jews and Christians in the Holy Land: Palestine in the Fourth Century*, tr. Ruth Tuschling (Edinburgh: T. & T. Clark, 2000), modified from the original German version of 1987.

[20]See, e.g., Eric M. Meyers, "Early Judaism and Christianity in the Light of Archaeology," *Biblical Archaeologist* 51 (1988): 69–79, esp. 76–79, on "religious pluralism in Palestine."

[21]See the valuable insights of Schwartz, *Imperialism and Jewish Society.*

pact of Michel Foucault and other proponents of discourse analysis on early Christian studies has drawn attention to nodes of power, knowledge, and resistance.[22] Power does not only mean the brute exercise of force; it also signals the ways in which language and practices can constrain and conform, the ways in which a universe of meanings and habits shapes and constructs reality. My study of Christians and Jews in the late ancient holy land emerges out of this concern for language and power, drawing in particular on a theoretical approach that has just begun to make an impact on premodern historical studies: postcolonial criticism.[23]

Postcolonial criticism, as it has evolved in the past twenty or thirty years, began as a way of establishing political and intellectual agency for colonized persons who had been subject to the cultural domination and appropriation of political powers.[24] Edward Said's groundbreaking *Orientalism* produced an intellectual archaeology of more than a century of Western hegemony, in which the "Oriental" object was both produced and manipulated to serve the cultural interests of imperial power (power defined as political, cultural, academic, and economic).[25] Taking his cue from Foucault, Said insisted that *knowledge* and *power* created a dominant imperial reality: the Oriental subject could only be "known" and thus controlled by his or her imperial master. Travel literature, novels, and academic sources were fruitfully plumbed in *Orientalism* for traces of this "knowing" and powerful hegemony.[26]

[22] Averil Cameron, "Redrawing the Map: Early Christian Territory After Foucault," *Journal of Roman Studies* 76 (1986): 266–71; idem, *Christianity and the Rhetoric of Empire: The Development of Christian Discourse* (Berkeley: University of California Press, 1991), esp. 1–15; and Elizabeth A. Clark, "Foucault, the Fathers, and Sex," *Journal of the American Academy of Religion* 56 (1988): 619–41.

[23] I prefer the terms *postcolonial criticism* and *postcolonial studies* to *postcolonial theory*, which would imply an overarching explanatory metanarrative (as in Marxism or Freudianism). See Robert Young, *Postcolonialism: An Historical Introduction* (London: Blackwell, 2001), 64.

[24] See Ranajit Guha, "On Some Aspects of the Historiography of Colonial India," *Subaltern Studies* 1 (1982): 1–8; more recently Gyan Prakash, "Subaltern Studies as Postcolonial Criticism," *American Historical Review* 99 (1994): 1475–90; and *A Subaltern Studies Reader, 1986–1995*, ed. Ranajit Guha (Minneapolis: University of Minnesota Press, 1997).

[25] Edward Said, *Orientalism* (New York: Pantheon, 1978; reprint, with an afterword, New York: Pantheon, 1991); and idem, *Culture and Imperialism* (New York: Alfred A. Knopf, 1993). For earlier influential writings see Patrick Williams and Laura Chrisman, eds., *Colonial Discourse and Post-Colonial Theory: A Reader* (New York: Columbia University Press, 1994).

[26] Said's work has not been without criticism, on both theoretical and historical grounds; see, e.g., Ahmad Aijaz, *In Theory: Classes, Nations, Literatures* (Verso: London, 1992); and John MacKenzie, *Orientalism: History, Theory, and the Arts* (Manchester: Manchester University

Theorists following Said have moved beyond the task of exposing the authoritative discourses of imperial subjects. They have attempted to discern whether the colonial object of imperial authority (the "subaltern") can achieve voice and agency from within these imperial constructions. Gayatri Spivak's influential essay "Can the Subaltern Speak?" suggested that the subaltern constructed through discourses of imperialism has been boxed into an essentially voiceless position.[27] Some of Spivak's later essays, focusing especially on gender as a politically "colonized" space, have been more optimistic about the possibilities of recovery and intellectual intervention.[28] Homi K. Bhabha has sought out spaces of "hybridity" from which the colonized subject can "speak back" to the colonizer, by which he or she can appropriate and manipulate the voices of dominant culture at that same point at which his or her own voice has been appropriated.[29] The quest for multifaceted political agency in the postcolonial (or, to some, neocolonial) world has occupied much of the energy of postcolonial critics, moving beyond the simple binary analysis of imperial discourse that originally occupied Said.[30]

I have chosen to draw on the critical historiographic insights of postcolonial studies in order to reorient our view of the early Christian holy land and ancient Christian writings about Jews. Certainly critical engagement with the construction of the "other" is not new to historical studies of antiquity: the sociological and anthropological methods em-

---

Press, 1995). For an overview see Bart Moore-Gilbert, "Postcolonial Cultural Studies and Imperial Historiography: Problems of Interdisciplinarity," *Interventions* 1 (1999): 397–411.

[27]Gayatri Chakravorty Spivak, "Can the Subaltern Speak?" in *Marxism and the Interpretation of Culture,* ed. C. Nelson and L. Grossberg (Basingstoke: Macmillan, 1988), 271–313; it has been reprinted in Williams and Chrisman, *Colonial Discourse,* 66–111.

[28]See her later essays and writings in *The Spivak Reader: Selected Works of Gayatri Chakravorty Spivak,* ed. Donna Landry and Gerald MacLean (New York: Routledge, 1996); and Gayatri Chakravorty Spivak, *A Critique of Postcolonial Reason: Toward a History of the Vanishing Present* (Cambridge, Mass.: Harvard University Press, 1999).

[29]See Homi K. Bhabha, *The Location of Culture* (London: Routledge, 1994), esp. the essays reprinted as chapters 2–7.

[30]Said, Spivak, and Bhabha remain central figures in postcolonial theory, as Robert Young notes: "[I]t would be true to say that Said, Bhabha and Spivak constitute the Holy Trinity of colonial-discourse analysis" (*Colonial Desire: Hybridity in Theory, Culture, and Race* [London: Routledge, 1995], 163). See also Robert Young, *White Mythologies: Writing History and the West* (London: Routledge, 1990); and idem, *Postcolonialism,* which is far more ambitious than its modest title suggests; Bart Moore-Gilbert, *Postcolonial Theory: Contexts, Practices, Politics* (London: Verso, 1997); Ania Loomba, *Colonialism/Postcolonialism* (London: Routledge, 1998).

braced by social historians of early Christianity often introduced precisely this attention to constructions of identity and difference.[31] One of the main advantages of postcolonial studies over other anthropological or sociological approaches, however, is its dual emphasis on the instability and materiality of colonialist identities. Postcolonial critics resist portraying imperial and colonial discourses as static and eternal, yet they also insist on the very real material and political consequences of those discourses. Although Said was dissatisfied with the ways in which Marx had narrated the relations between East and West, he found useful the Marxist connections among cultural, political, and economic subjugation. "Orientalism" could at the same time be a literary style, an artistic aesthetic, an academic discipline, and a method of political and economic exploitation. All of these discursive modes operated together to produce a pervasive imperial regime of knowledge and control, situated in real physical and material areas. At the same time, these discourses of normative power grounded in appropriation and difference produce an inherent instability and the constant process of recolonization required to maintain imperial control. Colonizer and colonized cannot remain fixed binary subjects in the perpetually shifting contest of power and identity. Materiality and instability have remained central components of postcolonial analyses. As a method of interrogating certain types of evidence, postcolonial criticism can be usefully applied to the textual and material construction of the Christian holy land in the Constantinian and post-Constantinian periods.

For my purposes I understand postcolonial criticism to be a "distinct set of reading practices . . . preoccupied principally with analysis of cultural forms which mediate, challenge, and reflect upon the relations of domination and subordination—economic, cultural and political—between (and often within) nations, races or cultures."[32] There is some debate as to whether postcolonial criticism, like other contemporary modes of critical analysis, is applicable to premodern societies, which were not part of the web of gendered, racial, and capitalist discourses that

---

[31]See, e.g., the recent foray of sociologist of religion Rodney Stark, *The Rise of Christianity: A Sociologist Reconsiders History* (Princeton, N.J.: Princeton University Press, 1996), esp. the debatable chapters on women and Jews.

[32]Moore Gilbert, *Postcolonial Theory*, 12.

mark out modernity.[33] I contend, however, that the holy land provides a particularly rich site for the analysis of asymmetrical power relations, based not only on theological or intellectual suppositions but on the very real material and economic configuration and appropriation of "other" space. I understand the Christian holy land to be what Mary Louise Pratt has dubbed a "contact zone": a "social space . . . where disparate cultures meet, clash, and grapple with each other, often in highly asymmetrical relations of domination and subordination."[34] This dual emphasis on the material realities of a "social space" and the intellectual capacities of power and culture suggests the rewarding avenues open for this sort of analysis.

Likewise, the recent attention to the interaction of Jews and Christians in the holy land can benefit from a differently theorized historical approach. There has been a tendency to avoid explicit discussions of Christians and political power in the holy land and to imagine either a disjunctive set of communities (Jews to the left, Christians to the right) or else a variously imagined patchwork of diverse communities.[35] Although any or all of these scenarios may obtain from site to site, there has been a reticence to explore how the formation of *imperial* Christianity—that is, a form of religious identification that is explicitly associated with the regimes and structures of the Roman Empire—might create a new set of assumptions on the part of Christians and Jews.[36] From the perspective of colonial discourse analysis, we can explore how, in the construction of imperial authority in the holy land, the figure of the Jew might play the part of the colonial "subaltern": that dominated object of fear, mistrust, and envy that, through disparate forms of intellectual construction, the

---

[33]Young, *Postcolonialism*, 56, presses for a more restrictive, modern definition of "postcolonialism as a form of knowledge." But see discussions in Moore-Gilbert, *Postcolonial Theory*, 9–13, as well as the premodern postcolonial studies in *The Postcolonial Middle Ages*, ed. Jeffrey J. Cohen (New York: Saint Martin's, 2000).

[34]Mary Louise Pratt, *Imperial Eyes: Travel Writings and Transculturation* (London: Routledge, 1992), 4.

[35]See, among other recent studies, Mordechai Aviam, "Christian Galilee in the Byzantine Period," in Meyers, *Galilee*, 281–300, which argues for a "sharp borderline" (297) between Christian and Jewish settlements in Galilee.

[36]G. G. Stroumsa, " 'Vetus Israel': Les juifs dans la littérature hiérosolymitaine d'époque byzantine," *Revue de l'Histoire des Religions* 125 (1988): 115–31, invokes administrative treatment of Jews in the empire under Christian rule but ultimately reintroduces the focus on separation and mixing of Jews and Christians in the holy land.

Christian can transform into his or her own indispensable shadow.

Before embarking on such an analysis, however, some definition and delimitation are in order to make clear what I am trying to accomplish and how I am doing it.[37] First, I should clarify my use of the term *imperial* throughout this book. Since I do not take the occasion at every use of the term to explain its meaning, I pause here to lay out the range of meanings I intend to invoke. First, I am referring to the political situation of the Roman Empire in the fourth through sixth centuries: the administrative structures vested ultimate power in a single office (sometimes held by more than one individual), with (ideally) crisp and sharply defined lines of political authority radiating out from that office to lesser officeholders in different positions of local and regional command throughout the empire. Power that operates from within this web of offices and structures is imperial, that is, deriving its authority from association with or investiture from political power descending ultimately from the figure of the emperor.[38] Second, I am using the term to designate a worldview that is self-consciously expansive as opposed to restrictive: *imperial,* in this case, refers to the expansiveness of the empire in (perceived) opposition to the restrictedness of the province. In this sense an imperial view takes the perspective of Roman totality in deliberate contrast with, for instance, Palestinian provinciality. The two views—from metropolitan center and provincial periphery—are understood to be stratified, with the imperial perspective enjoying intellectual and cultural privilege.[39] Finally, I am using the term *imperial* in a cultural sense: figures may be described as acting imperially, or behaving within imperial modes of discourse, when they are implicitly drawing on forms of cultural, economic, or political authority that transcend the needs or desires of a local or sub-

---

[37]I thank the many individuals who have pressed me on these points in the course of my research, particularly Daniel Boyarin, Virginia Burrus, and Eric Meyers.

[38]This sense of imperial authority represents an ideal, of course, and existed alongside nonimperial, but increasingly associated, forms of local political authority: see Peter Brown, *Power and Persuasion in Late Antiquity: Towards a Christian Empire* (Madison: University of Wisconsin Press, 1992); Michele Renée Salzman, *The Making of a Christian Aristocracy: Social and Religious Change in the Western Roman Empire* (Cambridge, Mass.: Harvard University Press, 2002).

[39]See the essays in Simon Goldhill, ed., *Being Greek Under Rome: Cultural Identity, the Second Sophistic, and the Development of Empire* (Cambridge, U.K.: Cambridge University Press, 2001).

altern figure. Tourists traveling to the provinces, therefore, may be described as acting imperial in terms of their interaction with "locals," even without any explicit connection to the capital of the empire or to the authority of the emperor. Here the term *imperial* is deliberately at its fuzziest, suggesting attitudes and ideologies as opposed to political office or geographic origin.

Throughout this study my goal is to underscore how Christian discourse about Jews, especially and specifically the Jews of the Christian holy land, instantiated and elaborated a new mode of Christian identity, one that was explicitly and unapologetically imperial in all of the senses I have just outlined. Through this exploration of Christian imperial identity, constructed over, through, and around holy land Jews, I am also hoping to trace the intricacies and instabilities of that imperial identity, and the possibilities for (Jewish) resistance that it constructed. I am restricting the scope of my study on two fronts: textually and geographically. I am going to discuss Christian texts: texts that are produced and circulated from a deliberately Christian point of view. I rarely analyze Jewish literature as part of my colonial analysis of Christian power in the holy land, even as I focus on the place of Jews in that construction of power. A persistent question I have heard as I pursued this subject over the past several years has been, "Why don't you cite Jewish texts?" I have been brought to task for imbalance, for the unfair exclusion of authentic Jewish voices from my analysis of Christians and Jews, and for naively reinforcing the triumph of Christian Empire by giving Christians the last (if not the only) word. Such queries are entirely valid and deserve a careful response.

My focus on Christian writings about Jews is certainly not intended to suggest that Jewish literature from the period is either nonexistent or irrelevant. But the introduction of Jewish "countertexts" either to validate or refute Christian texts potentially reifies these texts as a sort of neutral evidence, to be counted or discounted, and risks glossing over the effective power of colonialist discourse. Jerome's discussions of Jewish biblical interpretations in my analysis (Chapter 3) construct positions of scholarly and cultural authority and promote a particular notion of Christian imperialism from the holy land. Many scholars before me have carefully sifted through the rabbinic corpus of literature in order to verify whether

Jerome has accurately reported authentic Jewish interpretations or perhaps misunderstood or misrepresented the Jews of Palestine (or simply lied). In such an analysis Jerome's highly charged representations of Jews as instructors and consultants, and his effective display of cultural dominance, have been obscured in favor of a comparative approach that ignores the asymmetrical power relations at work. Such an approach potentially strips Christian literature of its ideological impact, in antiquity and today.

Of course, a subtle colonialist analysis may be possible that introduces Jewish literature not as a neutral or neutralizing countertext to Christian writings but as a substantive and even subversive instance of colonial resistance. Much of postcolonial criticism, after all, has been grounded in the cultural work of the colonized. That I have not attempted such an analysis here does not obviate the possibility, or even the great value and necessity, of such a project. I have been heartened in recent years to find scholars of ancient Jewish history approaching the history of Palestinian Jewry from the perspective of colonial discourse analysis.[40] My own restriction to Christian literature is partly practical and partly theoretical. Simply put, I am not trained in the analysis of late ancient Jewish literature to the degree that I am trained in patristic literature. To claim that my familiarity with ancient Jewish history (enhanced, perhaps in an unspoken way, by my ethnic or religious background) qualifies me to speak in an authoritative or persuasive manner about the extraordinarily dense and complex web of rabbinic writings would be to suggest that ancient Judaism is, after all, easily mastered and appropriated. It is perhaps, ironically, to justify and replicate the claims of the ancient Christian authors under examination here, who took it on themselves to "speak Jewishly" in the name of producing authoritative knowledge.

Furthermore, I believe that we can learn something about Jews, Judaism, and potential Jewish resistance to Christian imperial power from the writings of Christians. It is a fundamental argument of many postcolo-

---

[40]Specifically Drs. Cynthia Baker, Steven Fine, and Hayim Lapin have been gracious enough to share their work with me. Also important are Schwartz, *Imperialism and Jewish Society*, which does not employ postcolonial analysis but nonetheless incisively details the effects of imperialism (pre-Christian and Christian) on Jewish identity; and Daniel Boyarin's forthcoming *Border Lines: Hybrids, Heretics, and the Partition of Judaeo Christianity* (Philadelphia: University of Pennsylvania Press, 2004).

nial studies, and of this book, that imperial discourse is inherently ambivalent and destabilizing. My argument throughout this study is that
Christians staked their imperial claims on a self-conscious appropriation
of Jewish space and knowledge; that is, they embedded their power and
authority in the authenticated existence of a religious, political, and cultural "other." Christian imperial discourse was henceforth split against itself, between desire and need for the Jewish other that authenticated
Christian power and its fear and anxiety generated by Jewish otherness.
The Jewish land became the holy land, authenticating Christian Empire
even as it potentially disrupted Christian identity by remaining intracta-
bly Jewish. It is through Christian writings on Jews that I believe this simultaneous construction and deconstruction of Christian imperial identity emerges:

What is theoretically innovative, and politically [and, one might add, religiously
and culturally] crucial, is the need to think beyond narratives of originary and
initial subjectivities and to focus on those moments or processes that are produced in the articulation of cultural [religious, political] differences. These "in-
between" spaces provide the terrain for elaborating strategies of selfhood—
singular or communal—that initiate new signs of identity, and innovative sites
of collaboration, and contestation, in the act of defining the idea of society itself.[41]

As imperial Christianity is elaborated, so does the potentiality for Jewish
resistance emerge from that selfsame space. My focus on Christian writings will therefore not, I suggest, ultimately affirm and reinscribe Christian triumph. Christian writers of Empire are also the writers, in a fashion, of Jewish resistance.

    A second restriction of my scope relates to the geographic specificity of
holy land Jews. Again, it is not my claim that writings about Jews from
other geographic areas cannot be illuminating in terms of the formation
of imperial Christianity. I do think, however, that the discourse of Christian imperialism made particularly notable use of the Jews of Palestine,
the Jews in their "homeland," as it were. The paradoxes of inscribing this
provincial space simultaneously as the home of ethnic religious others,

---

[41] Homi K. Bhabha, introduction to *Location of Culture*, 1–2. The bracketed words are
mine.

Judaea ("Jew-land"), and as the holiest sites of Christian sanctity, *terra* sancta, create a promising field for the elaboration and problematization of Christian imperial identity. The inscription of identity and alterity, of sameness and difference, of imperial possession and colonial dispossession, makes the Jews of Palestine a particular focus of Christian imperial energy. The Christian focus on the "contact zone" of Jewish Palestine as the holy land also makes particularly visible the instabilities of imperial identity constructed through the "other." These Jews are at once the distant relatives of those Jews who called for Christ's blood and of Christ himself (as the Jews of Nazareth playfully point out to a sixth-century Christian pilgrim). In the land that is holy-but-Jewish the Jew materializes with sharp clarity into Christian consciousness, and it is in that land that we might perhaps imagine Jews most fruitfully exploiting that piercing clarity in order to assert their own autonomy and agency in the face of rising Christian imperialism.

It is worth pausing to consider again the real material impact of the colonialist discourses I am going to explore. This was a real empire, these were real Christians, and there were real Jews whom they attempted to construct and constrain through their imperialist discourses (and who could, in turn, resist such attempts). By all accounts there were prominent Jewish communities in Palestine from the period of Constantine to Justinian (just as there were prominent Jewish communities throughout the Roman and Persian Empires).[42] Specific population numbers in the ancient world are notoriously elusive, no less for Jews than for other groups. Archaeologists have argued for prominent Jewish populations in certain sectors of Palestine, more sparse representation in others.[43] The vitality of the Jewish population in Palestine, however, should not be in question. Nor, I hasten to add, should the visible presence of Jews be of-

---

[42]See Claudine Dauphin, *La Palestine byzantine: Peuplement et populations,* 3 vols. (Oxford: Archaeopress, 1998).

[43]See the recent estimates of Stemberger, *Jews and Christians,* 17–21; and Joan E. Taylor, *Christians and the Holy Places: The Myth of Jewish-Christian Origins* (Oxford: Clarendon, 1993), 48–56; in addition to earlier discussions in Zvi U. Ma'oz, "Comments on Jewish and Christian Communities in Byzantine Palestine," *Palestine Exploration Quarterly* 117 (1985): 59–68; and Dennis Groh, "Jews and Christians in Late Roman Palestine: Towards a New Chronology," *Biblical Archaeologist* 51 (1988): 80–96. Dauphin, *La Palestine byzantine,* 1:77–225, does not attempt hard numbers so much as comparative populations and overall population growth and decline.

fered as a causal explanation for representation of Jews in Christian literature in this period, as if Christian writings on Jews were responsive and
not in themselves performing specific ideological functions. By pointing
out the material reality of the Jews in question, I am reiterating the fact
that the imperialist discourse of Christians cannot, and should not, be
dismissed as "mere rhetoric." I am reminding us of the very real consequences of imperial practice, before turning to analyze its discursive in-
scriptions. I will return on occasion to the question of consequences, effects, and disruptions of the Christian discourse of Empire in the land of
the Jews throughout this book.

A few notes on the organization of the book are in order as well. Some
of the chapters are arranged thematically. At times I take particular authors to be emblematic of certain strategies for configuring Christian imperial identities, although it is never my intention to imply that such
texts can be read only in the manner I propose here. At other times I incorporate a wide range of Christian writings under a single rubric in order to trace the prevalence of particular understandings of Christian identity. Discourses of power and resistance are diffuse, and any feigned gesture on my part toward finitude and completeness would be futile and
unsatisfying.

The study is divided into two sections. In the first section (Chapters 2
and 3) I investigate discourses of knowledge, that is, the ways in which
Christians inscribed their own appropriation and construction of imperial knowledge through, around, with, or from the Jews of the holy land.
In Chapter 2 I explore the ways in which Christian authors of the fourth
century began to construct comprehensive or "totalizing" discourses of
the Christian empire and the significant roles played by Palestinian Jews
as focal points of these totalities. In Chapter 3 I attend to the ways in
which Christians created authoritative, scholarly knowledge through the
masterful, if perilous, appropriation of the knowledge of Jews. I also look
at how these ambivalent cultural representations might open up a space
for Jews to subvert the Christian order of Jewish knowledge. The second
section (Chapters 4 and 5) examines representations of Christian power
in the holy land. Chapter 4 looks at the travel literature of Christian pilgrims, focusing on the ways they configure their encounters with "local"
Jews. In Chapter 5 I look at how the city of Jerusalem was transformed

into a site of simultaneous religious and political authority, through the benefaction of emperors and the settlements of monks, as well as the discovery and distribution of relics. The position of the Jew as materially and culturally colonized object of Christian imperial authority will be made especially clear in the writings of the holy city and in the constructions of Jewish threat and Christian conquest. Here too the internally deconstructive ambivalence of Christian imperial discourses becomes evident in the convoluted, hybrid nature of space, identity, and control. In the concluding chapter I consider how the reading of Christian texts on Jews as documents of colonial power and resistance might change the perspective from which we write the history of Jews and Christians in the Roman Empire.

PART I

Knowledge

2 ⌐ "Full Knowledge": Jews and the Totality of Christian Empire

Christian Empire and Its Comprehensive Discourse

The legalization of Christianity at the beginning of the fourth century and Emperor Constantine's attendant patronage of Christian institutions were perceived as watersheds even by contemporaries. Eusebius of Caesarea could speak, in the triumphalist final book of his *Church History*, of the end of a dark era and a "bright and clear day" dawning for Christians.[1] The crowning sign of this new day was surely the unprecedented favor of the imperial house: "Even the emperors . . . strengthened yet still more the great munificence [*megalodōreas*] from God upon us, as imperial letters came steadily unto the bishops, and honors, and monetary gifts [*chrēmatōn doseis*]."[2] Yet this "new day" of Christian favor also brought with it a new set of demands from the new imperial patron: Constantine insisted that the church respond to him "without any sort of split at all or dissension in any place."[3] In terms of the material reality of

---

[1] Eusebius, *Historia ecclesiastica* 10.1.8 (GCS n.f. 6:858).

[2] Eusebius, *Historia ecclesiastica* 10.2.2 (GCS n.f. 6:860). For a recent discussion of Constantine's motives with respect to Christianity see H. A. Drake, *Constantine and the Bishops: The Politics of Intolerance* (Baltimore, Md.: Johns Hopkins University Press, 2000).

[3] Cited by Eusebius, *Historia ecclesiastica* 10.5.20 (GCS n.f. 6:888), in Greek translation of a presumed Latin original. Similar sentiments are expressed in *Vita Constantini* 3.17–20, 60–63 (GCS 7:89–93, 112–19). On Constantine's expectations of established uniformity see T. D. Barnes, *Constantine and Eusebius* (Cambridge, Mass.: Harvard University Press, 1981), 224–44; and Drake, *Constantine and the Bishops*, esp. 193–306. On the reliability of "Constantinian" documents in Eusebius's oeuvre see A. H. M. Jones and T. C. Skeat, "Notes on the Genuine-

imperial munificence ("honors and gifts"), this was a reasonable request: he could not be expected to lavish basilicas on each and every group that claimed Christian status. Likewise, he could not be expected to bestow the material benefits newly granted to Christian clergy (most significantly recusal from the burdensome and at times crushing monetary obligations of the decurionate) to rival bishops in the same city.[4] The demands of the empire, as they entered the sphere of religious identity, were perhaps unsurprisingly comprehensive and unitary: in the words of Eusebius, just as there was "one way of religion and salvation, the doctrine of Christ," so, too, "the entire rule of the Roman Empire rests in a single emperor."[5]

This call for totality and unity in the period of Christianity from the sole reign of Constantine through the first decades of the Theodosian dynasty (roughly 325–425) was answered and modulated by new forms of Christian discourse,[6] which allowed Christians to occupy positions of social and cultural power *as* Christians, to move from the church of martyrs to the Church Triumphant. I do not mean by this to suggest a sinister or unnatural collusion between politically interested bishops and statesmen, the degenerate and irreligious "politicization" of a previously unworldly church.[7] I signal instead the various processes and strategies employed by fourth- and fifth-century Christians to understand their place in a world radically different from the one described in their most sacred literature

---

ness of the Constantinian Documents in Eusebius's *Life of Constantine,*" *Journal of Ecclesiastical History* 5 (1954): 196–200; and B. H. Warmington, "The Sources of Some Constantinian Documents in Eusebius' *Ecclesiastical History* and *Life of Constantine,*" *Studia Patristica* 18, no. 1 (1986): 93–98.

   [4]See Barnes, *Constantine and Eusebius,* 44–61. Eusebius arranged the edicts and letters of Constantine to emphasize theological unity and monetary munificence: *Historia ecclesiastica* 10.5–7 (GCS n.f. 6:883–91). See also *Vita Constantini* 3.44–61 (GCS 7:102–16).

   [5]Eusebius, *De laudibus Constantini* 16.4 (PG 20:1424A). H. A. Drake, *In Praise of Constantine: A Historical Study and New Translation of Eusebius' Tricennial Orations* (Berkeley: University of California Press, 1976), has demonstrated that the *De laudibus Constantini* is actually a combination of two separate orations, "To Constantine" and "On the Holy Sepulcher" (Drake, *In Praise of Constantine,* 30–45). For convenience I refer to the speeches in their combined form. On the politics of Christian monotheism see Erik Peterson, *Der Monotheismus als politisches Problem: Ein Beitrag zur Geschichte der politische Theologie im Imperium Romanum* (Leipzig: Jakob Hegner, 1935), 70–82.

   [6]See Averil Cameron, *Christianity and the Rhetoric of Empire: The Development of Christian Discourse* (Berkeley: University of California Press, 1991).

   [7]See Drake, *Constantine and the Bishops,* 13–27, on nineteenth- and twentieth-century historiography of Constantine and Christianization.

and history.[8] If Christians of the second and third centuries understood themselves as "suffering" subjects,[9] Christians of the fourth and fifth centuries required a new authoritative identity.

One new mode of articulating Christian identity during this period acknowledged this need for unity and stability in Constantine's new world order by refashioning the Christian world in a newly comprehensive manner. This Christian view was comprehensive in two senses of the word: *totalizing,* seeking to gather together all that existed into clear and definable intellectual and cultural categories; and *knowing,* seeking to create a cognitive mastery of all that existed in the Christian world. Historians of ideology, including those who study the later Roman Empire, have long been familiar with the notion that "totalizing discourses" characterize imperial regimes. Averil Cameron has employed the term to signify a new Christian dependence "upon the idea of absolute truth" that allows "no waver or dissent."[10] Although Cameron's focus on the combination of various discourses into a single (enforced) "Truth" is provocative, my own use of the term here derives more immediately from twentieth-century critical theory (especially Marxist theories of imperialism), through the recent elucidation of postcolonial criticism. I am describing not only a discourse that forces unity but one that seeks to know and contain everything under its imperial gaze.[11] It aims to be total in scope and in knowledge, comprehensive in vision and in control. Totalizing attempts to construct knowledge and power in the Christian empire are perhaps aptly described by David Chidester in his study of nineteenth-

---

[8]Robert Markus, *The End of Ancient Christianity* (Cambridge, U.K.: Cambridge University Press, 1990), 85–135, discusses various means by which Christians after Constantine attempted to reclaim "their own past" (85).

[9]Judith Perkins, *The Suffering Self: Pain and Narrative Representation in the Early Christian Era* (London: Routledge, 1995).

[10]Cameron, *Christianity and the Rhetoric of Empire,* 2, 57–58, 220–21. See also Theodore S. de Bruyn, "Ambivalence Within a 'Totalizing Discourse': Augustine's Sermons on the Sack of Rome," *Journal of Early Christian Studies* 1 (1993): 405–21; and Drake, *Constantine and the Bishops,* 360–61, on Cameron's use of "totalizing discourse."

[11]See Patrick Wolfe, "History and Imperialism: A Century of Theory, from Marx to Postcolonialism," *American Historical Review* 102 (1997): 388–420, esp. 407–13. "Totality" and "knowledge" combine to form, through various "scientific" discourses, an "all-encompassing phylogenetic hierarchy" (410). See also Mary Louise Pratt, *Imperial Eyes: Travel Writing and Transculturation* (London: Routledge, 1992), 24–37; Robert Young, *White Mythologies: Writing History and the West* (London: Routledge, 1990), 1–20.

century comparative religions: "The conceptual organization of human diversity into rigid, static categories was one strategy for simplifying and thereby achieving some cognitive control over the bewildering complexity of a frontier zone."[12] The Christians of Empire sought unity and normativity through such "cognitive control," creating a culture of authority and domination through processes of comprehensive "knowing."

Some notable examples of such comprehensive discourses, and the nexus of power relations constructed within them, are already familiar to students of late antiquity: the invention of Christocentric "world histories,"[13] the codification of laws by Christian emperors,[14] and the attempts of "universal" church councils to craft totalizing creeds.[15] A universe of discourses engendered different disciplinary modes for establishing normativity, working in tandem to reorganize all aspects of life under a single, totalized, imperial Christian rubric.

These processes of conceptual organization positioned Christians as knowers and controllers by construing inferior objects as to-be-known and to-be-controlled. As one colonial historian has noted: "Domination is a relationship."[16] Christians in the fourth century began creating a

[12]David Chidester, *Savage Systems: Colonialism and Comparative Religion in Southern Africa* (Charlottesville: University of Virginia Press, 1996), 21–22.

[13]See Alden A. Mosshammer, *The* Chronicle *of Eusebius and Greek Chronographic Tradition* (Lewisburg, Pa.: Bucknell University Press, 1979); William Adler, "Eusebius' *Chronicle* and Its Legacy," in *Eusebius, Christianity, and Judaism*, ed. Harold Attridge and Gohei Hata (Detroit, Mich.: Wayne State University Press, 1992), 467–91; Brian Croke, "The Origins of the Christian World Chronicle," in *History and Historians in Late Antiquity*, ed. Brian Croke and Alanna Emmet (Sydney: Pergamon Press, 1983), 116–31.

[14]The "totality" of the Theodosian and Justinianic Codes—that is, their claim to include *all* relevant laws for *all* subject peoples—distinguishes them from other, earlier legal codifications, such as the *Codex Hermogenianus* or the collections of second- and third-century jurists. See *Gesta senatus urbis Romae* 2; *Codex Theodosianus* 1.1.5. Text from Theodor Mommsen, *Theodosiani Libri XVI* (Berlin: Weidmann, 1934), 2 vols., here 1.2:1, 28–29. See also Tony Honoré, *Law in the Crisis of Empire, 379–455 A.D.: The Theodosian Dynasty and Its Quaestors* (Oxford: Clarendon Press, 1998), 1–29; Jill Harries, "Introduction: Background to the Code," in *The Theodosian Code*, ed. Jill Harries and Ian Wood (Ithaca, N.Y.: Cornell University Press, 1993), 1–16.

[15]See Barnes, *Constantine and Eusebius*, esp. 191–260; idem, *Athanasius and Constantius: Theology and Politics in the Constantinian Empire* (Cambridge, Mass.: Harvard University Press, 1993); as well as Averil Cameron, "Constantinus Christianus?" *Journal of Roman Studies* 73 (1983): 184–90. See also Gillian Clark, " 'Let Every Soul Be Subject': The Fathers and the Empire," in *Images of Empire*, ed. Loveday Alexander (Sheffield: Sheffield Academic Press, 1991), 251–75.

[16]Wolfe, "History and Imperialism," 412.

world of imperial religious authority through new relational webs of knowledge and power. Thus, a common feature of such discourses was the description of deviant others, those figures who could be "known" and thus controlled by Christian discourses: criminals, heretics, "pagans" all emerge from the web of Christian totalizing discourses. This is not to suggest that the "other" him- or herself was not a matter of concern: Christian emperors no doubt genuinely feared dissidents and criminals. Christian discourses were not mere "fantasy" or hypothetical speculation. On the contrary: these totalizing discourses framed and contextualized reality for the imperial Christian and called that reality into existence (for better and for worse, as I will discuss at the end of this chapter). As significant as the varieties of comprehensive discourse was the very process of control elucidated through "conceptual organization." In the fourth century Christianity was learning to understand itself as a knowing, powerful institution. Comprehending the exercise of power as a Christian act underscored the fact that the world now could and should be understood as a thoroughly Christian world, with every part of life subsumed within a Christian totality.

In the Constantinian and post-Constantinian holy land the figure of the Jew became a remarkably pliable object through which Christians might "think through" issues of identity and power relations through the elaboration of comprehensive discourses. The Jew ranked high among the deviant figures of Christian discourse to be "known" and thus controlled by Christians.[17] As the Christian holy land rose in prominence, it served the functions of Chidester's "frontier zone," a complex site within which we find Christian authors producing knowledge about Jews in order to construct a comprehensive vision of Christianness.

I will take three of these writers and their discursive figurations of Palestinian Jews to sample different ways of constructing Christian power in

---

[17]Jews often served in the role of "proximate other" with regard to "absolute" others (e.g., pagans). On "proximate others" see Jonathan Z. Smith, "What a Difference a Difference Makes," in *"To See Ourselves as Others See Us": Christians, Jews, "Others" in Late Antiquity,* ed. Jacob Neusner and Ernest Frerichs (Chico, Calif.: Scholars Press, 1985), 3–48. The utility of Jews to "think through" the totality of Christianity has been extended in modern scholarship as, for instance, by the missiological compilation of A. Lukyn Williams, *Adversus Judaeos: A Bird's-Eye View of Christian* Apologiae *Until the Renaissance* (Cambridge, U.K.: Cambridge University Press, 1935).

the later Roman Empire. I am not arguing that each writer uniquely represents a certain position, nor am I trying to obviate other tendencies at work in their writings. These series of texts, however, do represent the most extensive and wide-ranging attempts on the part of fourth-century Christians in and around the holy land deliberately to reconceive their world as Christian totalities, a totalizing task in which Jews featured prominently. My intention here is to open up questions of how this new comprehensive vision of Christianity informed such writings and how the Jews of the holy land functioned in such a project. I will first attend to the historicizing strategies of Eusebius of Caesarea, whose writings in the early part of the fourth century press the Jew into service for the supersessionist Christian; next, Cyril of Jerusalem, writing in the middle of the century, whose sermons post devious and diabolical Jews at the literal and figurative threshold of Christian initiation; and, finally, Epiphanius of Salamis, whose heresiological writings of the last third of the century produce the "Jewish-Christian," that liminal figure whose ambiguous threat sharpens the categorical definitions of Christian and Jew. All three of these Christian writers of Empire exploited the pliable figure of the Palestinian Jew to "think" different aspects of the Christian subject, to produce that subject as whole, knowledgeable, and powerful.

Eusebius of Caesarea: Jews in Christian History

At the beginning of the fourth century Eusebius, bishop of Caesarea and self-appointed spokesperson for the new Christian dynasty of Constantine,[18] gave new life and depth to the Pauline slogan "neither Jew nor Greek" (Galatians 3.28). In his apologetic theological treatises *Gospel Preparation* and *Gospel Demonstration* Eusebius schematized the world's populace into three "types": Jew, the nonbeliever in Christ whose time had come and passed; Greek, the irreligious believer in myth and fancy; and Christian, the culmination and supersession of the previous two

---

[18]See Eusebius, *Vita Constantini* 1.17, 3.42–48, 4.51 (GCS 7:24–25, 101–4, 141). See Averil Cameron, "Eusebius' *Vita Constantini* and the Construction of Constantine," in *Portraits: Biographical Representation in the Greek and Latin Literature of the Roman Empire*, ed. M. J. Edwards and Simon Swain (Oxford: Clarendon Press, 1997), 145–74; and the commentary in Averil Cameron and Stuart G. Hall, *Eusebius, Life of Constantine, Translated with Introduction and Commentary* (Oxford: Clarendon Press, 1999), 192–200, 294–96, 342–49.

groups, the new people chosen by God to spread the truth toward which all of time and civilization had been leading.[19] These works, produced around the beginning of the fourth century, can be seen as the climax of an apologetic literary tradition stretching back to the beginning of the second century, accomplished with a new breadth and scope.[20] In Eusebius we see the tropes of apology extended into the comprehensive foundations of a Christian world:[21] "Jew and Greek," the straw opponents of Paul or Justin Martyr or the author of the *Epistle to Diognetus,* come to delimit entire populations that must (and can) be completely known and thereby contained.[22]

The vast scope of Eusebius's explicitly apologetic work signals his comprehensive aims: the *Gospel Preparation* and *Gospel Demonstration* together comprise thirty-five books, a massive historico-theological edifice of Christian truth.[23] For Eusebius, the "father of church history,"[24] this comprehensive view of Christian truth was essentially plotted along lines of historical progression. As one recent study remarks: "Theology is, for Eusebius, basically construction and reconstruction of history."[25] In Eu-

---

[19]Eusebius *Demonstratio evangelica* 1.2.1 (GCS 23:7); *Praeparatio evangelica* 1.5.12 (SC 206:136).

[20]See the close reading of these texts in Jörg Ulrich, *Euseb von Caesarea und die Juden: Studien zur Rolle der Juden in der Theologie des Eusebius von Caesarea* (Berlin: Walter de Gruyter, 1999). On Eusebius as "apologist" in general see Michael Frede, "Eusebius' Apologetic Writings," in *Apologetics in the Roman Empire: Pagans, Jews, and Christians,* ed. Mark Edwards, Martin Goodman, and Simon Price (Oxford: Oxford University Press, 1999), 223–50.

[21]Although Barnes, *Constantine and Eusebius,* 164, announces that "Eusebius was not primarily an apologist," this comes from a rather narrow reading of the term. For a significantly different appreciation of apologetic traditions in Eusebius's thought and writings see, among others, Arthur J. Droge, "The Apologetic Dimensions of the *Ecclesiastical History,*" in Attridge and Hata, *Eusebius,* 492–509.

[22]On comparison with earlier apologetic uses of the "Jew-Greek-Christian" divide see Ulrich, *Euseb,* 125–31, 255–70. On Jews in general in pre-Constantinian apologetic literature see Judith Lieu, *Image and Reality: The Jews in the World of the Christians in the Second Century* (Edinburgh: T. & T. Clark, 1996); and William Horbury, *Jews and Christians in Contact and Controversy* (Edinburgh: T. & T. Clark, 1998).

[23]It is generally agreed that Eusebius intended both the *Praeparatio evangelica* and *Demonstratio evangelica* to be understood as a single work: see the overview of Ulrich, *Euseb,* 30–34, and notes. Only ten books of the *Demonstratio evangelica* are extant.

[24]F. Winkelmann, *Euseb von Kaisareia: Der Vater der Kirchengeschichte* (Berlin: Verlags-Anstalt Union, 1991).

[25]Ulrich, *Euseb,* 133. See also Michael J. Hollerich, *Eusebius of Caesarea's Commentary on Isaiah: Christian Exegesis in the Age of Constantine* (Clarendon Press: Oxford, 1999).

sebius's scheme the "new day" of Christian triumph can only be understood in relation to all of the days that came before. Some of Eusebius's reliance on claims of historical progression derive from an earlier apologetic tradition. The need to refute accusations of novelty or innovation (so unseemly in the ancient world) had led second- and third-century Christians to insist, on the one hand, on their religious affiliation to the antiquity of the Jews (primarily through their monotheism and their Scriptures) and, on the other hand, on a philosophical truth that predated and anticipated the vaunted wisdom of the Greeks.[26] Eusebius's ambitious scope, however, exceeds earlier apologetic thought by transforming all of human history into the "proof" of Christian superiority and triumph.[27]

In Eusebius's historically totalizing vision Jews play an especially significant role as the descendants of the actors of Christian Scripture.[28] This historical interplay between "Jews then" and "Christians now" was not necessarily an innovation of Eusebius: Justin Martyr and Melito of Sardis in the second century, for instance, had constructed their religious identities over against "old Israel," embodied in the Jews of their day.[29] What we see in Eusebius, however, is a new epistemic totality that strives for an absolute and comprehensive historical vision of Christian identity and Jewish difference. Historical construction, and totalizing absorption of difference (that is, the Jew), becomes a towering structure, almost (but not quite) too unwieldy for the Christian historian to master; the achievement of control over this enormous history (and the others within it) thus demonstrates Christian cognitive control in a grand sense. The

[26]See, e.g., Justin Martyr, *Apologia* 1.23, 39–31, 59–60 (text in *Saint Justin, Apologies: Introduction, texte critique, traduction, commentaire et index*, ed. André Wartelle [Paris: Études Augustiniennes, 1987], 128–30, 136–38, 178–80).

[27]*Pace* Frede, "Eusebius' Apologetic Writings," 224: "[I]f we adopt a generously vague notion of 'apology,' we might end up seeing even the *Chronicle* classified as an apologetic writing. Obviously, though, a notion which is so diffuse is also of very little help." On the contrary, it is "of help" precisely in evaluating the degree to which history itself becomes a "defense" of Christian identity for Eusebius.

[28]Aryeh Kofsky, "Eusebius of Caesarea and the Christian-Jewish Polemic," in *Contra Iudaeos: Ancient and Medieval Polemics Between Christians and Jews*, ed. Ora Limor and G. G. Stroumsa (Tübingen: J. C. B. Mohr [Paul Siebeck], 1996), 59–84; and Ulrich, *Euseb*, for two very different approaches and conclusions concerning Eusebius and the Jews.

[29]See esp. Justin Martyr's *Dialogue with Trypho* and Melito of Sardis's *On the Pascha*.

objects of historical reconstruction become the objects of Christian imperial knowledge and control.

Scholars often point to Eusebius's famous distinction between Jews and Hebrews, by which "Hebrews" designate the pure, monotheistic people of the time before Moses and "Jews" the present-day scoffers and unbelievers subject to the Law.[30] His practical application of such terminology, however, is generally more flexible. Jörg Ulrich has recently highlighted the fuzziness of Eusebius's religious terminology, specifically the ways in which he distinguished (and blurred the distinctions between) "Hebrews," "Jews," "pagans," and "Christians." For Eusebius, "Hebrews" were the paradigmatic ur-monotheists, theologically and morally opposed to the deficient and derivative polytheistic "Greeks [*Hellēnes*]." "Hebrew" is thus a religiously positive category, the historico-theological, spiritual progenitor of the Christian. Yet the Hebrew is also the physical ancestor of the Jew, and Eusebius allows some slippage in terminology that indicates that Jews, even *after* the advent of Moses and the Law, remained important for the articulation of Christian identity. This terminological slippage gives us a sense of the ongoing utility of Jews in Eusebius's historically comprehensive view of Christian identity.

In Eusebius's apologetic and exegetical writings "Hebrews," as the spiritual progenitors of Christians, appear throughout the stream of history.[31] Following his "proper" distinction between "Hebrews" and "Jews" outlined in the *Gospel Preparation,* Eusebius refers to such figures as Abraham, Isaac, and Jacob as "Hebrews," believers in the one God in an age before Moses.[32] Moses himself is the pinnacle of the "Hebrew" peo-

---

[30]Eusebius, *Praeparatio evangelica* 7.6 (SC 215:168–70); see, among others, J. Parkes, *The Conflict of the Church and the Synagogue* (London: Soncino Press, 1934), 161–62; and James Pasto, "When the End Is the Beginning? or When the Biblical Past Is the Political Present: Some Thoughts on Ancient Israel, 'Post-Exilic Judaism,' and the Politics of Biblical Scholarship," *Scandinavian Journal of the Old Testament* 12 (1998): 165–67, where he cites *Praeparatio evangelica* 1.2 (SC 206:104–8). To some extent Eusebius is extending a terminological distinction suggested by his intellectual predecessor Origen; see Nicholas De Lange, *Origen and the Jews: Studies in Jewish-Christian Relations in Third-Century Palestine* (Cambridge, U.K.: Cambridge University Press, 1976), 29–31.

[31]See Ulrich, *Euseb,* 57–131; Kofsky, "Eusebius of Caesarea," 74–75; Hollerich, *Eusebius of Caesarea,* 120–24.

[32]See Eusebius, *Historia ecclesiastica* 1.4.5 (GCS n.f. 6:40), where "the children of the Hebrews claim Abraham as their very own ancestor." See also *Praeparatio evangelica* 9.16.1 (SC 369:230); and *Demonstratio evangelica* 4.7.3 (GCS 23:161), on Jacob/Israel as "that one pro-

ple, who spoke with God and ensured the monotheistic purity of God's people in the midst of Egypt's polytheistic decline.[33] But even after the institution of the Law, the supposed dividing mark between pure "Hebrews" and derivative "Jews," we find laudable Hebrew figures: Isaiah, Jeremiah, and other "prophets of the Hebrews in whom divine power resided";[34] David, the "king of the whole Hebrew nation";[35] and the blessed ranks of kings, prophets, and high priests down to the destruction of the Temple who presaged the divine offices of Christ.[36] The Maccabees also are "Hebrews," as are the seventy Alexandrian translators of the Old Testament.[37] Two favorite Jewish sources of Eusebius, Philo of Alexandria and Josephus, are among the "Hebrews" of recent times; so, too, is Justin Martyr's debate partner, the Jew Trypho.[38] Eusebius can even spot "Hebrews" in his own time, especially those contemporary Jews whose biblical interpretation he attempts to refute.[39] In addition to these time-traveling Hebrews there are numerous references in Eusebius's exegetical and apologetic texts to the "children of the Hebrews [*paides Hebraiōn*]," used of recent Jewish "philosophers," such as Philo and Aristobulus, as

claimed forefather of the whole nation of Hebrews."

[33]Eusebius, *Praeparatio evangelica* 7.7.1 (SC 215:172), even accords to Moses the Pauline epithet of Phil 3.5: "For that great theologian Moses was a 'Hebrew from among Hebrews' [*Hebraios ōn ex Hebraiōn*]," although it is unclear what he means by this (see Ulrich, *Euseb,* 62 and n. 19; and Kofsky, "Eusebius of Caesarea," 74). For Jerome's use of this phrase (generally of the evangelists and apostles) see below, Chapter 3, section 3.

[34]Eusebius, *Demonstratio evangelica* 5 prooem. 32 (GCS 23:209). On Isaiah: *Demonstratio evangelica* 1.4.7 (GCS 23:19); on Jeremiah: *Demonstratio evangelica* 1.4.5 (GCS 23:19); see also *Praeparatio evangelica* 13.7.5 (SC 307:290), where Eusebius refers to the "Hebrew prophet" when citing Ps 7.5.

[35]Eusebius, *Demonstratio evangelica* 4.15.34 (GCS 23:178).

[36]Eusebius, *Demonstratio evangelica* 8 prooem. 2 (GCS 23:349); and *Historia ecclesiastica* 1.3.9 (GCS n.f. 6:32).

[37]Eusebius, *Historia ecclesiastica* 3.10.6–7 (GCS n.f. 6:224), on the Maccabees; *Demonstratio evangelica* 5 prooem. 35, 7.1.31 (GCS 23:209, 303), on the LXX.

[38]On Philo and Josephus in particular see Ulrich, *Euseb,* 88–110. Josephus, like Moses, even merits the enigmatic Philippians 3.5 epithet, a "Hebrew from the Hebrews" (*Demonstratio evangelica* 6.18.36 [GCS 23:281], juxtaposed further with "Jewish *deuterōseis* accomplished elsewhere"). Other references to Philo and Josephus: *Historia ecclesiastica* 1.5.3 (GCS n.f. 6:44), where Josephus is the "most famous of the Hebrew historians"; and 2.4.2–3 (GCS n.f. 6:114–16) on Philo as a "Hebrew scholar." On Trypho, "one of the most eminent Hebrews of his day," see *Historia ecclesiastica* 4.18.6 (GCS n.f. 6:364).

[39]Eusebius, *Demonstratio evangelica* 4.1.12 (GCS 23:150), where "the Hebrews and ourselves hold the same and common understanding of the Messiah, which to some extent likewise even now those who follow Scripture among both of us confess."

well as what seem to be contemporary rabbinic sages in Caesarea.[40]

Some scholars have argued that when Eusebius calls such figures as Philo and Josephus "Hebrews" instead of "Jews," he is ceding to them a privileged religious status in recognition of their conceptual proximity to Christian truth. In essence, he is "promoting" them, claiming them as crypto-Christians, part of the theologically pure genealogy from Hebrew to Christian.[41] Or, perhaps more mundanely, the term *Hebrew* (despite Eusebius's theological emphases in his apologetic works) functions as a primarily linguistic marker: a "Hebrew" is, simply, someone who speaks the language of the Jews (Hebrew or Aramaic). Neither of these attempts to justify Eusebius's expansive use of the term *Hebrew,* however, attends carefully to the contexts in which Eusebius deploys the term. There is no question of "promoting" Trypho to privileged, quasi-Christian status when Eusebius describes the ways in which Justin "inveighs" against him and his people (called "Jews").[42] Nor is there much sense in claiming that those Jews who challenge Christian exegesis by producing the testimony of the Greek biblical translation of Aquila are primarily called "Hebrews" for their linguistic particularity.[43] Labeling contemporary Jews "Hebrews" does not necessarily render them any less acrimonious or oppositional to Christian truth.

So what does Eusebius gain by his extension of the historicizing label "Hebrew," eschewing the more straightforward label "Jew" with respect to persons who would (presumably) self-identify as such? I suggest that the terminological fuzziness is a conceptual tour de force by which Eusebius demonstrates the mastery and totality of his Christian historical vision. The sweep of Christian history is so all-encompassing that its shadow even falls over his contemporaries and allows Eusebius to nudge

---

[40]Eusebius, *Praeparatio evangelica* 7.14.2 and 8.12.22 (SC 215:236, 369:138), where he uses it of Philo, Aristobulus, and other "sages among the Jews"; *Demonstratio evangelica* 6.20.3 (GCS 23:285), used generically of exegetical debaters; and *Commentarius in Isaiam* 43 (7.8), 98 (30.1), 100 (30.30), 2.10 (36.3) (GCS 58:46, 194, 202, 222), where he uses it of contemporary (perhaps rabbinic) sources (on which see Hollerich, *Eusebius of Caesarea,* 147–53).

[41]Kofsky, "Eusebius of Caesarea," 75–77. See Ulrich, *Euseb,* 97–98, who points out that Eusebius gets much more mileage out of Philo as a Jew than as a quasi Christian.

[42]Eusebius, *Historia ecclesiastica* 4.18.6–7 (GCS n.f. 6:364).

[43]See Eusebius, *Demonstratio evangelica* 7.1.139 (GCS 23:324), when he refers to the Greek Bible of Aquila, "who is brought forward as a textual witness among the Hebrews even now [*eiseti nun*]."

those individuals into a remote and more "Christian-friendly" past.[44] Among all these "Hebrews" and "children of Hebrews" the common element seems to be not their historical distance from present-day Christians (and Jews) but rather their utility in constructing a historicizing authentication of Christian truth. Jews who can be usefully absorbed into Eusebius's historically totalizing vision—whether because of conceptual proximity, like Philo, or absolute otherness, like Trypho—are granted the gently historicizing label of "Hebrew." Despite Eusebius's own claims at semantic and chronological distinction, I suggest that it would be more accurate to say that "Hebrews" for Eusebius are Jews insofar as they relate to Christian identity—the Jews of any time, the time of Jesus or that of Eusebius himself. They embody the Christian past, and for this task any Jew will do.

This fuzziness between praiseworthy and quasi-Christian "Hebrew" and paradigmatically non-Christian "Jew" suggests a new way of interpreting the persistence of Jews throughout Eusebius's comprehensive vision of Christian history. In Eusebius's historical and panegyrical writings the best Jews "to think with" (that is, those Jews whose historical presence helps elucidate Christian truth) are in and around Palestine. This focus on Palestinian Jews resonates with Eusebius's episcopal proximity to the *loca sancta* and the original sites of biblical narrative.[45] This focus also suggests the growing significance of the holy land as a site for the elaboration of Christian identity, a "frontier zone" in which "Hebrew," "Jew," and "Christian" all mingle to produce the triumphant Christian self. The Jews of Palestine emerge, like the recurring "Hebrews" of Eusebian apologetic, at momentous junctures to act as foils to Christian identity. In his *Oration on the Holy Sepulcher* Eusebius positions Palestinian Jews at the epitome of the fractured, preimperial *oikoumenē*:

Before that time [that is, the coming of Jesus], some ruled separately in Syria, others reigned in Asia, still others in Macedonia; there a few isolated persons

[44]The "historicizing" label of choice among Jews of Eusebius's Caesarea would presumably be "Israel," a term occasionally but infrequently used by Eusebius (see Graham Harvey, *The True Israel: Uses of the Names Jew, Hebrew, and Israel in Ancient Jewish and Early Christian Literature* [Leiden: E. J. Brill, 1996]).

[45]On Eusebius's historical and theological focus on Palestine in the 320s and 330s see P. W. L. Walker, *Holy City, Holy Places? Christian Attitudes to Jerusalem and the Holy Land in the Fourth Century* (Oxford: Clarendon Press, 1990), 94–116.

held sway over Egypt, likewise others in Arab lands. Why, even the Jewish people ruled over Palestine: in every village, in every city, in every single place, just as if under some madness, truly possessed to the point of murdering each other, they waged battles and wars.[46]

In this oration the "madness" ceases with the ascension of Augustus and the concomitant arrival of Christ's message, at which point history reaches a new turning point and the world achieves a new wholeness. Just as Augustus's empire will heal the politically fractured remnants of Alexander the Great's kingdoms, so, too, the new Christian message will overwrite Jewish immorality and falsity. The image emerges of historical progression and evolution, a new world order born explicitly of the old.

This moment of salvific import, the correction of Jewish error, might be thought to signal the end of the Jews' significance for Christian history: after all, the "madness" of Jewish self-rule needed only last until the arrival of the "new Moses," the lawgiver Christ. But in Eusebius's *Church History* the tendentious and difficult history of the Jews stretches further, until the destruction of Jewish Jerusalem in the second century. Eusebius here suggests that this second historical fissure will provide a launching point for a more purely Christian chronology. Book four of the *Church History* begins with the contrast of Christian efflorescence and Jewish decrepitude in the second century: "Now on the one hand our Savior's teaching and church were flourishing daily and progressing quite well, while on the other hand Jewish tragedy [*tēs Ioudaiōn sumphoras*] was reaching its peak of serial catastrophes."[47] Eusebius then narrates the woes of the Jews in Alexandria and Cyrene and turns to the Jewish revolt against Hadrian in Palestine (again, Palestinian Jews become exemplary). Embedded in this account is the "parting of the ways" between Jews and Christians, set in the appropriate backdrop of Jerusalem. Here the history of the Jews, insofar as it informs Christian identity, comes to a conclusion (once again):

Until Hadrian's siege of the Jews there had been a succession of fifteen bishops there, of whom it is said all were originally Hebrews. . . . For in those days the

---

[46]Eusebius, *De laudibus Constantini* 16.5 (PG 20:1424B); see Drake, *In Praise of Constantine,* 178n3. If Drake is correct, and this part of the oration was delivered in Jerusalem, this connection would be made even more pointed by the prominent ruins of the Jerusalem Temple.

[47]Eusebius, *Historia ecclesiastica* 4.2.1 (GCS n.f. 6:300).

whole church consisted of Hebrew believers enduring from the days of the apostles down to the siege in which the Jews, rising up again against the Romans, were conquered in great battles. Since a break was at this time made from the bishops of the circumcision, *we now feel the need* to list their names from the first.[48]

After cataloguing the "Hebrew" bishops of Jerusalem, Eusebius goes on to narrate the fall of the city to Hadrian and the expulsion and elimination of its Jewish population.[49] He concludes this portion of the narrative by remarking on the ordination of "Markos, first of the bishops *after* those from the circumcision."[50] The eradication of Jews from the Jerusalem church marks another sea change for Eusebius: the catalogue of "circumcised" bishops, followed by the first "gentile" bishop of the city arising, as it were, out of the mass of Jewish destruction, projects these Jews entirely into a bygone era. The rest of book 4 becomes a narrative of martyrdom and heresy: Jews are comfortably inscribed into the Christian past, whereas pagans and heretics loom in the Christian present.

Yet if those "Hebrews" of the second century C.E. can be pushed into the safe Christian past, so too can the fourth-century Jews, who are Eusebius's contemporaries. History in its vast scope is a tool Eusebius implements to fashion even his own time and place, to make the present Christian through a manipulation of the Jewish past. Such historicization is accomplished most effectively by Eusebius on the holy sites of Palestine. Earlier in his career as a Christian writer, Eusebius had attempted to align biblical place-names with contemporary topography in his *Onomastikon*.[51] This tract was fourth in a series that had so far included a Greek translation of Hebrew names, a register of ancient Judaea by tribe, and a

---

[48]Eusebius, *Historia ecclesiastica* 4.5.2–5 (GCS n.f. 6:304–6), emphasis added.

[49]See Yohanan Lederman, "Les évêques juifs de Jérusalem," *Revue Biblique* 104 (1997): 211–22, on possible rabbinic sources for Eusebius's bishop list; Eusebius himself ascribes it to Hegesippus.

[50]Eusebius, *Historia ecclesiastica* 4.6.4 (GCS 6:308), emphasis added.

[51]On the early dating for this treatise see T. D. Barnes, "The Composition of Eusebius' Onomasticon," *Journal of Theological Studies,* n.s., 26 (1975): 412–14; and idem, *Constantine and Eusebius,* 110–11; Walker, *Holy City,* 42–43. Other scholars have dated the *Onomastikon* as late as the 330s (Peter Thomsen, "Palästina nach den Onomasticon Eusebius," *Zeitschrift des deutschen Palästina-Vereins* 26 [1903]: 131; Hollerich, *Eusebius of Caesarea,* 21). Confusion arises from contradictory statements by Eusebius and Jerome, which may be reconciled if the *Onomastikon,* like other works of Eusebius, was issued more than once.

plan of Jerusalem and the Temple.[52] As Dennis Groh has remarked, the *Onomastikon* forms part of Eusebius's comprehensive discourse on the history and identity of the fourth-century Christian: "In the *Onomasticon* Eusebius is doing spatially (and alphabetically) what he has already done chronologically in the *Chronicon* and what he will go on to do narratively in the *History*—namely, bring biblical, Roman, and Christian realities together in such a way that Christianity in his own day can be seen to be the successor of the biblical realities in the Roman world."[53] It is noteworthy that, within the schema described by Groh, the present-day Jews of Palestine would fall under the rubric of the "biblical," encoded into a scriptural past that is continuously making way for a Christian present. Much like the "children of the Hebrews" found in Eusebius's other apologetic/exegetical works, the Jews of Palestine are dislodged from the present into a Christian past. Here the historical sweep of Christian triumph is grounded in the physicality of the biblical holy land, brushing living Jews of Palestine along with it.

The *Onomastikon* lists locations alphabetically according to biblical book, such that sites in Palestine become "visible" only by virtue of their scriptural origins.[54] Christian sanctity is now played against the colorful background of ancient Israel. By layering biblical place-names over contemporary toponyms Eusebius transforms the Jewish present into the Christian past, initiating a sort of linguistic and historical telescoping.[55] The result is that when Eusebius makes mention of contemporary "Jewish villages,"[56] they are already positioned in the Christian past: for a Christian of Eusebius's day to look on a contemporary Jew in the holy land is thus to look through a window into a biblical reality. In this way Eusebius simultaneously absorbs the holy land Jews into a facet of Chris-

---

[52]Eusebius states this in *Onomastikon* 2.5–12 (page and line numbers refer to GCS 11.3, the critical edition of Eusebius's text and Jerome's translation). These three treatises are not extant.

[53]Dennis Groh, "The *Onomasticon* of Eusebius and the Rise of Christian Palestine," *Studia Patristica* 18 (1983): 29.

[54]Benjamin Isaac, "Eusebius and the Geography of Roman Provinces," in his *The Near East Under Roman Rule: Selected Papers* (Leiden: Brill, 1998), 284–309, also sees in the *Onomastikon* evidence for contemporary Roman administrative methods of provincial mapping.

[55]*Pace* Barnes, "Composition," 413.

[56]"Jewish towns" described by Eusebius are Accaron (22.9), Anab/Anea (26.9), Dabeira (78.6), Engaddi (86.18), Esthemo (86.21), Eremmon (88.17), Zeib/Zif/Carmelis (92.21), Thalcha (98.26), Jettan (108.9), Nineveh of Arabia (136.2), and Naaratha (136.25). See Thomsen, "Palästina," 164–65.

tian identity (much like fourth-century "Hebrews" and "children of Hebrews") and renders them safe for the contemporary Christian. In this biblicized and historicized context a "village mostly inhabited by Jews"[57] is not a threat to Christian *imperium* but rather a spectacle of entirely scriptural, "past-tense" import. Their historicized presence gestures impotently ever forward into the triumphal Christian present, like the intact ruins of the Jewish Temple in Christian Jerusalem or the carefully Christianized text of the "Old Testament."

We can understand Eusebius's textual "mapping" of contemporary Jews into a Christian past along the lines of historians who analyze the imperial functions of early modern mapping as "a 'projection' that reduced *terra incognita* to order, banishing the monster and converting space into place."[58] Just as his reordering of history served to contain and usefully integrate the Jew into the scope of Christian knowledge and identity, so, too, the spatial configurations of the *Onomastikon* exert a similar comprehensive control over Christianized (not just *Christian*) space. Through totalizing visions of Christian history and geography, Eusebius can inscribe the aptness of Christian power, marking out the Jew of Jerusalem and the holy places as the figure through which this Christian power can be quite naturally exerted. Christian power, for Eusebius, emerges out of its historical totality and mastery. As the object of that historical vision, the constant marker of the "past tense" that always precedes a Christian present, the Jew is pivotal to that historical totality. The Jew of Eusebius's day, inhabiting the most rarefied sites of Christian sanctity, remains in this sense still a *Hebrew,* a historical and tractable character from the Christian past.

---

[57]Of the cities listed in the previous note, all but four (Dabeira, Zeib/Zif/Carmelis, Nineveh, and Naaratha) are described as "great towns of Jews [*kōmē megistē Ioudaiōn*]," which would seem to be a comment on majority populations; compare his descriptions of cities as "wholly Christian [*holē Christianōn*]" (said of Aneim, Jereth, and Kariathaim [26.14, 108.2–3, 112.15]).

[58]Wolfe, "History and Imperialism," 409, speaking of Edward Said and other analysts of "Orientalist" imperialism.

Cyril of Jerusalem: Jews Outside Christian Ritual

If Jews under Eusebius's gaze slip constantly into a past over which impe-rial Christians have demonstrated their mastery, Jews in the rhetoric of Cyril of Jerusalem hover menacingly at the threshold of ritual transfor-mation. In one sense the distinction might be characterized as testamen-tary: Eusebius's Jews (as in the *Onomastikon* or the *Gospel Preparation*) become shades of the Hebrew ancestors of the Old Testament; Cyril's Jews behave like those paradigmatic unbelievers of the New Testament, the crucifiers of Jesus and tormentors of Paul and the apostles. Likewise, we might characterize the inscription of Jews in Eusebius as historical (Jews two thousand years ago or today are always part of "the past") and that of Jews in Cyril's writings as eschatological (Jews two thousand years ago or today are always harbingers of the impending judgment day). In either case it is noteworthy that Cyril's more alarmist stance toward the Jews of his day results in a totalizing discourse of knowledge and con-tainment not dissimilar to Eusebius's: to "know" the enemy, for Cyril, is ultimately to surmount that enemy's diabolical peril.

Just as Eusebius creates through his writings a discursive universe—a comprehensive framework for identity that comes into existence through Christian language—so Cyril, in his role as catechist for the church of Je-rusalem, uses the rigorous and intensive process of Lenten catechesis to form discursively the throngs of catechumens gathered in his church.[59] Late ancient society was in many respects a profoundly oral culture. This is not to paint a picture of "illiterates" communicating in unwritten (and therefore unsophisticated) manner but rather to emphasize the degree to which speech, particularly public oratory, shaped individual and cultural identities.[60] Even the most sophisticated readers and writers would learn

[59]Although I refer to Cyril's audience as "catechumens," technically these Christians were now *phōtēzomenoi* (illuminandi) until their baptism. Walker, *Holy City,* 410, dates the *Catecheses* to either 348 or 350 (and seems to prefer the earlier date: see the offhand dating, e.g., on 215); Alexis Doval, "The Date of Cyril of Jerusalem's Catecheses," *Journal of Theological Stud-ies,* n.s., 48 (1997): 129–32, proposes instead 351, after Cyril's ordination as bishop. On Cyril's life and works see Edward Yarnold, *Cyril of Jerusalem* (London: Routledge, 2000), 3–64; this volume also contains select translations of Cyril's writings.

[60]See Peter Brown, *Power and Persuasion in Late Antiquity: Towards a Christian Empire* (Madison: University of Wisconsin Press, 1993); Richard Lim, *Public Disputation, Power, and Social Order in Late Antiquity* (Berkeley: University of California Press, 1995); and idem, "Christian Triumph and Controversy," in *Late Antiquity: A Guide to the Postclassical World,*

to discern (and, perhaps, critique and subvert) their social boundaries through formal oratory performance. The precise context of prebaptismal oratory makes the identity-forming rhetoric of Cyril even more charged and transformative. In the late ancient Christian catechumenate, language very explicitly made correct Christians:[61] Cyril can speak on everything from biblical history to Trinity to heresy; but, above all, his lectures are designed to construct a totalizing form of Christian knowledge. When Cyril nears the end of his exposition of the creed, and turns to explain the phrase "in one holy catholic church [*eis mian hagian katholikēn ekklesian*]," this totalizing knowledge is given a universal Christian scope:

[The church] is called "universal" [katholikē], first of all, because it stretches from one end of the earth to the other, across the whole world; also because it teaches universally and without lack [katholikōs kai anellipōs] all the teachings which are meant to be brought into the knowledge of humanity [eis gnōsin anthrōpōn], concerning things seen and unseen, heavenly and earthly; and also because it brings every type of person [pan genos anthrōpōn] into piety, the rulers and those ruled, the learned and the ignorant; and also because it heals entirely [katholikōs], on the one hand treating every form of sin accomplished by the soul and the body, on the other hand possessing in itself every form of what is called virtue, in deeds and in words and in all manner of spiritual gifts.[62]

The "whole world" in Cyril's speeches becomes a Christian world, materially and spiritually, and so can be schematized by Cyril's *catecheses* into forms of knowledge uniquely transmissible in Christian form. The Christian produced on the other side of these lectures, ready for the Easter

---

ed. G. W. Bowersock, Peter Brown, and Oleg Grabar (Cambridge, Mass.: Belknap Press of Harvard University Press, 1999), 196–218.

[61] On the formative and stratifying nature of ritualized discourse see Catherine Bell, *Ritual Theory, Ritual Practice* (New York: Oxford University Press, 1992), 197–223; and Jonathan Z. Smith, *To Take Place: Toward Theory in Ritual* (Chicago, Ill.: University of Chicago Press, 1987), 75–95, 103–15. On Cyril and his relation to Jerusalem in this process see Thomas Finn, *From Death to Rebirth: Ritual and Conversion in Antiquity* (New York: Paulist Press, 1997), 188–211.

[62] Cyril, *Catecheses* 18.23. Text in *Cyrilli Hierosolymum Archiepiscopi Opera*, ed. J. Rupp, 2 vols. (Munich: Stahl, 1860), 2:324–26. The recitation of the creed seems to have (loosely) structured Cyril's eighteen lectures, with the last lecture containing a full recitation. On this creed (dubbed the "J" or "Jerusalem creed" by scholars) see J. N. D. Kelly, *Early Christian Creeds*, 3d ed. (New York: D. McKay, 1972), 183–84; and the introductory material of A. A. Stephenson in *The Works of Saint Cyril of Jerusalem*, vol. 1, tr. Leo P. McCauley and A. A. Stephenson (Washington: Catholic University of America Press, 1969), 4–6, 60–65.

baptismal font, is as "total" and universal as his or her instruction. This process encompasses the whole "mind, heart, and soul,"[63] resulting in a total and uniform spiritual structure: "Unless you construct in a united fashion, keeping in mind first and last things, the builder can go on building but your house will be dilapidated."[64] The well-built Christian "house" (the orthodox baptizand) will see and understand everything in a Christian manner, "things seen and unseen" and "first and last things."

The process of "total" formation, however, is distinctly dangerous. Cyril's lectures possess a singularly martial and threatening tone, highlighting the perils his audience will face in seeking Christian enlightenment. Christian construction is a struggle, both internal and external. From the first of his catechetical lectures, Cyril attempts to arm his spiritually vulnerable charges against the massing foes: "You take up arms against heresies, against Jews, against Samaritans, against Gentiles. You have many enemies: take up many arrows."[65] At times, as in this general warning, Jews appear lumped into a horde of "enemies" against which the catechumen must be armed, representing, it might seem, one particular facet of anti-Christianity. In a later lecture Cyril declaims on all of the "diabolical operations [*diabolikēn energeian*]" at work against the Christian, assigning each a particular province of evil influence: "Pay no attention to astrology, or augury, or omens, or the fanciful divination of the Greeks. . . . Do not fall in with Samaritanism or Judaism, for Jesus Christ ransomed you from all that: avoid all observance of sabbaths and speaking of any kind of meat as 'common' or 'unclean.' . . . Especially [*exairetōs*] hate all the assemblies of perverse heretics."[66] In this schema Greeks are superstitious, Jews and Samaritans are law-bound, and heretics are perverse.[67] Throughout the catechetical lectures Cyril elaborates

---

[63]Cyril of Jerusalem, *Procatechesis* 17 (Rupp, *Cyrilli,* 1:24).

[64]Cyril, *Procatechesis* 11 (Rupp, *Cyrilli,* 1:16). Cyril is explicit at the end of the lectures that spiritual *construction* does not equal spiritual *perfection.* His charges will be made "wholly" Christian, but their need for further instruction continues: Cyril, *Catecheses* 18.32 (Rupp, *Cyrilli,* 2:336). Absolute perfection, for Cyril, seems to be deferred to the *eschaton.*

[65]Cyril, *Procatechesis* 10 (Rupp, *Cyrilli,* 1:14).

[66]Cyril, *Catecheses* 4.37 (Rupp, *Cyrilli,* 1:130–32). I thank Jan Willem Drijvers for pointing out the significance of this passage to me. Although heretics seem the pinnacle of evil here, there is a wordplay between "heretics [*hairetikōn*]" and "especially [*exairetōs*]." Nonetheless, by focusing on Cyril's writings about Jews I do not want to imply that he does not address other "dangers" to his ritual charges.

[67]See, similarly, Cyril, *Catecheses* 4.2 (Rupp, *Cyrilli,* 2:90): "Now the Greeks lure away

on these points, granting each "diabolical" group particular attention in turn. The "Greeks and Samaritans" together become the foils for Cyril's defense of the doctrine of the resurrection of the body,[68] and the "Greek and heretics" together are the focus of Cyril's exposition of the nature of "God the Father."[69] Heretics alone, especially Manicheans, receive special notice for their theological and cosmological perversities, particularly their denigration of God's creation.[70]

Jews are therefore not the only "diabolical" threat against which Cyril's catechumens are being armed. The Jewish threat is, however, peculiarly imminent in Cyril's scheme. The danger of Jews builds on and extends the threat of the Greeks, Samaritans, and heretics. The Jews suffer from "total senselessness [*pasēs agnōmosunēs*]" and a "habitude of disbelief" with which they seek to coerce Christians into apostasy.[71] Jews are, in fact, the very embodiment and carriers of disbelief, "always in denial."[72] When the catechumens roam the streets of Jerusalem unattended between instructional lectures, Cyril imagines that the devious Jews will attack and sully every aspect of their inchoate formation. Often his theological instruction is framed for the occasions "whenever the Jews disparage you," as when he announces curtly that his Trinitarian exposition, for example, is being given "on account of the Jews."[73] The Greeks may be seductively foolish, and the heretics deviously perverse, but the disbelief of the Jew stands in direct and total opposition to the salvific narrative of the Christians: the Christians have Christ, whereas the Jews await the anti-Christ.[74] Total theological truth is positioned opposite malicious and

---

through glibness. . . . The circumcised [Jews and Samaritans?] deceive their followers through the holy Scriptures, which they interpret poorly. . . . And the children of the heretics, 'through fair speech and glibness deceive the hearts of the simple'" (Rom 16.18).

[68]Cyril, *Catecheses* 18.1–20 (Rupp, *Cyrilli,* 2:300–324). Jews are possibly acquitted from this accusation through a reading of New Testament passages on Pharisaic belief in resurrection of the dead (Acts 23.6–10, Matt 22.23 and par.).

[69]Cyril, *Catecheses* 8.1–7 (Rupp, *Cyrilli,* 1:228–34).

[70]Cyril's heresiology is laid out in *Catecheses* 6.12–34 (Rupp, *Cyrilli,* 1:170–204); some MSS of the *Catecheses* have even inserted the *titulus* "On Heresies" over this portion of the lecture. It is notable that Mani is given a heretical pedigree that marks him as "having nothing in common either with Judaism or Christianity" (*Catecheses* 6.22 [Rupp, *Cyrilli,* 1:184]).

[71]Cyril, *Catecheses* 7.2, 7.3 (Rupp, *Cyrilli,* 210).

[72]Cyril, *Catecheses* 13.7 (Rupp, *Cyrilli,* 2:58).

[73]Cyril, *Catecheses* 4.12, 10.8 (Rupp, *Cyrilli,* 1:102, 270).

[74]Cyril, *Catecheses* 12.2 (Rupp, *Cyrilli,* 2:4). Much of *Catecheses* 12 is directed at the Jews, to the point where Cyril finally exclaims: "This is going to be an even clearer response to the

divisive Jewish untruth.

The demonic presence of the Jews, unlike the Greek or heretics, is also inscribed spatially, making them particularly dangerous foes for the Christian catechumen learning his or her Christian identity at the foot of the ruins of the Jerusalem Temple. Cyril is even able to gesture to this menacing, empty space in his lectures: "Because of these words of Jesus, 'There will not be left here one stone upon another' (Matt 24.2) the Temple of the Jews just opposite us [*antikrus hēmōn*] is fallen."[75] If biblical inscription into the topography served to domesticate Eusebius's Palestinian Jews and created a landscape of historical mastery, for Cyril it makes manifest their persistent threat, even until the end of time:[76] "for if he [that is, the Antichrist] comes as Christ to the Jews and wants to be worshipped by the Jews . . . he will be very zealous to rebuild the Temple, giving the impression that he is of David's line and will rebuild the fully restored Temple of Solomon."[77] Cyril's Jews loom across time, made especially manifest (if never quite visible) by the catechetical setting of Jerusalem.[78]

For Cyril in Jerusalem, Jews make an exemplary enemy for the Christian formed within sight of the *loca sancta*. Cyril often gestures toward Golgotha, Mount Olivet, and other Christian sites,[79] and he makes the connection between catechetical illumination and the "first institution" of these mysteries in and around Jerusalem.[80] In the holy city of Jerusalem Christian discourse shines brighter; conversely, the Jewish threat looms darker. Cyril describes Jerusalem as a Christian epicenter, encom-

---

Jews—I know I'm going on a lot and my listeners are weary, but endure the length of my speech, since these things pertain to Christ and this speech isn't about everyday matters!" (*Catecheses* 12.22 [Rupp, *Cyrilli*, 2:30]).

[75] Cyril, *Catecheses* 10.11 (Rupp, *Cyrilli*, 1:276). See below, Chapter 5, on the Temple Mount.

[76] On the particularly eschatological dimension of Cyril's anti-Jewish rhetoric see the arguments of Oded Irshai, "Cyril of Jerusalem: The Apparition of the Cross and the Jews," in Imor and Stroumsa, *Contra Iudaeos*, 86–104.

[77] Cyril, *Catecheses* 15.15 (Rupp, *Cyrilli*, 2:172). Irshai, "Cyril of Jerusalem," 98n39, suggests that Cyril "updated" this fifteenth lecture in the 360s in light of Julian's attempts to allow the Jews to rebuild the Temple.

[78] On Cyril's theological and imperial promotion of Jerusalem as the "holy city" of the Christian Roman Empire see Walker, *Holy City*, 312–46.

[79] See Cyril, *Catecheses* 1.1, 5.10, 13.4, 22, 23, 39, 14.23 (Rupp, *Cyrilli*, 1:30, 146; 2:54, 80, 102, 138). See also Finn, *From Death to Rebirth*, 191–95.

[80] Cyril, *Catecheses* 18.33 (Rupp, *Cyrilli*, 2:336).

passing and then surpassing even the bounds of Empire: "Look, you who are illuminated by him [that is, the Holy Spirit] in your mind: how many Christians there are in this whole region, and how many in this whole province of Palestine! Extend your mind from this province into the whole Roman Empire, and from there out into the whole world."[81] The expansion of Christian truth outward from Jerusalem "into the whole world" stands in contrast to the provincial restriction of Jewish falsity: Cyril comments that the Jewish threat remains "bound in a certain region,"[82] the Jews' paradigmatic misdeeds concentrated and epitomized by their provincially located leader, the patriarch.[83] Christian transcendence, emanating from the Jerusalem *loca sancta,* comes into existence in direct opposition to Jewish limit and failure.[84]

Cyril projects all the dark fantasy of the catechumenate onto a knowable "other," thereby focusing and channeling all the danger and uncertainty of this liminal ritual process. The complete Christian comes into being in direct opposition to the Jew; it is ultimately this place and time of uncertainty, the catechetical schoolroom over the course of Lent, where the Jew is felt to exert his menace. The catechumens standing before Cyril are swept into the eschatological promises of Christian triumph over Jews. The implication is made that, on the other side of the baptismal font they, like Jesus at the *parousia,* will have the last word: "the Jews, seeing the one they dishonored, will beat their breasts in repentance . . . but we shall boast, taking pride in the cross, worshipping the Lord who was sent and was crucified for us."[85] The incomplete Christian must fear Jewish lies and deceit, but the Christian fully formed through ritual will prevail.

The centrality of the Jewish threat to the elaboration of Christian triumph is emphasized in a letter written by Cyril to Emperor Constantius

[81]Cyril, *Catecheses* 16.22 (Rupp, *Cyrilli,* 2:232). See also Walker, *Holy City,* 344–45.

[82]Cyril, *Catecheses* 10.6 (Rupp, *Cyrilli,* 1:282). The reference to demographic restriction seems to indicate that Cyril is thinking specifically of local (Palestinian) Jews. See the discussion of Jewish population and demographics in late ancient Palestine in Chapter 1 and in Seth Schwartz, *Imperialism and Jewish Society, 200 B.C.E. to 640 C.E.* (Princeton: Princeton University Press, 2001), 202–14.

[83]For Cyril's warning about the Jewish patriarch see *Catecheses* 12.17 (Rupp, *Cyrilli,* 2:24).

[84]See also Cyril, *Catecheses* 18.25 (Rupp, *Cyrilli,* 2:326–28).

[85]Cyril, *Catecheses* 13.41 (Rupp, *Cyrilli,* 2:104); see also *Catecheses* 15.11–12 (Rupp, *Cyrilli,* 2:168–70).

concerning a miraculous apparition of the cross that supposedly lit up the Easter skies of Jerusalem in 351.[86] Cyril writes joyously to the emperor:

An enormous cross, constructed entirely out of light, appeared in the heavens above holy Golgotha and stretched out to the holy Mount of Olives, not appearing to one or two people only, but shown most clearly to the whole population of the city. . . . As one great crowd at the same time, the whole population of the city ran into the holy church, overpowered by fear of the vision of God, and also by delight: the young along with the old, men and women of every age, and even maidens cloistered in their houses, locals and foreigners, Christians together with gentiles here visiting from elsewhere, of one disposition in unison, as if with a single mouth, they all praised Jesus Christ our Lord.[87]

The city of Jerusalem is a network of holy sites configured to make the totalizing and unifying Christian truth particularly visible, literally illuminating the hearts and minds of the inhabitants of the holy city. A sense of totality and fulfillment suffuses this scene of revelation and unanimity, and Cyril suggests in his letter that this moment of illumination conferred on Jerusalem is a foretaste of the *eschaton*.[88] Here, in a blaze of Christian glory, is the triumph and perfection promised to the catechumenate. This ultimate triumphal tone may explain a notable absence in this list of "the whole population of the city [*to tēs poleōs plēthos*]" of Jerusalem: those shadowy Jews who had stalked the catechumens throughout their Lenten formation.[89] In the luminescent Christian victory, it would seem, these Jews are no longer visible, no longer threatening.[90] The appa-

---

[86]On this letter and Cyril's motives in bolstering waning imperial support for Jerusalem see Jan Willem Drijvers, "Promoting Jerusalem: Cyril and the True Cross," in *Portraits of Spiritual Authority: Religious Power in Early Christianity, Byzantium, and the Christian Orient,* ed. Jan Willem Drijvers and John W. Watt (Leiden: Brill, 1999), 79–95.

[87]Cyril, *Epistula ad Constantium* 4 (Rupp, *Cyrilli,* 2:436–38).

[88]See Cyril, *Epistula ad Constantium* 6 (Rupp, *Cyrilli,* 2:438); and discussion in Irshai, "Cyril of Jerusalem.

[89]A later version of this miracle, a Coptic homily on Mary composed in Cyril's name, inserted both Jewish and Samaritan witnesses to be converted by the apparition: see my "Visible Ghosts and Invisible Demons: The Place of Jews in Early Christian *Terra Sancta,*" in *Galilee Through the Centuries: Confluence of Cultures,* ed. Eric M. Meyers (Winona Lake, Ind.: Eisenbrauns, 1999), 359–60.

[90]The deliberate elimination of Jewish presence in the context of Christian illumination may also explain the absence of Jews in the postbaptismal *Mystagogical Lectures,* if they are indeed to be attributed to Cyril and not his successor, John. On Cyrillian authorship see Yarnold, *Cyril,* 23–32; and Alexis Doval, *Cyril of Jerusalem, Mystagogue: The Authorship of the Mystagogic Catecheses* (Washington, D.C.: Catholic University Press, 2001).

rition of the cross, as Cyril describes it to the most pious emperor,[91] has given a glimpse of the eradication of those others to be fulfilled at the end of Christian time. The transformation, regeneration, and enlightenment that produce the whole and knowing Christian subject, symbolized in Cyril's letter by the celestial cross, also produce and restrain the threat of the Palestinian Jew. The comprehensive ritual process makes the Christian and simultaneously unmakes the sinister Jewish enemy.

Epiphanius of Salamis: Jews Among Christian Heretics

Eusebius uses the Palestinian Jew to vitalize the Christian sweep of history, whereas Cyril employs the same figure in the dangerous yet ultimately triumphant transformation of baptism, rebirth, and *eschaton*. If Eusebius tames the Jew in the past, and Cyril promises Jewish defeat in the future, Epiphanius, monk, bishop, and master heresiologist, inscribes the Jews of Palestine along a very careful conceptual edge, somewhere between Jewish past, heretical present, and Christian future. His massive "medicine-chest against heresies," the *Panarion,* lists eighty heresies and their "antidotes."[92] Like the history of Eusebius and the catechetical instruction of Cyril, this medicine chest is conceived of as absolute and complete.[93] Epiphanius declares as much at the beginning of the treatise:

To report on and speak of faith and unbelief, of orthodoxy and heresy, recalls to me the beginning of the world's creation and course. Not that I begin on the strength of my own ability or on the basis of my own reasonings. I do it as God, the Lord of all and the merciful, has revealed the complete knowledge [tēs tou

---

[91]Cyril's connection of imperial power and Christian piety is quite explicit: Constantius is "adorned with every virtue, and displaying customary concern for both the holy churches and the rule of the Romans" (*Epistula ad Constantium* 8 [Rupp, *Cyrilli,* 2:440]).

[92]See Aline Pourkier, *L'hérésiologie chez Épiphane de Salamine* (Paris: Beauchesne, 1992). Epiphanius draws the number eighty from Song of Songs 6.9 (see *Panarion* prooem. 1.1.3 [GCS 25:155]).

[93]Epiphanius compares his own medicine chest with the treatises *Theriaca* and *Alexipharmaca* of Nicander and Dioscurides (*Panarion* prooem. 2.3.1–3 [GCS 25:171]). J. Dummer, "Ein naturwissenschaftliches Handbuch als Quelle für Epiphanius von Constantia," *Klio* 55 (1973): 289–99, is less certain that Epiphanius had access to these particular authors but posits another "natural science" source.

pantos gnōseōs] to his prophets, and vouchsafed it to me through them, so far as human nature allows.[94]

Against this sweeping opening, Epiphanius's modest claim that he "certainly" does not "promise to teach everything in the world"[95] rings somewhat hollow. Epiphanius's heresiology in fact constructs the whole world along comprehensive Christian lines similar to Eusebius's. In fact, he pushes the Pauline slogan of Galatians 3.28 further even than Eusebius by incorporating other similar "Pauline" passages, such as Colossians 3.11: "No longer is there Greek and Jew, circumcised and uncircumcised, barbarian, Scythian, slave, free; but Christ is all in all."[96] Epiphanius's orthodox taxonomy of "all in all" employs such biblical categories to create both diachronic and synchronic conceptual maps of the Christian world.

Heresy, for Epiphanius, is understood so broadly as to encompass all of history and geography: the first "heresies," in fact, began with Adam himself.[97] To the extent that "heresy" defines the un-Christian, Epiphanius the heresiologist can expand notions of Christian truth across all time and space, as well.[98] Epiphanius first employs the Colossian categories of "barbarian, Scythian, Greek, and Jew" as historical epochs, ways of charting all doctrinal deviance from Adam to Jesus: "from Adam until Noah there was barbarism; from Noah until the tower [that is, of Babel], and until Serug, two generations after the tower, came the Scythian superstition; after that, from the tower, Serug and Terah until Abraham, Hellenism. From Abraham on, a fear of God ascribed to Abraham: Judaism, after Judah, Abraham's descendant."[99] The first twenty heresies in the *Panarion* are grouped according to these categories, divided from the

---

[94]Epiphanius, *Panarion* prooem. 2.1.1 (GCS 25:169). Translations of Epiphanius are adapted from Frank Williams, *The Panarion of Epiphanius of Salamis*, 2 vols. (Leiden: E. J. Brill, 1987–94), here 1:11–12.

[95]Epiphanius, *Panarion* prooem. 2.2.1 (GCS 25:170; Williams, *Panarion*, 1:12).

[96]Epiphanius, *Ancoratus* 12.8; *Panarion* 1.9, 8.3.3 (GCS 25:21, 173, 188). This last version of the phrase ("In Christ Jesus there is neither barbarian, Scythian, Greek, nor Jew, but a new creation") is a conflation of Gal 3.28, 6.15, and Col 3.11: see Frances M. Young, "Did Epiphanius Know What He Meant by 'Heresy'?" *Studia Patristica* 17, no. 1 (1982): 202.

[97]Epiphanius *Panarion* 1.4, 9 (GCS 25:173). Pourkier, *Hérésiologie*, 87, remarks: "[Epiphanius] a en effet une notion très large de l'hérésie."

[98]On pre-Constantinian heresiological discourses of "alterity and strangeness" see Alain le Boulluec, *La notion d'hérésie dans la littérature grecque (IIe–IIIe siècles)*, 2 vols. (Paris: Études Augustiniennes, 1985).

[99]Epiphanius, *Panarion* 8.3 (GCS 25:188; Williams, *Panarion*, 1:24).

other sixty heresies by a recitation of the life of Christ. In a way Epiphanius's rhetoric recalls the extreme historicization of Jews in Eusebius's *Church History*: he prefaces his account of Christ's incarnation and ministry with an account of the formation and demise of the "four Samaritan and seven Jewish sects," leaving, as it were, a clear playing field for Jesus and his ministry.[100] The sweeping and triumphant historical works of Eusebius were known to Epiphanius,[101] and in some ways Epiphanius can be seen to take up and modulate the historicizing view of his predecessor.

Yet, although Jewish deviance is made to bow out before Jesus' message (insofar as the "heresy" of Judaism is one of the pre-Christian "mother-heresies"), Judaism continues to play a role throughout the *Panarion* as the baseline of absolute difference by which to gauge Christian truth and heretical error.[102] Epiphanius casually remarks that "the facts about the Jews are obvious to practically everyone,"[103] and by this he signals the great utility of Judaism in his sweeping survey of heresy and orthodoxy. Jews exist as the paradigmatic "to-be-known" in the overwhelming project of conceptualizing the "all in all" of orthodoxy. This comes out most clearly in the accounts of "Jewish-Christian" heresies,[104]

---

[100]Epiphanius, *Panarion* 20.3, locates the various heresies of Jews and Samaritans in the same geographical places as the account of Jesus, finishing with the statement "none of them exists any longer" (GCS 25:227; Williams, *Panarion,* 1:50).

[101]Pourkier, *Hérésiologie,* 477, lists Eusebius as one of Epiphanius's principal sources.

[102]Later hagiography even portrayed Epiphanius as a convert from Judaism (*Vita Epiphanii* 2–7 [PG 41:25–32]). Judith Lieu, "Epiphanius on the Scribes and Pharisees (*Pan.* 15.1–16.4)," *Journal of Theological Studies,* n.s., 39 (1988): 509–24, plausibly suggests this is an "imaginative development" from Jerome's description of Epiphanius as *pentaglōssos* (*Apologia contra Rufinum* 3.6 [SC 303:230]), that is, knowing Greek, Latin, Hebrew, Aramaic (or Syriac), and Coptic. On Epiphanius's biography see Jon F. Dechow, *Dogma and Mysticism in Early Christianity: Epiphanius of Cyprus and the Legacy of Origen* (Macon, Ga.: Mercer University Press, 1988), 25–43.

[103]Epiphanius, *Panarion* 8.3.6 (GCS 25:189).

[104]The term *Jewish-Christianity* is a modern coinage: see Joan E. Taylor, "The Phenomenon of Early Jewish-Christianity: Reality or Scholarly Invention?" *Vigiliae Christianae* 44 (1990): 313–34. Simon C. Mimouni, *Le judéo-christianisme ancien: Essais historiques* (Paris: Editions du Cerf, 1998), 42, attributes the term to Ferdinand Christian Baur, "Die Christuspartei in der korinthischen Gemeinde, der Gegensatz des petrinischen und paulinischen Christentums in der ältesten Kirche, der Apostel Paulus in Rome," *Tübinger Zeitschrift für Theologie* 5, no. 4 (1831): 61–206. Baur himself, however, draws on the work of Johann Ernst Christian Schmidt, *Bibliothek für Kritik und Exegese des Neuen Testaments und ältesten Christengeschichte,* 2 vols. (Hadamar: Neue Gelehrtenbuchhandlung, 1797–1803), 1:91.

Panarion 29–30, two chapters nestled in the midst of a bewildering mass of "gnostic" heretical groups.[105] The Nazoraeans, Epiphanius informs us, are to be found around the city of Pella, east of Jerusalem, "where all the disciples had settled . . . after they left Jerusalem."[106] Although the Nazoraeans believe in Christ, their main fault is that they remain "under the curse"—that is, the Old Testament Law. This single, glaring flaw allows Epiphanius to limit himself to "a brief discussion," since "people like these are refutable at once and easy to cure—or rather, they are nothing but Jews themselves."[107] Their conceptual proximity to the fully comprehended Jews makes them both easy to know and easy to defeat: if they must be analogized to a poisonous creature, they are most like "an insect that is small," fittingly "squashed with the words of truth."[108] To be Jewish (or so conceptually close to Jewishness as to render the difference negligible) is thus to be "obvious," easily known and therefore easily controlled.[109]

The Ebionites present a more complicated problem, since their alleged founder, Ebion, stands "practically midway between all the sects," that is, defying easy definition, cognitive control, and refutation.[110] The Ebionite *seems* Jewish, but he is in fact "the opposite of Jews."[111] The categorical

[105]The two groups, Nazoraeans and Ebionites, are placed between the Cerinthians (*Panarion* 28) and the Valentinians (*Panarion* 31). For a study of the sources of these heresies in Epiphanius, especially the Ebionites, see Glenn Alan Koch, "A Critical Investigation of Epiphanius' Knowledge of the Ebionites: A Translation and Critical Discussion of *Panarion* 30" (Ph.D. diss., University of Pennsylvania, 1976).

[106]Epiphanius, *Panarion* 29.7.8 (GCS 25:330). The "flight to Pella" is narrated in Eusebius, *Historia ecclesiastica* 3.5.3 (GCS n.f. 6:196). Scholars still wrangle over the veracity of this tradition: see Jürgen Wehnert, "Die Auswanderung der Jerusalemer Christen nach Pella—historisches Faktum oder theologische Konstruktion?" *Zeitschrift für Kirchengeschichte* 102 (1991): 231–55; and Craig Koester, "The Origin and Significance of the Flight to Pella Tradition," *Catholic Biblical Quarterly* 51 (1989): 90–106.

[107]Epiphanius, *Panarion* 29.9.1 (GCS 25:331; Williams, *Panarion*, 1:119).

[108]Epiphanius, *Panarion* 29.9.5 (GCS 25:333; Williams, *Panarion*, 1:119).

[109]Nor should we consider the violent language of "squashing" merely incidental or colorful on Epiphanius's part: see Young, *White Mythologies*, 13, on the "ontological violence" of totalizing discourses.

[110]Epiphanius, *Panarion* 30.1.4 (GCS 25:333–34; Williams, *Panarion*, 1:120). Earlier texts on the Ebionites had pointed out that *Ebion*, which means "poor" in Hebrew, is not an eponym: see, e.g., Eusebius, *Historia ecclesiastica* 3.27.6 (GCS n.f. 6:256). Epiphanius insists that the founder "really was named Ebion" (*Panarion* 30.17.3 [GCS 25:356; Williams, *Panarion*, 1:133]). Sources on "Ebionites" and other "Jewish-Christian sects" are collected in A. F. J. Klijn and G. J. Reinink, *Patristic Evidence for Jewish-Christian Sects* (Leiden: E. J. Brill, 1973); and Mimouni, *Judéo-christianisme ancien*.

[111]Epiphanius, *Panarion* 30.1.5 (GCS 25:334; Williams, *Panarion*, 1:120).

slipperiness of the Ebionites makes them an ideal test case for the organizational control of the comprehensive discourse of Christian orthodoxy and the utility of Jews as the baseline of difference. In order to produce useful knowledge (and an "antidote") for this mystifying heresy, somewhere uncomfortably "between" Christianity and Judaism, Epiphanius uses his own knowledge produced at the margins: the anecdotes of Count Joseph of Tiberias, a Jewish convert to Christianity who had himself "suffered a great deal from the Jews."[112] Count Joseph, it would seem, is perfectly positioned to provide countervailing knowledge about these slippery Ebionites: whereas they seem Jewish but are not, he *was* Jewish but is so no longer.[113] Whereas the Ebionites combine all manner of heresy, Joseph remains pure in his Christian orthodoxy. He embodies the knowledge of Jew and Christian necessary to define and combat heresy.

Epiphanius does not himself initially invoke Joseph in order to concoct his "antidote" for the Ebionites. Instead, it is the mention of Ebionite use of Hebrew translations of New Testament books that sparks Epiphanius's memory and leads him into a "digression" about Joseph's religious conflicts.[114] Joseph had once been a "man of rank" in service to the Jewish patriarch in Palestine.[115] When this patriarch secretly arranged his own deathbed baptism, Joseph began protracted years of confused exploration of Christianity.[116] His long spiritual struggle (during which he discovered, in a hidden Jewish treasury, the Hebrew gospel translations that have prompted Epiphanius's digression) was punctuated by the heinous deeds of the secretly converted patriarch's son and successor.[117] This scoundrel not only engaged in "seductions of women and unholy sexual unions"[118] but even attempted to seduce a Christian virgin through

---

[112]Epiphanius, *Panarion* 30.4.1 (GCS 25:338; Williams, *Panarion,* 1:122). The only full-length study of Joseph of Tiberias is Stephen Goranson, "The Joseph of Tiberias Episode in Epiphanius: Studies in Jewish and Christian Relations" (Ph.D. diss., Duke University, 1990); see also idem, "Joseph of Tiberias Revisited: Orthodoxies and Heresies in Fourth-Century Galilee," in Meyers, *Galilee,* 335–43; and the brief article by T. C. G. Thornton, "The Stories of Joseph of Tiberias," *Vigiliae Christianae* 44 (1990): 54–63.

[113]See Epiphanius, *Panarion* 30.5.3 (GCS 25:340; Williams, *Panarion,* 1:123).

[114]Epiphanius, *Panarion* 30.3.8–9 (GCS 25:340); see also *Panarion* 30.12.10, 13.1 (GCS 25:348).

[115]Epiphanius, *Panarion* 30.4.2 (GCS 25:338).

[116]Epiphanius, *Panarion* 30.4.5–7 (GCS 25:339–40).

[117]Epiphanius, *Panarion* 30.6–8 (GCS 25:340–44).

[118]Epiphanius, *Panarion* 30.7.4 (GCS 25:342; Williams, *Panarion,* 1:124).

magic.[119] The magician seducing the Christian virgin is an image of heresy common in the fourth century, drawing on the legends of the proto-heretic Simon Magus.[120] That the image of the archheretic is projected onto the Palestinian Jewish patriarch (the "arch-Jew," as it were) shows how amenable Epiphanius found Jews for theorizing heresy. Similarly, Epiphanius can relate the "insider" testimony of a Jew—a *former* Jew—who can thus speak authoritatively and disarm the Jewish/heretical threat with the same expertise with which he once disarmed the young patriarch's various magical implements.[121]

After the tribulations of sickness, healing, and the young patriarch's oversexed adolescence, Joseph received baptism and went to Constantine's court. There he exchanged his "highest rank among the Jews" for "rank in [Constantine's] Empire."[122] He moved, physically and politically, from the provincial and colonial margin to the imperial center. He requested and received from Constantine a special commission to "build Christ's churches in the Jewish towns and villages where no one had ever been able to found churches, since there are no Greeks, Samaritans, or Christians among the population."[123] Here we see, once again, the holy places of Palestine acting as the quintessential "frontier zone" of Christian power, the place where the Jew as object-to-be-known and -to-be-controlled is manipulated as the counterpoint to the dominant Christian subject. Jewish space becomes the proving ground for the unity and totality of Christian orthodoxy. These spaces in Galilee are marked as uniquely Jewish, and that Christian who best knows the Jew—the convert Joseph—is best suited to carry out the imperial desire for Christian

---

[119]Epiphanius, *Panarion* 30.8 (GCS 25:343–44).

[120]See, e.g., the famous line of Hegesippus quoted in Eusebius, *Historia ecclesiastica* 4.22.4 (GCS n.f. 6:370): "For this they called the church a virgin: for in no way had she been corrupted by hearing foolishness." On the intersection of heretical representation and gender in the fourth century see Virginia Burrus, "The Heretical Woman as Symbol in Alexander, Athanasius, Epiphanius, and Jerome," *Harvard Theological Review* 84 (1991): 229–48.

[121]Epiphanius, *Panarion* 30.8.7 (GCS 25:343; Williams, *Panarion,* 1:125). Joseph urinates on the young man's "implements of sorcery," nullifying their effects. Epiphanius does not state whether this was a "common" remedy (known to Epiphanius and his readers) or part of Joseph's particular knowledge of Jewish magic.

[122]Epiphanius, *Panarion* 30.11.7–9 (GCS 25:346–47; Williams, *Panarion,* 1:128). Joseph's imperial rank is emphasized several times: *Panarion* 30.4.1, 5.6, 12.1 (GCS 25:338, 340, 347).

[123]Epiphanius, *Panarion* 30.11.9 (GCS 25:347; Williams, *Panarion,* 1:128).

uniformity demanded by Constantine.[124] Joseph first went to Tiberias, his hometown, where the Jews (unsurprisingly) devised diabolical resistance: "The ingenious Jews, who are ready for everything, did not spare their continual sorcery. Those natural-born Jews wasted their time on magic and jugglery to put a spell on the [lime-pit] fire, but did not entirely succeed."[125] Naturally, Joseph's Christian faith triumphed over Jewish chicanery, and several small churches were built in Galilee under his supervision.[126] The imperial mission of the Christian church makes manifest and displaces the powerlessness of the Jews.

The placement of this story in the middle of the *Panarion*—a story that ostensibly has nothing to do with heresiology proper, except by "coincidence" and digression—is not, of course, accidental.[127] This anecdote demonstrates how a comprehensive discourse of heresiology, an attempt at a totalizing production of knowledge about the dangerous heretical "others" of Christian identity, so effectively makes use of the figure of the Jew as the entirely knowable and subjectable sign. Jewish knowledge—*from* a converted Jew, *of* other "natural-born" Jews—provides the Christian reader with a familiar and understandable discourse of power. That the power is explicitly Christian and imperial is embodied in the convert Joseph, who goes from a high-ranking Jew, serving a degenerate and duplicitous Jewish provincial leader, to the specially commissioned count of Emperor Constantine. Just as knowledge of "things Jewish" is "practically obvious" to everyone, so the exercise of imperial power as Christian

---

[124]The cities listed by Epiphanius as devoid of non-Jewish presence are Tiberias, Diocaesarea/Sepphoris, Nazareth, and Capernaum: *Panarion* 30.11.10 (GCS 25:347). The Nazoraean and Ebionite heretics themselves are localized in these chapters to the areas in and around Palestine: see *Panarion* 29.7.7–8, 30.2.7–9 (GCS 25:330, 335).

[125]Epiphanius, *Panarion* 30.12.4 (GCS 25:348; Williams, *Panarion*, 1:128). It is tempting to read this impotent magic of the Jews interfering with church building as a counterpart to God's miraculous collapse of the Jewish Temple-building project under Julian the Apostate.

[126]Epiphanius, *Panarion* 30.12.9 (GCS 25:348). Taylor, *Christians and the Holy Places,* 288–90, suggests that the remains of an earlier house-church in Capernaum might be the structure built by Joseph. For other attempts to verify Joseph's building projects (all inconclusive) see Goranson, "Joseph of Tiberias," 99–125.

[127]Epiphanius ends his "digression" by "returning" to the subject of Ebionite Scriptures (*Panarion* 30.13–15 [GCS 25:348–53]) and Ebionite practices, such as daily baptisms, vegetarianism, and circumcision (*Panarion* 30.16–19 [GCS 25:353–59]); he then refutes all of these practices and the docetic Christology of Ebion and his followers (*Panarion* 30.20–34 [GCS 25:359–82]).

power becomes equally "obvious," and so instructive on how to exert orthodox power.

The instructive value of the exercise of Christian power over Jews is brought home in Epiphanius's discussion of Joseph's later life. After his construction of Christian churches in Jewish towns, Joseph became an emblem of orthodoxy in his new town of Scythopolis: "Joseph was not only privileged to become a faithful Christian, but a despiser of Arians as well. In that city, Scythopolis, he was the only orthodox Christian—they were all Arian."[128] At the time when Epiphanius met Joseph and heard these stories, many years before the writing of the *Panarion,* Jews had ceded their villainous place to the Arians of Palestine. Significantly, the only other Jew Epiphanius mentions in Joseph's Scythopolis is in fact an anonymous convert from Judaism who was forced to hide his pious orthodoxy from his Arian neighbors.[129] The entire fabric of Joseph's story in the *Panarion* prepares us to understand how the imperial Christian is to overcome the onslaught of the unorthodox "other": Jews then, Arians now, a bewildering multitude of Gnostics, Jewish-Christians, Encratites, Origenists, or any other theological deviant who might cross the Christian's future path. If they can be as thoroughly comprehended as the Jew, their threat will be as easily squashed as an annoying insect.

Ideology and the Nature of Christian Empire

Marxist literary critic Terry Eagleton was most likely not thinking of Epiphanius's image of heretics (and Jews) as poisonous insects when he wrote: "What persuades men and women to mistake each other from time to time for gods or vermin is ideology."[130] Nevertheless, Eagleton's

---

[128]Epiphanius, *Panarion* 30.5.5 (GCS 25:340; Williams, *Panarion,* 1:123). Epiphanius actually recounts Joseph's "anti-Arian" troubles before going back further in time to his conversion and church building later in *Panarion* 30: his orthodoxy is established early on.

[129]Epiphanius, *Panarion* 30.5.7 (GCS 25:340). On the chronology of Joseph's life, Epiphanius's meeting with Joseph, and the composition of the *Panarion* see Goranson, "Joseph of Tiberias," 70–72. Epiphanius mentions that he met Joseph while visiting Eusebius of Vercelli in exile in Scythopolis (*Panarion* 30.5.2 [GCS 25:340]), placing the meeting somewhere between 355 and 361 (Goranson prefers a date closer to 361). The events narrated by Joseph must have taken place before the death of Constantine (337), and the *Panarion* was composed ca. 377.

[130]Terry Eagleton, *Ideology: An Introduction* (London: Verso, 1991), xiii.

insistence on the significance of ideology in political discourse can help elucidate some of the motives, strategies, and consequences of the totalizing language of Christian Empire that I have outlined.[131] Eagleton provides what he calls a "broad definition" of ideology "as a body of meanings and values encoding certain interests relevant to social power," and then he "fine-tunes" this definition somewhat: "Ideologies are often thought . . . to be *unifying, action-oriented, rationalizing, legitimating, universalizing* and *naturalizing*."[132] All of these "ideological strategies," as he calls them, are evident in the totalizing project of early Christian imperialism, the unifying and justificatory attempts to create a discourse of religious power that "speaks for itself." Particularly significant for this first blush of Christian Empire in the fourth century, I think, is the notion of *naturalizing*, the ways in which "successful ideologies are often thought to render their beliefs natural and self-evident—to identify them with the 'common sense' of a society so that nobody could imagine how they might ever be different."[133]

This ability to cloak the production of knowledge in the anonymity of "common sense" was one way in which the radical transformation of Christianity from dissident sect to imperial religion was effected. The authors I have selected as examples of comprehensive discourses of Christian Empire from the fourth-century holy land could not construct theories of "why Christians should possess power," as this might highlight the constructedness and artificiality of such power. They could only portray themselves as "discovering" this information and mediating it to their wider audience. The presentation of Christian authority as self-evident rendered that Christian authority more effective at this moment of ideological transition: "Power is tolerable only on condition that it mask a

[131]Definitions and discussions of ideology proliferate almost faster than one can type. Useful are David McLellan, *Ideology*, 2d ed. (Minneapolis: University of Minnesota Press, 1995); Eagleton, *Ideology*; Gary Lease, "Ideology," in *Guide to the Study of Religion*, ed. Willi Braun and Russell T. McCutcheon (London: Cassell, 2000), 438–47. See also Elizabeth A. Clark, "Ideology, History, and the Construction of 'Woman' in Late Ancient Christianity," *Journal of Early Christian Studies* 2 (1994): 155–84.

[132]Eagleton, *Ideology*, 45 (Eagleton's emphasis); see also 5–6, 202, 222.

[133]Eagleton, *Ideology*, 58. See also the definition in David Spurr, *The Rhetoric of Empire: Colonial Discourse in Journalism, Travel Writing, and Imperial Administration* (Durham, N.C.: Duke University Press, 1993), 156: "the process whereby a theory about how the world works is assumed implicitly by a text, as what is 'natural' within the system of cultural values which the text represents."

substantial part of itself. Its success is proportional to its ability to hide its own mechanisms."[134] Eusebius does not present himself as *inventing* the theological reading of all history as Christian history but as merely "the first now to embark on the undertaking and to set out on this deserted and untrodden path [*hodon*]," ultimately relying on the eternal God as his "guide [*hodēgon*]."[135] The path is there: it is merely "untrodden." Likewise, Cyril and Epiphanius rarely allow themselves explicit agency in their production of forms of totalizing knowledge. The knowledge they transmit is already always "out there," needing only to be drawn in from the periphery, catalogued, categorized, and presented in an orderly manner to the Christian reader.

The naturalness of this collation and presentation serves to naturalize the discourses of Christian power that are embedded within these texts. Epiphanius, for instance, does not need to explain why Joseph of Tiberias is able to countermand the diabolical magic of the Jews. The power of Jesus and the Christians is evident, "commonsensical," even to the scoffing crowd of Tiberian Jews who realize without prompting that their "one God" has become "the aid of the Christians."[136] The "natural" exercise of power over the Jews by Joseph becomes the natural exercise of power by Christian orthodoxy, the ability to crush heresy under the Christian boot. Likewise, the sweep of history "makes its needs" felt to Eusebius, so that his own historiographic agency is occluded by the theological press of the divine: the imperative of history becomes fittingly realized in the culmination of Christian Empire. In Eusebius's scheme, there can be no other outcome. There is no "outside" to the ideology constructed and naturalized by these authors at the dawn of Christian Empire.

If there is no "outside," there is, however, an "other" maintained inside, a tool with which the mechanisms of the new Christian ideology of Empire might be at once constructed and concealed. The Christian reader could come to understand through the representation of the known and dominated figure of the Jew that Christians have power. The production of naturalized and totalized forms of Christian knowledge,

[134]Michel Foucault, *The History of Sexuality*, vol. 1, *An Introduction*, tr. Robert Hurley (New York: Pantheon, 1978), 86.

[135]Eusebius, *Historia ecclesiastica* 1.1.3 (GCS n.f. 6:8).

[136]Epiphanius, *Panarion* 30.12.8 (GCS 25:348; Williams, *Panarion*, 1:129).

significantly oriented around the paradigmatically known figure of the Palestinian Jew, delineated the first crude outlines of imperial Christian power: "The realm of order, of what was signified, was the new realm of authority, of the certainty of political power."[137] The comprehensive nature of these discourses, as sweeping and inclusive as they are knowledgeable, serves to naturalize Christian power, in history, ritual, and theology, as well as law, art, or any other area of Christian life.[138] The Jew emerges throughout the fourth century, the "Age of Constantine," as a malleable "shadow-other" of the Christian-in-power; in the totality of the new Christian worldview, power from the Christian is articulated through imperial power over the Jew of the "frontier zone" of the holy land.[139]

My point in emphasizing naturalization and the construction of a Christian ideology of knowledge and mastery in the holy land is precisely to begin to denaturalize, unravel, and problematize this "new realm of authority." Analysis of ideology since Marx has served to unmask, not to fortify. Particularly ideologies that may be described as explicitly colonial—that is, articulated, as these comprehensive discourses were, through the active articulation and appropriation of an inferior "other" subject, the Jew—bear the seeds of their own deconstruction. The comprehensive discourses emanating from the fourth-century holy land derive their force through a delicate act of construction and containment. Empty Eusebius's Palestine of its "great Jewish villages," deprive Cyril of his devious Jewish lurker or Epiphanius of his squashable Jewish heretics, and the triumph of mastery rings hollow. The dangerous other must be called into existence, comprehended, and controlled in order for an ideology of power to be meaningful.[140] The new Christian self is inextricably

---

[137]Timothy Mitchell, *Colonising Egypt* (Cambridge, U.K.: Cambridge University Press, 1988), 179.

[138]A few examples of the expansive nature of this totalizing ideology and its Jewish "other" in such arenas must suffice here: see Margaret Miles, "Santa Maria Maggiore's Fifth-Century Mosaics: Triumphal Christianity and the Jews," *Harvard Theological Review* 86 (1993): 155–75, on Jews in Christian art; David Brakke, " 'Outside the Places, Within the Truth,'": Athanasius of Alexandria and the Localization of the Holy," in *Pilgrimage and Holy Space in Late Antique Egypt*, ed. David Frankfurter (Leiden: Brill, 1998), 445–81, on Jews in Christian cult; Rudolf Lorenz, *Arius Judaizans? Untersuchung zur dogmengeschichtlichen Einordnung des Arius* (Göttingen: Vandenhoek & Ruprecht, 1980), on Jews in Christian heresy.

[139]See the discussion in Young, *White Mythologies*, 12–18, on the "self-centred" construction of the imperial "other."

[140]This dangerous flipside emerges in an early text of Eusebius, *De martyribus Palaestinae*,

bound up in the certain knowledge of the Jewish other. Once called into existence, however, this Jewish other cannot be quietly shelved and forgotten: the carefully naturalizing project of containment evokes the fear of breach and loss of control.[141] As I turn now to a different facet of Christian knowledge production, the biblical scholarship of fifth-century monastic *émigré* Jerome, we will see the ephemerally conjured holy land Jews of these comprehensive discourses materialize more solidly, and menacingly, into Christian perception. We will also, perhaps, perceive some of the ways in which Christian discourses of imperial knowledge might result not just in the naturalization of power, but in the invocation of resistance.

---

in which the "great villages of Jews" (here, Lydda/Diospolis) are present as witnesses to Christian suffering, not Christian triumph: see *History of the Martyrs in Palestine by Eusebius, Bishop of Caesarea Discovered in a Very Antient* [sic] *Syriac Manuscript,* ed. and tr. William Cureton (London: Williams and Norgate, 1861), 29–30 (Syr.), 27–28 (Eng.). This episode survives only in the long, Syriac recension. Eusebius seems to have abbreviated and edited the work himself after 313, and this section was not included (see Barnes, *Constantine and Eusebius,* 148–58). It nonetheless stands as an important reminder of the shadows that haunted Eusebius's historicized ideology.

[141] See the discussion of ideology, interpellation, and colonial discourse in Robert J. C. Young, *Postcolonialism: An Historical Introduction* (London: Blackwell, 2001), 412–16.

3 ∽ "Captive Judaea": The Production of Jewish Knowledge

Christian Knowledge as Imperial Power

From his monastic cell in fifth-century Bethlehem, that renowned (and infamous) ascetic man of letters Jerome made a reputation for his biblical interpretations and translations produced "according to the Jews," *iuxta Hebraeos*. Jerome frequently provided his readers with a solidly anti-Jewish justification for this noteworthy linguistic practice: "so that you might respond word-by-word to Jewish slanders [*Iudaeis . . . calumniantibus*]."[1] Surely any good Christian of Jerome's day and age would accept such a religiously grounded argument: churches both East and West had long invested their Christian interpretation of the Bible, especially the Old Testament, with strong anti-Jewish sentiment.[2] What then should we make of a corollary justification, often found in these Vulgate prefaces and elsewhere in Jerome's corpus, crafted as "preemptive" defenses of Jerome's Hebrew learning?[3] More than once he rails at the hypothetical

---

[1] Jerome, *Praefatio in libro Psalmorum (iuxta Hebraeos)* 33–34. Line numbers follow the editions of the prefaces found in *Biblia sacra iuxta Vulgatam versionem,* ed. R. Weber et al., 2 vols. (Stuttgart: Würtembergische Bibelanstalt, 1964), here 1:769. This preface is addressed to Sophronius, who had himself recently been frustrated in debates with Jews (18–20 [Weber, *Biblia,* 1:768]). See also *Praefationes in libro Iosue* 19–20, *in libro Isaiae* 31 (Weber, *Biblia,* 1:285, 2:1096). J. N. D. Kelly, *Jerome: His Life, Writings, and Controversies* (London: Duckworth, 1975), 160–61, seems to accept this as Jerome's main motivation for his Hebrew studies, as well.

[2] See Marc Hirshman, *A Rivalry of Genius: Jewish and Christian Biblical Interpretation in Late Antiquity,* tr. Batya Stein (Albany: SUNY Press, 1996).

[3] That Jerome considered these *praefationes* part of a larger *apologia pro lingua hebraica* is evident by their inclusion in his *Apologia contra Rufinum* 2.25–32 (SC 303:172–94).

(or, at times, not so hypothetical) detractors: "If you don't believe *me*, read the Greek and Latin versions and compare them with these little works [*opusculis*], and whenever you find them in disagreement, *go ask any Jew*, in whom you ought to have more trust, and if he confirms our view, I imagine you won't consider him a soothsayer who has conjured up the very same translation as myself!"[4]

This retort recurs throughout Jerome's career: "Go ask the Jews!"[5] Could a Christian of Jerome's day be expected to hold Jews in the most thorough theological and cultural contempt yet still find them helpful and useful as linguistic and even interpretive guides to the Bible? We know, from Jerome's own insistence on the fact, that the solitary of Bethlehem did just that. He can protest to friends in Rome that "if it is expedient to hate any people and to detest any nation, I have a notable hatred for the circumcised; even now they persecute our Lord Jesus Christ in the synagogues of Satan"; even so, he asks immediately afterward, with apparent sincerity, "Yet can anyone object to me for having had a Jew as a teacher?"[6] Of course, people did object: both his purported foes, such as Rufinus of Aquileia, Jerome's fierce enemy in the Origenist controversy of the early fifth century, and his supposed allies, such as his younger anti-Pelagian contemporary Augustine of Hippo Regius. Against all challenges Jerome maintained a framework of Christian scholarship and identity in which it was permissible simultaneously to "hate" the Jews and to

---

[4]Jerome, *Praefatio in libris Samuel et Malachim* 69–73 (Weber, *Biblia*, 1:365–66, emphasis added). See also esp. his *Praefatio in libro Paralipomenon (iuxta LXX)* (PL 29:404A). Even though this latter preface (addressed ca. 388 to Domnio and Rogatianus) is appended to a Latin translation of Greek Chronicles, Jerome is already introducing his defenses of Hebrew learning and, for the first time, makes his oft-repeated challenge: *Interroget Hebraeos.*

[5]Jerome, *Praefationes in Pentateucho* 43, *in libris Samuel et Malachim* 70–71, *in libro Ezrae* 31, *in libro Psalmorum (iuxta Hebraeos)* 28 (Weber, *Biblia*, 1:4, 365–66, 638, 768); *Commentarius in Ezechielem* 10.33.1300–1301 (CCL 75:475); and *ep.* 112.20.5 (CSEL 55:391), to Augustine. This last instance will be discussed more fully below. It is variously phrased: *interrogent quemlibet Hebraeorum, interroga Hebraeos, interroga quemlibet Hebraeorum, interrogent Hebraeos.* Stefan Rebenich, "Jerome: The 'Vir Trilinguis' and the 'Hebraica Veritas,'" *Vigiliae Christianae* 47 (1993): 74n84, draws the social historical conclusion that "in Rome and in other cities of the Empire Jewish scholars could be found who offered their assistance in tackling difficult textual problems." The degree to which and context in which such assistance was "offered" is more or less unrecoverable: I focus instead on the rhetorical effect of such defiant proclamations from Jerome.

[6]Jerome, *ep.* 84.3.3 (CSEL 55:123), in one of the opening salvos of the Origenist controversy (on which see more below).

rely on them for certain types of instruction.

Scholars have posited several explanations for Jerome's dedication to the *Hebraica veritas,* the "Hebrew truth" of the Old Testament, and his reliance on contemporary Jewish teachers and informants. Jerome himself claims that his inspiration for the study of Hebrew was, in part, the studious effort of Origen at mastering this *lingua contra gentis naturam;*[7] but pointing out that Jerome has modeled himself on a literary giant does not explain why Jerome found such literary enormity so laudable. Some scholars have suggested that mastery of difficult and arcane literary knowledge afforded Jerome access to the more aristocratic circles of Roman clergy and aristocracy.[8] Some explanations point to the necessities of rhetoric: Jerome was, after all, the master of invective and polemic, with a vicious repertoire of responses always at hand for his "detractors [*obtrectatores*]."[9] His peculiarly "pro-Jewish"-sounding defense might be merely a part of this rhetorical apparatus,[10] some might argue, along with defenses ranging from the dismissive,[11] to the practical,[12] to the satirical.[13] Still oth-

---

[7]Jerome, *De viris inlustribus* 54 (TU 14.1:32–33); *Hebraicae quaestiones in libro Geneseos,* preface (CCL 72:2). See Mark Vessey, "Jerome's Origen: The Making of a Christian Literary Persona," *Studia Patristica* 28 (1993): 135–45. Adam Kamesar, *Jerome, Greek Scholarship, and the Hebrew Bible: A Study of the* Quaestiones Hebraicae in Genesim (Oxford: Clarendon Press, 1993), 43, suggests that this description of Origen refers to Greek monolingualism.

[8]Christine Steininger, *Die ideale christliche Frau,* virgo-vidua-nupta: *Eine Studie zum Bild der idealen christlichen Frau bei Hieronymus und Pelagius* (St. Otillien: EOS Verlag, 1997), 195; Stefan Rebenich, *Hieronymus und sein Kreis: Prosopographische und sozialgeschichtliche Untersuchungen* (Stuttgart: Franz Steiner Verlag, 1992), 208; idem, "Jerome," 60–65. On Jerome's low social origins in comparison with that of his aristocratic ascetic companions see Elizabeth A. Clark, *Jerome, Chrysostom, and Friends: Essays and Translations* (New York: Edwin Mellen Press, 1979), 61–64; Rebenich, *Hieronymus,* 154–92.

[9]See, e.g., *epp.* 48–49 (CSEL 54:350–87), and discussion in David S. Wiesen, *St. Jerome as a Satirist: A Study in Christian Latin Thought and Letters* (Ithaca, N.Y.: Cornell University Press, 1964), 200–44; and Ilona Opelt, *Hieronymus Streitschriften* (Heidelberg: Carl Winter-Universitätsverlag, 1973).

[10]Jerome answers his *obtrectatores:* Jerome, *Praefationes in Pentateucho* 4, 39; *in libro Paralipomenon (iuxta Hebraeos)* 32, *in libro Iob* 8, *in libro Psalmorum (iuxta Hebraeos)* 24 (Weber, *Biblia,* 1:3, 4, 547, 731, 768).

[11]Jerome, *Praefationes in libro Ezrae* 46, *in Iob* 52–53 (Weber, *Biblia,* 1:639, 732).

[12]Jerome, *Praefatio in libro Iosue* 11–12 (Weber, *Biblia,* 1:285), on the confusion of Latin translations. See also *Praefationes in libro Paralipomenon (iuxta Hebraeos)* 5–16; and *in libro Heremiae* 12 (Weber, *Biblia,* 1:546, 1166); and *Praefatio in Evangelio* 12–13 (Weber, *Biblia,* 2:1515), on the need for standardized translations. In his correspondence with Jerome, Augustine admits to the baffling multiplicity of Latin translations of the LXX: Augustine, *ep.* 71.4.6 (CSEL 34.2:254); see also *De doctrina christiana* 3.10.16 (CCL 32:87–88).

[13]Jerome, *Praefatio in libro Iob* 48–51 (Weber, *Biblia,* 1:732), mocking those who buy ex-

ers have even imagined Jerome had psychological reasons for bolstering his own "self-worth" in the face of more aristocratic or popular opponents.[14] Usually, however, modern scholars attribute a more or less sympathetic motive of "academic curiosity" to Jerome, as one recent study remarks: "Jerome's persistence with his belief in the correctness and authenticity of what he termed the *Hebraica veritas* . . . is a memorial to his scholarly integrity and resolute convictions."[15] It seems natural to us, as we struggle to achieve our own "scholarly integrity," that our ancient "counterparts" should also find philological accuracy significant for its own sake.[16] I would like to propose a different (although by no means exclusive) interpretation for Jerome's strangely scholastic "double vision"[17] with regard to his Jewish contemporaries, one we might dub "academic imperialism."

I outlined in the previous chapter how the production of knowledge about Jews held a delicate place in Christian imperial discourses of the fourth century. I suggested that the very process of producing knowledge of the inferior or deviant "other" constructed Christians into new positions of social power and authority. Jews were good "to think" Christian domination into existence: "to know a thing is to dominate it, to have authority over it. And authority means here for 'us' to deny autonomy to 'it' . . . since we know it and it exists, in a sense, *as* we know it."[18] This understanding of colonialist forms of knowledge as appropriation and

pensive books that are poorly edited.

[14]Neil Adkin, "A Note on Jerome's Knowledge of Hebrew," *Euphrosyne* 23 (1995): 245.

[15]Dennis Brown, *Vir Trilinguis: A Study in the Biblical Exegesis of Saint Jerome* (Kampen: Pharos, 1992), 55.

[16]See Benjamin Kedar-Kopfstein, "Jewish Traditions in the Writings of Jerome," in *The Aramaic Bible: Targums and Their Historical Context,* ed. D. R. G. Beattie and M. J. McNamara (Sheffield: Sheffield Academic Press, 1994), 420–30, esp. 420–23.

[17]On "doubled vision" see Joan Kelly, "The Doubled Vision of Feminist Theory," *Feminist Studies* 5 (1979): 216–27 (repr. in *Women, History, and Theory: The Essays of Joan Kelly* [Chicago, Ill.: University of Chicago Press, 1984], 51–64). That such "doubling" is apparent on the "top" of social relations (male, colonizer) as well as the "bottom" (female, colonized) has been elucidated in subsequent analyses of colonialist discourse. See, e.g., Laura Chrisman, "The Imperial Unconscious? Representations of Imperial Discourse," *Critical Quarterly* 32, no. 3 (1990): 38–58 (repr. in *Colonial Discourse and Post-Colonial Theory: A Reader,* ed. Laura Chrisman and Patrick Williams [New York: Columbia University Press, 1994], 498–516).

[18]Edward Said, *Orientalism* (New York: Pantheon Books, 1978), 32 (emphasis in original); see also idem, *Culture and Imperialism* (New York: Alfred A. Knopf, 1993); and Bernard S. Cohen, *Colonialism and Its Forms of Knowledge: The British in India* (Princeton, N.J.: Princeton University Press, 1996), ix, 22.

domination can likewise provide a new way of interpreting Jerome's
scholarly reliance on Jews. Jerome's stubborn display of Hebrew language
and contemporary Jewish interpretive sources, I suggest, is best read as a
simultaneous strategy of mistrust and appropriation, analogous to and
wound up in the strategies of imperial Christian totalization discussed in
the previous chapter. Jerome's "double vision" of Jews and Jewish knowledge enacts a sort of academic imperialism on the part of the Christian
scholar in the fourth and fifth centuries. Unlike his more tentative predecessors and contemporaries (such as Origen and Augustine), Jerome,
from his particular vantage point in the holy land at the beginning of the
Theodosian age, was able to construct Jews as an object of Christian
knowledge in such a way as to configure them into the thought-world of
a Christian Empire. For Jerome in Bethlehem, to "know" Jews was to exert religious and cultural authority over them, to acknowledge their
threat and to master it. As the expert Roman Christian "man on the
spot,"[19] Jerome positioned himself and his scholarly endeavors as the
boundary and conduit for the appropriation of this knowledge. Through
these endeavors Jerome was able to incorporate Jews—for all his "hatred"—into a component of imperial Christian identity. This process of
knowledge and power exerted over Jews could also be directed inward, to
establish new lines of hierarchy and power within the Christian empire.
Jerome's literary production was an academic discourse of power, suited
to the ideological turn of the post-Constantinian Christian empire.

Origen: "In Conversation with the Jews"

As I noted above, Jerome gestured to the scholarly model of Origen in his
use of Hebrew sources and texts. Before simply homologizing these two
intellectual efforts, however, it is worth pausing to consider the very different social and political context in which Origen wrote and the particular way he used his "Jewish knowledge" to construct Christian identity.
From his ecclesiastical position in the Roman city of Caesarea Maritima,
Origen produced a particularly authenticated form of Christian interpretive knowledge based on the Hebrew language and direct contact with

---

[19]A felicitous phrase of David Chidester, "Colonialism," in *Guide to the Study of Religion,*
ed. Willi Braun and Russell T. McCutcheon (London: Cassell, 2000), 432.

Jewish "informants."[20] I want to suggest, however, that this form of Christian knowledge did not ultimately ascribe intellectual authority to Origen or other Christians in his day. Instead it created a Christian discourse of justification and defense—of resistance—from a situation of explicit political powerlessness: through his use of Jewish knowledge from "real Jews," Origen sought to resist the intellectual and cultural hegemony represented by pagan (and, it is likely, Jewish) critique.

Origen's long work of Christian apology, the *Contra Celsum*, is telling in this regard. The second-century philosopher Celsus, in his anti-Christian *True Discourse*, had introduced a hypothetical Jew to indict Christians for their misuse of Scripture and their abandonment of Jewish religious traditions. Origen objects to Celsus's prosopopoetic Jew on several counts, particularly accusing Celsus of getting his Jewish voice wrong.[21] To bolster his defense, Origen marshals his Christian knowledge about Jews to counter the arguments of a pagan critic. This careful reappropriation of a Jewish voice based on Christian knowledge does not serve to establish a hierarchy of power—Christian over Jew, or Christian over pagan—but rather to establish legitimacy for Christians while maintaining difference between Jew, Christian, and pagan. For instance, when Origen responds to Celsus's criticisms about Jewish history (despite his use of a fictitious Jewish witness against Christianity, Celsus was hardly sympathetic to Judaism), Origen counters Celsus's fiction with his own truth, derived "from the Jews": "Now, I learned the history of the aforementioned [patriarchs] and the meanings of their names from the Jews [*apo Hebraiōn*], who have exalted and narrated them in their native letters and native dialect. For even until today Jewish names, being of the

---

[20]See E. E. Urbach, "The Homiletical Interpretation of the Sages and the Expositions of Origen on Canticles, and the Jewish Christian Disputation," *Scripta Hierosolymitana* 22 (1971): 247–75; Nicholas De Lange, *Origen and the Jews: Studies in Jewish-Christian Relations in Third-Century Palestine* (Cambridge, U.K.: Cambridge University Press, 1976), 39–47, elaborated by Reuven Kimelman, "Rabbi Yohanan and Origen on the Song of Songs: A Third-Century Jewish-Christian Debate," *Harvard Theological Review* 73 (1980): 567–95; Hayim Lapin, "Jewish and Christian Academics in Roman Palestine: Some Preliminary Observations," in *Caesarea Maritima: A Retrospective After Two Millennia*, ed. Avner Raban and Kenneth G. Holum (Leiden: E. J. Brill, 1996), 496–512.

[21]Origen, *Contra Celsum* 1.28, 23–44, 56–71; 2.1, 3–79 (SC 132:150–52, 162–92, 228–74, 276–80, 286–476). That the cultural critique Origen resists may have come from "pagans" as well as Jews is not impossible but is also not significant in my reading of Origen: he certainly ascribes cultural "sovereignty" to Jews as well as Romans (see below).

Hebrew dialect, are written in these same letters."[22]

Origen can, quite literally, speak like a Jew, with knowledge of their "native dialects" and foreign names, which (he suggests) remain unchanged from biblical times. Palestinian Jews, with whom Origen has his informative contact, are still inherently biblical, so by learning their language Origen can defend Christian use of Scripture against Celsus's attacks. Throughout his many exegetical projects Origen refers to "local" Palestinian Jewish life and society, continually promoting his own firsthand knowledge of Jewish language and interpretation.[23] The knowledge of local Jews even helped Origen produce a more "authentic" biblical text on which to base his often astonishing biblical exegesis.[24] At the same time that Origen complained that Jewish understanding of the Bible was too "fleshly"—that is, too focused on the literal, nonspiritual interpretation of the text[25]—he relied on their philological and geographical expertise in his own interpretive efforts to produce a thoroughly spiritualized interpretation of the Old and New Testaments.[26]

It might be argued that such blatant appropriation of Jewish knowledge in defense of Christian truth constitutes an act of aggression and domination: is not Origen, like Celsus before him, merely pressing the Jew into service against his will? On the contrary, I suggest that Origen's copious and repeated references to Jewish knowledge and teachers, and his claims to be able to speak with their voice, constitute an act of resis-

[22]Origen, *Contra Celsum* 4.34 (SC 136:270).

[23]See Gustave Bardy, "Les traditions juives dans l'oeuvre d'Origène," *Revue Biblique* 34 (1925): 217–52; De Lange, *Origen and the Jews,* presses these sources for social-historical reconstruction of Jewish life and Jewish-Christian relations. See also Roger Brooks, "Straw Dogs and Scholarly Ecumenism: The Appropriate Jewish Background to the Study of Origen," and Paul Blowers, "Origen, the Rabbis, and the Bible: Towards a Picture of Judaism and Christianity in Third-Century Caesarea," both in *Origen of Alexandria: His World and Legacy,* ed. Charles Kannengeisser and William L. Petersen (Notre Dame: University of Notre Dame Press, 1988), at 63–95, and 96–116.

[24]The so-called Hexapla. Kamesar, *Jerome,* 4–28, argues that Origen's goal in producing the *Hexapla* was exegetical accuracy and "healing [*iasasthai*]" of the corrupt LXX text (see Origen, *Commentarius in Matthaeum* 15.14 [GCS 40:388], cited by Kamesar, *Jerome,* 5), not the promotion of a truly "Hebrew" Bible. See also C. P. Bammel, "Die Hexapla des Origenes: Die *Hebraica Veritas* im Streit der Meinungen," *Augustinianum* 28 (1988): 125–49.

[25]Most famously in *De principiis* 4.3.2, 6–7 (SC 268:346–52, 364–68).

[26]A few of many examples: *Selecta in Genesim* 2.8 (PG 12:100A); *Selecta in psalmo 1* (PG 12:1084A); *Homiliae in Ezechielem* 1.4 (SC 352:62); *Homiliae in Ieremiam* 13.2 (SC 238:56); *Commentarius in Matthaeum* 11.19 (SC 162:312–14); and *Commentariorum series in Matthaeum* (PG 13:1777D).

tance against a perceived regime of Jewish and pagan persecution. Origen's use of Jews to decry Jewish "fleshly" reading of the Bible is akin to acts of colonial mimicry, not imperial domination.[27]

Origen's intellectually resistant construction of Christian knowledge of Jews is most evident when Origen is pressed from within the Christian fold, as in his correspondence with Julius Africanus, another learned Christian of Origen's day. Africanus wrote to Origen following a public debate between Origen and some "witless" person (*agnōmōn,* as Africanus characterizes him).[28] We know very little about the debate itself,[29] only that, in the course of making his argument, Origen referred to the story of Susanna in the Greek book of Daniel. Africanus, presumably in the audience, withheld comment at the time but soon after wrote to Origen in "amazement."[30] Surely, Africanus writes, Origen of all people must realize that the story of Susanna and the elders is a Greek forgery and not part of the authentic Bible. As Origen himself should know, Africanus continues, the story of Susanna is not part of the Jewish Old Testament, the Hebrew Bible, and thus should not be cited as real Scripture.[31] Africanus suggests that the preeminent mark of scriptural authenticity is linguistic and cultural connection to the authors of Scripture, the Jews.

Africanus's other arguments build on this central link between Jews and "their" Bible: Jewish language (the puns in this story do not translate from Greek to Hebrew), Jewish style (the prophetic form of speech is all wrong), and Jewish culture and politics (Jews in exile would never behave in the way depicted in this story).[32] Africanus approaches Origen as one intellectual to another and invites him to revise his biblical interpretation in light of Origen's vast knowledge of Jewish language and culture.[33] The modern scholar reading Africanus's letter might be sympathetic, not least

[27]On mimicry see discussion of Homi Bhabha below, and the important nuances of Anne McClintock, *Imperial Leather: Race, Gender, and Sexuality in the Colonial Contest* (London: Routledge, 1995), 61–71.

[28]Africanus, *Epistula ad Origenem* 2 [SC 302:514]). Origen calls him "my friend Bassus" (*Epistula ad Africanum* 3 [SC 302:522]).

[29]See the discussion of the *Sources chrétiennes* editor, Nicholas De Lange, SC 302:475–78.

[30]Africanus, *Epistula ad Origenem* 2 (SC 302:514).

[31]A point made twice: Africanus, *Epistula ad Origenem* 5, 7 (SC 302:516, 518).

[32]Africanus, *Epistula ad Origenem* 4–8 (SC 302:516–20).

[33]For a refutation of the theory that Africanus was himself Jewish see E. Habas (Rubin), "The Jewish Origins of Julius Africanus," *Journal of Jewish Studies* 45 (1994): 86–91.

of all in the assumption that the Greek book of Daniel contains significant later additions that are not "authentic" to the original Hebrew text.
Had not Origen himself made similar arguments using Jewish language
and culture to support authentic Christian interpretation? Based on Origen's own triangulation among the Hebrew Bible, Jewish knowledge, and
Christian exegesis, Africanus writes in a sympathetic and surprised tone
to request a revised argument from Origen.

Origen declines Africanus's invitation to make such a revision. He instead takes this opportunity to explain to Africanus (and to others, presumably) precisely why he has paid such close attention to Jewish texts
and interpretations: certainly not in order to "judaize" the Christian Bible but rather

lest we be ignorant of what is found in their versions, so that when we are in
conversations with the Jews [*pros Ioudaious dialegomenoi*] we don't offer forth
something not found in their Scriptures and, likewise, so we will be prepared for
whatever they might bring forth from their versions that is not found in our Bible. We have made this sort of preparation for our debates with them [*pros aut-
ous en tais zētēsi*] so they won't scorn us or laugh at the gentile believers (as is
their custom), saying that they are ignorant of the true readings in their texts.[34]

Thus, according to Origen the Christian appropriation of a Jewish textual tradition serves, paradoxically, to define more clearly Jewish-
Christian difference by establishing a meaningful language of debate.
Laying out a common text allows Christians and Jews to be "in dialogue," to open up lines of contest that Jews would otherwise not allow
to Christians. This is not an arena in which the Christian can exert power
over the Jew—by, for instance, insisting that Jews adhere to the Septuagint—but one in which the Christian textually "submits" to the Jews in
the hope of establishing intellectual legitimacy.[35] At the same time, this
act of textual submission signals the vitality of Christian opposition and
resistance. By accepting Jewish terms for debate, the Christian gains a
foothold to resist Jewish control of the text: it is by speaking "Jewishly
[*hebraïkon*]" that Origen can plausibly argue against Jewish fleshly interpretation.

    [34]Origen, *Epistula ad Africanum* 9 (SC 302:534).
    [35]On "dialogues" and "debates" between Christians and Jews see also *Contra Celsum* 1.44,
55 (SC 132:192, 224–28).

That the text under consideration here is the story of Susanna—with its condemnation of the "unjust elders" of the Jews—accentuates Origen's ultimately resistant attitude toward Jews through their own texts. Origen can even use contemporary Palestinian Jews' linguistic proximity to the Hebrew Bible to defend his own preference for a story found only in the Greek Old Testament, a true subversion of their textual claims to authority. He says that he consulted a certain "learned Jew" who considered the Susanna story authentic[36] and "another Jew" who testified to the mendacity of the elders in captivity.[37] Both of these Jewish witnesses not only support Origen's textual practices against Africanus, by granting the authorizing stamp of Jewish approval, but they also allow Origen to turn around and protest the unreliability of the Jews' text of the Old Testament, since the Jews have "clearly" expurgated unwanted and unflattering material from their versions.[38]

Origen invokes his own experience among Jews as well. "Living for a long time among this nation" has given him insight into their devious political and social practices, affirming the behavior of the elders in Babylon:[39] "Why even now, while Romans run their Empire [*basileuontōn*] and Jews pay the drachma tribute to them, with Caesar's agreement their Ethnarch rules over them, no differently than as if he were king of the nation [*basileuontos tou ethnous*]."[40] By using the same term to characterize the dominion of the Romans and the Jews—*basileia* (sovereignty)—Origen positions himself, and other Christians, as the objects of their homogenized authority. Christian-Jewish debate now rings in the same register as Origen's defense against the pagan critic Celsus, both as attempts to inscribe intellectual legitimacy to Christians against their more well-established detractors (philosophers and Jews). Origen's Palestinian Jew is historicized and biblicized, but he still determines the terms of intellectual interaction between Jew and Christian. Origen's locally produced Jewish knowledge is not a knowledge of power but of resistance. Through "dialoguing" and debating with the Jews, Origen can achieve a

---

[36] Origen, *Epistula ad Africanum* 11 (SC 302:538).
[37] Origen, *Epistula ad Africanum* 12 (SC 302:540).
[38] Origen, *Epistula ad Africanum* 13–15 (SC 302:542–50).
[39] Origen, *Epistula ad Africanum* 12 (SC 302:540).
[40] Origen, *Epistula ad Africanum* 20 (SC 302:566).

measure of intellectual respectability and resistance within and against that power.

For Origen the superiority of Christian interpretations of the Bible does not amount to the language of appropriation and domination that we find in later Christian imperial writings or that was evident in the writings on Jews of Epiphanius or Eusebius. Although the Jews may in some sense be "known," their voice comprehended and perhaps even plausibly replicated or mimicked, this knowledge does not enable Christian access to power. Origen seeks to establish an independent Jewish vitality with which to contrast, yet in which to ground, Christianity's own legitimacy. Origen's works come from a notably uncertain period of Christian history. Although persecutions are not rampant, the church is still configured as consisting "of martyrs," and the common discourse of Christianity is one of powerlessness and suffering.[41] Christians are careful to define themselves over against Jews for social and religious reasons, but in the face of "pagan persecution" the Jews and their vast antiquity can be deployed as defenses against accusations of Christian novelty and subversion.[42] In both cases, ultimately, Origen prefers to place Caesar and the Jewish patriarch in the same dominant political position with respect to the politically powerless Christian. Origen's use of Jewish knowledge may, perhaps, be a rare instance in which "the subaltern speaks" (to borrow Gayatri Chakravorty Spivak's now famous phrase):[43] the object of imperial authority creates for him- or herself a voice from the very position of cultural and political inferiority to which he or she has been rele-

[41]Origen, *Exhortatio ad martyrium* 5 (GCS 2:6–7); *Commentarius in psalmo 37* 2.8 (SC 411:322). See Judith Perkins, *The Suffering Self: Pain and Narrative Representation in the Early Christian Era* (London: Routledge, 1995); and Averil Cameron, *Christianity and the Rhetoric of Empire: The Development of Christian Discourse* (Berkeley: University of California Press, 1991), 111–12.

[42]Origen does this most famously in the *Contra Celsum:* see esp. 1.14–26, 3.3–7 (SC 132:112–44; 136:18–26). Origen's apologetical ambivalence is described by Louis Feldman, "Origen's *Contra Celsum* and Josephus' *Contra Apionem:* The Issue of Jewish Origins," *Vigiliae Christianae* 44 (1990): 105–35.

[43]See Gayatri Chakravorty Spivak, "Can the Subaltern Speak?" originally in *Marxism and the Interpretation of Culture,* ed. C. Nelson and L. Grossberg (Basingstoke: Macmillan, 1988), 271–313; cited here from Williams and Chrisman, *Colonial Discourse,* 66–111. In 1988 the answer was "no"; Spivak has since simultaneously defended and revised this answer, most recently in her *A Critique of Postcolonial Reason: Toward a History of the Vanishing Present* (Cambridge, Mass.: Harvard University Press, 1999), 246–311.

gated. The subaltern learns to mimic in order to resist and even subvert. In the end a more careful examination of Origen's particular relation to Jews and Jewish knowledge indicates that intellectual genealogies can take us only so far: Jerome's "double vision" of the Palestinian Jew must be viewed in its own context of fourth- and fifth-century imperial Christian power relations.[44]

Jerome and the *Judaeus Biblicus*

Jerome, who moved to Bethlehem near the end of the 380s from Rome,[45] shared with Origen the sense that the Palestinian province was more "biblical" than any other place in the Roman Empire and so more conducive to the serious study and interpretation of Scripture. As he wrote to his friends Domnio and Rogatianus:

Just as Greek histories are better understood by those who have seen Athens, and the third book of Vergil by those who have sailed from Troy, through Leucates, and Acroceraunia to Sicily, and finally to the ports of the Tiber: so, too, will he gaze with greater clarity upon holy Scripture who has contemplated Judaea with his own eyes, and come to know the memorials of ancient cities, and the places by both their indigenous and successive appellations.[46]

The Bible, for Jerome, is a cultural "classic" to be understood (as were the Greek and Latin classics of his day) more fully by those who had experienced the original *loci* of the narrative. Text and land cohered and completed each other. Yet, for all the fittingness of the Bible in its "native" land, the acquisition and production of biblical knowledge from within

[44]John Wright, "Origen in the Scholar's Den: A Rationale for the Hexapla," in Kannengeisser and Petersen, *Origen of Alexandria*, 48–62, at 61–62; and De Lange, *Origen*, 135: "It is not profitable to speculate on how different Origen's treatment of the Jews might have been had he lived after the triumph of the Church, at a time when Christians treated the Jews much as they had themselves been treated by pagans. In his day political power was in the hands of pagans, and the Church vied with the more favoured Synagogue by polemical means to win the minds, hearts and souls of the entire world."

[45]The standard chronologies of Jerome's life and works can be found in Georg Grützmacher, *Hieronymus: Eine biographische Studie zur alten Kirchengeschichte*, 3 vols. (1901–8; repr. Darmstadt: Scientia Verlag, 1969), 1:99–102; and Ferdinand Cavallera, *Saint Jérôme: Sa vie et son oeuvre*, 2 vols. (Louvain: Spicilegium Sacrum Lovaniense, 1922), 2:153–65. All of the Vulgate prefaces as well as prophetic commentaries were executed after Jerome's arrival in Palestine.

[46]Jerome, *Praefatio in libro Paralipomenon (LXX)* (PL 29:401A).

the holy land is never simple or natural for Jerome. The strangeness of
the Hebrew text always lingers on its surface, most often embodied for
him, as for his opponents and friends, by the living and alien bodies of
Jews.[47] Jerome's linguistic and exegetical expertise as he comes to inscribe
it in this holy-land environment is thus always self-conscious. Constant
protests of "travail" and "difficulty," as well as the "modest" concession
that he has learned the Hebrew language only "partly," although common rhetorical *topoi,* also contribute to an ongoing emphasis on the foreignness and otherness of Hebrew learning.[48] Jerome must seek out and
appropriate this knowledge and reformulate it for his Latin Christian
brethren.[49] In this important sense Jerome is never "native" to the Bible
and its land of origin: he must actively colonize it. There is something essentially different about the holy land and its "native" texts and languages, something that Jerome must acquire through outstanding erudition: "who does not know on what account I have sweated in learning
this foreign language?"[50] Only through this process can he mediate and
transmit "home" this new Christian knowledge to friends in Rome or
elsewhere in the Latin West.[51]

Adam Kamesar has suggested that Jerome's linguistic understanding,
especially his affinity for the original Hebrew text of the Old Testament,

---

[47]Compare Jerome's description, later in life, of how he learned the "hissing, gasping"
sounds of Hebrew: *ep.* 125.12 (CSEL 56:131); Patricia Cox Miller, "The Blazing Body: Ascetic
Desire in Jerome's Letter to Eustochium," *Journal of Early Christian Studies* 1 (1993): 21–45, at
37–38, makes good use of this passage in her exploration of the transference of bodily erotics
into textual metaphor. This passage from *ep.* 125 serves the complementary purpose of transfer-
ring textual signs into bodily strangeness. Interestingly, James Barr, "St. Jerome and the
Sounds of Hebrew," *Journal of Semitic Studies* 12 (1967): 1–36, concludes by *dis*embodying
Jerome's Hebrew linguistics, pointing out how (at times) Jerome's method for describing Hebrew "pronunciation" is more driven by a textual concern for orthography than by an auditory
concern for "soundedness."

[48]"Travail and difficulty": *Praefationes in libro Iosue* 19; *in Daniel* 11–19, citing Vergil, *Geor-
gica* 1.146: *labor omnia vicit improbus* (Weber, *Biblia,* 1:285, 2:1341). "Partial" Hebrew knowledge: *Praefationes in libro Ezrae* 42–43, *in Iob* 39–40 (Weber, *Biblia,* 1:639, 732). On the trope
of modesty in Latin Christian writing see Tore Janson, *Latin Prose Prefaces: Studies in Literary
Conventions* (Stockholm: Almquist & Wiksell, 1964), 124–47.

[49]See also Homi K. Bhabha, *The Location of Culture* (London: Routledge, 1994), 136–37:
"But cultural authority is also un*heimlich,* for to be distinctive, significatory, influential and
identifiable, it has to be translated, disseminated, differentiated, interdisciplinary, intertextual,
international, inter-racial."

[50]Jerome, *Praefatio in libro Isaiae* 30–31 (Weber, *Biblia,* 2:1096).

[51]See Said, *Orientalism,* 71–72, on the "vacillation between the familiar and the alien."

relates directly to his cultural formation as an educated Latin-speaking male of the late ancient Roman Empire.[52] Formed in a bilingual cultural context that emphasized the "'vertical' gap separating the Latin from the Greek,"[53] Jerome was sensitized to the profound significance of linguistic origins and difference. Although I find this to be an extremely persuasive description of Jerome's cultural and linguistic context, I believe it tells only part of the story. The gap between educated Latin males (especially in Rome) and Greek language and literature was "vertical" (with Greeks "on top") only in an abstract sense. The cultural politics of Greekness in the Roman Empire, as many recent studies of the "Second Sophistic" have shown, embedded the theoretical superiority of Greek learning in a political matrix of Roman domination.[54] As erudite as the Greeks might be, they were always the political and economical subjects of a Roman imperial master.

Romans did not just admire and aspire to the erudition and linguistic grace of the Greeks: they actively appropriated it in a manner that might also fittingly be described as "academic imperialism."[55] For Jerome, at the end of the fourth century, Horace's words still rang true: *Graecia capta ferum victorem cepit et artis / intulit agresti Latio* (Captive Greece captured the beastly victor, and introduced / The arts to rustic Latium).[56] Greece

[52]Kamesar, *Jerome*, 43: "Why did Jerome attach so much importance to the study of the Hebrew text when no one before him in the Greek Church had done so? It seems there can be only one explanation for this. He was part of a culture in which sensitivity to a foreign language was an integral element. The Romans had developed one of the most sophisticated bilingual cultures in the history of man [*sic*]. Jerome was heir to that culture."

[53]Kamesar, *Jerome*, 46.

[54]See the introduction by Simon Goldhill to his edited volume, *Being Greek Under Rome: Cultural Identity, the Second Sophistic, and the Development of Empire* (Cambridge, U.K.: Cambridge University Press, 2001).

[55]See Greg Woolf, "Becoming Roman, Staying Greek: Culture, Identity, and the Civilizing Process in the Roman East," *Proceedings of the Cambridge Philological Society* 40 (1994): 116–43, esp. 118–25, where Woolf argues that in the early empire "a belief that, in some sense, Rome had civilized the west was compatible with, and in some sense necessitated, the notion that Greeks were overcivilized, and that Romans were balanced between barbarism and decadence" (121). Although Woolf does not refer in this piece to Said's work on "cultural imperialism," the sensitivity to ideological scholarship and power/knowledge is nonetheless present.

[56]Horace, *Epistularum liber* 2.1.156–57 (LCL 2:408). Jerome makes a veiled reference to such linguistic "capture" when discussing the Greek-to-Latin translations of Hilary of Poitiers: *ep.* 57.6.3 (CSEL 54:512). For a study of Jerome's appropriation and transformation of literary *topoi* in his writings from Palestine see B. P. Nugent, "Jerome's Prologues to his Commentaries on the Prophets" (Ph.D. diss., University of Texas at Austin, 1992), esp. 419–33. On

may have tamed rustic Latium, but it did so as a "captive": it did not render the "beastly victor" any less victorious.[57] From the late republic through the height of the western empire, Latin-speaking Romans actively cultivated and appropriated Greek language and culture as a status marker in a manner that reinforced their own Latin superiority. Just as the late republican politician Cicero had praised Greek as the "height of eloquence," while criticizing dandies who "disdained Latin letters" and became almost *too* Greek,[58] so the late imperial politician Symmachus could demonstrate his family's cultural status by bragging about his son's Greek lessons while retaining his own proud Latinity by playfully sitting down with his son and "relearning" Greek along with him.[59] An important aspect of Roman domination was the possession of enough cultural temperance to appropriate Greek knowledge without becoming Greek. As Romans took in Greek knowledge, it remained distinctly "foreign" to them,[60] inscribing a certain ambivalence in the mastery of Greekness that

Jerome's use of Horace (and other Latin "classics") to shape his own writerly "persona" see Vessey, "Jerome's Origen," 138–39 and nn. 11–12, which helpfully nuances the earlier study of Harald Hagendahl, *Latin Fathers and the Classics: A Study on the Apologists, Jerome, and Other Christian Writers* (Göteborg/Stockholm: Almqvist and Wiksell, 1958), 91–328 (on Jerome in general) and 281–83 (on Horace in particular), as well as idem, "Jerome and the Latin Classics," *Vigiliae Christianae* 28 (1974): 216–27, which consists mainly of addenda and acknowledgment of subsequent scholarship. As far as I can tell, Jerome does not cite this particular Horatian passage in his extant corpus, although he certainly knew this work (see the index of works in Hagendahl, *Latin Fathers*).

[57]Further exploration of Roman-Greek imperialism could go far in explaining some of the paradoxes of Romano-Greek relations (political mastery and cultural mistrust/envy). Some of this work has been done by Susan E. Alcock, *Graecia Capta: The Landscapes of Roman Greece* (Cambridge, U.K.: Cambridge University Press, 1993).

[58]Cicero, *De oratore* 1.4.13, *De optimo genere oratorum* 4.13, *Brutus* 70.247 (LCL 3:10, 2:364, 5:212); and see Elizabeth Rawson, *Intellectual Life in the Late Roman Republic* (Baltimore, Md.: Johns Hopkins University Press, 1985); and M. H. Crawford, "Greek Intellectuals and the Roman Aristocracy in the First Century B.C.," in *Imperialism in the Ancient World*, ed. P. D. A. Garnsey and C. R. Whittaker (Cambridge, U.K.: Cambridge University Press, 1978), 193–207 and 330–39 (notes).

[59]Symmachus, *ep.* 4.20.2. Text in *Symmaque: Lettres*, ed. J.-P. Callu (Paris: Société Édition Belles Lettres, 1972–95), 2:101. See Alan Cameron, "The Roman Friends of Ammianus," *Journal of Roman Studies* 54 (1964): 15–28, esp. 17; and Gerd Haverling, "Symmachus and Greek Literature," in *Greek and Latin Studies in Memory of Cajus Fabricius*, ed. Sven-Tage Teodorsson (Göteborg: Acta Universitatis Gothoburgensis, 1990), 188–205.

[60]See Augustine's (plaintive? rhetorical?) claims concerning his difficulty in learning Greek: *Confessiones* 1.13.20, 1.14.23 (CCL 27:11–12); see M. Lamberigts, "Augustine as Translator of Greek Texts," in *Philohistôr: Miscellanea in honorem Caroli Laga septuagenarii*, ed. A. Schoors and P. van Deun (Leuven: University Press, 1994), 151–61.

became central to high Roman status.[61] This desire to emulate Greek foreignness (to a point) may have granted abstract "vertical" superiority to "Greekness," but the process of mastery emphasized the domination and authority of "Romanness."

By the same token, the valuation of Greekness as a symbol of Roman mastery also gave "native" Greeks the opportunity to manipulate and subvert Roman authority. The ambivalence of Roman desire for Greek culture—intellectual emulation without total assimilation—perhaps provided "real" Greeks some access to resistance and subversion, as the arbiters of a desirable cultural capital.[62] If we apply this grid of domination, authority, and resistance over Kamesar's persuasive grid of "culture" and Latin education, Jerome's eagerness both to make visible and then to bridge the vertical "gap" between Latin, Greek, and Hebrew acquires a sharper contour. His scholarly endeavor enlarges to envelop not only "culture" in an abstract academic sense but the very materiality of Palestine and its "natives," as well. *Graecia capta* makes way in Jerome's Christian empire for *Judaea capta,* and the Palestinian "natives"—the Jews—become the domesticated bearers of Christian scriptural truths. The "natives" in turn may be reconsidered as active agents—and not passive embodiments of knowledge—in a complex struggle over culture and politics set in the very real scene of colonial encounter.

In Jerome's massive body of writings we can find two strategies of "academic imperialism" at play to effect the knowledgeable production of *Judaea capta.*[63] First, in his exegetical and translational writings Jerome builds on the totalizing historical discourse of such predecessors as Eusebius of Caesarea in order to project the present-day materiality of Pales-

---

[61]See Jorma Kaimio, *The Romans and the Greek Language* (Helsinki: Societas Scientiarum Fennica, 1979), esp. 195–331; Simon Swain, *Hellenism and Empire: Language, Classicism, and Power in the Greek World, A.D. 50–250* (Oxford: Clarendon Press, 1996); and Goldhill, introduction to *Being Greek Under Rome.*

[62]But see McClintock, *Imperial Leather,* 67: "Ambivalence may well be a critical aspect of subversion, but it is not a sufficient agent of colonial failure."

[63]I do not treat here the straightforward polemical refutation of "Jewish knowledge," which can also be found in Jerome's writings: see for discussion Ralph Hennings, "Rabbinisches und antijüdisches bei Hieronymus Ep 121,10," in *Christliche Exegese zwischen Nicaea und Chalcedon,* ed. J. van Oort and U. Wickert (Kampen: Kok Pharos, 1992), 49–71. Hennings uses this letter of Jerome's to examine some of his broader "anti-Jewish" interpretive themes, especially the question of "purity" and Sabbath observance and how they relate to contemporary rabbinic halachah.

tinian Jews into a comfortable, ever-receding Christian past. Second, in his more polemical writings, Jerome nuances his scholarly project with the more alarmist, yet equally totalizing, discourse of Epiphanius or Cyril of Jerusalem's heresiological writings on Jews. These two methods of Jerome's "academic imperialism" are not distinct or discontinuous but rather complementary strategies for producing Christian power through the domesticated representation of the non-Christian object.[64] They also give a sense of that delicate balance between the appropriation of foreign knowledge and the fear of assimilation into the other's foreignness; the result is a fractured discourse of knowledge and power, within which it might be possible to infer more than a little "native" resistance.

In his old age, when recalling learning Hebrew, Jerome represented this task as cultivating the "sweet fruits" from the "bitter seed" of the Jews.[65] As scholars for almost a century have demonstrated, much of Jerome's own representation of his contact with and knowledge of Palestinian and Syrian Jews cannot be taken at face value. He often cites directly from the exegetical works of Eusebius of Caesarea or Origen and claims their interactions as his own. Jerome's veracity aside, it is important to consider how Jerome uses Jewish interaction to craft an authoritative image of his own activity.[66] For Jerome to strive for a posture of academic imperialism that is at once triumphant yet cautious, it suffices for him to represent himself as culling the "sweet fruit" from the "bitter seeds" himself.

Jerome thus frequently frames his contacts with living Jews and their language as a strenuous yet ultimately rewarding journey into Christian prehistory. The holy land itself, every hill and peasant, is made to bear

---

[64]See Bhabha, *Location of Culture*, 70: "[Colonial discourse] seeks authorization for its strategies by the production of knowledges of colonizer and colonized which are stereotypical but antithetically evaluated." Compare also the efforts of British imperialists to "mark the social and political map of nineteenth-century India" through the production of linguistic knowledge, as described by Cohn, *Colonialism*, ch. 2: "The Command of Language and the Language of Command" (16–56).

[65]Jerome, *ep.* 125.12.2 (CSEL 56:131).

[66]Gustave Bardy, "Saint Jérôme et ses maîtres hébreux," *Revue Bénédictine* 46 (1934): 145–64; and, more recently, Günter Stemberger, "Hieronymus und die Juden seiner Zeit," in *Begegnungen zwischen Christentum und Judentum in Antike und Mittelalter: Festschrift für Heinz Schrechenberg*, ed. Dietrich-Alex Koch and Hermann Lichtenberger (Göttingen: Vandenhoeck & Ruprecht, 1993), 347–64. See Megan Hale Williams, "Jerome's Biblical Criticism and the Making of Christian Scholarship" (Ph.D. diss., Princeton University, 2002), 256–62.

some of the weight of this omnipresent past. Jerome sings the inimitable praises of Jerusalem and its environs in the voices of his companions Paula and Eustochium, soon after their arrival in the area, to their friend Marcella back in Rome: "Certainly, if that preeminent orator considers so-and-so at fault for having learned Greek not at Athens, but at Lilybaeum, and Latin not at Rome, but in Sicily—seeing that each province has its own idiom, all things *not* being equal—why would we consider that someone has been fully educated away from our own 'Athens'?"[67] Like Greek learned in Athens, Christian culture acquired in Jerusalem ("our own 'Athens'") possesses the purest accents. Jerome, crafting an ecclesiastical reputation as an expert commentator on Scripture, places great emphasis on "seeing" the biblical sites, and concludes that the holy sites are those places where Christians reach their intellectual and spiritual pinnacle *as* Christians.[68] The land is inescapably biblical, and even its quotidian sights and sounds convey echoes of scriptural tones: "Wherever you turn, the farmer at his plow keeps chanting, 'Alleluia!' The sweaty harvester distracts himself with Psalms, and the vine-dresser pruning the vine with his curved hook sings any of David's songs. These are the songs of the province [*haec sunt in hac provincia carmina*]: these, as they say, are the love ballads. This is the whistling of shepherds, these are the tools of husbandry."[69] If the essence of Scripture inheres even in the common plowman and shepherd, how much more will it flourish in the erudite monk Jerome? If the vine-dresser chants psalms like love ballads, how much knowledge will Jerome harvest with a little of his own scholarly "sweat"?

Jerome distinguishes himself from the native "chanting plowman" by a subtle spatial and temporal collapsing within the bounds of the holy

[67]Jerome, *ep.* 46.9.2 (CSEL 54:339), quoting Cicero in his condemnation of Caecilius (*in Caecilio* 39).

[68]See Jerome, *ep.* 46.13 (CSEL 54:343–44), with its constant emphasis on Marcella "seeing" the *loca sancta* (forms of the verb *videre* occur six times in this single paragraph). Visuality and Christian identity are insightfully discussed by Georgia Frank, *The Memory of the Eyes: Pilgrims to Living Saints in Christian Late Antiquity* (Berkeley: University of California Press, 2000), 107–8 for discussion of this passage in particular.

[69]Jerome, *ep.* 46.12.3 (CSEL 54:342–43). This passage can be read literally—as I have done—or figuratively, assuming that Jerome is metaphorically describing the "labors" of the simple "rustic" monastic houses that have sprung up in Palestine. Even the metaphorical reading, however, constructs a reality in which it is grounded: monks are like the biblical peasantry that is native to the holy places.

land, similar to the linguistic and geographic telescoping of Eusebius in his *Onomastikon*.[70] His goal is to construct the holy land as a biblical space, in which all the geographical and literary particularity of the books of the Bible can become transparent to the Christian scholar. To this end he frames the present-day Palestinian Jews as a population of a primarily linguistic and literary character: the "chanting plowman" is a cipher for what we might term the *Judaeus biblicus,* the Jew whose appropriable subjectivity frames Jerome's linguistic and literary edification of the Christian Bible.[71] The present-day *Judaeus biblicus* serves to mediate for Jerome the biblical past inscribed in this foreign landscape, to authenticate Christian *loca sancta.*[72]

One function Jerome's Jewish informants serve throughout his Palestinian exegetical writings is that of native guides to the foreign sights and sounds, inscribed in the text of the Bible and the landscape of Palestine. They "translate" biblical sites into contemporary Christian *loca sancta* by verifying and authenticating their original meaning for Jerome.[73] Jerome had himself, soon after arriving in Palestine, translated Eusebius's own *Onomastikon;* within only a few years he undertakes two further treatises designed to connect contemporary sites with their biblical counterparts: the *Book of Hebrew Names* and the *Book of Hebrew Questions on Genesis.* Both treatises specifically rely on "local" Jewish knowledge in order to provide justification for contemporary Christian piety at the holy places.

[70]Jerome had himself translated Eusebius's *Onomastikon* soon after arriving in Palestine and in his own preface acknowledges and appropriates the historically "flattening" procedure of Eusebius: Jerome, *Onomasticon Eusebii* praef. (GCS 11:3). On his translation and additions to the text see Grützmacher, *Hieronymus,* 2:71–74.

[71]See David Spurr, *The Rhetoric of Empire: Colonial Discourse in Journalism, Travel Writing, and Imperial Administration* (Durham, N.C.: Duke University Press, 1993), 32: "[Colonial discourse] seeks to dominate by inclusion and domestication rather than by a confrontation which recognizes the independent identity of the other." This distinction is useful in considering the differing approaches of Origen and Jerome toward "Jewish" sources of knowledge.

[72]With, as we will see, no appreciable loss of his constant disdain for the Jews themselves. Remarking on Jerome's *Commentary on Obadiah,* in which Jerome frequently refers to "Jews" and their interpretation, Georg Grützmacher observes: "Der Judenhaß der alten Kirche, den Hieronymus trotz seines Verkehrs mit den Rabbinen von ganzer Seele teilt, kommt hier zu scharfem Ausdruck" (*Hieronymus,* 2:206); elsewhere Grützmacher notes "ein fanatischer Judenhaß" on the part of Jerome (2:126–27).

[73]On the question of languages in fifth-century Palestine see Claudine Dauphin, *La Palestine byzantine: Peuplement et populations,* 3 vols. (Oxford: Archaeopress, 1998), 1:133–55, who argues that linguistic identity in this period became increasingly tied to religiocultural identity (Christian, Jewish, "Hellene," Samaritan) rather than to geographic origin.

That both texts are also framed as biblical commentaries serves to intensify the scriptural aura of the land. Jews, by acting as a sort of living lexicon for these projects, are themselves also embedded in the biblical space
and time of Jerome's newly Christian province.[74] Often the references are
subtle: an anonymous Jewish source here and there adds a shade of linguistic authenticity.[75] But Jerome can also press his Jewish geographers
into authenticating specifically Christian (and, as often, anti-Jewish) interpretation:

I myself once heard a Jew speaking in this way about this passage [*istum locum*]:
Because Bethlehem is situated towards the south, in which the Lord and Savior
was born [*natus est*], so there it is said of him: "The Lord will come from the
south"; that is, he will be born [*nascetur*] in Bethlehem, whence he shall rise.
And since he who was born in Bethlehem also gave the former law on Mount
Sinai, he also is "holy who comes from Mount Pharan," since Pharan is in the
area of Mount Sinai.[76]

It is entirely unclear where "the Jew" stops speaking and Jerome begins.
It is difficult to imagine that a Jew would speak of the "former Law" of
Moses or of "the Lord and Savior" as having already been born.[77] Jerome

---

[74]On the "dual axes of time and space" in colonial discourse see Spurr, *Rhetoric of Empire*,
64–67.

[75]See, e.g., *Hebraicae quaestiones in libro Geneseos* 10.6, 19.30, 22.2, 35.21, 46.28, 49.21 (CCL
72:12, 23, 26, 43–44, 50, 55); *Liber interpretationis hebraicorum nominum,* presented more as a
straight list of names and their meanings, refers directly to no sources, but in his prologue
Jerome configures the entire project as a Christian "completion" of Jewish knowledge (CCL
72:59–60). See also *Commentarii in Ioelem* 3.4, 12 (CCL 76:200, 204); *in Hieremiam* 2.45
(CCL 74:84) offers an interesting passage on "Gehinnom," providing essentially a Jewish geography of hell.

[76]*Commentarius in Abacuc* 2.3.3 (CCL 76A:623). Jerome has translated Hab 3.3 as *Deus ab
austro veniet, et sanctus de monte Pharan;* the NRSV reads: "God came from Taman, the holy
one from Mount Paran" (Jerome translates *Taman* as "south"). Jerome refers to this same interpretation (that Jesus would be born in Bethlehem) in *Tractatus de psalmo 106* 3 (CCL
78:197) but without mentioning his Jewish informant.

[77]But see *Talmud Yerushalmi* Berakhot 2:4 (text in *Talmud Yerushalmi,* 7 vols. [Vilna:
Romm, 1922; repr. Jerusalem: N.p., 1970], here 1:34), which recounts the strange story of a
man who moved to Bethlehem after hearing that, on the same day, Jerusalem had been destroyed and the "king and messiah" had been born. The story ends with the mother of this
messianic child weeping over the destruction of Jerusalem and claiming that her child had
been taken away by "spirits." The story could be read as a reaction to Christian nativity stories
and increasing pilgrimage to Bethlehem in the fourth and fifth centuries. My point here is not
to justify Jerome's readings with rabbinic "countertexts," but I also do not want to rule out the
possibility of textual resistance on the part of Palestinian Jews.

presumably relies on his Jewish informant here for geography, not Christology. Nonetheless, the Jew's local (and biblical) geographical knowledge becomes evidence for Jerome's supersessionist vision of the two testaments and the coming of the Christian "savior." That he could write these words from his monastery in Bethlehem, in view of the thickening trail of Christian pilgrims to this holy site, adds a certain immediacy to this Christian appropriation of local "Jewish" knowledge.[78]

Jews also serve in Jerome's exegetical writings to give proper, contemporary names to local Palestinian flora and fauna named in the biblical books. Various bushes and shrubs, otherwise obscured in both Hebrew and Septuagint texts, are restored to their original meaning, such as the "branch [flos]" in Isaiah 11.1 that Jerome claims has muddled interpretation of the prophetic passage cited in Matthew 2.23.[79] As he did with his geographical informants, Jerome can also compel his Jewish experts on local plant and animal life into explicitly Christianized, anti-Jewish interpretations of prophetic texts. In commenting on Isaiah 22.17 Jerome executes the following exegesis:

Moreover, a Jew who instructed me in the reading of the Old Testament translated this word [that is, geber] as "domestic rooster" [gallum gallinaceum]. He says: just as a domestic rooster, on the shoulder of its carrier, is moved from one place to another, so the Lord will cast you lightly from your own place. And you who formerly possessed the priestly crown and sanctification in the gold breastplate, on which was written God's name, you shall be crowned with tribulation and anguish. And, just as a ball when thrown on a wide, sloping place cannot stand still, but rolls off into the void, so all of

[78]Jerome remarks on the resurgence of Bethlehem as a Christian site in what seems to be the post-Constantinian period: see *ep.* 58.3.5 (CSEL 54:532). It is placed in a list of sites (like the Holy Sepulcher) previously obscured by "pagan persecutors." See also *epp.* 108.14.4, 121.praef. (CSEL 55:325, 56:3), and *Commentarius in Ezechielem* 3.prol. (CCL75:91); and discussion below in Chapter 5. On sources for pilgrimage to Bethlehem in this period see Pierre Maraval, *Lieux saints et pèlerinages d'Orient: Histoire et géographie des origines à la conquête arabe* (Paris: Éditions du Cerf, 1985), 272–74 (and note the lovely ninth-century illustration on the cover depicting Jerome embarking for Palestine).

[79]Jerome, *Commentarius in Isaiam* 4.11.1 (CCL 73:147); Matt 2.23: "There he made his home in a town called Nazareth, so that what had been spoken through the prophets might be fulfilled, 'He will be called a Nazorean'" (NRSV); this *logion* confused previous interpreters—who could not find this "prophecy"—but Jerome related it to Isaiah 11.1, in which the Hebrew for "branch" is *nêṣer*, whence Matthew's "Nazorean." See also *Commentarius in Ioelem* 3.18 (CCL 76:207).

your populace [that is, the Jews] has been scattered to the ends of the earth.[80]

Once again, a local informant has (unwittingly?) provided grist for Jerome's anti-Jewish exegetical mill. Roughly contemporary rabbinic sources do debate whether *geber* should be translated as "man" or "rooster,"[81] and one reference from Palestinian rabbinic literature even gestures toward such a translation for this Isaiah passage.[82] I do not, however, want to provide Jerome with Jewish "countertexts" that somehow relieve his interpretations of their own ideological burden. Jerome does not claim to act as a stenographer neutrally cataloguing and transcribing exegesis, nor should we view him as such. Even assuming Jerome did learn this interpretation of Isaiah from a Jewish teacher, it has now been repackaged in Jerome's commentary, recontextualized for Christian consumption—including the reference to a Jewish teacher. Jerome claims the assistance of a local Jewish linguistic "expert" (an Old Testament instructor) to authorize an anti-Jewish interpretation of the Bible. With the highly visible assistance of the *Judaeus biblicus* Jerome can interpret a prophetic passage as a prediction of the transformation of Palestine from a Jewish into a Christianized space: our lightly tossed rooster becomes a symbol of contemporary, not prophetic, Jewish exile.

Jerome is not only adept at transforming "Jewish" place-names and

---

[80]Jerome, *Commentarius in Isaiam* 7.22.17 (CCL 73:306). Isa 22.17: "The Lord is about to hurl you away violently, my fellow" (NRSV).

[81]*Geber* as "rooster" or "man": *Talmud Yerushalmi* Sukkah 5:5 (*Talmud Yerushalmi,* 4:48); *Talmud Bavli* Yoma 20b (text in *Talmud Bavli,* 20 vols. [Vilna: Almanah & Romm, 1880–92; repr. Jerusalem: N.p., 1980], here 5:40). Yet more highly gendered rabbinic interpretations of Isa 22.17, in which *geber* as "man" is generally opposed to "woman," necessitate the more obvious understanding of the word: see *Talmud Bavli* Ketubot 28a, Sanhedrin 26a (*Talmud Bavli,* 8:54, 15:51).

[82]*Leviticus Rabbah* 5.5 is the only reference I have found to the *geber* in Isa 22.27 as "rooster"; the passage is attributed to R. Samuel, b. Nahman (fourth-century *amora*), and is a secondary reading with merely the phrase, "Just like a *geber,* that is, a rooster (*tarnāglā'*) is tossed from one place to another" (see Louis Ginzberg, "Die Haggada bei den Kirchenvätern, VI.: Der Kommentar des Hieronymus zu Jesaja," in *Jewish Studies in Memory of George A. Kohut,* ed. Salo Baron and Alexander Marx [New York: Alexander Kohut Memorial Foundation, 1935], 279–314, at 302). Given the general difficulty in dating rabbinic midrashim, it is almost impossible to posit a connection between R. Samuel's interpretation and Jerome's, beyond noting that Palestinian rabbis did, at times, make this translation. We may continue to assume that the anti-Jewish interpretation derived from it is entirely Jerome's. On the date of *Leviticus Rabbah* see H. L. Strack and G. Stemberger, *Introduction to the Talmud and Midrash,* tr. Markus Bockmuehl (Edinburgh: T. & T. Clark, 1991), 313–17.

farm animals into simultaneous props of native authenticity and tools for anti-Jewish interpretation. In addition, as several students of Jerome's exegesis have noted, Jerome further equates the Jews themselves with their own historical particularity, which is closely associated with their linguistic proximity to the *Hebraica veritas.*[83] Both the interpretive mentality and the linguistic authenticity of Jerome's contemporary Jews are characterized as "streams," the "sources [*fontes*]" of which can still be sought *ad Hebraeos:* "Therefore let us have recourse to the Jews [*ad Hebraeos*], and seek true knowledge from the source rather than from the small streams, particularly since this is not a prophecy about Christ, about which they tend to be evasive and to hide the truth with lies, but the historical order of events is being woven together out of what goes before and after."[84] The assumption here is that Jews are naturally untrustworthy, and will, of course, lie about matters pertaining directly to Christ;[85] but they are also essentially historical and biblical subjects, possessing a direct connection to the past that can be teased out through learned interrogation. A veritable Dr. Livingstone of biblical exegesis, Jerome can trace Christian history back to its Jewish sources thanks to—and in spite of—his native informants.

The metaphor of "streams" and their "sources" is an important image in Jerome's linguistic endeavors, as well.[86] Just as the Old and New Testaments are better understood at their respective Hebrew and Greek "sources," the language of the Bible as a whole is better comprehended (on some levels) through its "native" speakers. The familiar charge that Jews tend to read the text of the Bible "historically" instead of "spiritually" acquires a new significance: Jerome does not merely condemn their

---

[83]Kamesar, *Jerome,* 182–83, 188; Pierre Jay, *L'exégèse de Saint Jérôme d'après son "Commentaire sur Isaïe"* (Paris: Études Augustiniennes, 1985), 145–46; Ralph Hennings, *Der Briefwechsel zwischen Augustinus und Hieronymus und ihr Streit um den Kanon des Alten Testaments und die Auslegung von Gal. 2,11–14* (Leiden: E. J. Brill, 1994), 120–21.

[84]Jerome, *Commentarius in Zachariam* 2.8.19 (CCL 76A:820). The question here concerns the "fasts" prescribed for the Jews in Zech 8.19, about which (Jerome complains) Christian commentators have previously provided only "disagreement [*dissonantia*]" among themselves.

[85]Spurr, *Rhetoric of Empire,* 34: "for the threat of distrust or violence remains inherent in this classic colonial situation.

[86]See, e.g., Jerome, *Commentarius in Ecclesiasten* praef. (CCL 72:249). The concept of linguistic *fontes* and *rivuli* appears already in *ep.* 28.5 (CSEL 54:229), written to Marcella while still in Rome. In *ep.* 106.2.3–4 (CSEL 55:249), the *fons hebraicae veritatis* is more explicitly linked to *Hebraeorum auctoritas.* See Kamesar, *Jerome,* 182.

"historical" (or "fleshly") reading, but rather he makes his contemporary Jews the embodiments of this more basic scriptural reality. In his biblical commentaries executed in the holy land Jerome refers often to the *veritas historiae* that he has received "from the Jews [*ab Hebraeis*]."[87] Although sometimes he refers neutrally or dismissively to "Jewish fables,"[88] he more often equates the biblical knowledge of Jews with the Christian "historical" level of biblical interpretation. Even the recent interpretations of Jews executed in Jerome's day are always already "historicized" and can thus be appropriately combined with Christian spiritual interpretation:

So desiring to imitate the head of household who brought forth from his treasury both old and new things (Matt 13.52), and the bride in the Song of Songs who says, "new as well as old have I saved for you, my beloved" (Song 7.13), I have mixed Jewish history [*historiae Hebraeorum*] with our own moral interpretation [*tropologiam*], so that I might build on stone and not on sand (Matt 7.24–27), and so I might establish a stable foundation, just as Paul the architect wrote that he was able to do (1 Cor 3.10).[89]

Just as passages from the Old and New Testaments blend here to instruct on the fitting and stable synthesis of "old" and "new," so Jerome can justify seeking the "old"—the *historia*—with which to authenticate his own scriptural interpretation. That this "old" foundation should come from contemporary Jews serves at the same time to ameliorate the dangers of consulting Jewish interpreters (even present-day Jews are locked into a bygone past) and to demonstrate the ultimate Christian authority over all

[87] Jerome, *Commentarii in Isaiam* 5.23.18 (CCL 73:223), *in Abdiam* 20 (CCL 76:372), *in Abacuc* 2.3.2 (CCL 76A:620), *in Sophoniam* 2.5 (CCL 76A:681), *in Zachariam* 1.4.8 (CCL 76A:793–94), *in Malachiam* 2.13.16 (CCL 76A:924). In employing certain "narrative aggadah" as interpretive *historia,* Jerome falls within a particular Christian exegetical tradition: see Adam Kamesar, "The Evaluation of the Narrative Aggada in Greek and Latin Patristic Literature," *Journal of Theological Studies,* n.s., 45 (1994): 37–71.

[88] Jerome, *Commentarii in Isaiam* 5.14.18, 8.27.1 (CCL 73:169–70, 346), *in Ezechielem* 8.25.8, 9.28.19 (CCL 75:338, 398–99), *in Danielem* 2.5.2 (75A:821), *in Amos* 1.2.12 (CCL 76A:239–40), *in Abacuc* 1.2.15 (CCL 76A:610). This last reference seems to refer specifically to contemporary rabbinic midrash, as it is attributed to "a wise man who is called a *deuterōtēs* among them," which seems to signify *tanna* (see Stemberger, "Hieronymus," 354–55). Not all references to *fabula* were necessarily negative: see Kamesar, "Narrative Aggada," 51n49. The *Hebraica veritas* of Jewish sources could in fact be deployed against pagan *fabula:* see *Commentarius in Amos* 2.5.7/9 (CCL 76:280–81).

[89] *Commentarius in Zachariam* prol. (CCL 76A:748); see also *in Amos* 3.7.9 (CCL 76A:318–19), *in Naum* 1.11 (CCL 76A:536).

things biblical. Jews and their history—like their vocabulary, geography, and agronomy—become props for Christian identity; that Jerome serves to mediate this process and the knowledge produced within it demonstrates his own mastery of both Jewish *historia* and Christian *sanctitas*.[90]

One of the most significant Christianizing uses to which Jerome can put his *Judaeus biblicus* is the recovery of authentic dominical speech. Jerome will insist, throughout his career and in the face of much resistance, that Jesus and the apostles spoke Hebrew and referred to the Hebrew text of the Old Testament. His constant justification for this belief is the discovery that several New Testament passages that purport to refer to the Old Testament, but are not found in the Septuagint, can be restored by a careful reading of the Hebrew text. On numerous occasions he can trot out a string of dominical and apostolic pronouncements beginning with, "It is written . . . " and ask, "So: where is it written? It's not in the Septuagint, and the church does not recognize apocrypha. So we must go back to the Hebrew [*ad Hebraeos igitur revertendum est*], since this is what the Lord speaks and his disciples follow his example."[91] That Jerome can turn to Jewish sources [*ad Hebraeos*] to recover the original language of Jesus and the apostles should be read, in part, as a cultural triumph of the Christian over the Jewish: at no time does the Bethlehem monk intend to suggest that the apostles and evangelists were simply *Jews* and that discovering their original language will initiate some sort of religious rapprochement between Jew and Christian. On the contrary: the citations in the New Testament that are to be "clarified" by Jerome's linguistic archaeology are Christological and often pressed into anti-Jewish service.[92] Using the inherently biblical nature of the Palestinian Jew to

---

[90]Jerome had earlier (ca. 380) translated Eusebius's *Chronikon* and later referred to this translation in some anti-Jewish "historical" prophecy: *Commentarius in Danielem* 3.9.24 (CCL 75A:875–78). He can additionally push Jewish "historical" interpretation into anti-Jewish meanings, as at *in Isaiam* 5.22.2 (CCL 73:210).

[91]Jerome, *Praefatio in libro Paralipomenon (iuxta Hebraeos)* 30–31 (Weber, *Biblia*, 1:547). The New Testament passages cited here are Matt 2.15, 23; John 19.37; 1 Cor 2.9; and John 7.38. The same passages are cited in *Praefatio in Pentateucho* 11–17 (Weber, *Biblia*, 1:3), where Jerome again invokes "the authority of the evangelists and apostles" in bringing forth "the Jewish books [*libris hebraicis*]."

[92]Kamesar, *Jerome*, 62–65, places Jerome's discussion of Hebrew as the apostolic and dominical language in the context of his attitude toward the LXX and the appropriate "Christian" Bible. These passages had long been mainstays of "orthodox" Christological polemic, as evident in Tertullian: see *Adversus Marcionem* 4.8.1 (CCL 1:556), on Matt 2.22; *De carne Christi*

justify such passages as "Out of Egypt I have called my Son" (Matt 2.15), "He will be called a Nazarene" (Matt 2.22), and "They will look at him whom they have pierced" (John 19.37) forces the *Judaeus biblicus* to defend Christ as God and Christians as the possessors of biblical truth. As Jerome remarks to his inevitable detractors:

These passages and others like them are to be found in the books of the Jews [*in Hebraeorum libris*]. Certainly the apostles and evangelists were familiar with the Seventy translators [*septuaginta interpretes*]. But from where do they speak of texts not found in the Seventy? Christ our God, founder of both Testaments, says in the Gospel according to John: "Whoever believes in me, as Scripture says, rivers of living water will flow from his belly" (John 7.23). Obviously whatever the Savior testifies to is scriptural![93]

The "God" is still "ours"—that is, the Christians'—but knowledge of him has been appropriated from the Jews.

Indeed, Jerome's entire endeavor for appropriating the "source" of Jewish knowledge is grounded in the authority of the evangelists and apostles.[94] He attempts to distinguish between the proposition that they were "really" Jewish and the notion that they (like Jerome) drew on the foundational knowledge of Jews. In retranslating the passage of Zechariah (12.10) that he finds to be the root of John 17.39, Jerome casts himself and the evangelist in analogous roles:

The evangelist John moreover, who drank his wisdom from the Lord's breast, a Jew from the Jews [*Hebraeus ex Hebraeis*] whom the Savior loved above all others (cf. John 19.26), did not care much for Greek letters; but he translated what he read in the Hebrew word for word, and said that the time of the Lord's passion had been fulfilled. But whoever doesn't receive this, let him bear witness as to what passage in holy Scriptures John is offering up here![95]

Like John, Jerome "drinks his wisdom" from the Lord's breast, knowl-

---

34.4 (CCL 2:916) and *De resurrectione mortuorum* 26.4–5 (CCL 2:954), on John 19.37; and *De resurrectione* 24.7–8 (CCL 2:954–55), on 1 Cor 2.9.

[93]Jerome, *Praefatio in libro Paralipomenon* 24–29 (Weber, *Biblia,* 1:546).

[94]See Jerome, *Praefatio in Pentateucho* 11–17 (Weber, *Biblia,* 1:3).

[95]Jerome, *Commentarius in Zachariam* 3.12.10 (CCL 76A:868). Jerome also attributes the Pauline epithet *Hebraeus ex Hebraeis* (Phil 3.5) to the evangelist Matthew: *sed quasi Hebraeum ex Hebraeis, et in Lege Domini doctissimum ea gentibus protulisse, quae in Hebraeo legerat* (*ep.* 121.2.5 [CSEL 56:9]).

edge derived *ex Hebraeis*. The phrase *Hebraeus ex Hebraeis,* a Pauline epithet drawn from Philippians 3.5, characterizes Jerome's own position as
local "expert" on Jewish language and interpretation. As will become
clear from Jerome's debates with Augustine, Paul is *not* Jewish in
Jerome's eyes. The apostle speaks "*as* a Jew from the Jews" or (sometimes) "*as if* a Jew from the Jews."[96] It is a form of knowledgeable mimicry, and by likewise mastering this mimicry of the Jews Jerome too can
attain the knowledge and wisdom that characterizes apostolic speech,
speaking "as if a Jew from the Jews."[97] He crafts a role for himself as the
transmitter of a particular form of appropriated knowledge, from an
original source to those less trained. So Jerome can remark, when discussing Matthew's reference to Jeremiah 31.15 (Matt 2.17–18): "Matthew draws
his testimony here neither from the Hebrew nor the Septuagint. . . . From
this it is clear that the evangelists and apostles did not always follow some
Hebrew translation; but, as if Jews from the Jews [*quasi Hebraeos ex
Hebraeis*], because they read Hebrew, they expressed themselves in their
own speech."[98] In describing how Matthew and other apostles and evangelists could speak "as if Hebrews from Hebrews," Jerome is generally
signaling not their religious or ethnic affiliation but rather their ability to
adapt themselves linguistically to their audience.[99]

Jerome, too, shares this linguistic adaptability, executed with finesse
and care. This production of knowledge from within the colonial context
establishes lines of hierarchy between Jew and Christian (power and
knowledge is made to flow uniquely from Jewish periphery to Christian
center) and between the Christian "on the scene" and the Christian "at

[96]Jerome, *Commentarius in epistolam ad Galatas* 2.3.13: *ut Hebraeus ex Hebraeis;* 2.4.29–31:
quasi Hebraeus ex Hebraeis (PL 26:363A, 392B).

[97]See Jerome, *Commentarius in Isaiam* 17.64.4–5 (CCL 73A:735). Homi Bhabha employs
the term *mimicry* to describe a colonial response to imperial domination (see Bhabha, *Location
of Culture,* 85–92), in which the imperial representation of the colonial other is in turn appropriated and used to open up a space of colonial resistance. My own use of the term focuses on
the slippage of imperial representations and identifications (what Bhabha, *Location of Culture,*
80–81, calls "fetishistic identification").

[98]Jerome, *Commentarius in Hieremiam* 18.2 (31.15) (CCL 74:306–7).

[99]See also *Commentarii in epistolam ad Galatas* 3.6.1 (PL 26:455B), *in epistolam ad Ephesios*
2.3.1, 3.5.3 (PL 26:509B, 553B), *in epistolam ad Titum* 2.11, 3.3 (PL 26:622C, 628B–C). On Eusebius's use of this Philippians phrase to describe ancient "Hebrews" (including Moses and
Josephus) see Chapter 2 above.

home" (Jerome alone can speak both imperially and colonially).[100] Jewish knowledge produces Christian power; and, for Jerome, this process is truly only possible "on the spot," in the biblical (and Jewish) land itself, the Christian *terra sancta* of Palestine: "What we read in his prose is the history of a consciousness negotiating its way through an alien culture by virtue of having successfully absorbed its systems of information and behavior."[101] Both "local Jew" and Jerome, the knowledgeable Christian, come into being in relation to one another, and Jerome's construction of the *Judaeus biblicus* through this form of "academic imperialism" is a construction of Jerome the imperial Christian, as well. The sweet fruits of Jerome's alien negotiations are prized, at least by Jerome and his circle of Roman scriptural devotees; but they are also culled from "bitter seeds" of the knowledgeable yet treacherous Jewish informants. A deep ambivalence remains at the core of Jerome's enterprise—sweetness and bitterness, desire and fear—that marks mastery of Christian scholarship with the danger of the Jewish frontier from which it has been extracted.

The Disciple of Barabbas and His Jewish Consultants

The suggestion that Jerome could use contemporary Jews as a tool for reconstructing the words of Jesus and the apostles (and the foundations of Christian identity) did not go unchallenged, nor did it fail to raise concerns in the minds of other fifth-century Christians. Some members of the Christian literate classes explicitly resisted attempts to formulate Christian power through knowledgeable mimicry of the colonized Jews. Yet unlike Origen, who could ultimately disconnect his Christian identity from the Hebrew Scriptures of the Jews when pressed (as by the inquiries of Julius Africanus), Jerome persists in linking his pristine, holy land Christian Bible with the Jews who served as his linguistic and exegetical informants. Two specific challenges in Jerome's career focused on his troublesome mixing with Jews and forced him to defend his particular

---

[100] See Mary Louise Pratt, *Imperial Eyes: Travel Writing and Transculturation* (London: Routledge, 1992), 189–92, on the unidirectionality of colonial representation.

[101] Said, *Orientalism*, 196 (a comment on Sir Richard Burton). We might understand Jerome, in this fashion, as an ancient Christian version of Sir Richard, walking the edge of colonial "imitation" through his superior and, at times, contentious "knowledge" of the East: see the rest of the discussion in Said, *Orientalism*, 194–97.

"Christian judeography."[102] The first came from his erstwhile schoolmate, Rufinus of Aquileia, at the beginning of the fifth century in the context of the early Origenist controversy.[103] Rufinus focused his harsh criticism on Jerome's persistent and (according to Rufinus) un-Christian reliance on "foreign" learning and erudition. The second challenge, beginning at about the same time but extending over a longer period, came from the bold and (from Jerome's perspective) upstart bishop of Hippo Regius in North Africa, Augustine.[104] Here the issues between ostensible theological allies related to the most reliable and theologically appropriate text of the Old Testament and the bounds of Christian exegesis of the entire Bible. In response to these two challenges Jerome nuanced his perilous endeavor by acknowledging the danger of his Jewish contacts and highlighting his own hyper-Christian "zeal [*studium*]" in both knowing and surmounting the peril of the Jews.[105] If the Jerome who so carefully crafted the *Judaeus biblicus* emphasized his own powers of colonialist mimicry, the Jerome of Christian controversy underscored more fully the hazards to be encountered on the colonial horizon.

It was a matter of cultural and linguistic translation that initially embroiled Rufinus and Jerome in the controversy over the problematic theological speculations of Origen. When Rufinus modestly invoked his "brother and colleague" Jerome in the preface to his translation of Origen's *On First Principles*, his flattering tone was likely shaded with irony.[106] By citing Jerome's own "smooth" and "emending" style of

---

[102]I borrow the term *judeography* (to signify ideologically laden, authoritative writings about Jews) from James Pasto, "Who Owns the Jewish Past: Judaism, Judaisms, and the Writing of Jewish History" (Ph.D. diss., Cornell University, 1999), some arguments of which are rehearsed in "Islam's 'Strange Secret Sharer': Orientalism, Judaism, and the Jewish Question," *Comparative Studies in Society and History* 40 (1998): 437–74.

[103]For an outline and analysis (both social and theological) of this controversy see Elizabeth A. Clark, *The Origenist Controversy: The Cultural Construction of an Early Christian Debate* (Princeton, N.J.: Princeton University Press, 1992), 11–17, 121–51, 159–93.

[104]See Hennings, *Briefwechsel;* and Alfons Fürst, *Augustins Briefwechsel mit Hieronymus* (Münster: Aschendorffsche Verlagsbuchhandlung, 1999).

[105]See the remarks of Bhabha, *Location of Culture,* 88–92, on "the *menace* of mimicry" and the responses of imperial authority.

[106]Rufinus, *Praefationes in libros Origenis Periarchon* 1.1 (CCL 20:245). Pierre Courcelle, *Late Latin Writers and Their Greek Sources,* tr. Harry E. Wedeck (Cambridge, Mass.: Harvard University Press, 1969), speaks of Rufinus taking "malicious delight . . . in posing as continuator of Jerome's vast design" (10). For a literary analysis of the controversy and Jerome's *apologia* see Opelt, *Hieronymus,* 82–118.

Greek-to-Latin translation, "observing the same disciplinary rules if not
with the same force of eloquence,"[107] Rufinus ultimately drew his former
schoolmate into a rabid controversy that was as much about the bounds
of Christian culture as it was about theology. As the debate achieved an
increasingly ad hominem pitch, Rufinus craftily pointed out that not
only had Jerome in his youth relied on the exegesis and sophistication of
Origen, whom Jerome now hypocritically dubbed a heretic, but he continued to depend on the most un-Christian of intellectual sources: pagans
and Jews. On the pagan side Rufinus remarked acidly that despite
Jerome's now famous account of the dream in which he renounced "Ci-
ceronianism,"[108] there remains not "a single page of a work where he does
not confess himself a Ciceronian, where he does not say, 'But our Cicero
. . . ,' 'but our Horace . . . ,' 'but our Vergil. . . . '"[109] As for Jerome's dis-
tasteful association with Jews, this has already become so notorious in
Rufinus's circles that he can successfully mangle the name of Jerome's
former Hebrew teacher in order to make a scathing point about Jerome's
loyalty to his Christian faith:

But why, like a fool, do I enumerate holy Christian men? It is not on account of
such men that he says we taught ourselves, but because we did not receive
Barabbas as a teacher from the synagogue and because we were not introduced
to logic through Porphyry's *Isagogē*. Forgive me for this, that I preferred to appear ignorant and unlearned rather than to be called a disciple of Barabbas![110]

Rufinus creates a charged parallel between Jerome's "heathen" learning
(Porphyry) and his fraternizing with Jews. The insinuation is that he has
breached the permissible borders of Christian identity and therefore has
rendered any of his knowledge suspect, heretical, tainted. Rufinus can
even invert the language of *Judaea capta,* clucking mockingly at Jerome:
"Who else would dare to tamper with the tools of the church, handed
down by the apostles, but that Jewish spirit [*Iudaicus spiritus*]? It is they,
brother most dear to me before you were captured by the Jews, they who

[107]Rufinus, *Praefationes in libros Origenis Periarchon* 1.2 (CCL 20:246).

[108]Jerome, *ep.* 22.30 (CSEL 54:189–91).

[109]Rufinus, *Apologia contra Hieronymum* 2.7 (CCL 20:88).

[110]Rufinus, *Apologia contra Hieronymum* 2.15 (CCL 20:95). Jerome had written about
Baraninas in a letter to Roman allies (*ep.* 84) around 398.

are rushing you into these evil matters!"[111] That Jerome refers so casually to Jewish learning shows, for Rufinus, not his erudition but his scandalous lack of Christian integrity. In Rufinus's scheme of Christian identity there is no way to bring Jews into such close proximity to Christian truth without compromising the very essence of Christianity.

In the face of Rufinus's attack Jerome does not renounce his Christian reliance on Jewish knowledge in order to safeguard his Christianness. That such knowledge was perilous he had conceded from the beginning, and in his various responses to Rufinus (and corollary defenses to friends) he admits to the danger of consorting with Jews. In the preface to one of his earliest translations from Hebrew, the book of Job, Jerome had already begun the process of aligning his reliance on Jews and Jewish knowledge with an explicit defense against Jews and their contrary interpretations and translations.[112] After mentioning the "great expense" he has gone to in order to acquire a "preeminent" Hebrew instructor from Lydda,[113] he lashes out against his detractors:

Surely if, after the Septuagint was published and after the gospel of Christ shone forth, the Jew Aquila and the judaizing heretics Symmachus and Theodotion had been received—who covered over the many mysteries of the Savior by their wily translation [subdola interpretatione]—and, what's more, they are kept in the hexapla in churches and interpreted by churchmen; if this is so, how much more should I—I who am Christian, born of Christian parents and bearing the insignia of the cross on my forehead, whose zeal has been to restore what is lost, correct what is corrupted, to disclose with pure and faithful speech the mysteries of the Church—how much more should I not be rebuked either by disdainful or malicious readers?[114]

Jerome chooses to play the Jews against themselves: if their "wily translations" seek to undo the majesty of Christ's gospel, Jerome will use their own knowledge to construct a "pure and faithful" translation. It is a task of daring Christianness on Jerome's part, and it is this aspect—of danger,

---

[111]Rufinus, *Apologia contra Hieronymum* 2.41 (CCL 20:115).

[112]Cavallera, *Saint Jérôme*, 1:147–48, 2:28–29, and 157, places this translation work around the year 390; P. Jay, "La datation des premières traductions de l'Ancien Testament sur l'hébreu par saint Jérôme," *Revue des Études Augustiniennes* 28 (1982): 208–12, argues that it was the middle work in a series of veterotestamentary translations accomplished by 392.

[113]Jerome, *Praefatio in libro Iob* 20–23 (Weber, *Biblia*, 1:731).

[114]Jerome, *Praefatio in libro Iob* 41–48 (Weber, *Biblia*, 1:732).

of reckless zeal—that he highlights in his response to Rufinus. It is a posture of *bravura,* of domination, of cultural conquest.[115] He includes in his *Apology Against Rufinus* the prefaces to his Latin translations *iuxta Hebraeos,* as the proverbial "antidote before the poison," ready responses to whatever charges might be brought against him.[116] All the danger he has courted by consorting with Jews he insists was done with the most Christian of intentions: "my own familiar friend should just receive from a Christian and a friend what he has taken great pains to obtain and transcribe from the Jews."[117] Most important, Jerome never subordinated himself to the Jews: this would, he admits, be an act of Christian "disloyalty," a perversion of the rightful relationship between Jews and Christians: "Listen then, you pillar of wisdom and standard of Catonian severity. I did not say that he [that is, Baraninas] was my *master;* but I wanted to prove my zeal for the Holy Scriptures in order to show that I had read Origen just in the same way as I had studied with that one."[118] If Rufinus can claim to have tamed the heretical and overly speculative portions of Origen's writing through learned translation and "editing," surely Jerome can use his authority as monk and Christian to appropriate selectively the knowledge of Jews for good Christian purposes. At no time are they his "masters [*magistri*]," but rather his "teachers [*praeceptores*]," a relationship that can retain connotations of subordination and hierarchy.[119]

To demonstrate how he has maintained a hierarchical relationship between himself and the Jews who gave him "lessons" in Palestine, Jerome,

---

[115]My thinking in this area has been helped by David Chidester, *Savage Systems: Colonialism and Comparative Religion in Southern Africa* (Charlottesville: University of Virginia Press, 1996).

[116]Jerome, *Apologia contra Rufinum* 2.34 (SC 303:194). This *proverbium* (*ante antidotum quam venenum*) seems to be a Christian commonplace by this time: see the notes of Pierre Lardet, *L'apologie de Jérôme contre Rufin: Un commentaire* (Leiden: E. J. Brill, 1993), 84n146, 235n432. The prefaces in *Apologia contra Rufinum* 2.25–32 are to the Pentateuch, Kings, Chronicles, Ezra, Job, Psalms, the books of Solomon, Isaiah, and Daniel (SC 303:172–94).

[117]Jerome, *Apologia contra Rufinum* 2.35 (SC 303:198).

[118]Jerome, *Apologia contra Rufinum* 1.13 (SC 303:38). This understanding remains implicit in later references to this preceptorial relationship. See, e.g., *Commentarius in Isaiam* 5.13.10 (CCL 73:163): "That Hebrew whom I employed [*usus sum*] as my instructor [*praeceptore*]."

[119]Again, we might invoke the parallel between Jerome's knowledge of Hebrew and the educated Roman male's knowledge of Greek (see above): see Woolf, "Becoming Roman," 132–35; and Kaimio, *Romans and the Greek Language,* 322–31; as well as the helpful observations of Robert Kaster, *Guardians of Language: The Grammarian and Society in Late Antiquity* (Berkeley: University of California Press, 1988), 51–61.

during his debates with Rufinus, increasingly emphasizes the risk of his encounters with those Jewish "teachers." One of the first references to a "Hebrew teacher" seems to be in the preface to a Latin translation of the LXX book of Chronicles (ca. 388), where he describes how he secured a local Jew to help him correct the "defective" transliteration of names in the LXX and Latin versions of Chronicles:[120] "Since you had recently been entreating me by letter to translate the book of Chronicles into Latin for you, I had brought in from Tiberias a certain doctor of the Law, who was held in great esteem among the Jews; and when I had consulted with him from 'head to toe,' as they say, and thus confirmed my translation, I dared to do as you commanded me."[121] There is no question of inappropriate subservience or even collegiality in these remarks: the Jew is an *instrumentum interpretationis,* to be acquired like a scroll or codex.[122]

At the beginning of the fifth century Jerome heightens this subservient relationship, highlighting for the benefit of Rufinus and other detractors the danger he risked in this venture. In a defensive letter to Roman friends Pammachius and Oceanus Jerome describes anew the process by which he learned Hebrew. As in his earlier preface to the Chronicles translation, the endeavor is explicitly linked to his arrival in the holy land. Here, however, the "Jew learned in the law" is transformed from an exegetical tool into a form of Christian contraband: "Back in Jerusalem and Bethlehem, with what trouble and at what cost I acquired Baraninas as my nocturnal instructor! He so feared the Jews that he showed himself as a second version of Nicodemus."[123] This is the same Baraninas (or Bar

---

[120]According to a later account Jerome began his Hebrew studies as a monk in the desert of Chalcis with the aid of "a certain brother who had once been a believer among the Jews" (*ep.* 125.12.1 [CSEL 56:131]). Kamesar, *Jerome,* 41–43, insists that Jerome must have begun his study of Hebrew seriously by the time he was back in Rome. It is worth pointing out, however, that live Jewish instructors only become visible in his writings once Jerome migrates to Palestine. The notable exception is *ep.* 36.1 (CSEL 54:268–69), which may actually have been written later: see Pierre Nautin, "Le premier échange épistolaire entre Jérôme et Damase: Lettres réelles ou fictives?" *Freiburger Zeitschrift für Philosophie und Theologie* 30 (1983): 331–47.

[121]Jerome, *Praefatio in libro Paralipomenon (iuxta LXX)* (PL 29:401B).

[122]Kamesar, *Jerome,* 181, on Jerome's rabbinic "informants" as "tools" at his disposal.

[123]Jerome, *ep.* 84.3.2 (CSEL 55:123), referring to John 3.1–2. Ilona Opelt, "San Giraolamo e i suoi maestri ebrei," *Augustinianum* 28 (1988): 327–38, assumes that these are two different Jewish instructors under discussion (she actually counts "at least five" in Jerome's writings [338]). As Jerome only mentions the name of his instructor once, this enumeration must remain more

Hanina) whom Rufinus rhetorically transformed into Barabbas, symbol of all that is Jewish and opposed to Christ in the New Testament; yet in this daring narrative of Jerome's acquisition of "native" knowledge, there is no question that he is fraternizing with the "synagogues of Satan." The knowledge is no less Jewish (in the sense that Nicodemus and Barabbas are both Jews), and it is accessible at great cost and peril only "on the spot," among the *loca sancta* that generated the Scriptures. Just as the ritual discourse of Cyril of Jerusalem had brought to light devious Jews on the fringes of the *loca sancta* in order to master their threat on the margins of Christian identity, so, too, Jerome's intimate knowledge becomes a form of Christian domination.[124]

The literary confrontation with Rufinus exemplifies how Jerome developed this second strategy for possessing Jewish knowledge while protecting his own inherent Christianness: he is the expert on the scene, able to brave the dangers of contact with Jews in order to save the secrets of the Bible that they have hoarded and corrupted. Around the same time that Rufinus launched his acerbic attacks on Jerome, a younger and less well-known priest in the hinterlands of North Africa sent his first tentative epistle to the "great man" of Bethlehem, posing two specific questions: Augustine queried Jerome first on the necessity for retranslating the Old Testament from the Hebrew, when his translations of the Septuagint were already so successful, and second on Jerome's interpretation of the quarrel between Paul and Peter at Antioch (Gal 2.11–14) as "playacting" before the believers of Galatia.[125] As the course of the letters themselves reveals, these two issues are not unrelated: the quarrel between Paul and Peter relates (at least in the minds of Jerome and Augustine) directly to the question of the present-day "Jewishness" of Christian faith and prac-

---

or less unprovable. I would instead point to Jerome's own rhetorical emphases in this period and the manner in which his Jewish informant(s) is (are) variously characterized. See the comments of Jay, *Exégèse*, 39–43.

[124]Jay, *Exégèse*, 42–43, contrasts the flat and lackluster descriptions of Jerome's *praeceptores Hebraei* with the "admiration ou . . . attachement personel" found in his (much less frequent) references to such *magistri* as Donatus or Gregory Nazianzen.

[125]That is, as *simulatio:* see Jerome, *Commentarius in epistolam ad Galatas* 1.2.11–13 (PL 26:363C–367C). See Hennings, *Briefwechsel*, 249–56; and Fürst, *Augustins Briefwechsel*, 2–64, on early Christian interpretation of the Peter-Paul Galatian conflict in general, and 29–36 on interpretation of Gal 2.11–14 as *simulatio/hupokrisis*.

tice.[126] As in Epiphanius's *Panarion* 30, knowledge of Jews reveals a crucial boundary between orthodoxy and heresy. Likewise, the introduction of Hebrew texts into the Christian liturgy raises for Augustine the same prickles of discomfort that Rufinus attempted to generate around Jerome's project. Jerome's response to Augustine builds on his replies to Rufinus: Jews are *of course* completely untrustworthy, treacherous, and deceitful—all the more reason to correct their own "wily interpretation" using the very knowledge they attempt to hide from Christians. To know the Jews is to render their threat impotent and thus demonstrate Christian potency. By contrast (as Jerome emphasized in his discussion of Gal 2.11–14), to accept Jewish ways without first mastering them is to risk sliding down the heretical slope of judaizing.

Augustine eagerly approaches Jerome as a student of Scripture, seeking a literary "conference" on behalf of "the whole studious society of African churches."[127] Augustine's first query concerning Jerome's philological and exegetical inquiry, written around 395, is imbued with concerns particular to his North African situation. On the one hand, Augustine's desire to retain the Septuagint because of its "greater harmony of purpose and spirit" resonates with his ecclesiological concern over the Donatist schism.[128] On the other hand, the suggestion that the scene between Peter and Paul depicted in Galatians 2.11–14 might signal an "advocacy of lying"[129] could ultimately lead the Christian "not to believe the authorities of the divine Scriptures at all."[130] Augustine immediately adduces the example of Paul's declarations on marriage, indicating that he has in mind here the exegetical duplicity of the Manicheans.[131] That the reliance on

[126]See Hennings, *Briefwechsel,* 107–10, esp. 107–8, nn. 2–3, for a review of previous literature on the correspondence.

[127]Augustine, *ep.* 28.2.2 (CSEL 34.1:105); see also *ep.* 28.4.6 (CSEL 34.1:112), for mention of a "conference of Christian study." To avoid confusion, I refer to Augustine and Jerome's letters by their respective enumerations (i.e., I refer to Augustine, *ep.* 28.4.6, and not Jerome, *ep.* 56.5.1). See Mark Vessey, "Conference and Confession: Literary Pragmatics in Augustine's 'Apologia contra Hieronymum,'" *Journal of Early Christian Studies* 1 (1993): 175–213.

[128]Augustine, *ep.* 28.2.2 (CSEL 34.1:106). According to Peter Brown, *Augustine of Hippo* (Berkeley: University of California Press, 1967), 212–32, Augustine became embroiled in refuting Donatist ecclesiology soon after his return to North Africa.

[129]*Patrocinium mendacii:* Augustine, *ep.* 28.3.3 (CSEL 34.1:107). Also *officiosa mendacia* (*ep.* 28.3.4 [CSEL 34.1:109]).

[130]Augustine, *ep.* 28.3.4 (CSEL 34.1:110).

[131]Augustine, *ep.* 28.3.4 (CSEL 34.1:109).

Hebrew texts and Jewish experts might be used to defend Jerome's hermeneutical peculiarities (such as calling the apostles "liars") underscores further for Augustine the ecclesiological dangers of breaching the cultural canons of Christian Scriptures.

Augustine received no reply to his first two inquiries to Jerome. The first letter was entrusted to a North African pilgrim who apparently never found his way to Bethlehem.[132] The second letter circulated in Rome and eventually reached Jerome through his own agents in that city. Jerome reacted so violently to Augustine's "brotherly" injunction that he "sing" to Augustine a "*palinōdia* of correction and emendation"[133] that Augustine (underestimating the effect of his words on Jerome) assumed that someone had circulated a forged *liber adversus Hieronymum* in his name.[134] After writing to assure Jerome (wrongly, as it turns out) that he would never write any offensive words against him, Augustine composed a third letter, around 403, in which he compiled more concerns and queries for the master exegete of Bethlehem.

In this epistle Augustine (who has taken on the mantle of the episcopacy since initiating this correspondence) expresses dismay that his churches, when faced with textual variants in Jerome's new translations *iuxta Hebraeos,* might actually have to rely on Jews as scriptural mediators. Differences in Latin translations are more easily resolved, he claims, "by bringing forth the Greek [version of the] book, since this language is well-known."[135] On the other hand,

if anyone should be disturbed by something strange in what has been translated from the Hebrew, and should bring charges of deceit, scarcely if at all could Hebrew witnesses [*hebraea testimonia*] [that is, texts] be brought forth against which the objection might be defended. But even if such should be found, who will endure that as many Latin and Greek authorities would be condemned? Besides all this, even if Jewish consultants [*consulti Hebraei*] could respond to the matter, it would be necessary for you yourself to be present, you alone who could be convincing, but even then, by any judg-

---

[132]Augustine recounts the misadventure of his correspondence in *ep.* 71.1.2 (CSEL 24.2:249). On the lost pilgrim who was to have delivered the first letter (*ep.* 28 in Augustine's corpus) see *ep.* 40.5.8 (CSEL 34.2:78).

[133]Augustine, *ep.* 40.5.7 (CSEL 34.2:77–78).

[134]See Augustine, *ep.* 67.2.2 (CSEL 34.2:238).

[135]Augustine, *ep.* 71.2.4 (CSEL 34.2:252).

ment it would be a marvel if you could successfully intervene.[136]

Augustine's concern for ecclesiological unity would be completely un-
done, it would seem, by the introduction of non-Christian arbiters of
scriptural correctness: even if Jerome could (somehow) be present in
every church in which his translation was being read in order to mediate
between the "consultants" and the Christians, Augustine doubts that
such pronouncements would be efficacious. Augustine introduces a scandalous local incident to prove to Jerome the ecclesiological peril of "Jewish consultants." On reading a recent translation of a certain word in
Jerome's translation of the book of Jonah

such a tumult was made among the congregation—especially the Greeks, arguing and inflaming charges of falsehood—that the bishop was forced (this was in
the city of Oea) to press for the testimony of Jews [*Iudaeorum testimonium*].
Now these ones, from ignorance or malice, responded that the Hebrew books
read just as the Greek and Latin versions. What more is there to say? The man
was forced to correct the passage as if it were fraudulently done, wishing to avert
the great danger of losing his entire congregation! From this indeed it seems to
us that from time to time even you might make a few mistakes. And look how
enormous the consequences are for such texts as cannot be compared to the tes-
timonies of languages actually in use.[137]

Enormous consequences indeed: an African church nearly fractured or
emptied by the questionable translation of a single word. But Augustine
seems to imply that the damage is, in some sense, already done. The dissolution of the church of Oea would have been the "great danger"; the
"lesser danger," that of corrupting Christian witness with *testimonium Iudaeorum,* was disastrously realized. Ecclesiastical unity has been broken,
and a chain of tradition called into question: after all, Augustine asks near
the end of this letter, was not the Septuagint the same Bible used by the
apostles?[138] Let Jerome continue as he had done before and provide fresh

---

[136]Augustine, *ep.* 71.2.4 (CSEL 34.2:252).

[137]Augustine, *ep.* 71.3.5 (CSEL 34.2:253). The references to *calumnia falsitatis* and *crimen
falsi* link this discussion of translation with the exegetical question of Peter and Paul "play-
acting" before the believers of Galatia and Augustine's (anti-Manichean) concerns over the
possibility of *officiosa mendacia.* Jerome will remain generally unconcerned about this criticism.

[138]Despite Jerome's insistence in other contexts on the matter, he declines to press the theory that the apostles (as well as Jesus) in fact cited from the Hebrew text of the Old Testa-

and "useful" Latin translations of the Greek Old Testament to maintain the western churches in intellectual communion with each other and the apostolic tradition.[139]

After first receiving word of Augustine's various epistles, circulating throughout the Mediterranean world, and then finally multiple copies of them (as Jerome complains: "You keep sending me letters!"[140]) Jerome eventually composes a full response to Augustine's specific, and persistent, inquiries.[141] Much of this letter, composed around 404, addresses the question of Peter and Paul "acting" (or, according to Augustine, lying) to the Galatians. Here Jerome is particularly incensed at Augustine's belief that Peter, who was Jewish, was correct in following Jewish Law and only incorrect in attempting to persuade gentiles to do the same. As Jerome fairly summarizes:

Your whole argument, which you have protracted into such a long disputation, boils down to this: Peter did not err in supposing that the Law should be kept by those who had first believed as Jews, but that he deviated from the right path when he compelled the gentiles to judaize [*gentes cogeret iudaizare*]; moreover he compelled them not by force of teaching but by example of conduct; and that Paul didn't speak against this, which he himself was also doing, but rather against the manner in which Peter compelled those who had been gentiles to judaize.[142]

To Jerome this immediately suggests that there is nothing wrong with "judaizing [*iudaizare*]": if Peter and Paul could keep dietary laws, circumcise, shave their heads in the fulfillment of arcane Old Testament votive legislation, what is to stop present-day Christians from being so ju-

---

ment. I believe his insistence on the character of Peter and Paul themselves serves the same function as his linguistic characterizations of the apostles described above.

[139]Augustine, *ep.* 71.4.6 (CSEL 34.2:254). It is in roughly this same period that Augustine is attempting to theorize the quality of linguistic scriptural "signs," thus leading him to specify which biblical texts are most appropriate: see *De doctrina christiana* 2.14.21–15.22 (CCL 32:46–48). See Hennings, *Briefwechsel,* 206–9.

[140]Jerome, *ep.* 105.1.1 (CSEL 55:242).

[141]In the course of Augustine's succession of letters, Jerome had composed a few shorter responses. One is sent after Jerome has received a copy of Augustine's *ep.* 40: Jerome therein asks for confirmation that Augustine actually wrote this "challenge." With this epistle Jerome also sends drafts of the first books of his *Apologia contra Rufinum,* apparently in an attempt to enlist Augustine's support (*ep.* 102 [CSEL 55:234–36]).

[142]Jerome, *ep.* 112.12.3 (CSEL 55:381).

daized? "If this is true," Jerome complains, "we shall lapse into the heresy of Cerinthus and Ebion."[143] Augustine's offhand comment that "Paul was a Jew"[144] Jerome finds particularly offensive: "*I* shall say to the contrary, even if the world shouts me down in a single voice in response, that the ceremonies of the Jews are harmful and fatal to Christians and that whoever observes them, whether from among Jews or gentiles, is cast down into the devil's pit."[145] Jews and their customs, Jerome insists, are now and have always been contrary to Christian identity: any other opinion constitutes heresy. This was as true for Paul the apostle as it is for Augustine the bishop: "So indeed, wretched and pitiably lamentable are they who, by contention and love of the Law that has been abolished, have made Christ's apostle into a Jew!"[146] Since Augustine is so willing to abandon Paul to the Jews and heretics, no doubt he will also welcome Jews into his own church who will circumcise their sons, observe the sabbath, abstain from meat, and celebrate Passover by slaughtering a lamb![147] Augustine's understanding of the Bible, Jerome concludes, pushes Christian identity across that fluctuating heretical boundary that Epiphanius had worked so hard to delimit, through the "judaizing" heresies of the Nazarenes straight into the "synagogues of Satan."[148] Jerome woefully informs Augustine: "Although indeed you fear Porphyry's blasphemy [that is, devaluing Scripture], you rush into the traps of the Ebionites, deciding that the Law is to be observed by those believers from among the Jews."[149] Augustine, it seems, is no better than the Galatian enemies of Paul for whom the drama described in Galatians 2.11–14 was originally enacted.[150]

---

[143]Jerome, *ep.* 112.13.1 (CSEL 55:381). See above, Chapter 2, on Epiphanius and "Jewish Christian" heresy.

[144]Augustine, *ep.* 40.4.4 (CSEL 34.2:73), cited by Jerome, *ep.* 112.14.1 (CSEL 55:382), although for clarity (and, perhaps, rhetorical emphasis) Jerome changes *Iudaeus erat* to *Iudaeus erat Paulus.*

[145]Jerome, *ep.* 112.14.2 (CSEL 55:382).

[146]Jerome, *ep.* 112.17.2 (CSEL 55:387).

[147]Jerome, *ep.* 112.15.2 (CSEL 55:384).

[148]Jerome, *ep.* 112.13.2–3 (CSEL 55:381–82). Not only does Jerome rely on standard Christian heresiology at this point, but he even invokes rabbinic condemnations of heresy: "Even today, through all the synagogues of the east among the Jews this is considered a heresy, which is called Minaeite and continues to be condemned by the Pharisees [i.e., rabbis]" (112.13.1 [CSEL 55:381]). Jerome can deploy his local ("eastern") Jewish knowledge against judaizing scriptural interpretation.

[149]Jerome, *ep.* 112.15.3 (CSEL 55:386).

[150]Jerome's rhetorical flourish is in full force in these letters. For more nuanced evaluations

To understand why the offhand reference to Paul's Jewishness (certainly plausible from a straight reading of Paul's epistles) should so offend Jerome, we must consider again the relationship he has constructed between himself and the Palestinian *Judaeus biblicus*. Jerome has configured himself to be like Paul, the evangelists, and even Jesus: one who can so perfectly know and control the colonized Jew that he can speak *quasi Hebraeus ex Hebraeis*. But this knowledgeable control must somehow guard against slipping down the scale of power into actually being Jewish: it must remain the privilege of Empire to know without becoming, to mimic without metamorphosis. For Jerome the question of Peter and Paul actually *being* Jewish and the authenticity of his own translations *iuxta Hebraeos* are intimately connected. The heretical threat of judaizing with which Jerome brands Augustine thus leads immediately into a defense of his use of Jewish informants and his translations of the Old Testament *iuxta Hebraeos*. Straightaway he provides one of his standby defenses: he has produced new translations so that his fellow Latin-speakers "might know what has been omitted or corrupted by the Jews, and what the Hebrew truth [*Hebraea veritas*] contains."[151] This reliance on "Hebrew truth" to overcome "Jewish corruption" reinforces the boundary between *knowing* and *becoming*, between appropriating the knowledge of Jews and actually being Jewish. He likewise refers Augustine to his translational prefaces (although he does not append them, as he did in his *Apology Against Rufinus*), and he makes the famous defense he has already used so many times in the past: "If you doubt me, ask the Jews!"[152] By reiterating this old challenge, Jerome signals to Augustine that he does not

---

of Augustine's theological positions vis-à-vis Jews, Judaism, and "Judaizing," including analysis of this correspondence from Augustine's perspective, see the essays of Paula Fredriksen: "*Excaecati Occulta Iustitia Dei:* Augustine on Jews and Judaism," *Journal of Early Christian Studies* 3 (1995): 299–324; "*Secundum Carnem:* History and Israel in the Theology of St. Augustine," in *The Limits of Ancient Christianity. Essays on Late Antique Thought and Culture in Honor of R. A. Markus*, ed. William Klingshirn and Mark Vessey (Ann Arbor: University of Michigan Press, 1999), 26–41; and "Augustine and Israel: *Interpretatio ad litteram*, Jews and Judaism in Augustine's Theology of History," *Studia Patristica* 38 (2001): 119–35, as well as her forthcoming *Augustine and the Jews* (New York: Doubleday, 2004).

[151]Jerome, *ep.* 112.20.4 (CSEL 55:390). This is, perhaps, the one argument that Augustine finds ultimately persuasive: see Augustine, *ep.* 82.5.34 (CSEL 34.2:385), although note that he still insists on knowing "by which Jews [*a quibus Iudaeis*]" this textual "mutilation" has been perpetrated.

[152]*Sicubi dubitas, interroga Hebraeos: ep.* 112.20.5 (CSEL 55:391).

share the North African bishop's fears about "Jewish consultants": "You might say: 'What if the Jews either don't want to respond, or wish to lie?' Will the whole throng of Jews keep silent about my translation? Will not one be found who has some familiarity with the Hebrew language? Or will all of them imitate those Jews whom you say were found in that little town in Africa and conspire to slander me?"[153] Jerome also refuses to admit, as Augustine has implied, that Hebrew is not among the "living languages [*usitatae linguae*]" of Christianity. Jerome laments sarcastically the awakening of an old "slumbering" accusation about mistranslating the word *gourd* in the book of Jonah (Jonah 4.6), a charge against which he has already thoroughly defended himself.[154] He implies that the problem is not with "Jewish consultants" at all but rather with Augustine's particular relationship to Jews: "If, as you yourself suggest, your Jews [*Iudaei vestri*], either through 'malice or ignorance,' have said that the same word is found in the Hebrew scrolls as in the Greek and Latin books, clearly they don't know their Hebrew letters, or else they wanted to lie in order to make fun of the gourd-keepers!"[155] The problem, it seems, is that Augustine has uncontrolled Jews, Jews who likely do not even know Hebrew (unlike the more authentic Palestinian Jews who act as Jerome's teachers). It is a question of Christian mastery and ability to appropriate effectively Jewish knowledge despite the Jews' "wily interpretation." If Augustine knew the Jews better (or accepted Jerome's painstakingly acquired knowledge), they would pose less of a danger to his churches; trifles such as Jonah's gourd could not rise up and rend the fabric of North African Christianity.

The Wily Jew: Knowledge and Resistance

In his conflicts with Rufinus and Augustine over the potential conse-

---

[153]Jerome, *ep.* 112.21.1 (CSEL 55:391).

[154]Jerome had translated the word as *hedera* (ivy) instead of *cucurbita* (gourd): *Commentarius in Ionam* 4.6 (SC 323:296–300, 419–20nn1–3), drawing criticism for (it seems) decades after. See Y.-M. Duval, "Saint Augustin et le Commentaire sur Jonas de Saint Jérôme," *Revue des Études Augustiniennes* 12 (1966): 9–40; Alfons Fürst, "Kürbis oder Efeu? Zur Übersetzung von Jona 4:6 in der Septuaginta und bei Hieronymus," *Biblische Notizen* 72 (1994): 12–19; Bernard P. Robinson, "Jonah's Qiqayon Plant," *Zeitschrift für die Alttestamentliche Wissenschaft* 97 (1985): 391–94.

[155]Jerome, *ep.* 112.22.3 (CSEL 55:393).

quences of his colonial "mimicry" among the Palestinian Jews of the *loca sancta* Jerome demonstrated how precarious and delicate was the production and appropriation of "other" knowledge.[156] As David Spurr comments, "The temptations of the colonizer are both narcissistic and therapeutic. They betray a desire to recreate in these unconquered territories or in these unsubdued hearts and minds, one's own image, and to rewrite the pieces of a cultural identity divided from itself."[157] In his articulation of the *Judaeus biblicus* Jerome attempted to inscribe a Christian discourse of power onto the very real Jews of the Christian Roman Empire by assimilating Jewish knowledge into Christian texts; in doing so, however, Jerome risked slipping too far into that space of Christian otherness. The dual awareness of Jews as a font of Christian origins and a threat to Christian orthodoxy signaled the dangers of this power/knowledge nexus. For Jerome the project of imperial Christian power became increasingly a project of containment, connected to and operating within the totalizing Christian discourses of Empire:[158] localizing, so that the "best" Jews became those Jews most intimately connected with the original scriptural *loci;* historicizing, so that the Jews themselves constantly drifted back into a comfortable and interpretable biblical (and Christian) past through custom and language; and, finally, hereticizing, so that these localized, historicized Jews were placed on the same totalizing boundary of Christian "right thinking" by which Christians in the later Roman Empire were themselves beginning to "know," and thus dominate, the deviant proximate other lingering in the shadows.[159] Despite Jerome's damage control—perhaps because of this damage control—these boundaries are nonetheless revealed to be frighteningly permeable. This anxious edge of Jerome's academic imperialism gives us a sense of how Christian discourses of knowledge might engender the very real threat of resistance from Jews. The dangerous gap between "knowing" and "becoming" that

---

[156]See the discussion of "colonial ambivalence" in Bhabha, *Location of Culture,* 123–38.

[157]Spurr, *Rhetoric of Empire,* 41–42.

[158]See Bhabha, *Location of Culture,* 70–71: "There, despite the 'play' in the colonial system which is crucial to the exercise of power, colonial discourse produces the colonized as a social reality which is at once an 'other' and yet entirely knowable and visible. It resembles a form of narrative whereby the productivity and circulation of signs are bound in a reformed and recognizable totality."

[159]See Hillel I. Newman, "Jerome's Judaizers," *Journal of Early Christian Studies* 9 (2001): 421–52.

haunted Jerome's appropriation of Jewish knowledge, and was so fruitfully exploited by Rufinus, signals the deeper dangers of Jewish resistance
to Christian power.

Augustine's anecdote from Oea is telling in this respect, as we see Jews
summoned for their authorizing expertise (as Jerome had done throughout his writings) and offering Jewish knowledge that serves not to uphold
but rather disrupt Christian authority: a church is nearly fractured, all
because of the "wily interpretation" of Jews. Jerome's increasingly repetitive answer is knowledgeable containment and mastery of the sort he
claims to have executed on the frontier zone in Palestine. But Jerome's
solution, and the imperial construction of scholarly mastery and containment in general, is ultimately self-defeating and unstable. Jerome's
academic mastery depends directly on the perils of his endeavor: the
fruits of his Jewish knowledge are made all the sweeter in contrast to the
"bitter seeds" from which they have been cultivated (the Jews themselves,
the "bitter seed" of Christian power). Jerome must construct and delineate the "wily interpretation" before he can successfully master it. It is no
great leap to infer that, from time to time, Jews in the fifth century might
themselves appropriate and subvert that mantle of interpretive wile for
their own purposes. We begin to discern through the mystification of
Christian scholarly discourse "what kind of *agency* is possible in situations
of extreme social *inequality*."[160]

In these two chapters I have traced how Christians produced knowledge about Jews in the fourth and fifth centuries as a means of manufac-
turing a new and powerful Christian identity. To accomplish this I have
used the insights of contemporary philosophers and theorists of Empire,
for whom "the fundamental problem concerns the way in which knowledge—and therefore theory, or history—is constituted through the com-
prehension and incorporation of the other."[161] "Knowledge, theory, and
history" were not uninterested or objective categories of investigation for
the ancient Christian, any more than they have been for modern scholars
and historians. The construction of new identities through the acquisi-

[160]McClintock, *Imperial Leather*, 140 (McClintock's emphasis). McClintock's critiques of
Homi Bhabha's notions of ambivalence, mimicry, and resistance (on which I am, obviously,
dependent) provide an important caveat in postcolonial studies.

[161]Robert Young, *White Mythologies: Writing History and the West* (London: Routledge,
1990), 12.

tion of knowledge forges and reconstitutes social relations and hierarchies.

A focus on constructions and representations does not mean that knowledge so produced—and resistance so provoked—was therefore "untrue," that the Palestinian Jews so "known" by these Christian writers did not exist, or that they existed as "mere" rhetorical devices of Christian literature. To the contrary: this knowledge about Jews created a new and forceful reality for the Christians of the period, and this, too, is one of the characteristics of imperial discourse that must be recognized. Jerome and Augustine did not just debate Jews "in theory": as scholars have been at pains to demonstrate, the theology of Jews and Judaism that emerges from these debates, most important for Western Christendom in the writings of Augustine, was to have immense and very real impact on the lives of medieval Jews for centuries to come.[162] So, too, the possibilities for resistance—whether we can plausibly verify them or maintain them as imaginative potentialities—remain equally real. In addition to outlining the shadows of a new discourse of Christian power, one that uses the Palestinian Jew as the ultimate object-to-be-known, I have attempted to demonstrate the fissures and cracks in this discourse, those points at which Christians became unsure, disconcerted, and anxious. I do not simply point the accusing finger at a new Christian "will to knowledge" or "will to power" arising in the fourth and fifth centuries; in the study of the Christian Roman Empire, as in the study of modern empires, we must keep in mind that "the text speaks ambiguously. . . . Hence the uneasiness, the instability, the frequent hysteria of colonial discourse."[163] The faceless and usually nameless Jews who (wittingly or otherwise) consult for Jerome are deliberately veiled and ostentatiously contained, yet the production of knowledge on the frontier zone invokes the instability of that containment. Even blinded, we sense the capacity of those Jews (like the Jews in Oea who casually dismissed Jerome's ivies and gourds)

---

[162]See Bernhard Blumenkranz, *Die Judenpredigt Augustins: Ein Beitrag zur Geschichte der jüdisch-christlichen Beziehungen in den ersten Jahrhunderten* (Basel: Helbing & Lichtenhahn, 1946); and idem, "Augustin et les Juifs, Augustin et le judaïsme," *Recherches Augustiniennes* 1 (1958): 225–41; also Fredriksen, "*Excaecati Occulta Justitia Dei*"; Jeremy Cohen, *Living Letters of the Law: Ideas of the Jew in Medieval Christianity* (Berkeley: University of California Press, 1999), 19–65.

[163]Spurr, *Rhetoric of Empire*, 11.

to resist the mechanisms of academic imperialism on their very terms. Knowledge, as a form of Christian domination, is haunted by that gap between emulation and assimilation, between knowing and becoming the other: in that gap, no longer coherently visible to us, the Jewish potential for agency and resistance cannot be fully eradicated.

PART II

Power

4   "A Province like Paradise":
Jews in Christian Travel Writing

Charting Imperial Christian Space

In the intriguing and idiosyncratic *Christian Topography,* composed in
the sixth century by the otherwise unknown merchant and traveler called
Cosmas Indicopleustēs, the physical world is at once entirely Christian
and entirely imperial.[1] The physical space of the universe is scriptural:
from his own travels and intense piety he has inferred that the cosmic
space of the universe is laid out in the shape of the tabernacle as described
in the Christian Old Testament.[2] The political space of the known world
is understood through the rise and success of the Christian Roman Empire:

> The Roman Empire shares in the honors of the empire of the Master, Christ,
> surpassing all others as much as is possible in this life, remaining invincible until
> the consummation of time. . . . As for the Roman Empire, insofar as it grew up
> together with Christ, it will not be destroyed in this time. Boldly do I declare
> that, if, for the sake of a little instruction on account of our sins, barbarian ene-
> mies rise against Rome, even still the Empire remains invincible in its ruling

---

[1]Wanda Wolska, *La Topographie chrétienne de Cosmas Indicopleustès: Théologie et science au
VIe siècle* (Paris: Presses Universitaires, 1962), 1–12, 28–29.

[2]Cosmas Indicopleustēs, *Topographia christiana* 2.35–36 (SC 141:343); illustrations from the
manuscript (perhaps based on Cosmas's own drawings) are reproduced at the end of Wolska,
Topographie chrétienne. The theoretical foundation is the validity of Scripture over "pagan" science (*Topographia christiana* 1.4–6 [SC 114:265–67]), but Cosmas also introduces his own
travel experiences [*peirai*] as corroboration (*Topographia christiana* 2.29 [SC 114:335]).

power, as long as the Christian world does not grow narrow but rather continues to expand.[3]

This alignment of Roman and Christian success was suggested already by the historiographic framework of Eusebius.[4] In the interval between Eusebius and Cosmas, however, the universal notion of Christian Empire acquired a more explicit material dimension, as evident in one of Cosmas's arguments for the power and extension of the Christian Roman Empire: "Here is another sign of the domination [*dunasteias*] of the Romans with which God has graced them, for I say indeed that it is in their coin that all the nations trade, and in every place, from one tip of the land to the other, it is accepted, admired by every person and every kingdom, of which no other kingdom can boast."[5] Roman money has come to signal Roman power; since Roman rule also reflects Christian domination, the universal exchange of Roman coin is a gleaming symbol of the triumphant Christian message.

The process by which Christian triumph could come to be expressed in terms of material expansion necessitated building on the Christian discourse of knowledge under examination in the previous chapters. Abstract notions of dominion and Empire were manifested through discursive configurations of material control.[6] In and around the Christian holy land this Christian idea of material dominion was scripted through various forms of travel writing, moving back and forth across the Mediterranean in the fourth through sixth centuries. Through religiously oriented travel writing to the holy land, the ideology of Christian Empire could be literally mapped in material terms; the Roman *provincia* came to be ven-

[3]Cosmas Indicopleustēs, *Topographia christiana* 2.75 (SC 141:391).

[4]See Philip S. Alexander, "Jerusalem as the *Omphalos* of the World: On the History of a Geographical Concept," in *Jerusalem: Its Sanctity and Centrality to Judaism, Christianity, and Islam*, ed. Lee I. Levine (New York: Continuum, 1999), 104–19, esp. 112–13.

[5]Cosmas Indicopleustēs, *Topographia christiana* 2.77 (SC 141:393–95). See Lena Cansdale, "Cosmas Indicopleustes: Merchant and Traveller," in *Akten des XII. internationalen Kongresses für Christliche Archäologie (Bonn 22.-28. September 1991)*, ed. Josef Engemann (Münster: Aschendorffsche Verlag, 1995), 609–16.

[6]See Jaś Elsner and Joan-Pau Rubiés, introduction to *Voyages and Visions: Towards a Cultural History of Travel* (London: Reaktion Books, 1999), 9: "Whatever the actualities of life, the ideologies within the empire strove towards new forms of universalism which would be the bedrock for the universal and imperial Christianity established by Constantine and his successors in the fourth century."

erated as the earthly manifestation of "Jerusalem above."[7]

The texts that scholars label "pilgrimage narratives" did not arise ex nihilo in the literary landscape of the Mediterranean world.[8] Throughout the ancient Roman period, forms of travel writing, textual cartographies, served to negotiate local identity within an increasingly omnipresent empire.[9] Travel writing produced forms of knowledge about other places and other times that situated the author (and audience) in a particular cultural location. Before turning to our Christian travel writing, it is worth examining one pre- (or, better, para-) Christian text that can help illuminate the discursive effect of travel writing in the limits of Empire. Pausanias's *Description of Greece* was probably completed sometime near the end of the second century C.E.[10] Understandably mined by scholars for centuries for its descriptions of lost works of private and monumental art,[11] this document has more recently been studied for its perspective on provincial-imperial relations, as "a guide to the formation of Greek reli-

---

[7]Cosmas addresses his work to a certain Pamphilos, "currently residing in the earthly Jerusalem, but inscribed with the firstborn as a citizen of the heavenly one" (*Topographia christiana* 2.1 [SC 141:305]). On this inscription of "Jerusalem above" (see Galatians 4.26) onto the earthly Palestinian city see Lorenzo Perrone, " 'The Mystery of Judaea' (Jerome, *ep.* 46): The Holy City of Jerusalem Between History and Symbol in Early Christian Thought," Levine, *Jerusalem*, 221–39, building on the study of N. Brox, "Das 'irdische Jerusalem' in der altchristlichen Theologie," *Kairos*, n.s., 28 (1986): 152–73.

[8]See E. D. Hunt, "Travel, Tourism, and Piety in the Roman Empire: A Context for the Beginnings of Christian Pilgrims," *Echos du Monde Classique* 28 (1984): 391–417; idem, "Were There Christian Pilgrims Before Constantine?" in *Pilgrimage Explored*, ed. J. Stopford (Suffolk: York Medieval Press, 1999), 25–40; and Georgia Frank, *The Memory of the Eyes: Pilgrims to Living Saints in Christian Late Antiquity* (Berkeley: University of California Press, 2000), esp. 37–59.

[9]See Elsner and Rubiés, *Voyages and Visions,* 9–11; and Jaś Elsner, "The *Itinerarium Burdigalense:* Politics and Salvation in the Geography of Constantine's Empire," *Journal of Roman Studies* 90 (2000): 181–95.

[10]Christian Habicht, *Pausanias' Guide to Ancient Greece* (Berkeley: University of California Press, 1985), 8–13; K. W. Arafat, *Pausanias' Greece: Ancient Artists and Roman Rulers* (Cambridge, U.K.: Cambridge University Press, 1996), 8–10; and Simon Swain, *Hellenism and Empire: Language, Classicism, and Power in the Greek World, A.D. 50–250* (Oxford: Clarendon Press, 1996), 330–33. Elsner, "*Itinerarium Burdigalense,*" 186, 191, 193–94, compares Pausanias and the Bordeaux pilgrim.

[11]Perhaps most famously by Heinrich Schliemann, as in *Mykenae: Bericht über meine Forschungen und Entdeckungen in Mykenae und Tiryns* (1878; repr., Darmstadt: Wissenschaftliche Buchgesellschaft, 1964), e.g., at 3–4, 28–29, and 143–44. Schliemann views Pausanias's descriptions (like the Greece of Schliemann's day) as something beneath which he must excavate to arrive at authentic Homeric history (see, e.g., 64–69, on the royal graves of Mycenae). On Schliemann and later classical archaeologists see Habicht, *Pausanias' Guide,* 29–31 and notes.

gious identity as resistance to the realities of Roman rule"[12] or a description of Pausanias's personal "view of the very institutions of the Republic
and the Empire themselves."[13] His *periēgēsis* has been interpreted as a
form of cultural mapping, the inscription of a deliberate and ideological
landscape, an "imaginative geography."[14] By constructing a "view" of
Greece from a particular stance (that of a learned provincial), Pausanias is
able to shape his material world, to depict a landscape cluttered with
monuments, tombs, and statues into an identity useful for his present social and political situation.[15]

This provincial-imperial setting emerges notably in the way Rome appears in Pausanias's narrative description, not so much as a main subject
but rather as an ancillary actor in a primarily Greek drama. When narrating the Roman capture of Athens by Sulla, for instance, Pausanias acknowledges that the "cause of the war" was "Mithridates, a king of the
barbarians from around the Euxine Sea." He suggests, however, that the
cause of Sulla's conflict with Mithridates be left to "those who wish to
investigate Mithridatic affairs, since I myself shall confine the narrative to
the fall of Athens."[16] Roman wars, even when they destroy Greek land,
are not within Pausanias's descriptive view (indeed, they are not even
"Roman" here but rather "Mithridatic"). Likewise, the fact that present-
day Corinth is not inhabited by "ancient Corinthians, but rather Roman
colonists [*epoikoi*]," is not primarily a result of Roman activity but "has as
its cause the Achaean League."[17] K. W. Arafat can argue that Pausanias
seems to bear no specific malice toward all Romans,[18] but this framing of

---

[12]Jaś Elsner, *Art and the Roman Viewer* (Cambridge, U.K.: Cambridge University Press, 1995), 127. See also Swain, *Hellenism and Empire*, 330–56.

[13]Arafat, *Pausanias' Greece*, 3. Arafat takes a somewhat dim view of Elsner's reading of the *Graeciae Descriptio* as a culturally "resistant" text, preferring to underscore "in Pausanias a more even-handed view of matters Greek and Roman than is generally acknowledged" (215).

[14]See Edward Said, *Orientalism* (New York: Pantheon Books, 1978), 71–72, on "imaginative geography"; and Alan R. H. Baker and Gideon Biger, eds., *Ideology and Landscape in Historical Perspective: Essays on the Meanings of Some Places in the Past* (Cambridge, U.K.: Cambridge University Press, 1992).

[15]See also the analysis of Lucian's *De Dea Syria* by Jaś Elsner, "Describing Self in the Language of Other: Pseudo(?) Lucian at the Temple of Hierapolis," in *Being Greek Under Rome: Cultural Identity, the Second Sophistic and the Development of Empire*, ed. Simon Goldhill (Cambridge, U.K.: Cambridge University Press, 2001), 123–53.

[16]Pausanias, *Graeciae descriptio* 1.20.4 (LCL 1:98).

[17]Pausanias, *Graeciae descriptio* 2.1.2 (LCL 2:246).

[18]Arafat, *Pausanias' Greece*, 202: "Pausanias does not feel negatively towards Rome *per se*."

Roman colonialism and military aggression in Greece as *Greek* history nonetheless sets a certain tone in provincial-imperial relations.[19] The long and involved Roman conquest of Greece, which takes up a large section of the book "describing" Achaea, is in fact, for Pausanias, merely the last chapter of "Achaean military history,"[20] and once he has finished with his historical "results," he can resume his geoartistic survey: "The boundary between Achaea and Elis is the river Larisos."[21] Roman history for Pausanias functions as a sort of inverse *ekphrasis,* breaking up his description of the timeless landscape of Greek culture and identity with the incidental and distracting history of the Roman Empire. Greece becomes a contiguous network of sacred and historical objects, a visible chain of the past that can, perhaps, transcend the ineluctable and imperial Roman present. The result is an eternal Greece in high relief, and a temporal Roman Empire irrupting into the shadows and crevices.

I do not want to argue that Christian travel writers deliberately worked from or appropriated or somehow "Christianized" earlier Greek modes of travel writing. Rather I wish to point out some of the ways in which travel itself functioned in the ideological workings of the Roman Empire, whether Christian, Greek, or Roman.[22] Pausanias sought to fix the provincial view in response to a sweeping imperial gaze, to give the colonial past coherence and significance in the present. I will read the writings of holy land pilgrims as the slow and, at times, halting construction of an imperial view and voice in the provinces. As veneration of the holy land took on a sacred and material importance to Christians after Constantine, interaction with the holy places and objects could be employed by Christians to tell themselves a new story of religious Empire. In this newly constructed imperial identity, the encounter with the Palestinian Jew (or the conspicuous erasure of such encounters) allowed the pious Christian traveler to inhabit a material world in which the Christian possessed power. These encounters encode materially enacted "con-

---

Arafat's study takes all mentions of Roman rulers on a case-by-case basis, arguing that Pausanias has feelings about individual Romans in history but that, together, these do not portray a particular emotion toward *Rome.*

[19] See Habicht, *Pausanias' Guide,* 117–26.

[20] Pausanias, *Graeciae descriptio* 7.6.3 (LCL 3:200).

[21] Pausanias, *Graeciae descriptio* 7.17.5 (LCL 3:264).

[22] On this see also Frank, *Memory of the Eyes,* 37–49; and Elsner, *"Itinerarium Burdigalense.*

figurations of power" through which we can evaluate the various strategies employed to construct the imperial Christian subject in relation to a
colonial Jewish "other."[23] Importantly, not just the authors but the texts
themselves are designed to "travel," to view a material reality and translate it back "home," where they can emerge as "a primary ground for the
production of new cultural forms."[24] Like Cosmas's universally accepted
"Roman coin," the material representations of encounter and appropriation inscribed in these Christian travel writings of late antiquity impress
and circulate an authoritative economy of Christian Empire. "Travel
writing needs to be perceived as a discourse in which imperatives of
knowledge and power intersect in a constitutively reciprocal manner,"
modern colonial theorists write.[25] In these particular forms of Christian
travel writing—pilgrimage texts—we find these intersections of knowledge and power "made flesh," as it were, in the physical landscape of the
holy land. This incarnation of Christian power in the holy land also creates a space within which the Jew of Christian Empire is also inscribed
and animated: we will return to this enlivened Jew of Christian Empire
later.

I have divided my overview of these Christian travel writings under
four rubrics, according to various strategies for narrating the encounter
between Christian subject and Jewish "other": historicization, by which
the Jew, or the Jew's remains, is made to embody a Christian past; textualization, by which the Jew and his or her vestiges are dissolved into the
text of Christian Scriptures; aestheticization, by which the Jew and the
Jewish world are encoded into the sensory experience of the Christian;
and ritualization, by which Jewish religious practice (as represented by
the Christian author) is made to reflect or reinforce the imperial religious
conduct of the Christians themselves. Individual pilgrimage accounts will

---

[23]See Said, *Orientalism,* 5: "Ideas, cultures, and histories cannot seriously be understood or
studied without their force, or more precisely their configurations of power, also being studied."

[24]Dean MacCannell, *Empty Meeting Grounds: The Tourist Papers* (London: Routledge, 1992),
1, speaking of "tourism." See also Said, *Orientalism,* 99–100, 177: "Pilgrimage is after all a form of
copying." See also Edward Said, *Culture and Imperialism* (New York: Alfred A. Knopf, 1994); and
E. D. Hunt, "Saint Silvia of Aquitaine: The Role of a Theodosian Pilgrim in the Society of East
and West," *Journal of Theological Studies,* n.s., 23 (1972): 351–73, esp. 362–73.

[25]Wimal Dissanakyake and Carmen Wickramagamge, *Self and Colonial Desire: Travel
Writings of V. S. Naipaul* (New York: Peter Lang, 1993), 7.

be used to exemplify these discrete textual strategies, although it is not my intention to impose univocity on these pilgrim narratives or argue for a simple developmental model of the travel literature of the Christian Roman Empire. In choosing to focus on narrative typologies rather than constructing some sort of linear or chronological explanatory model, I hope to demonstrate that these texts, in fact, produce multiple and even, at times, conflicting representations: the figural Jew of Christian travel literature is not a stereotyped or fixed icon of the Christian imagination but rather a fluctuating and elusive figure (for ancient Christian as for modern scholar). In this fluctuation we shall trace the instability of early imperial Christian subjectivities, as well.

"You Would Say It Happened Today": Historicization of the Jew

We know very little about the pilgrim from Burdigala (modern Bordeaux) who made the overland journey to see the holy places in the year 333, at the height of the sole reign of Constantine the Great.[26] Details such as name, status, age, and gender are lost to us, although we can make some assumptions: the traveler was a Christian from the western half of the Empire, who had the time, leisure, and (presumably) funds to make a long and possibly costly journey for reasons of piety and curiosity.[27] Scholars tend to give much attention to this document because it is "the earliest surviving Christian account of travel to what came to be known as the Holy Land."[28] In form it is something of a hybrid: a long

[26]E. D. Hunt, *Holy Land Pilgrimage in the Later Roman Empire, A.D. 312–460* (Oxford: Clarendon Press, 1982), 57–58, assumes that the Bordeaux pilgrim did not enjoy the "privileges" of the *cursus publicus,* the state-supported travel network. See also Laurie Douglass, "A New Look at the *Itinerarium Burdigalense,*" *Journal of Early Christian Studies* 4 (1996): 313–33, who suggests, among other things, that the pilgrim may have been a woman; and Susan Weingarten, "Was the Pilgrim from Bordeaux a Woman? A Reply to Laurie Douglass," *Journal of Early Christian Studies* 7 (1999): 291–97.

[27]On the costs and difficulties of overland travel see generally Lionel Casson, *Travel in the Ancient World* (London: George Allen & Unwin, 1974), 176–86; and A. H. M. Jones, *The Later Roman Empire, 284–602: A Social, Economic, and Administrative Survey* (Norman: University of Oklahoma Press, 1964), 824–34, 841–44.

[28]Douglass, "New Look," 313. Mary Campbell, *The Witness and the Other World: Exotic European Travel Writing, 400–1600* (Ithaca, N.Y.: Cornell University Press, 1988), 27–31, minimizes the potential impact of the text due to its form; likewise Robert Wilken, *The Land*

table of rest stops and cities, with little in the way of actual detail, is interrupted in the middle by a denser account of the significant sites of the holy land.[29] The difference between the narrative core of the document and the long, dry list of place-names and distances inscribes a certain tension between imperial geography and Christian history.[30] E. D. Hunt has pointed out the "contrast" this formal organization creates between "Christian core" and "secular" list of routes,[31] and I concur that this juxtaposition and tension are integral to understanding the effect of this document in constructing a place for Christian material piety within the limits of Empire. Connections between the "secular" and the Christian are perceptible in the text, just as the famous Roman roads are allowed to penetrate the more thickly textured space of the holy land.[32] This connection is fragile, however, and this fragility tells us something about the nature of this vision of Christianity and Empire.[33]

This tenuous bridge between Christian and imperial identities inscribed by the form of this document is also executed through the treatment of the pilgrim's "figural Jews." Blake Leyerle, in her excellent study

---

Called Holy: Palestine in Christian History and Thought (New Haven, Conn.: Yale University Press, 1992), 110, finds little interest in the text. By contrast Glen Bowman and Jaś Elsner have extracted thoroughly complex ideological and theological agendas from even the barest lists of place-names. See Glenn Bowman, " 'Mapping History's Redemption': Eschatology and Topography in the *Itinerarium Burdigalense*," in Levine, *Jerusalem*, 163–87; and Elsner, "*Itinerarium Burdigalense.*"

[29]See Tom B. Jones, *In the Twilight of Antiquity: The R. S. Hoyt Memorial Lectures (1973)* (Minneapolis: University of Minnesota Press, 1978), 22–25; and Elsner, "*Itinerarium Burdigalense,*" 183–86. On *itineraria* in general see Annalina Levi, *Itineraria picta: Contributo allo studio della Tabula Peutingeriana* (Rome: Brettschneider, 1967), 25–33, 35–38. Modern production of critical editions underscores the *Itinerarium*'s literary liminality: it has been edited with "classical" texts in the Teubner series (*Itineraria Romana* I, ed. Otto Cuntz [Lipsius: Teubner, 1929]) and with "Christian texts" in the *Corpus Christianorum,* series Latina (vol. 175).

[30]See Mary Louise Pratt, *Imperial Eyes: Travel Writing and Transculturation* (London: Routledge, 1992), 148–49: "the itinerary itself [can become] the occasion for a narrative of success, in which travel is a triumph in its own right. What are conquered are destinations, not kingdoms; what are overcome are not military challenges, but logistical ones." See also Douglass, "New Look," 318–19; and Elsner, "*Itinerarium Burdigalense,*" 186–90.

[31]Hunt, *Holy Land Pilgrimage,* 58.

[32]There are four *mansiones* and *mutationes* ("lodging-posts" and "changing-posts") on the Roman road between Caesarea and Jerusalem (*Itinerarium Burdigalense* 589.5–6 [CCL 175:14]). On these different grades of stops on the Roman road see Casson, *Travel,* 184–85. On Roman roads in Palestine see Israel Roll, "The Roman Road System in Judaea," *Jerusalem Cathedra* 3 (1986): 136–61; and idem, "Roads and Transportation in the Holy Land in the Early Christian and Byzantine Times," in Engemann, *Akten,* 1166–70.

[33]See also Elsner, "*Itinerarium Burdigalense,*" 188–90.

of the sociology of pilgrim literature, noted that the pilgrim's account "lacks any real interest in the native terrain, flora, fauna, or people."[34] This seeming lack of "real interest" is perhaps made more conspicuous because of our familiarity with such garrulous texts as those of Egeria or the Piacenza pilgrim, from a later period. When considered on its own, however, the Bordeaux pilgrim's holy land is, in fact, densely populated by the dead heroes of the Bible, mostly figures from the Old Testament. Indeed, they crowd his landscape as semivisible phantoms. The pilgrim's first narrative description of his travels comes when he reaches the city of Neapolis, and he remarks: "There is Mount Gerizim. There (say the Samaritans) Abraham offered his sacrifice, and 300 steps rise up to the summit of the mountain. Then, at the foot of the mountain, is the place called Shechem. There is the monumental tomb [*monumentum*] where Joseph is buried, in the estate which his father Jacob gave to him. There was Dinah, Jacob's daughter, abducted by the sons of the Amorites."[35] A host of biblical characters run hither and yon through the landscape, up and down the mountain, ordered through the mediating lens of Scripture[36] and grounded in the material reality of the visible graves. Although the landscape may be described as "lifeless," it is not depopulated. The native population has been historicized, made to inhabit an ever-receding past, in such a way as to empty the land of live bodies. They have left remains, such as steps in a mountainside and monumental tombs. *Monumentum* is the Bordeaux pilgrim's preferred term for these biblical graves, emphasizing at once their historicity and their public visibility.[37] As Mary Louise Pratt has remarked, in writing about early modern travel literature, "to revive indigenous history and culture as archaeology is to revive them *as dead*. The gesture simultaneously rescues them from

[34]Blake Leyerle, "Landscape as Cartography in Early Christian Pilgrimage Narrative," *Journal of the American Academy of Religion* 64 (1996): 123–24, 126, and n. 9.

[35]*Itinerarium Burdigalense* 587.2–588.2 (CCL 175:13–14).

[36]It is notable, though, that the pilgrim does not specifically cite Scripture by verse or in general (with the formulaic *scriptum est*, for example). This provides a strong contrast with Egeria, as we will see below.

[37]*Itinerarium Burdigalense* 595.2–4 (Isaiah and Hezekiah), 596.5 (Lazarus), 598.4–5 (Rachel), 598.7 (Ezekiel, Asaph, Job, Jesse, David, and Solomon) (CCL 175:17–18, 19–20). The pilgrim also uses *cripta* (596.2: Lazarus; 598.8: Ezekiel et al. [CCL 175:18, 20]) and *memoria* (599.8: Abraham, Isaac, Jacob, Sarah, Rachel, and Leah [CCL 175:20]).

European forgetfulness and reassigns them to a departed age."[38] If the Jews are dead, they cannot stand up and interact with the Christian pilgrim; they can only be viewed, displayed, and catalogued for future observers. The pilgrim thus creates a terrain populated by ghosts, past-tense inhabitants that are in some sense still visible, still significant to his own vision of the holy land but now frozen and inactive.[39]

Indeed, their sluggish and immobile shadows at Neapolis obscure what must be contemporary Samaritans, who have provided the pilgrim or his guides with an alternative location for the biblical story of the binding of Isaac.[40] Even these helpful Samaritans are gently nudged into the scriptural past in the next passage, where the pilgrim describes "Shechar, where the Samaritan woman went down to the same place where Jacob dug a well, and she drew water from it and our lord Jesus Christ spoke with her."[41] The "real" inhabitants of this land are throughout the itinerary the long-dead Jews of the Old Testament, and their specters show that the Bordeaux pilgrim has traveled not only across Roman roads but through Christian time. In this way imperial travel has the power to access sacred history.

In the pilgrim's long description of the Temple Mount in Jerusalem the ghostly presence of the Jews accomplishes a complex looping of imperial space and sacred time. The passage is worth quoting in full:

There are in Jerusalem two great pools on the side of the Temple, that is, one to the right and the other to the left, which Solomon built. But inside the city there are the twin pools, having five porches, which are called Bethsaida. There those sick for many years used to be healed. Moreover these pools have water churned up, a sort of scarlet color. There is also a crypt, where Solomon used to torture demons. There is the corner of a very tall tower, where the Lord climbed up and said to the one who was tempting him, "And the Lord said to him: You

---

[38]Pratt, *Imperial Eyes*, 134 (Pratt's emphasis). See also 64–65: "indigenous peoples are abstracted away from the history that is being made."

[39]I am aware of the nearly unpardonable anachronistic shorthand of calling these historicized shadows "ghosts" and certainly intend no theological reference to early Christian beliefs about the afterlife. By *ghost* I mean inert, yet paradoxically *present,* absences in the view of the Christian traveler.

[40]See John Wilkinson, *Egeria's Travels to the Holy Land* (Warminster: Aris & Phillips, 1981), 154–55, nn. 8–11; and Pierre Maraval, *Lieux saints et pèlerinages d'Orient: Histoire et géographie des origines à la conquête arabe* (Paris: Éditions du Cerf, 1985), 288–89, on this tradition.

[41]*Itinerarium Burdigalense* 588.2–5 (CCL 175:14), referring to John 4.

will not tempt the Lord your God, but him only will you serve."[42] There is also the great corner stone, about which it was said: "That which the builders rejected, this same stone is the head of the corner" (Matt 21.42) and under the pinnacle of the tower are many chambers where Solomon had his palace. There also remains the chamber in which he sat and wrote Wisdom,[43] and its roof is of a single stone. You also have there great underground cisterns and pools built with great toil, and in the building itself where was the Temple that Solomon built, before the altar in marble is the blood of Zacharias—you would say it had been shed today [*ibi dicas hodie fusum*]. Also all around are the traces of the hobnails of the soldiers who killed him, throughout the area, so that you might think they had been pressed in wax. There are there also two statues of Hadrian. There is also not far off from the statues a pierced stone, to which the Jews come every year, and they anoint it, and they cry out with a groan, and they tear their own garments, and in this way they withdraw. There is also there the house of Hezekiah, king of Judaea.[44]

This single site exists at several different chronological moments, and its ghostly inhabitants practically career into each other in frenzied activity. Solomon the Temple builder alone is several places at once: building the Temple, torturing demons, writing placidly of wisdom. Every place we see Solomon, however, he is generally found next to Christian figures, such as Jesus on the Temple tower or Zechariah, who likely here signifies the father of John the Baptist, murdered in Christian legend by Herod the Great's soldiers.[45] "You would think" his blood was shed "today," so

---

[42]A conflation of two of Jesus' responses to the devil: "from the highest mountain" on being offered "all the kingdoms of the world" and on being tempted to throw himself from the "pinnacle of the Temple" (Matt 4.5–11, Luke 4.1–8).

[43]Presumably the canonically problematic "Wisdom of Solomon," although the Latin is ambiguous: *in quo sedit et sapientiam descripsit*, which might simply refer to Solomon's "office," where he wrote various works *about* wisdom (e.g., Proverbs). A less ambiguous variant reading is *et sapientiam scripsit*.

[44]*Itinerarium Burdigalense* 589.7–591.7 (CCL 175:14–16).

[45]A complicated matter of scriptural confusion between a priest named Zechariah, who was stoned to death (not by soldiers) in the Temple courtyard (2 Chr 24.20–22, Luke 11.50–51), the minor prophet Zechariah (Matt 23.35), and the father of John the Baptist, murdered by Herod's soldiers at the altar. The death of the Baptist's father was well known from the *Protoevangelium Iacobi* 23.1–3. Latin text in Émile Stycker, "Une ancienne version latine du protévangile de Jacques," *Analecta Bollandiana* 83 (1965): 351–410, here 400–401. Greek text in idem, *La forme la plus ancienne du Protévangile de Jacques* (Brussels: Société de Bollandistes, 1961), 177–83. Such intertestamental confusion, however, fits well with the Bordeaux pilgrim's multitemporal narrative of the Temple mount. See Günter Stemberger, *Jews and Christians in the Holy Land: Palestine in the Fourth Century*, tr. Ruth Tuschling (Edinburgh: T. & T. Clark,

vivid and real are the ghosts that occupy this charged "contact zone."[46]
The past exists on display in the present, yet the pilgrim need not fear
that these ghosts could act in any other manner than expected—they are,
after all, still dead. As the pilgrim proceeds through the Temple, he pro-
gresses also through time: we are next confronted with the incongruous
statues of Hadrian, the emperor who expelled the last living Jews from
Jerusalem and remade the city into an imperial Roman colony bearing
his name, Aelia Capitolina. Yet Hadrian's historical significance as deju-
daizer of Jerusalem is undermined by the sudden presence "not far from
his statues" of our only glimpse of contemporary Jews, mourning at a
pierced stone.[47] Time, for the moment, seems to exist in an imperial present, marked by live Jews bereft by imperial force of their Temple.

Except that the Jews are no more "alive" in this passage than the scriptural ghosts surrounding them; the pilgrim has been told about them. It
is, of course, entirely possible that the Bordeaux pilgrim visited the Temple Mount in time to witness this public mourning festival firsthand. Presumably it would have been on the ninth of Ab, which would have fallen
in early August in 333; the pilgrim reports leaving Constantinople on
May 30 and returning in December, so his presence in Jerusalem in August is certainly possible.[48] The fact remains, however, that he does not
say that he saw it; he merely reports that "the Jews come every year," and
he does not employ the second-person verbal forms ("you go up," "you
enter in") more typical of the personal visual experiences he wishes to
share with his readers. Indeed, as quickly as he has evoked the shadowy
presence of these Jews, mourning in typical Old Testament fashion
(weeping and rending their garments), they are gone; the pilgrim has
imagined their presence only to underscore their material absence from a
Christian space.[49] The Jews then "depart" as quickly as they came from
his imagination, and the mention of Hezekiah returns us to a scriptural

---

200), 91–95.
    [46]On this term see Chapter 1 above.
    [47]Elsner, "*Itinerarium Burdigalense*," 193, reads the pairing of Hadrian and Hezekiah as "a
conflation of pre-Christian realities (Roman and Jewish)," but I think Hadrian's particular
significance *within* Jewish "reality" (especially as they are "mourning") is signaled here as well.
    [48]*Itinerarium Burdigalense* 571.5–10 (CCL 175:8); see Stemberger, *Jews and Christians*, 93.
    [49]See the imaginative reconstruction of Erich W. Cohn, "Second Thoughts About the Per-
forated Stone on the Haram of Jerusalem," *Palestine Exploration Quarterly* 114 (1982): 143–46.

ambience: the only present Jews are now the dead biblical ones.[50]

Scholars have long noted the Bordeaux pilgrim's interest in sites relating to the Old Testament and have proffered various explanations; interestingly, many of them return to the question of contemporary Palestinian Jews. Either this pilgrim is supposed to have derived information directly from these (unnamed and, more important, uncited) Jews,[51] or else he is himself alleged to be a Jew (or a converted Jew, or Jewish-Christian).[52] The assumption that attention to Jews in their Old Testament guise bespeaks Jewishness on the part of the pilgrim does not allow for the possibility that, in fact, a particular Christian identity is being inscribed through these representations.[53] The representation of Jews as Old Testament figures, and their ambivalent placement within the imperial province of Palestine, allows the Bordeaux pilgrim to articulate some of the power dynamics of imperial Christianity.

At very few places in his description does the Bordeaux pilgrim allow an explicitly imperial presence to exert itself within these holy places. Apart from "Hadrian's statues," the pilgrim mentions four churches recently built "by command of Constantine";[54] these mentions are casually inserted between longer descriptions of nearby biblical events and catalogues of Old Testament tombs. The description of the Golgotha church follows a lengthy (for the Bordeaux pilgrim, at least) description of the crucifixion; the Eleona church is found between the tomb of "Hezekiah, king of the Jews," and the sites of the Transfiguration and tomb of Lazarus; the Bethlehem church is wedged between a long list of local Old Testament tombs (Rachel, Ezekiel, Asaph, Job, Jesse, David, and Solo-

[50]See Homi K. Bhabha, *The Location of Culture* (London: Routledge, 1994), 51: "The image is at once a metaphoric substitution, an illusion of presence, and by that same token a metonym, a sign of its absence and loss.

[51]John Wilkinson, "Jewish Holy Places and the Origins of Christian Pilgrimage," in *The Blessings of Pilgrimage*, ed. Robert Ousterhout (Urbana: University of Illinois Press, 1990), 41–53; followed by Wilken, *Land Called Holy*, 110–11.

[52]Herbert Donner, *Pilgerfahrt ins Heilige Land: Die ältesten Berichte christlicher Palästinapilger (4.-7. Jahrhundert)* (Stuttgart: Verlag Katholisches Bibelwerk, 1979), 42.

[53]See Stemberger, *Jews and Christians*, 88–95.

[54]*Itinerarium Burdigalense* 594.2–3, 595.5–6, 598.7, 599.5–6 (CCL 175:17, 18, 20), the churches at Golgotha, Eleona, Bethlehem, and Terebinth/Mamre. See John Wilkinson, "Christian Pilgrims in Jerusalem During the Byzantine Period," *Palestine Exploration Quarterly* 108 (1976): 80.

mon, whose names are "written in Hebrew letters");[55] and the Terebinth church is between the spring where Philip baptized the eunuch and the tombs of the Old Testament patriarchs and matriarchs.[56] Imperial construction, like Roman roads, has encroached but little on the sacred space of the Christian holy land. Like Hadrian, the Bordeaux pilgrim cannot successfully manage to purge the land of its former inhabitants, the Jews; he is constantly surrounded by their ghosts, especially on the Temple Mount, where they threatened to burst in and mourn like ancient Israelites.

In his study of early modern and modern travel writing David Spurr has described the colonialist textual strategy of "insubstantialization": "the object of representation is seen as an immaterial counterpart to the dissolving consciousness of the subject, a dissolution which can be joyful . . . or profoundly disorienting."[57] The "disorientation" of seeing the colonized object as if in a dream can be both empowering and humbling. For the Bordeaux pilgrim this ambivalent representation of the Jew as always historicized—as dead, yet somehow still *there*—underscores the ambivalent manifestation of imperial power in the Christian holy land. The itinerary format of the document inscribes the material significance of Roman roads and stopping stations, of the imperial function of travel itself; yet that power exerts itself only fitfully in the limits of the holy places.

Robert Markus has argued that Christian holy places themselves are a by-product of Christian historical ambivalence, the attempt to "bridge this generation gap" between "the triumphant Church of the fourth and later centuries" and "its persecuted predecessor."[58] In a manner similar to Eusebius's *Church History* and *Onomastikon* the itinerary of the Bordeaux pilgrim neutralizes the presence of the Jew through strategies of historicization and creates a Christian subjectivity with the ability to view the Jewish presence on historical display. At the same time, however, this historicization keeps the sites of Christian sanctity cut off from the full im-

---

[55] *Itinerarium Burdigalense* 598.7–9 (CCL 175:20).

[56] *Itinerarium Burdigalense* 593.2–594.2, 595.4–596.3, 598.5–9, 599.1–9 (CCL 175:17, 18, 20).

[57] David Spurr, *The Rhetoric of Empire: Colonial Discourse in Journalism, Travel Writing, and Imperial Administration* (Durham, N.C.: Duke University Press, 1993), 142.

[58] Robert Markus, "How on Earth Could Places Become Holy? Origins of the Christian Idea of Holy Places," *Journal of Early Christian Studies* 2 (1994): 269.

pact of imperial authority, allowing contemporary Jews the opportunity to slip in on occasion, groaning, mourning, and then vanishing.

"Just the Man for the Place": Textualization of the Jew

If the Bordeaux pilgrim's representation of Jews serves to encode historical ambivalence between Christianity and Empire, between "then" and "now," the more lively travel account of Egeria demonstrates how the Jewish past can be pressed into more immediate service for the Christian present through processes of textualization. The pilgrim most likely named Egeria came to the holy places from Spain or Gaul in the early reign of Theodosius I,[59] whose unified rule at the end of the fourth century ushered in an officially "Christian Empire." E. D. Hunt has called her narrative "an authentic witness of 'Theodosian' Christianity,"[60] that is, a public form of piety that deliberately elaborated affiliations between imperial authority and Christian identity.[61] As a representative of this stream of Western piety and Eastern *imperium,* Egeria and her textualized representation of the Palestinian Jew create a purely Christian space for the exercise of religious piety and authority.

The seventh-century monk Valerius, in his letter praising "the virtue and fragility" of this fearless woman,[62] remarks that, driven by the "flame of desire that burned in her holy heart," Egeria "accordingly read through all the books of the Old and New Testaments with all intrepidity, and sought out all the places to which holy miracles had been ascribed [*conscripta*], in whatever diverse parts of the world they might be found—in provinces, cities, mountains, and desert places."[63] Scholars have subsequently concurred that "the main impetus" for Egeria's travel "was the influence of the Bible."[64] Of all our Christian travel writers, Egeria stands

---

[59]P. Devos, "La date du voyage d'Égérie," *Analecta Bollandiana* 85 (1967): 165–94; Hagith Sivan, "Who Was Egeria? Piety and Pilgrimage in the Age of Gratian," *Harvard Theological Review* 81 (1988): 59–72; Hunt, *Holy Land Pilgrimage,* 164–65; E. D. Hunt, "The Date of the *Itinerarium Egeriae,*" *Studia Patristica* 38 (2001): 410–16.

[60]Hunt, *Holy Land Pilgrimage,* 165, and see 157–79 on "Theodosian piety."

[61]See also John Matthews, *Western Aristocracies and Imperial Court, A.D. 364–425* (Clarendon: Oxford, 1975; repr., Clarendon: Oxford, 1990), 139.

[62]Valerius, *Epistula de beatissima Egeria* 1 (SC 296:336).

[63]Valerius, *Epistula de beatissima Egeria* 1 (SC 296:338).

[64]Hunt, *Holy Land Pilgrimage,* 120. See also Martin Mulzer, "Mit der Bibel in der Hand?

as the preeminent example of a "textual attitude" toward the holy land.[65] Not only does "sacred writing make this topography meaningful" for Egeria, as Blake Leyerle has demonstrated;[66] it very simply *makes* this topography. Even sites completely devoid of monument or marker are made noteworthy by their scriptural resonance. This is demonstrated most fully in the first extant section of the travel diary, as Egeria travels through "Moses-country." Here empty vistas are imbued with significance solely due to their correlation to the "books of Moses":

Then . . . we were led to another place not far off, where priests and monks showed us that very spot [*id est ad eum locum*] where holy Aaron stood with the seventy elders, when holy Moses accepted the Law from the Lord for the children of Israel. So on that spot, although there is not even a structure, nevertheless there is a big, round rock, with a flat ridge on top, on which these very same saints stood![67]

A big, flat rock leaps out of an otherwise unremarkable landscape, animated by the scriptural text (and the accommodating local guides).

At times it is clear that the text remains in some sense even *more* authentic than "the very place." Wearied by her descriptions of "Moses-country," Egeria tells her "sisters" back home: "All these things, one by one, it has sufficed to write down, since no one could keep all this in their memory. But when Your Affection reads the holy books of Moses, she will perceive more diligently what happened there."[68] The most striking place where the text of Scripture creates landscape is in an empty plain near the village of Livias, where Egeria and her party pause to read a passage from Deuteronomy since "this was the very place where Moses *wrote the book* of Deuteronomy."[69] Here the site is devoid of any visual marker but claims significance as a textual monument to the text itself. Throughout these "Moses" sections, especially, Egeria speaks of the "cus-

---

Egeria und ihr 'Codex,'" *Zeitschrift der deutsches Palästina-Vereins* 112 (1996): 156–64.

[65]Said, *Orientalism*, 83–84, on "textual attitude."

[66]Leyerle, "Landscape as Cartography," 127; see also 129: "the emphasis still rests on how the land supports the facticity of scripture."

[67]*Itinerarium Egeriae* 4.4 (SC 296:138–40).

[68]*Itinerarium Egeriae* 5.8 (SC 296:146). See Leyerle, "Landscape as Cartography," 127.

[69]*Itinerarium Egeriae* 10.6 (SC 296:168), emphasis added. Egeria apparently correlates this site with Deut 31.24: "Moses had finished writing the words of this law in a book, to the very end."

tom" of her company: to arrive at a site, say a prayer, read an appropriate passage [*ipse locus*] from the Bible, say another prayer, and move on.[70] Egeria's Moses, Aaron, and children of Israel inhabit texts, and they are invoked from and contained within the portable codex of Egeria's Bible, like amiable genies.[71]

In a manner similar to the Bordeaux pilgrim, Egeria is constantly aware of the Old Testament dead: but where the Bordeaux pilgrim would see a *monumentum*, a material trace of Jewish natives, Egeria sees empty spaces and texts that inscribe the Jewish dead into her landscape. The closest she (and her readers) comes to viewing the material remains of a tomb is at Carneas, identified as the home of long-suffering Job. She relates the story of the *inventio* of Job's tomb. The discovery was made by the local clergy, following the ecstatic instructions of a hermit: "As they were digging in the place that was revealed to him [that is, the local monk], they discovered a cave, which they followed through for about a hundred paces; suddenly, a stone appeared before the diggers. When they took a closer look at the stone, they discovered engraved on top of it the name JOB."[72] Significantly, however, the tomb itself is no longer visible to Egeria: "Nowadays, in Job's honor in this spot that church has been built which you can see, however it was built so that the stone and the body itself were not moved to another place but left here where they were found."[73] Job's body is now entirely invisible, replaced by the text of Job left in Egeria's possession.

This Jewish absence is made fruitful for the production of Christian identity precisely by its absorption into biblical text: substituting textual Jews for Jewish remains allows Egeria to push her Christian appropriation of the holy places further than the Bordeaux pilgrim. The overlay of a Christian church on top of Job's body represents quite graphically Egeria's entire vision of the Christian holy places. On the level of the material text itself, we can contrast Egeria's notice with the Bordeaux pilgrim's method of historicizing his dead Jews: in his account, he was care-

---

[70] *Itinerarium Egeriae* 10.7 (SC 296:168). Other "books of Moses" scenes in this section: *Itinerarium Egeriae* 4.8, 6.3, 11.3, 12.3, 14.1 (SC 296:142, 154, 172, 174, 186).

[71] See Catherine Schmidt, "The Guided Tour: Insulated Adventure," *Urban Life* 7 (1979): 441–68.

[72] *Itinerarium Egeriae* 16.6 (SC 296:194).

[73] *Itinerarium Egeriae* 16.6 (SC 296:196).

ful to note that the graves, still visible, were inscribed with Hebrew characters of the names of the entombed.[74] In Egeria's account the name
"Job" is not only invisible, because it is covered by a church, but there is
no attempt to "historicize" Job's presence through the dead language of
Hebrew. Indeed, in Egeria's holy land the "native" language seems to be
Greek: she remarks several times on terms and names of sites "as they are
called here" in Greek, and provides a Latin translation.[75] The absorption
of Hebrew text into Greek, while certainly not unique to Egeria, nonetheless reveals her assumptions about Christian text and Jewish past.[76]

So, too, just as a church covers Job's tomb, we find that, at every site
where she "recognizes" the scriptural presence of Old Testament Jews,
there are Christians installed in their place, Christians who fit the scriptural bill as well as—if not better than—the Old Testament's original actors.[77] Our extant manuscript of Egeria's travel diary begins with her
traveling party scaling Mount Sinai: we have already seen how rich and
textured "Moses-country" was for Egeria. When her party reaches the top
of Mount Sinai, she finds only the "cave of holy Moses"; instead of some
material remains of Moses himself, there is in his place "a healthy old
man, a monk from his boyhood and an 'ascetic' as they call it here—in

[74]*Itinerarium Burdigalense* 598.7–9 (CCL 175:20): *hebraeis litteris scriptum.*

[75]*Itinerarium Egeriae* 3.4, *ascitis;* 8.4, *dendros aletheias;* 13.4, *opu Melchisedek;* 15.3, *cepos tu agiu Iohanni;* 24.1, *monazontes et parthenae;* 24.4, *lychnicon;* 24.5, *kyrie eleison;* 27.1, *heortae;* and 46.2, *catechesis* (SC 296:132, 160, 184, 188, 238, 240, 258, 308). See also A. Ernout, "Les mots grecs dans la Peregrinatio Aetheriae," *Emaerita* 20 (1952): 298–307, on Egeria's late Latin context.

[76]A point for further study is Egeria's division of canonical and apocryphal texts within and outside the holy land, respectively: the three sites where she explicitly refers *extra canonem* are in Edessa, Harran (in Mesopotamia), and Isaurian Seleucia (19.2, 20.10, 23.6 [SC 296:202, 218–20], 230]). All other "appropriate readings" are inside the holy land and inside the canon. Since Egeria herself mentions "canonical Scriptures" in Mesopotamia, I cannot simply argue that she was *unaware* of such divisions or that she embraced apocrypha because she was a Priscillianist (*pace* Henry Chadwick, *Priscillian of Avila: The Occult and the Charismatic in the Early Church* [Oxford: Clarendon Press, 1976], 166–68). The link between holy land venera-tion and construction of canonical/apocryphal distinction (quite prominent in Jerome, for in-stance) deserves further study. See also Leo Spitzer, "The Epic Style of the Pilgrim Aetheria," *Comparative Literature* 1 (1949): 245–46.

[77]See Andrew Palmer, "Egeria the Voyager, or the Technology of Remote Sensing in Late Antiquity," in *Travel Fact and Travel Fiction: Studies on Fiction, Literary Tradition, Scholarly Discovery, and Observation in Travel Writing,* ed. Zweder von Martels (Leiden: Brill, 1994), 39–53, who argues against Mary Campbell's claim (see *Witness and the Other World,* 8–9, 20–33) that Egeria's text is in any way "exotic."

fact, just the man for the place [*qualis dignus est esse in eo loco*]."[78] Like-wise, at the spot where Melchizedek met Abraham, she meets a priest who is "now older and well versed in Scriptures, who presided over this spot after being a monk; about this priest numerous bishops, whose ac-quaintance we made later, bore favorable witness to his way of life, for concerning him they said that he was just the man to preside in this spot [*dignus qui presit in hoc loco*]."[79] While in transit, she stops her guides to ask what "special reason" there might be for a solitary monk's cell in the Jordan valley, and is told that this was where Elijah hid from Ahab.[80] Al-though in some measure Egeria's vision of the holy land reproduces the effacing and historicizing gestures of the Bordeaux pilgrim, the ghosts that haunted the pilgrim from Bordeaux have now graciously ceded their place to more fitting Christian tenants.[81] It is noteworthy that the only active and mobile agents of Egeria's travel diary are, in fact, the monks and clergy who act as her holy land tour guides. Jews, as contemporary residents of the land, have been completely textualized into the Christian past.[82] The land is totally scriptural; Scripture is entirely Christian; the land becomes the site for Christians to *be* the texts they venerate.[83]

It is significant that this forceful appropriation of Jewish time and space occurred in the holy land of Theodosius I, the physical site where Christianity as "new Israel" attained a literal and potent reality not seen in the days of Constantine. The flood of imperial interest and money into the holy land in this period surpasses Constantine's day, and Egeria's voyage is best viewed in the context of the concerted efforts of Theodo-sius and his family to portray themselves as both ultraorthodox and ul-

[78]*Itinerarium Egeriae* 3.4 (SC 296:132).

[79]*Itinerarium Egeriae* 14.2 (SC 296:186).

[80]*Itinerarium Egeriae* 16.1–4 (SC 296:193).

[81]See E. D. Hunt, "The Itinerary of Egeria: Reliving the Bible in Fourth-Century Palestine," in *The Holy Land, Holy Lands and Christian History* (Suffolk: Boydell Press, 2000), 34–54.

[82]An additional instance of textualization, effacement, and appropriation is recounted in Carrae/Harran at Abraham's house, which has been covered over with the martyrium of Helpidius (*Itinerarium Egeriae* 20.5 [SC 296:214–16]).

[83]Jerome's representation of Christian monastic settlement reproduces this textualization, with the often problematic retention of "local Jews" (see Chapter 3); but *epp.* 46 and 108 (his *epitaphium Paulae*) resonate with Egeria's textualized cartography. On the significance of "bib-lical realism" in early Christian pilgrimage see Frank, *Memory of the Eyes*, esp. 6–11, 29–33, 69–75, and 168–73.

traimperial.[84] Not even the rumored "ghosts" of mourning Jews on the Temple Mount remain to haunt Egeria's rich landscape; the shadows of Moses and Elijah appear only as empty spaces next to the more apt Christian monks, through the process of appropriation and textualization.[85] As Christians traveled through a reunified and securely orthodox empire at the end of the fourth century, the holy land emerged as a nexus for this ideally homogeneous orthodox *imperium*.[86] The cacophony of languages into which the Jerusalem liturgy is translated at Easter testifies not so much to a diversity of Christian identities as to a unity of Christian imperialism.[87] All "otherness" is absorbed and thus erased within a robust and totalizing Christian identity.[88] In Egeria's travel diary it is the unifying force of Scripture, subsuming all otherness into wholly Christian text, that accomplishes this absorption and erasure: "To posit the land as a text is to claim its readability, and thence to arrogate power over it."[89]

Despite this thorough textualization, however, Egeria's textualized landscape fails, in the end, to accommodate successfully contemporary Jews into her Christian land. The Bordeaux pilgrim had been able to invoke the ghosts of Jewish mourners at the site of their empty Temple Mount, achieving in this way some measure of consonance between his scriptural cadavers and their Jewish descendants.[90] When we read Egeria,

---

[84]See Matthews, *Western Aristocracy*, 107–45; Hunt, *Holy Land Pilgrimage*, 155–79, 221–48. See also E. D. Hunt, "Theodosius I and the Holy Land," *Studia Patristica* 29 (1997): 52–57.

[85]See Bhabha, *Location of Culture*, 44: "It is always in relation to the place of the Other that colonial desire is articulated: the phantasmic space of possession that no one subject can singly or fixedly occupy, and therefore permits the dream of the inversion of roles."

[86]On the "imperial" subtext of the whole document see Spitzer, "Epic Style," 258.

[87]*Itinerarium Egeriae* 47.3–4 (SC 296:314).

[88]So, too, the thrill of discovering "new" and even unexpected elements of this Christian imperial identity (see Hunt, *Holy Land*, 20) might be read in a manner similar to Pratt, *Imperial Eyes*, 201–9: "Crudely, then, discovery in this context consisted of a gesture of converting local knowledges (discourses) into European national and continental knowledges associated with European forms and relations of power" (202).

[89]Simon Ryan, "Inscribing the Emptiness: Cartography, Exploration, and the Construction of Australia," in *De-Scribing Empire: Post-Colonialism and Textuality*, ed. Chris Tiffin and Alan Lawson (London: Routledge, 1994), 126. See also Spurr, *Rhetoric of Empire*, 92.

[90]Cf. Pratt, *Imperial Eyes*, 52: "Out of the corner of the landscanning eye, Khoikhoi servants move in and out on the edges of the story. . . . Apart from their ghostly presence as members of 'the party,' the Khoikhoi inhabit a separate textual homeland in these books, where they are produced as objects of formal ethnographic description." See also Anne McClintock, *Imperial Leather: Race, Gender, and Sexuality in the Colonial Contest* (London:

we learn (presumably erroneously) that there simply are *no* Jews in the Theodosian holy land. Such an assertion displays the power of textualization to rewrite the religious and cultural landscape yet at the same time reveals the tension involved in articulating this space, as, at the same moment, entirely Christian and profoundly "other."[91] If all Jews are supposed to have been replaced with more "fitting" Christians, it is unclear what a good imperial Christian is supposed to do when confronted with an *actual* Jew. Such a situation could certainly arise in places such as Galilee, home to an increasing host of pilgrimage sites, as well as the highest concentration of Jewish populations in this period. Our only indication that Egeria visited Galilee herself remains in excerpts of her travel journal preserved by Peter the Deacon, the twelfth-century librarian of Monte Cassino. According to these excerpts Egeria twice sees synagogues that are apparently no longer in use by contemporary Jews. One synagogue, she reports, was actually cursed by Jesus so that it would never be completed.[92] Even in a strongly Judaized part of the holy land, Jews fade away into the biblical background, subsumed by and replaced with the sacred texts. Although Egeria had a remarkable capacity for seeing, and *not* seeing, through the lens of Scripture, it is less certain that her biblical blinders would have sufficiently protected other Christian travelers from the spectacle of live Jews not replaced by Christian monks and bishops. Other strategies of landscape formation developed in early Christian travel writing to compensate, on some level, for this disjunction between domination and appropriation.

Routledge, 1995), 30–31, 40–42, on the "presiding dilemma" of " 'empty' lands [that] were visibly peopled" in the Victorian context, and 232–46 on "anachronistic space."

[91]Bhabha, *Location of Culture,* 66–84, and 98: "If the idea of despotism homogenizes India's past, the colonialist present requires a strategy of calculation in relation to its native subjects."

[92]Peter the Deacon, *Liber de locis sanctis* V 2, V 4 (CCL 175:98–99); see Blake Leyerle, "Pilgrims to the Land: Early Christian Perceptions of the Galilee," in Meyers, *Galilee,* 348–53. On the demography of Jews in Galilee from the later fourth century onward see M. Avi-Yonah, *The Jews of Palestine* (New York: Schocken, 1976), 17; Zvi Ma'oz, "Comments on Jewish and Christian Communities in Byzantine Galilee," *Palestine Exploration Quarterly* 117 (1988): 59–68; Dennis Groh, "Jews and Christians in Late Roman Palestine: Towards a New Chronology," *Biblical Archaeologist* 51 (1988): 80–96; and Mordechai Aviam, "Christian Galilee in the Byzantine Period," in Meyers, *Galilee,* 281–300.

"The Most Beautiful Jewesses": Aestheticization of the Jew

I turn now to a later travel account, that of the so-called Piacenza pilgrim, who traveled from Italy to the holy land and Egypt sometime between 560 and 570, in the wake of Justinian's reconquest of Italy and the brief reunification of Italian and Byzantine orthodoxy and *imperium*.[93] The travel writing of the Piacenza pilgrim is not centered on historical monuments, like the Bordeaux pilgrim's,[94] nor on scriptural texts, like Egeria's.[95] Although there is no particular reason to doubt that his motives for travel were as pious as those of either of these two pilgrims, the Piacenza pilgrim's judgment of the holy sites is more grounded in sensory experience and pleasure. His vision of the holy land incorporates the presence of cultural and religious others through strategies of aestheticization and appropriation. By "aestheticization" I mean the representation of the holy land as a primarily sensory (often visual) experience, one that gratifies an individual, whether that experience is of sites, persons, objects, sounds, or any other stimulus.[96] The reduction of material realities to aesthetic judgment inscribes at once distance and appropriation (consumption), as well as authenticity: the holy land offers up new, strange sensory data and the pilgrim receives and evaluates them ("good," "bad," "delicious"). The pilgrim is the consumer, and the holy land is consumed.[97]

As the Piacenza pilgrim moves through the self-consciously foreign land, his conclusions about cities and their populations revolve around their being "good" or "bad," based not on some notion of biblical history or textual appropriateness but on the pilgrim's own experiences. This different mode of imperial appropriation as aesthetic, sensual, and experiential allows this pilgrim to align less problematically his ideals of imperial

---

[93]See Celestina Milani, *Itinerarium Antonini Placentini: Un viaggio in Terra Santa del 560–570 d.C.* (Milan: Università Cattolica del Sacro Cuore, 1977), 31–46. The pilgrim has been posthumously called Antoninus, from a mention of the Placentine martyr-saint Antoninus in the opening lines of the text.

[94]He does, however, see his share of Old Testament corpses: see *Itinerarium Antonini Placentini* 28 (Rachel), 30 (Abraham, Isaac, Jacob, Sarah, and Joseph's bones) (CCL 175:143, 144).

[95]See Leyerle, "Landscape as Cartography," 134: "Compared to our earlier authors, the Piacenza pilgrim's knowledge of scripture is strikingly modest." This is a generous appraisal.

[96]See Frank, *Memory of the Eyes,* esp. 102–33.

[97]See Spurr, *Rhetoric of Empire,* 42–60.

domination and Christian identity. The ability to evaluate a site or object's aesthetic value is sometimes connected with its history or holiness but often through no more than the suggestive juxtaposition of sentences. The first stop out of Constantinople is "the island of Cyprus, the city of Constantia, where Saint Epiphanius has his resting place. A beautiful city, delightful [*deliciosa*], garlanded with date palms."[98] Is the city *deliciosa* for its date palms or for Epiphanius's tomb? The author does not specify, and it probably does not matter: both aspects of Constantia made it enjoyable in terms of the pilgrim's own experience. On the fringes of the holy land, cities generally receive such blanket judgments about their "goodness": passing through the cities of Tyre and Ptolemais, for instance, on his approach to Galilee, the Piacenza pilgrim finds Tyre to be characterized by "the worst sort of living, with so much decadence that it's impossible to speak of it"; Ptolemais is, in contrast, "an honest city, with good monasteries."[99] Likewise, near the end of his journey, as his party passes through Egypt, he remarks that Alexandria is a "shining city, with the shiftiest populace, but kind to pilgrims, at least."[100] Similarly he evaluates Gaza as a "splendid and delightful city, all the most honest people of a decent and generous sort, lovers of pilgrims."[101] Here it is clear that such evaluations of cities and their populations in toto are based on the pilgrim's experience: the Alexandrians were kind to him, so he can forgive (to some degree) their general "shiftiness."

Throughout this engaging piece of travel writing it is often the experience of the senses that marks a site or an object for this pilgrim. Sight, smell, sound, touch, and taste permeate his account and allow him to evaluate and appropriate his holy land experience. He sees images of both

---

[98] *Itinerarium Antonini Placentini* 1 (CCL 175:129).

[99] *Itinerarium Antonini Placentini* 2 (CCL 175:129–30). The pilgrim condemns the Tyrians for *genecia publica*, which John Wilkinson, *Jerusalem Pilgrims Before the Crusades* (Warminster: Aris & Philips, 1977), 79, mistranslates as "brothels" but is more likely "weaving factory" (*gunaikeion*); so the moral contrast between Tyre and Ptolemais is between shameless working women and humble (male?) monastics. Linda Jones Hall discusses the nineteenth-century origins of this mistranslation in her Ph.D. dissertation "Berytus, 'Mother of Laws': Studies in the Social History of Beirut from the Third to Sixth Centuries A.D." (Ohio State University, 1996) and her article in progress entitled "Of Weaving and Women: A Cautionary Tale About Misconstruction of Gender and Place in the Mistranslation of the *Genicia* of Tyre" (personal communication).

[100] *Itinerarium Antonini Placentini* 45 (CCL 175:152).

[101] *Itinerarium Antonini Placentini* 33 (CCL 175:145).

Mary and Jesus; the former is among several relics of Mary housed at Golgotha;[102] the latter is an imprint on linen on which Jesus had wiped his face: "We venerated it, but could not gaze upon it on account of its splendor, since, as soon as you look upon it, it shifts before your eyes."[103] The engagement of the visual sense makes the experience pleasurable, even when that experience is marked by disorientation. The pilgrim also delights in the tactile sensation of Jesus' footprints, noting that the shape of Jesus' foot was "beautiful, well-measured, and delicate."[104] Smells also give dimension to the pilgrim experience, as demonstrated by the sanctifying "incense and lights" of the liturgy at Mamre and the isolated healing shrine at Clysma, which "has a certain sulfuric odor."[105] The pilgrim also has the remarkable capability of layering aural experience on top of the tactile and visual: twice he inclines to touch stones marked by sanctity and remarks on the uncanny sounds that reach his ears.[106]

In addition, the tastes of the holy land permeate the Piacenza pilgrim's account at the level of sense perception. He drinks from the skull of the martyr Theodota; he partakes of the "indescribably sweet water" near Rachel's tomb in Ramah; he learns how to sweeten water that has turned bitter during his trek through Egyptian desert; and he tastes green nuts straight off the boat from India "which men believe come from paradise, of such grace that as soon as you eat them, you are full."[107] It is perhaps the portability of these tastes of the holy land that has made them so memorable and remarkable to the Piacenza pilgrim: he is constantly fill-

[102] *Itinerarium Antonini Placentini* 20 (CCL 175:139).

[103] *Itinerarium Antonini Placentini* 44 (CCL 175:152). See also *Itinerarium Antonini Placentini* 46 (CCL 175:153), where the pilgrims gaze through a clear, glass jar at the head of John the Baptist, "with our own eyes [*nostris oculis*]."

[104] *Itinerarium Antonini Placentini* 23 (CCL 175:141).

[105] *Itinerarium Antonini Placentini* 30 and 42 (CCL 175:134, 151). On sensory experience in hagiographic and liturgical literature see Susan Ashbrook Harvey, "The Stylite's Liturgy: Ritual and Religious Identity in Late Antiquity," *Journal of Early Christian Studies* 6 (1998): 523–39; idem, "Olfactory Knowing: Signs of Smell in the *vitae* of Simeon Stylites," in *After Bardaisan: Studies on Continuity and Change in Syriac Christianity in Honour of Professor Han J. W. Drijvers,* ed. G. J. Reinink and A. C. Klugkist (Leuven: Peeters, 1999), 23–34; and idem, "St. Ephrem on the Scent of Salvation," *Journal of Theological Studies,* n.s., 49 (1998): 109–28.

[106] He hears "streams of water" through a crack in Abraham's altar, which he places at Golgotha (*Itinerarium Antonini Placentini* 19 [CCL 175:139]) and "the murmuring of a crowd of people" from the "cornerstone rejected by the builders" in James's house on Mount Zion (*Itinerarium Antonini Placentini* 22 [CCL 175:140]).

[107] *Itinerarium Antonini Placentini* 22, 28, 36, 41 (CCL 175:141, 143, 147, 151).

ing up jugs of water to take home, and his description of the delights of
Jericho emphasizes the transportability of holy land sweetness:

The spring of water, which Elisha made sweet, waters all of Jericho. There they
grow grapes for wine, which is given to those suffering from fever. There they
grow dates that weigh a pound, some of which I took with me back home [*in
provincia*], and I gave one to my lord, the patrician Paterius. There they grow a
citron that weighs forty pounds and the branch of the fruit is two feet long and
two fingers wide. There is a vine there, from which they fill whole baskets for
sale on the Mount of Olives, and at Pentecost they make new wine out of it and
sell it by the jarful.[108]

This passage on the agricultural wonders of Jericho signals what is so significant for the Piacenza pilgrim about the sensory experience of the holy
land: it is a materiality that is at once entirely "natural" and native to the
site (Jericho grapes sell by the bushel to pilgrims on Mount Olivet) and
entirely exportable (Paterius can show his fellow Placentine nobles the
one-pound date from the holy land). This material appropriation by the
privileged traveler resonates with Cosmas's proud declaration of the uni-
versality of Roman coin, and we should not be surprised to see the
Piacenza pilgrim exclaim that "this province is like paradise!"[109] It is a
paradise from which the traveler may purchase and transport paradisiacal
souvenirs of a sensuous and material variety.

    In addition, the repeated presence of Jews sets the tone for this pil-
grim's triumphant journey through the Christian province. The journey
starts at Constantinople, with a trip overland through Syria; this makes
the cities of Galilee his first pilgrimage stops. He sees Mary's "breadbas-
ket" in Diocaesarea/Sepphoris, and the nuptial water pots at Cana; next
his party arrives in Nazareth, "where there are many miracles."[110] The
first stop in Nazareth is, in fact, the Jewish synagogue:

In the synagogue there sits the book in which the Lord wrote his ABCs, and in
this synagogue there is a bench on which he sat with other children. This table
can be lifted and moved around by Christians, but the Jews are completely unable to move it, and it doesn't allow them to drag it outside. The house of Saint

    [108] *Itinerarium Antonini Placentini* 14 (CCL 175:136–37).
    [109] *Itinerarium Antonini Placentini* 5 (CCL 175:131): *provincia similis paradiso.*
    [110] *Itinerarium Antonini Placentini* 4–5 (CCL 175:130).

Mary is now a basilica, and her clothes are the cause of frequent miracles.[111]

We might invent any number of scenarios to explain the Jews' "inability" to lift the bench of their own synagogue. Some scholars have suggested that the Jews themselves operated this particular "tourist" attraction for Christian visitors, charging them for the privilege of watching Jews (play-acting) at struggling with their own bench.[112] Such Jewish participation is not implied in the text, however, and would certainly have detracted from this pilgrim's own perception of the tactile thrill of lugging a bench on which Jesus sat with the other (less memorable) children. In fact, the pilgrim seems to envision resistance on the part of the Jews: they are attempting, unsuccessfully, to drag the bench outside, to remove the spectacle from their synagogue. As far as the Piacenza pilgrim is concerned, the Christian visitors are appropriating Jewish space for their own delight and pious amusement, insisting the whole time that it remain Jewish space. Unlike Egeria's "converted" spaces, where the once-Jewish had become completely Christian, the aesthetic experience of the pilgrim here would not be complete without the recognition and appropriation of the Jewish space as continually Jewish.

This delight in the Jewish is made even clearer when he incorporates the Jewish "natives" into his pleasurable experience of Nazareth:

The Jewesses of this city are better looking than any other Jewesses in the whole country. They declare that this is Saint Mary's gift to them, for they also say that she was a relative of theirs. Though there is no love lost between Jews and Christians, these women are full of kindness [caritae]. This province is like paradise, in wheat and in fruits like Egypt, a province of modest size, but that eclipses Egypt in terms of wine and oil and apples.[113]

[111]*Itinerarium Antonini Placentini* 5 (CCL 175:130–31). The most famous ancient account of Jesus learning to read is found in the *Infancy Gospel of Thomas* 6.2–7.1, the Greek text of which is now updated by Ronald F. Hock, *The Infancy Gospels of James and Thomas* (Santa Rosa, Calif.: Polebridge Press, 1995), 112–18. See also Brian McNeil, "Jesus and the Alphabet," *Journal of Theological Studies*, n.s., 27 (1976): 126–28.

[112]Joan E. Taylor, *Christians and the Holy Places: The Myth of Jewish Christian Origins* (Oxford: Clarendon Press, 1993), 228–29. But see also Robert Graves's novelization of this account: *Count Belisarius* (London: Penguin, 1954), 44–45: "[Barak the relic-seller] had a Jew or two always within call to prove the truth of one-half of this assertion; the pilgrims themselves could prove the other half, if they paid for the privilege."

[113]*Itinerarium Antonini Placentini* 5 (CCL 175:131).

The Piacenza pilgrim's delight in Nazareth centers on its pleasurable Jewishness: from the synagogue and its miracles, to the astounding agro-
nomic production, to the pretty Jewish girls whose very beauty is at once
undeniably Jewish—they are, after all, the "most beautiful Jewesses" in
the country[114]—but there, like the apples, wine, and synagogue, for the
enjoyment of Christian men.[115] It is Saint Mary's "gift" to these men
which preserves their beauty for Christian visitors, just as Mary's clothes
in her old Jewish house cure disease.

This mode of aesthetic appropriation of space creates a new type of
Christian landscape, one in which the "otherness" of the Jews is brought
into a fruitful proximity to the imperial, Christian self. Jews become the
"good" natives of this Christian province, now in contrast to the sinister
Samaritans. After leaving the welcoming embrace of the beautiful Jewesses of Galilee, the pilgrim's party passes through Samaritan country:
"Going down through the countryside, there were cities and villages of
the Samaritans; and wherever we passed, whether it was us or Jews, they
burned up our footprints with straw, so great is their loathing of both."[116]
Samaritans in earlier Christian discourses of heresy and historiography
had acted as a sort of "shadow-double" of the Jews.[117] Under Justinian,
however, they became the specific object of imperial persecution, making
them particularly apt receptacles for the "terrifying stereotypes of sav-
agery, cannibalism, lust and anarchy"[118] in the Piacenza pilgrim's account.[119] What is striking here, however, is the positioning of Jews with
Christians—"us and them" on one side, the Samaritans on the other.

[114]Simon Mimouni's theory is that the "Jewesses [Hebraeae]" of this passage are, in fact,
"Jewish-Christians" of some sort (see "Pour une définition nouvelle du judéo-christianisme
ancien," New Testament Studies 38 [1992]: 171–82). I think this somewhat misses the point of
this anecdote.

[115]See Spurr, Rhetoric of Empire, 173–77, on the colonialist "fantasy of seduction."

[116]Itinerarium Antonini Placentini 8 (CCL 175:133).

[117]Codex Theodosianus 16.8, e.g., legislates on "Jews and Samaritans" together (with the
mysterious Caelicoli), although only two of the laws (16.8.16 and 16.8.28) specifically mention
the Samaritans. Similarly, Epiphanius makes the Samaritans the "seventh heresy to spring
from Hellenism" but passes most of his argument against them marking out their distinctions
from other Jews (mostly idiosyncrasies: "they have a bad case of insanity" [9.3.6]) (Panarion 9
[GCS 25:197–203]).

[118]Bhabha, Location of Culture, 72.

[119]See Nathan Schur, History of the Samaritans (Frankfurt am Main: Peter Land, 1992), 78,
82–92.

Leyerle has noted that "the Piacenza pilgrim is attentive to native peoples" in a manner that distinguishes his account from that of his pilgrim predecessors.[120] But the Jews are not just another *populus* under the pilgrim's gaze. He may be intrigued by the outlandish appearance of the Ethiopians[121] and fascinated by the "utterly marvelous" and idolatrous rites of the Saracens near Mount Sinai.[122] In the scope of this pilgrim's narrative these are sights as wondrous and foreign as the "lions, leopards, wild asses, and gazelles."[123] The foreign quality of the Palestinian Jews, however, is quite distinct from this utter strangeness. Their spectacle can be made into Christian spectacle, and their presence can add a particular appropriate flavor to the sites of Christian pilgrimage.

This is made especially clear in the pilgrim's description of the Oak of Mamre, where his travels bring "us and the Jews" once more into close physical and conceptual proximity:

The basilica there was built with four porticos, with no roof over the central atrium. Through the middle runs a little screen and the Christians enter in one side, and the Jews on the other, carrying a lot of incense. For the deposition of Jacob and David is also celebrated in that place most devotedly, on the day after the Lord's birthday, such that from that whole land the Jews come together, an innumerable crowd, offering a lot of incense and lights and giving gifts to the ministers there.[124]

Nothing but a "little screen [*cancellus*]" divides Christian worship from Jewish—one day apart, footsteps away. The rites of the Jews pleasantly echo Christian celebration of the Nativity: Jewish culture becomes a particular facet of the pilgrim's own delight and piety, the familiar made strange, the exotic domesticated. The sights and sounds of the holy land are there to be consumed by the pilgrim, and the sensory and aesthetic experience of Palestinian Jews seasons this consumption.

The protest might be lodged that this is mostly imperialism and only tangentially "religion": surely the pilgrim's accounts seem to sacrifice "Christianness" for the sake of touristic gratification? The famous story,

---

[120]Leyerle, "Landscape as Cartography," 135.
[121]*Itinerarium Antonini Placentini* 35 (CCL 175:147).
[122]*Itinerarium Antonini Placentini* 38 (CCL 175:148–49).
[123]*Itinerarium Antonini Placentini* 39 (CCL 175:149).
[124]*Itinerarium Antonini Placentini* 30 (CCL 175:144).

for instance, of one of the pilgrim's traveling companions and the sisters
of the monastery at Sinai illustrates this nexus of Christian identity and
power that some may find troubling. At this monastery the sisters possessed not only their lone donkey but also a lion, "huge and fearsome to
look at," whose roar was so horrible that, upon the party's approach, all
of the pilgrims' own animals "either pissed or fell to the ground." Since
the sisters had been feeding the lion since it was a cub, it was tame, and
even shepherded their donkey out to pasture. The pilgrim's companion
[*ille christianissimus cum quo fui*] offered the sisters one hundred *solidi* for
the two animals. The response of the sisters was to tell stories about
"Mary, who was wandering around the desert."[125] "That most Christian
man" fetched from Jerusalem for the sisters tunics, legumes, lamp oil,
dates, baskets of roasted chickpeas, lupines, all without managing to secure the beasts. He was so inconsolable, after his two days of failed negotiations, that he cried out to his companions, "My rotten luck! Why do I
even call myself a Christian?"[126] The pilgrim narrator expresses neither
approval or disapproval,[127] but the story does make clear a sense of Christian privilege pervading the atmosphere of these pilgrims' journey
through the holy land and the fact that the privileges of Empire and
those of Christianity were indistinguishable. Power in Christians' hands
has become naturalized to the extent that we might paraphrase Edward
Said: "The cumulative effect of decades of so sovereign an imperial han-
dling has turned the holy land from alien into colonial space."[128] Sending
home a basket of enormous dates, or the lion tamed by a conventful of
nuns, registers on the same level of cultural appropriation and religious
domination. The aesthetic appropriation of the holy land by the Piacenza
pilgrim, especially marked in his representation of the Jewish population
of the Palestinian provinces, is one strategy by which Christian power
and Empire achieve their fullest expression.

[125]Mary was a local ascetic whose husband died on their wedding night and who, immediately after her seven-day period of mourning, went out to wander the desert: *Itinerarium Antonini Placentini* 34 (CCL 175:145).

[126]*Itinerarium Antonini Placentini* 34 (CCL 175:146).

[127]The pilgrim seems to suggest that he participated in the negotiations: *Quibus* (sc. *puellae*)
per me centum solidos offerebat ille christianissimus cum quo fui, sed noluerunt accipere.

[128]Said, *Orientalism,* 211. Although I would, perhaps, not so quickly apply the word *cumulative,* as if only time and practice allowed a figure to narrate and encode imperialist concerns
"better."

"According to Our Custom": Ritualization of the Jew

In her discussion of early Christian maps of the holy land Dorothea French remarked that "just as with maps drawn on a flat surface, metaphorical mappings reflect the biases and idealized view of the sacred held by each mapper."[129] In this chapter I have examined only some of the ways in which Christian travelers to the holy land mapped their own imperial desires and fears, using the local Jew as the metaphorical legend to their maps. One impression I wish to avoid is that this was a process that solidified and became more secure over time: that, somehow, the Piacenza pilgrim managed this imperial mapping "better" than the Bordeaux pilgrim or Egeria precisely because he and his pilgrim companions had more practice or had acquired more colonialist expertise. These three strategies—historicization, textualization, and aestheticization—were neither entirely discrete nor qualitatively more or less successful. Although I may claim that Egeria's textual holy land fails to incorporate contemporary Jews into Christian space, I may also point out the Piacenza pilgrim's failure to retain an effective aura of religious reverence, or the Bordeaux pilgrim's failure to allow imperial power to permeate and structure his sacred space. Each text is embedded in a historical particularity, and it constructs its Christian topography accordingly. To demonstrate both the overlap and instability of these topographies and their different strategies for metaphorical mapping, I would like to supplement the above analyses with a fourth strategy for mapping this imperial Christian space that is shared by all three of the authors I have examined.

The Bordeaux pilgrim, Egeria, and the Piacenza pilgrim all engage in processes of ritualization in their representations of the holy land and in their articulations of Christian identity therein. These textually represented rituals inscribe hierarchies into their holy land, hierarchies that reinforce the imperial presence of Christian cultural domination in the holy places. Jonathan Z. Smith has drawn attention to the significance of ritual and ritualization in the Constantinian construction of the Christian holy land. It was, according to Smith, a cultural production that

---

[129]Dorothea R. French, "Mapping Sacred Centers: Pilgrimage and the Creation of Christian Topographies in Roman Palestine," in Engemann, *Akten*, 797.

emphasized at once antiquity and novelty, materiality and ideology: "Constantine created, for the first time, a Christian 'Holy Land,' laid palimpsest-like over the old, and interacting with it in complex ways, having for its central foci a series of imperial dynastic churches. . . . [W]hat Constantine accomplished with power and wealth was advanced by rhetors like Eusebius who built a 'Holy Land' with words."[130] One crucial intersection of "power" and "words" came in the enunciation of Christian ritual: "In the Christian Jerusalem of the fourth century, gesture and story could be brought together in a unique fashion. . . . In Jerusalem, story, ritual, and place could be one."[131] Here, Smith posits, doing ("gesture") and telling ("story") were brought into conjunction in order to subsume the time and place of biblical antiquity into a new sort of Christian identity.

One vital aspect of this ritualization of the *loca sancta* is the production of hierarchies: "Ritual is, above all, an assertion of difference. . . . Ritual is systematic hierarchy par excellence."[132] It is no surprise, then, that our pilgrim authors use the representation of ritual to construct appropriate hierarchies between the "others" of their travel writing and their own Christian selves. The more laconic and historicized itinerary of the Bordeaux pilgrim has infrequent mentions of contemporary activity, but two instances listed in close proximity portray the hierarchical relations of Christian and Jew, as well as the problematic intervention of imperial domination. Near the end of the description of the Temple Mount, cited above, comes the reference to the "mourning Jews" who come every year to anoint the pierced stone "not far off [*non longe*]" from the two statues of Hadrian: "the Jews come every year, and they anoint it, and they cry out with a groan, and they tear their own garments, and in this way they withdraw."[133] Groaning and tearing of garments are typical Old Testament indications of ritualized mourning, appropriate gestures for Jews who are made to shrink back into their own biblical history.[134]

---

[130]Jonathan Z. Smith, *To Take Place: Toward Theory in Ritual* (Chicago, Ill.: University of Chicago Press, 1992), 79.

[131]Smith, *To Take Place*, 86.

[132]Smith, *To Take Place*, 109–10. This point is elaborated by Catherine Bell, *Ritual Theory, Ritual Practice* (Oxford: Oxford University Press, 1992), 169–223.

[133]*Itinerarium Burdigalense* 591.5–6 (CCL 175:16).

[134]The locus classicus of such mourning is David mourning Abner (2 Sam 3.31–36): see Ei-

Leaving the Temple Mount, and passing by Pontius Pilate's *praetorium,* the Bordeaux pilgrim looks at Golgotha, "where, by order of Emperor Constantine a basilica was built, that is a church [*dominicum*], having on its side reservoirs of remarkable beauty, from which water is drawn, and a bath behind it, where the *infantes* are washed."[135] The baptistery of the Church of the Holy Sepulcher seems to be indicated here,[136] although there is a notable lack of precision in the ritual terminology: *balneum* instead of *fons, lavantur* instead of *baptizantur;* even *basilica* needs to be glossed. The key indication seems to be *infantes,* which would refer to "newly born" Christian baptizands and not literal children.[137]

So the juxtaposition lies between the ancient mourning of ghostly Jews and the joyous washing of newly created Christians. The discourse of ritualization seems to reinforce the Bordeaux pilgrim's historicizing tendencies. Yet we should also note the increased significance of the imperial presence here: although the significance of Empire can be characterized as, at best, ambiguous in the totality of the itinerary, in these isolated passages of ritual representation imperial might takes on heightened significance as the instigator of ritual. Hadrian (through his two statues) is indicated as the responsible party for the mourning of the Jews, and Constantine has provided the physical structure for Christian initiation, and even made the reservoirs "remarkably beautiful." Not only ritual itself but the juxtaposition of rituals through imperial agency impresses on the reader Christian triumph and Jewish despair.

Egeria's travel diary is notoriously heavy with ritual: her detailed description of the Easter celebration in Jerusalem, appended to the travel portions of the diary, has been mined by liturgiologists and historians as confirmation or extrapolation of the ritual texts of Cyril of Jerusalem.[138] The totalizing and comprehensive sweep of Empire seems to be repre-

---

leen F. Ward, "Mourning Customs in 1, 2 Samuel," *Journal of Jewish Studies* 23 (1972): 1–27 and 146–66, esp. 8–10, 15–17, 153–54; and Emanuel Feldman, "The Rabbinic Lament," *Jewish Quarterly Review* 63 (1972): 51–75.

[135] *Itinerarium Burdigalense* 594.3–4 (CCL 175:17).

[136] See Annabel Jane Wharton, "The Baptistery of the Holy Sepulcher in Jerusalem and the Politics of Sacred Landscape," *Dumbarton Oak Papers* 46 (1992): 313–25.

[137] As pointed out by Wharton, "Baptistery of the Holy Sepulcher," 315 and nn. 13–14.

[138] See, e.g., Maxwell E. Johnson, "Reconciling Cyril and Egeria on the Catechetical Process in Fourth-Century Jerusalem," in *Essays in Eastern Initiation,* ed. Paul Bradshaw (Nottingham: Grove Books, 1988), 18–30.

sented by these Jerusalem gatherings: on the anniversary of the dedication
of the Golgotha church (called the *Encaenia*), for instance, not only
monks, but "layfolk, as many men as women, faithful of soul, on account
of the holy day from every province gather together at the same time in
Jerusalem."[139] The *Encaenia* "ranks equal with Easter or Epiphany," according to Egeria;[140] of course, it is a feast that is uniquely suited to celebration in post-Constantinian Jerusalem, a ritual celebrating the very institution of holy land ritual. The dedication feast celebrates Empire and
Christian ritual at the same moment, a sort of "national holiday" for the
Christian holy land.

The Jerusalem rituals are described with painstaking detail, but the
more pervasive form of ritualization in Egeria's account centers on the
alignment of Scripture and site or, to use Leo Spitzer's phrase, the affinity
between *locus* (passage) and *locus* (locality).[141] In her description of
Mount Sinai Egeria sets the tone for the rest of her journey: "Therefore
on this very spot [*ipso loco*] we read the whole passage from the book of
Moses, and we made the offering in the appropriate order."[142] This juxtaposition of site, text, and Eucharist seems to be Egeria's idea: "There [at
Elijah's cave] we made the offering and a most earnest prayer, and a reading was done from the appropriate passage [*ipse locus*] from the book of
Kings: indeed, for our group this was what I desired most of all, that,
wherever we went, the appropriate passage [*ipse locus*] would always be
read from its book."[143] This performance of reading and prayer (sometimes with communion and the recitation of a psalm) becomes "customary" for Egeria's travel party, serving to transform the holy places into
Christian sites through simultaneous textualization and ritualization.[144]
This interaction of text and ritual in Egeria's account even serves to provide the appropriate scriptural foundation for what seems a thoroughly

[139] *Itinerarium Egeriae* 49.2 (SC 296:318).

[140] *Itinerarium Egeriae* 49.3 (SC 296:318): *per pascha vel per epiphania*.

[141] Spitzer, "Epic Style," 239.

[142] *Itinerarium Egeriae* 3.6 (SC 296:132–34). See Paul Devos, " 'Lecto ergo ipso loco': A
propos d'un passage d'Égérie (*Itinerarium* III,6)," in *Zetesis: Album amicorum* (Antwerp: Nederlandsche Boekhandel, 1973), 646–54.

[143] *Itinerarium Egeriae* 4.3 (SC 296:138); on *ipse* as a rhetorical mark of "authenticity" or
"awe and precision" see Spitzer, "Epic Style," 228–31.

[144] *Itinerarium Egeriae* 14.1 (SC 296:186); see also *Itinerarium Egeriae* 15.4, 19.2, 20.3, 21.1,
and 23.5 (SC 296:188, 202, 214, 222, 230).

imperial celebration: the feast of *Encaenia,* mentioned above (the anniversary of the Golgotha church dedication), is transformed through ritual textualization into a feast with its own "appropriate reading": "It is found in the holy Scriptures that this very day was the *Encaenia,* when also holy Solomon had the house of God dedicated, which he had built, and he stood before the altar of God and he prayed, just as it is written in the books of Chronicles."[145] Here Egeria's texts reinstitute the erasure of the Jewish past by overlaying Solomon and his Temple with Constantine and his church: the emperor now becomes "just the man for the place," and Solomon gracefully and prayerfully bows out before him.[146]

Just as the Bordeaux pilgrim and Egeria reinforce and nuance their textual strategies through the hierarchical processes of ritualization, so, too, the Piacenza pilgrim employs ritual to bolster his thoroughly material alignment of imperial and Christian interests. I have already mentioned above how Jews in his account are distinguished from other "peoples" encountered on the road by their special proximity to Christians. After visiting Elijah's cave and participating in the Eucharist as well as a customary depilatory rite with other pilgrims and monks,[147] the Piacenza pilgrim immediately launches into a description of a Saracen rite that takes place on Mount Sinai:

And on this mountain, on part of the hill, the Saracens have set up their own marble idol, as white as snow. Their priest remains there as well, dressed in a dalmatic and a linen cloak. When the time of their festival arrives, at the new moon, before the moon has risen, on the day of their feast that marble begins to change color: as soon as the moon has appeared, when they begin to worship, the marble has become as black as pitch. When the time of the festival has been completed, it is returned to

---

[145]*Itinerarium Egeriae* 48.2 (SC 296:316). For Solomon's dedication of the Temple see 2 Chr 6–7 (2 Chr 7.9 is the only part of this passage in the LXX that uses the specific term, here *enkainismon*); the term is also used of the walls of Jerusalem (see Neh 6) and the Maccabean rededication of the Temple (1 Macc 4.36, 56, 59), where it is the Greek equivalent of *ḥănûkâ(h).*

[146]According to Pierre Maraval, Constantine chose the date of the *Encaenia* to dedicate this church not based on the biblical date but because it was the date of the dedication of the Capitoline Temple in Rome: SC 296:316–17n1.

[147]*Itinerarium Antonini Placentini* 37 (CCL 175:148). Following the suggestion of Maraval (SC 296:134n1) I understand *opus dei* in this passage to refer to the "daily office."

its original color, at which we were entirely amazed.[148]

The Saracen ceremony is exotic, miraculous, idolatrous (yet there is no overt condemnation of such idolatry), but it is mostly foreign: the final amazement of the pilgrims themselves encodes the entire ceremony as spectacle, amusement, completely "other" entertainment. The ceremonies of the Jews, by contrast, are extremely close: recall that the "little screen" dividing Jewish from Christian worshippers at the Oak of Mamre, ritualized into the "single day" that separates the Jewish celebration of the deposition of Jacob and David from the celebration of Christmas. Aesthetic appropriation is stratified, and ritualized description separates the proximate from the distant other, marking out the proper domain of Christian domination and appropriation from the realm of the utterly exotic and strange.

   All three of these documents make use of ritual to emphasize and reiterate hierarchy and difference. In conclusion I want to note also that, as "traveling texts,"[149] records of travel writing that were themselves made to travel across the Mediterranean, these documents are themselves ritually effective.[150] They enact, for readers, these instances of appropriation and differentiation; they become themselves sites of difference and *loci* of power.[151] The potential for discursive power that traveling texts and texts of travel might bear in the ancient world should not be underestimated,[152]

[148]*Itinerarium Antonini Placentini* 38 (CCL 175:148–49).

[149]See Edward Said, *The World, the Text, and the Critic* (Cambridge, Mass.: Harvard University Press, 1983), 226–47; idem, "The Text, the World, the Critic," in *Textual Strategies: Perspectives in Post-Structuralist Criticism*, ed. Josué V. Harari (Ithaca, N.Y.: Cornell University Press), 161–89: "texts are fundamentally facts of power, not of democratic exchange" (178); "texts are a system of forces institutionalized at some expense by the reigning culture, not an ideal cosmos of ideally equal poems" (189).

[150]See Stemberger, *Jews and Christians*, 87: "Their accounts could be intended as handbooks for the preparation of further trips to Palestine, or—probably in most cases—could be read as a literary substitute for the journey itself." See also Frank, *Memory of the Eyes*, 4, on "armchair pilgrims." Elsner, "*Itinerarium Burdigalense*," 181, also points out the physical "journey" involved in "moving through" a scroll or codex, replicating the "movement" of the travel narration itself.

[151]On the significance of reading practices in such hierarchical ritualization see Elizabeth A. Clark, *Reading Renunciation: Asceticism and Scripture in Early Christianity* (Princeton, N.J.: Princeton University Press, 1999), 204–32.

[152]Spurr, *Rhetoric of Empire*, 93: "This metaphorical notion of writer as colonizer ought to be considered as more than a mere figure of speech, given the practical role which writing plays in the actual processes of colonial expansion and administration. In fact, the structures of

and I have attempted in this chapter to suggest ways in which these particular textual maps of the holy land encode configurations of power and religious domination: as Robert Wilken has astutely remarked, "Space is never ideologically neutral."[153] Like the heresiology of Epiphanius or the biblical interpretation of Jerome, these are texts that, on the most fundamental level, naturalize and authenticate Christian power. But, more than that, they also give that knowledge and power a physical shape; they mold the contours of a sacred landscape into the site of Christian dominance.

---

writing and those of political power can never be wholly distinguished from one another."
[153]Wilken, *Land Called Holy,* 114.

5 ☞ "This Exalted City": Christian Jerusalem and Its Jews

Christian Jerusalem: Erasure and Appropriation

In the Transjordanian city of Madaba survives a representation of a map of the holy land, a carpet mosaic that was likely created around the middle of the sixth century, near the time that Cosmas Indicopleustēs was writing his *Christian Topography* and the Piacenza pilgrim was weighing dates on his journey through Palestine's *loca sancta*.[1] At the center of this unique artistic production, amid the various cities and monuments of Palestine, Syria, and Egypt, stands the city of Jerusalem, labeled in Greek *Hagiapolis Ierousalēm*.[2] Jerusalem stands out in the mosaic because of its central position, as well as its distinctive representation: recognizable amid the crowded thirty or so buildings and towers in the walled city are, among other structures, the church of the Anastasis, originally dedicated

---

[1] Herbert Donner, *The Mosaic Map of Madaba: An Introductory Guide* (Kampen: Kok Pharos, 1992); Michael Avi-Yonah, *The Madaba Mosaic Map with Introduction and Commentary* (Jerusalem: Israel Exploration Society, 1954); and the collected papers in Michele Piccirillo and Eugenio Alliata, eds., *The Madaba Map Centenary: Travelling Through the Byzantine Umayyad Period. Proceedings of the International Conference Held in Amman, 7–9 April 1997* (Jerusalem: Studium Biblicum Franciscanum, 1998). Scholarly consensus dates the mosaic to the reign of Justinian, but see Pauline Donceel-Voûte, "La carte de Madaba: Cosmographie, Anachronisme, et Propagande," *Revue Biblique* 95 (1988): 519–42.

[2] Different theories still abound, a century after the mosaic's discovery, as to what it is intended to represent. An early interpretation, recently revived and defended, is that the map represents the "vision of Moses" recounted in Num 34.1–2 and Deut 34.1–4: Irfan Shahid, "The Madaba Mosaic Map Revisited: Some New Observations on Its Purpose and Meaning," in Piccirillo and Alliata, *Madaba Map Centenary*, 147–54.

under Constantine the Great, as well as the *Nea,* or "new" church, dedicated to the Virgin Mary by Justinian.[3]

Yet one element of the Jerusalem cityscape, which scholars agree would have been prominent in the city's urban topography at the time, is most conspicuous by its absence: the ruins of the Temple Mount.[4] At most, scholars such as Michael Avi-Yonah have posited that a thin strip of mosaic tile in the southeast corner of the mosaic might represent a piece of the western retaining wall of Herod's Temple (the "wailing wall"), and a stretch of mosaic on the border might indicate the empty plaza before the Temple.[5] Other commentators on the map are less certain: Herbert Donner is willing to concede only that, based on its location, this small portion of the Jerusalem vignette might be a staircase leading up to the Temple Mount.[6] Some scholars are entirely unsurprised at this omission (or, at best, compression) of the Jewish Temple, assuming that it mirrors a typically unrealistic Christian theology: "Eliminating the Temple Mount from the Madaba Map reflects its elimination from Christian memory, although such an act was in total contradiction with the actual topographical situation," notes one commentator.[7] Some scholars have assumed that a pictorial representation of Revelation's "city with no Temple" (21.22) has been imposed on the landscape, although such an interpretation seems rather flimsy.[8] The paradox remains, however, between the representational "elimination" and the physical retention of this troublesome space in the "real" Jerusalem: if it was so natural for Christians in nearby Jordan to "eliminate" this space in art (presumably because of its unpalatable Jewishness), then why did it remain so

---

[3]Donner, *Mosaic Map,* 87–94; Avi-Yonah, *Madaba Mosaic,* 50–60; Noël Duval, "Essai sur la signification des vignettes topographiques," in Piccirillo and Alliata, *Madaba Map Centenary,* 134–36; and Yoram Tsafrir, "The Holy City of Jerusalem in the Madaba Map," in Piccirillo and Alliata, *Madaba Map Centenary,* 155–63.

[4]Tsafrir, "Holy City," 158.

[5]Avi-Yonah, *Madaba Mosaic,* 59, and see the figures on 51.

[6]Donner, *Mosaic Map,* 94; he finds the (unattributed) opinion of Avi-Yonah, that this represents the "Wailing Wall," to be a "much less probable solution."

[7]Tsafrir, "Holy City," 158.

[8]Wendy Pullan, "The Representation of the Late Antique City in the Madaba Map: The Meaning of the Cardo in the Jerusalem Vignette," in Piccirillo and Alliata, *Madaba Map Centenary,* 165. Not only does this assume a normative place for Revelation in the sixth-century East that may not be supportable, but it also introduces an eschatological motif into an otherwise scrupulously presentist depiction of the city.

prominent in the physical landscape of sixth-century Jerusalem? Late antique cities in Jordan were certainly not averse to wholesale appropriation of Jewish space: the prominent synagogue at Jerash was "converted" into a church in 530–531 (near the time the Madaba mosaic was produced).[9] The argument might be made that this Jewish space, the Temple Mount, was also important as Christian space, the site of events from the life of Jesus. In addition to the fact that many fifth- and sixth-century Christians imbued the site primarily with a sense of Jewish failure and resistance to Christian truth (as I will discuss), this counterargument also fails to explain why the Madaba artisans could so easily eliminate the Temple from their detailed mosaic. Surely nothing prevented any Christian emperor, from Constantine through Justinian, from entirely appropriating and Christianizing this space, to the point where "contradictory elimination" would no longer be necessary in any representation. By its very "contradictory elimination," reducing the site of Jerusalem's Jewishness to, at best, a few marginal *tesserae,* the Madaba map highlights the tensions inherent in the material and ideological construction of the Christian city of Jerusalem: tensions between old and new, between imperial and ecclesiastical, between Jewish and Christian.

We have seen in previous chapters how some Christians used the Jews of the newly conceived holy land to understand new forms of imperial religious dominion, employing strategies of totalizing discourse, academic imperialism, and the realized fantasy of travel. I have also tried to suggest, in places, how such discourses of appropriation are frequently destabilized by the anxiety of otherness on which they depend. The ambivalence and incompleteness of these discourses of Christian Empire leave a space in which we might infer resistance (real or potential) by the Jews themselves. Once conjured by discourses of Christian power, Jews continue to insinuate themselves problematically in Christian imagination, like the tiles that may or may not represent a Jewish Temple that may or may not be present in the mosaic landscape of Christian Jerusalem. The city of Jerusalem, the "holy city" of the Madaba mosaic map, became in the period from Constantine to Justinian a particular focus of imperial reimagining of religious and cultural identity in late antiquity, particularly im-

---

[9]Annabel Jane Wharton, *Refiguring the Post Classical City: Dura Europos, Jerash, Jerusalem, and Ravenna* (Cambridge, U.K.: Cambridge University Press, 1995), esp. 98–100.

bued with this ambivalence and anxiety. In ways impossible for Rome, Constantinople, or any other imperial residence, Jerusalem was figuratively and literally built up into a Christian capital for the late ancient empire. This is not to say that other imperial residences were not concentrated loci of Christian religious and political power. Rome and Milan in the fourth century, and Ravenna in the fifth and sixth centuries, were sites of complex entanglements between ecclesiastical and imperial authorities. I do believe, however, that Jerusalem posed both unique problems and opportunities for imperial Christianity, a singular ideological and topographical palimpsest.[10] On the site of the veritable birth of Christianity, as well as the site of some of the most spectacular displays of imperial wrath and conquest of the Jews,[11] Christianity attempted to negotiate the difficult process of its own authoritative identity. Here, too, at moments of crucial self-awareness Jews irrupted into Christian imagination and consternation, sometimes squeezed into a conceptual corner tighter than the few bare tiles allotted by the Madaba artisans to the Temple Mount, other times exploding larger than life into Christian imperial consciousness. Just as the actual topography of Jerusalem was reconceived in the Madaba mosaic through "abstractions, omissions, emphases, repetitions,"[12] so, too, Christian identity in the "holy city" absorbed and transmuted the local Jews to create a new political and religious reality. The conceptualization of Christian Jerusalem demonstrates how imperial Christian culture on many fronts emerged from "a dialectical process, inscribing and expelling its own alterity."[13] The Jewish "other" was at once expelled and internalized, erased and appropriated, the signifier of Christian difference that could never be totally eradicated but must always leave traces for the imperial Christian to master.[14]

[10]Richard Krautheimer, *Three Christian Capitals: Topography and Politics* (Berkeley: University of California Press, 1983); and Wharton, *Refiguring the Post Classical City*, 105–47.

[11]See Tacitus, *Historia* 5.1–13 (LCL 2:174–98) (including his ethnography of Judaea); and the surviving epitome of Cassius Dio, *Historia Romana* 65.4–7, 69.13–15 (LCL 8:264–70, 448–50), who places the two Jewish wars in the context of imperial military activity.

[12]Pullan, "Representation of the Late Antique City," 165.

[13]Robert J. C. Young, *Colonial Desire: Hybridity in Theory, Culture, and Race* (London: Routledge, 1995), 30.

[14]Cf. Wharton, *Refiguring the Post Classical City*, 147, on Ravenna: "The obvious traces of the earlier mosaic are as much about presence as absence. They are an index of the evisceration of meaning, the evacuation of an earlier signification. These pitiable remnants of an alternative ideology equally denote the triumphant establishment of a hegemonic orthodoxy."

To elucidate this complex phenomenon of erasure and appropriation, I will first explore ways in which Jerusalem acted as a focus of imperial identity in the early Christian era, emerging in the fourth through sixth centuries as a sort of alternative Christian capital for pious emperors ruling from Byzantium. A major part of this religious and political construction can be credited to the monks from around the empire who "colonized [*polisthēnai*]" the wilderness around Jerusalem: for the monks settling the Judaean desert, the fiction of "empty space" in and around the holy city provided a blank template for Christian (self-)mastery. The activities of emperors and monks delineate an important set of tensions operative in the way imperial power was inscribed in Jerusalem: for the emperors Jerusalem was a site to be appropriated through triumphant gestures of power and piety; for the monks the space was configured quite differently, through the narrative erasure of a space left open for Christian settlement. This tension between overt triumph and gentle succession, between conquest and erasure, highlights the ways in which Christians attempted to incorporate the otherness of the past into their present, imperial identity in their holy capital. The difficulty and otherness of that past, and the ways in which it could be integrated into a new Christian identity of power and authority, appear most vividly in the ways in which the historical remains of Jews—living and dead—were resurrected in Christian myth and devotion, emanating from the city of Jerusalem to provide concrete sites for the construction of Christian imperial power. Finally, the instability of this imperial power comes through at moments of political uncertainty, in which Jews narratively serve to generate the identity and fate of an imperial Christian capital from the moment of its conception through its fall to "barbarian" enemies.

Building a Christian Capital: Imperial Munificence

Modern historians remain as uncertain about Constantine's motives for creating his new capital city of Constantinople as they are about his reasons for reversing previous imperial policy and embracing the hitherto illicit Christian movement.[15] Ancient Christian writers, however, had few doubts that the two moves were related. Eusebius remarked in his *Life of Constantine* on how the city bearing the great emperor's name was "purified of all idolatry so that nowhere in it appeared images of those thought to be gods worshipped in shrines."[16] For the Christians of the fourth-century Roman Empire, Old Rome was tainted by nearly a millennium of idolatry, whereas for these same Christians, New Rome could be represented (probably inaccurately) as unsullied from its foundation: a new capital for a new imperial religion.[17]

Yet by its very newness "New Rome" lacked the triumphal sense of history that characterized the imperial Christianity emerging from the holy land.[18] The Christianity of Empire was not about novelty; it was about antiquity and authority. Without the ability to incorporate the religious past of Christianity into imperial ideology, Constantinople could not properly instruct its subjects on how to be Christians of Empire. In order to master the Christian past and construct a truly imperial Christianity, Constantine and his successors turned to Jerusalem. Jonathan Z.

---

[15]See H. A. Drake, *Constantine and the Bishops: The Politics of Intolerance* (Baltimore, Md.: Johns Hopkins University Press, 2000), on Constantine's conversion. On Constantinople: Krautheimer, *Three Christian Capitals*, 40–43; Averil Cameron, *The Later Roman Empire, A.D. 284–430* (Cambridge, Mass.: Harvard University Press, 1993), 170, 224; Gilbert Dagron, *Naissance d'une capitale: Constantinople et ses institutions de 330 à 451* (Paris: Presses Universitaires de Frances, 1974); Cyril Mango, *Le développement urbain de Constantinople, IVe–VIIe siècles* (Paris: Diffusion de Boccard, 1990). One of our earliest sources gives as the sole motive for the city's foundation Constantine's desire to build a "New Rome" and to memorialize his military victories: *Origo Constantini* 6.30, text in *Origo Constantini, Anonymus Valesianus*, part 1, *Text und Kommentar*, ed. Ingemar König (Trier: Verlag Trierer Historische Forschungen, 1987), 48.

[16]Eusebius, *Vita Constantini* 3.48.2 (GCS 7:104). By the time Sozomen wrote his history, he could refer to Constantinople not only as "equal in glory to Rome" and "New Rome" (*Historia ecclesiastica* 2.3.2, 2.3.5 [GCS 50:51, 52]) but also as "that newly-built city of Christ" (*Historia ecclesiastica* 2.3.8 [GCS 50:53]). Krautheimer, *Three Christian Capitals*, 67, agrees with these assessments; Mango, *Développement urbain*, 36, is more dubious.

[17]Historians remain skeptical as to how Christian Constantinople truly was in Constantine's lifetime: Sozomen's explanation for the display of frankly pagan treasures "for decoration [*pros kosmon*]" (*Historia ecclesiastica* 2.5.3 [GCS 50:56–57]) can sound strained, and the later anti-Christian historian Zosimus claimed that ancient religious customs (i.e., non-Christian ones) were executed in the new city (*Nova historia* 2.31.2–3, text in *Zosime: Histoire nouvelle*, ed. François Paschoud [Paris: Editions "Les Belles Lettres," 1971], 104, and see 227–29n42).

[18]Church historians paid little attention to the foundation of Constantinople: see Eusebius, *Vita Constantini* 3.25–47, 50–53 (GCS 7:94–107); Socrates, *Historia ecclesiastica* 1.16–17 (GCS n.f. 1:54–55); Sozomen, *Historia ecclesiastica* 2.1–4 (GCS 50:47–56); Theodoret, *Historia ecclesiastica* 1.15, 17–18 (GCS 44:59, 61–65), does not even mention the foundation of Constantinople in his list of church benefactions.

Smith has articulated this conceptual gap between Constantine's "New Rome" and his "new Jerusalem": "It was, in effect, the foundation of Constantinople that allowed experimentation in the development of a new Christian architectural idiom in the period from Constantine to Justinian. The same freedom of utter novelty was not available in Constantinian Jerusalem, and it is the relationship between the new and the old in that venerable city that concerns us here."[19] Constantinople was understood by Eusebius and like-minded Christians as shining and new, open to unfamiliar form and idiom; Jerusalem, by contrast, was "venerable," and its very stones hearkened back to a rich, divinely ordained past. Constantinople might obliquely draw on shades of "Old Rome" to authenticate its imperial significance,[20] but it was an Old Rome that had been uprooted, purified, and replanted. "Old" and "new" Jerusalem, however, occupied the same physical space: Constantine's Christian city was the ancient city of the Jews, the site of biblical majesty, the city of Kings David and Solomon, of Jesus' triumphal entry, of the holy cross and the holy tomb.[21] Constantine and his successors were, in essence, erecting an alternative Christian capital for their empire in Jerusalem, a site from which imperial authority could emanate in proper religious dress. In the words of Byzantinist Gilbert Dagron: "Constantine had not set out to make Byzantium a Christian capital. This Christian capital was Jerusalem."[22]

An overview of the ways in which Christian emperors crafted a distinctive presence in this religious capital reveals important strategies of Christian imperialism. One method for establishing imperial presence in the Christian capital consisted of monumental construction, by which the emperor displayed to his subjects the empire's triumphant stability. In Jerusalem that triumph was over a particular religious past, often embodied by living and dead Jews. Another method for establishing this

[19]Jonathan Z. Smith, *To Take Place: Toward Theory in Ritual* (Chicago, Ill.: University of Chicago Press, 1992), 76.

[20]See Dagron, *Naissance d'une capitale,* 43–47.

[21]See the comments of Robert Wilken, *The Land Called Holy: Palestine in Christian History and Thought* (New Haven, Conn.: Yale University Press, 1992), 88: "For Constantinople . . . was created ex nihilo. . . . Jerusalem was the work of God, and its stones displayed the grainy texture of the city's past."

[22]Dagron, *Naissance d'une capitale,* 389.

presence was the direct patronage of female members of the imperial household, who honed the religious nature of imperial authority through association (real or fictive) with the rising tide of asceticism in the holy land. Both of these strategies for manifesting a peculiarly Christian form of imperial power in a Christian capital reveal an essentially aggressive and triumphal manner in which Christian dominance was crafted in the holy land.

Although Constantine is credited by ancient and modern sources as the imperial builder of a "new Jerusalem" opposite the old city,[23] Christian Jerusalem never enjoyed an imperial *adventus* from its "founder," Constantine.[24] In fact, it is likely that Constantine only set foot in the province of Palaestina once in his life, as Diocletian's military tribune on his way to Egypt in 301–2.[25] Likewise, Constantine's later successor Theodosius I, who by law Christianized the Roman Empire and under whose reign the holy places of Palestine filled with pilgrims and monks, probably never saw Jerusalem or any of the holy places.[26] Nevertheless, soon after Theodosius's death, panegyric and legend transformed him into a great imperial patron of the holy city, a fitting successor to the first Christian emperor, Constantine.[27] Without setting foot in the city emperors succeeded in establishing a presence in Christian Jerusalem that made the city into a center of imperial religiosity.

As the examples of Constantine and Theodosius suggest, emperors

[23]See Eusebius, *Vita Constantini* 3.33 (GCS 7:99); followed by Socrates, *Historia ecclesiastica* 1.17.7, 11 (GCS n.f. 1:56, 57); see also Wilken, *Land Called Holy,* 82–100.

[24]On imperial *adventus* as a stabilizing feature of late ancient *imperium* see Sabine Mac-Cormack, *Art and Ceremony in Late Antiquity* (Berkeley: University of California Press, 1981), esp. 15–89. A locus classicus for late ancient adventus is Ammianus Marcellinus, *Res gestae* 16.10.1–17 (LCL 1:242–52), on Constantius II's arrival in Rome.

[25]See E. D. Hunt, "Constantine and Jerusalem," *Journal of Ecclesiastical History* 48 (1997): 406–8.

[26]See E. D. Hunt, "Theodosius I and the Holy Land," *Studia Patristica* 29 (1997): 52–57. On the upsurge in pilgrimage during Theodosius's reign see E. D. Hunt, *Holy Land Pilgrimage in the Later Roman Empire, A.D. 312–460* (Oxford: Clarendon Press, 1982), 155–79; on the connections of these pilgrims geographically and politically to Theodosius I and his Constantinopolitan court see John F. Matthews, *Western Aristocracies and Imperial Court, A.D. 364–425* (Oxford: Clarendon Press, 1975; Oxford: Clarendon Press, 1990), 121–45 (page citation is to the 1990 edition).

[27]See Ambrose, *De obitu Theodosii* 41–51 (CSEL 73:391–98). Elaborations continued in the middle Byzantine period: see Hunt, *Holy Land Pilgrimage,* 158–59, supplemented by Hunt, "Theodosius and the Holy Land," 54–55.

constructed this presence in the holy city, to a great extent, not through personal appearance but through remote gestures of discovery and monumentalization: "by Constantine's command" churches were erected, holy places purged and sanctified, relics uncovered and then distributed through imperial channels.[28] Constantine's Palestinian munificence at first resembled building projects throughout the empire, an eastern continuation of his earlier construction in the West, meant to mark his unified rule.[29] Aelia Capitolina, like other small Roman cities of the East, was perhaps at first yet one more recipient of the emperor's largesse.[30] In cities large and small the emperor's presence was traditionally signified through such benefaction. The imperial presence that monumentalized Christian Jerusalem, however, took on a singular depth and purpose, denoting the triumphant appropriation (indeed, conquest) of a rich and resistant religious past.[31]

That the past should be "conquered" was fundamental to late antique imperial ideology. Constantine had already trumped and surpassed the majestic founders of Rome, Romulus and Augustus, by staking out a "New Rome" in the East.[32] Yet if Augustus had boasted that he found Rome in brick and "left her clothed in marble,"[33] Constantine could perhaps claim to have found Jerusalem mired in impious obscurity and left her gleaming in marble sanctity. In rebuilding Jerusalem Constantine, through his monuments, laid claim to a new past, a more significant religious history that now dovetailed with the history of the Roman Empire. It was a history that resisted Christian imperialism, that necessitated conquest and monumental gestures of triumph. Eusebius, ever the rhetorical

[28]See *Itinerarium Burdigalense* 594.2–3, 595.5–6, 598.7, 599.5–6 (CCL 175:17, 18, 20).

[29]Wharton, "Baptistery of the Holy Sepulcher," 322–23.

[30]See Wharton, *Refiguring the Post Classical City*, 88–90; and John Wilkinson, "Christian Pilgrims in Jerusalem During the Byzantine Period," *Palestine Exploration Quarterly* 108 (1976): 75–101.

[31]Wilken, *Land Called Holy*, 88 (following Hunt, *Holy Land Pilgrimage*, 7–8), finds it plausible that Macarius, bishop of Jerusalem, first prompted Constantine at the Council of Nicaea in 325 to invest Jerusalem with particular euergetism.

[32]The simultaneous affirmation and supersession of prior imperial munificence had long been established in imperial building projects: see M. T. Boatwright, *Hadrian and the City of Rome* (Princeton, N.J.: Princeton University Press, 1987), esp. 19–32, 237–38.

[33]As reported by Suetonius, *De vita Caesarum: Divus Augustus* 28 (LCL 1:192). See Paul Zanker, *The Power of Images in the Age of Augustus*, tr. Alan Shapiro (Ann Arbor: University of Michigan Press, 1988), esp. 101–238.

craftsman of this religious *imperium*,[34] captured this particular idea as he described Constantine's construction of the Church of the Holy Sepulcher: "So then on that very spot of salvific witness the new Jerusalem was raised up, facing opposite the famous one of old, which, following the foul pollution of the Lord's murder, had experienced the extremes of desolation, a judgment upon its impious inhabitants [*dussēbōn oikētorōn*]. So just opposite this the emperor raised up a monument to the savior's victory over death with rich and lavish munificence [*philotimiais*]."[35] The "new Jerusalem," centered on the new church at Jesus' tomb, stands not only as witness to the birth of Christianity but to the "lavish munificence" of the first Christian emperor. To build the new Jerusalem was to convert imperial power and money into Christian piety and triumph. Moreover, to monumentalize the link between imperial authority and Christian piety was to triumph over this past. An integral element of classical *triumphi* was the display of those enemies whom the *triumphator* had defeated.[36] At the site of the Holy Sepulcher, as commemorated by Eusebius, the humiliated prisoners paraded before triumphant Christian eyes are the "impious inhabitants" of old Jerusalem, on whom a new imperial judgment has been cast. These Jewish inhabitants of the old city, rhetorically conjured to witness Constantine's Christian triumph, validate and testify to the shining imperial piety of the new holy city; they embody the past that the emperor has conquered and rebuilt.

By inscribing their imperial presence through the construction of churches and sacred monuments in Jerusalem, Christian emperors from Constantine onward attached their majesty to an older and more profound source of imperial power than was available in Old or New Rome. Perhaps uniquely visible in Christian Jerusalem was the dual Romanness and Christianness of imperial power: the "extremes of desolation" Eusebius invokes at the Temple Mount are the handiwork of Titus and Hadrian, now viewed as the instrument of God's (Christian) "judgment." Constantine's church marks the intersection and collusion of these two forces. This religious dominion also appeared when Constantine sought

[34] Smith, *To Take Place*, 79.

[35] Eusebius, *Vita Constantini* 3.33 (GCS 7:99).

[36] See, in general, Michael McCormick, *Eternal Victory: Triumphal Rulership in Late Antiquity, Byzantium, and the Early Medieval West* (Cambridge, U.K.: Cambridge University Press, 1986), 36–64.

to "depaganize" the shrine at Mamre; here he deliberately connected his own Roman *maiestas* with the religious authority of the patriarch Abraham and their combined triumph over pagans (past and present). In his letter to Macarius, bishop of Jerusalem, and the other Palestinian bishops Constantine writes:

You are not unaware that there first God the Lord of all things both appeared to Abraham and spoke with him. It was there, accordingly, that first the religion [*thrēskeia*] of the holy law had its origin, there first that the savior himself with two angels first freely manifested his own appearance to Abraham, there that God began to reveal himself to humanity, there that he spoke to Abraham about his future seed and right away he fulfilled the promise, and there that he predicted that he would be the father of very many nations. This being the case, it is right, as it seems to me, that *through our care* this place should be both maintained as pure from every defilement and restored to its ancient sanctity.[37]

It seems natural and right to Constantine that promises made by God to Abraham, the "father of nations," should be commemorated by the generosity and political power of the emperor. The letter itself represents Constantine's imperial authority, and he instructs Macarius that, once the area of Mamre is cleared, the bishop is to design "a basilica worthy of my munificence."[38] Constantine's imperial authority, his monumentalized presence, is the will of the Christian God. As at the site of his "new Jerusalem," it is a masterful, triumphal presence: just as the Jews, the "impious inhabitants" of the old city, are symbolically reconquered through the invocation of their desolated Temple Mount, so Mamre will be the site of Constantine's (and Abraham's, and God's) triumph over the "superstitious persons [*deisidaimonōn*]" who have defiled the holy places.[39]

Insofar as the emperor's presence in the holy places was inscribed

---

[37]Preserved by Eusebius, *Vita Constantini* 3.53.3–5 (GCS 7:107), emphasis added. Although this letter appears toward the end of Eusebius's account of Constantine's church building, the reference in it to Eutropia, Constantine's mother-in-law (*Vita Constantini* 3.52.1 [GCS 7:105]), dates it earlier, most likely before 326 and the death of Fausta: see Averil Cameron and Stuart G. Hall, *Eusebius, Life of Constantine, Translated with Introduction and Commentary* (Oxford: Clarendon Press, 1999), 300.

[38]Eusebius, *Vita Constantini* 3.53.2 (GCS 7:106). On the letter as imperial proxy see *Vita Constantini* 3.53.2 (GCS 7:106).

[39]Eusebius, *Vita Constantini* 3.53.1 (GCS 7:106).

through the Roman monumentalization of the Christian past, it is fitting that one of Constantine's most important constructions in the holy city, the Church of the Holy Sepulcher, commemorates a sacred absence: the celestial body of the risen Jesus. The ceremony of the dedication of the Church of the Holy Sepulcher likewise took place with its dedicator absent: although speeches were delivered "to" Constantine, the emperor was not in Jerusalem at the time.[40] A physically absent emperor received praise for uncovering the tomb of a physically absent Christ. Yet just as the absence of Christ's body signified a supernal, divine omnipresence throughout the Christian world, so, too, the absent emperor partakes in this omnipresent absence in the holy city.[41] Literal *adventus* is rendered superfluous by such juxtaposition of absences and presences, inaugurating imperial Christian authority through the munificent monumentalization of an imperial Christian past, overspilling with a transcendent hyperreality.[42]

Successive emperors likewise inscribed their presence monumentally, associating their patronage of the holy city not only with an imperial tradition but also with the Christian history they were attempting to master and memorialize.[43] Theodosius I had a church constructed at Gethsemane, on the other side of the Temple Mount from Constantine's Church of the Holy Sepulcher and down the hill from Constantine's church on the Mount of Olives, placing his own imperial monument in the stream of Jesus' earthly life and in view of Jewish failure.[44] Theodosius

---

[40]H. A. Drake, *In Praise of Constantine: A Historical Study and New Translation of Eusebius' Tricennial Orations* (Berkeley: University of California Press, 1976), 35–36, 42–45.

[41]On the theology of Constantine-as-Victor-as-Christ see Drake, *In Praise of Constantine*, 61–74.

[42]See Homi K. Bhabha, *The Location of Culture* (London: Routledge, 1994), 102–22: "the colonial presence is always ambivalent, split between its appearance as original and authoritative and its articulation as repetition and difference" (107).

[43]For an overview of church building see Günter Stemberger, *Jews and Christians in the Holy Land: Palestine in the Fourth Century,* tr. Ruth Tuschling (Edinburgh: T. & T. Clark, 2000), 48–120; Ephraim Stern, ed., *The New Encyclopedia of Archaeological Excavations in the Holy Land* (Jerusalem: Israel Exploration Society, 1993), 2:768–85 (by Hillel Geva and Michael Avi-Yonah); and Eric Meyers, ed., *Oxford Encyclopedia of Archaeology in the Near East* (Oxford: Oxford University Press, 1997), 3:235–37, supplementing Hugues Vincent and F.-M. Abel, *Jérusalem: Recherches de topographie, d'archéologie et d'histoire,* vol. 2, *Jérusalem nouvelle* (Paris: Gabalda, 1912–26).

[44]Vincent and Abel, *Jérusalem,* 306; and Stern, *New Encyclopedia of Archaeological Excavations,* 2:783–84. Hunt, "Theodosius," is skeptical of the attribution of this church.

I's grandchildren, Theodosius II and Pulcheria, donated a golden cross to adorn Constantine's church at Golgotha, thus not only invoking the first Christian emperor but also the crucified Jesus, as well as the "first man" whose skull was (in some traditions) said to lie under the hill.[45] Theodosius II's wife, Eudocia, restored the walls of the city of Jerusalem,[46] in the tradition of biblical kings of the city, and built shrines and churches seemingly wherever she could find tradition of a saint there.[47] Justinian, in the sixth century, sought to outshine his imperial predecessors, building in Jerusalem a great church dedicated to Mary (the "new church," or *Nea*) that sat higher and prouder than any other church in Jerusalem; the historian Procopius's description makes it clear that Justinian sought in this building (as in the Hagia Sophia in Constantinople) not only to outdo previous emperors but Solomon the Temple builder as well.[48] These doubled gestures of triumph and appropriation imbued the person of the emperor with religious authority, with ties to a past that served not only to demonstrate his personal piety but to Christianize the authority of the imperial house.[49] The imperial monumentalization of the past was by no means restricted to Jerusalem, but the degree to which emperors could fuse their religious and political authority into single, triumphant gestures was particularly effective there during this period.

[45]See Hunt, *Holy Land Pilgrimage*, 228–29. On Golgotha as the resting place of Adam's skull see Hunt, *Holy Land Pilgrimage*, 19 and n. 74.

[46]See *Itinerarium Antonini Placentini* 25 (CCL 175:142), who calls her *Eudoxia* (further confused in the MS tradition, in which she is called *Eudoxia uxor imperatoris Iustiniani: recensio altera* 25 [CCL 175:166]); see also Hillel Geva's comments in Stern, *New Encyclopedia of Archaeological Excavations*, 2:772.

[47]See Kenneth G. Holum, *Theodosian Empresses: Women and Imperial Dominion in Late Antiquity* (Berkeley: University of California Press, 1982), 219. Cyril of Scythopolis, *Vita Euthymii* 35, claims "the blessed Eudocia built many churches for Christ, and monasteries and poorhouses and elder hostels, so many that I am unable to count them." Texts of Cyril's *vitae* come from Eduard Schwartz, *Kyrillos von Skythopolis*, TU 49.2 (Leipzig: J. C. Hinrichs, 1939), here 53.

[48]Procopius, *Aedificia* 5.6 (LCL 342–48). Justinian supposedly exclaimed on the completion of the Hagia Sophia, "I have outdone you, Solomon [*enikēsa se Solomōn*]!" (*Anonymi narratio de aedificatione templi sancti Sophiae* 27, in *Scriptores originum constantinopolitanarum*, ed. Theodor Preger, 2 vols. [Leipzig: Teubner, 1901–7], here 1:105). On competition with Solomon among patrons at the sixth-century imperial court see M. Harrison, *A Temple for Byzantium: The Discovery and Excavation of Anicia Juliana's Palace-Church in Istanbul* (Austin: University of Texas Press, 1989), 137–44.

[49]See Gregory Armstrong, "Imperial Church Building in the Holy Land in the Fourth Century," *Biblical Archaeologist* 30, no. 3 (1976): 90–102.

Imperial presence was not only inscribed through the revitalization and monumentalization of historical space but also through the agency of the female members of the imperial household. This second manner in which imperial presence was crafted in Jerusalem combined late Roman ideologies of imperial dynasty with Christian concepts of sanctity newly opened up to women by the ascetic movements of the fourth and fifth centuries. The women of the emperor's household became the particular agents of imperial identity in the holy city, serving as proxies of the emperor's piety and demonstrating once more the fluidity and particularity of imperial piety in this Christian capital city. Like the monumentalized presence of their male relatives, these imperial women demonstrated how Roman mastery of a Christian past could suitably frame imperial Christian identity.

The fountainhead of female imperial piety of Jerusalem was, of course, the empress Helena, mother of Constantine. We will perhaps never know the original impetus for Helena's journey to the holy land.[50] Even the most pious of contemporary accounts carefully retained an imperial air in their descriptions of Helena's travels, in addition to what would become traditional "pilgrimage" motivations.[51] Not long after her death, Eusebius could almost effortlessly combine her motives as *Augusta* and as pious traveler: "The elderly woman, with youthful eagerness, came with her exceeding intellect, making inquiries into the admirable land, inspecting the eastern provinces and the nations and peoples there with imperial consideration [*basilikēi promētheiai*]. Indeed she accorded suitable adoration [*proskunēsin*] to the savior's footsteps."[52] The juxtaposition of "suitable adoration" and "imperial consideration" marks out Helena's activity in the environs of Jerusalem as both eminently pious and entirely

---

[50]For various ascriptions of motive see Barnes, *Constantine and Eusebius,* 221; Hunt, *Holy Land Pilgrimage,* 30–49; Kenneth G. Holum, "Hadrian and St. Helena: Imperial Travel and the Origins of Christian Holy Land Pilgrimage," in *The Blessings of Pilgrimage,* ed. Robert Ousterhout (Urbana: University of Illinois Press, 1990), 66–81; Jan Willem Drijvers, *Helena Augusta: The Mother of Constantine the Great and the Legend of Her Finding of the True Cross* (Leiden: E. J. Brill, 1992), 55–72.

[51]Holum, "Hadrian and St. Helena," 76–77, assumes that stories of Helena's travels directly inspired "long-distance" pilgrimage in later centuries.

[52]Eusebius, *Vita Constantini* 3.42.1 (GCS 7:101). Helena probably made her tour of the holy land after 326 and was likely dead by 329: see Drijvers, *Helena Augusta,* 55–73; and Hunt, *Holy Land Pilgrimage,* 29–30.

imperial. She is the *Augusta Christiana,* the "God-beloved mother of the God-beloved emperor,"[53] and her memorialized presence in the holy city of Jerusalem serves the same purpose as Constantine's building projects (with which she became associated): the authoritative recovery and mastery of the Christian past by the emperor, in order to combine the operations of dominion and piety.[54] Like the buildings themselves, the Christian empress on tour of the holy places became an embodied symbol of imperial Christian authority in the holy land.

A tradition of female imperial patronage in Jerusalem and the holy land subsequently built on Helena's example.[55] Successive generations of *Augustae* visited the holy city without their fathers, brothers, or husbands, carrying the standard of Christian imperial authority. Especially during the reign of Theodosius II the women of the imperial house forged tight bonds between the imperial capital of Constantinople and the Christian capital of Jerusalem.[56] Theodosius's wife, Eudocia, spent much of her career as Augusta in the holy land, doubtless in conscious imitation of her predecessor Helena.[57] Although historians often attribute Eudocia's long Palestinian sojourns to marital strife, and competition and animosity with her sister-in-law Pulcheria,[58] we should not view Eudocia's patronage in and around Jerusalem solely from the vantage point of Constantinopolitan politics. Church historians viewed her as the emperor's agent in the holy land and as a faithful pilgrim in her own right. Like Helena,

[53]Eusebius, *Vita Constantini* 3.43.4 (GCS 7:102).

[54]On Helena as "overseer" of Constantine's constructions in the holy land see Eusebius, *Vita Constantini* 3.42–43 (GCS 7:100–101); and Drijvers, *Helena Augusta,* 63–66.

[55]See Leslie Brubaker, "Memories of Helena: Patterns in Female Imperial Matronage in the Fourth and Fifth Centuries," *Women, Men, and Eunuchs: Gender in Byzantium,* ed. Liz James (London: Routledge, 1997), 52–75; and Jan Willem Drijvers, "Helena Augusta: Exemplary Christian Empress," *Studia Patristica* 24 (1993): 85–90.

[56]On tightening of imperial connections between Constantinople and Jerusalem in the fifth century see Dagron, *Naissance d'une capitale,* 409.

[57]See Gerontius, *Vita Melaniae Iunioris* 56, 58–59 (SC 90:238, 241–46); John Rufus, *Vita Petri Iberi* 33.3–15 (numbers refer to Syriac page and line numbers in *Petrus der Iberer: Ein Charakterbild zur Kirchen- und Sittengeschichte des fünften Jahrhunderts,* ed. Richard Raabe [Leipzig: J. C. Hinrichs, 1895]). On the conflicting representations of Eudocia in these sources see Elizabeth A. Clark, "Claims on the Bones of Saint Stephen: The Partisans of Melania and Eudocia," in *Ascetic Piety and Women's Faith: Essays on Late Ancient Christianity* (Lewiston, N.Y.: Edwin Mellen Press, 1986), 95–123. See generally Hunt, *Holy Land Pilgrimage,* 221–43; and Holum, *Theodosian Empresses,* 185–89, 217–21.

[58]Holum, *Theodosian Empresses,* 175–209. Eudocia's two stays in Palestine occurred in 438–39 and then from 441/42–60 (at her death).

she combined in her person imperial munificence and piety: "And he [Theodosius II] sent his wife Eudocia to Jerusalem: for she had also promised to fulfill this vow if she should see her daughter married. Now she honored the churches around Jerusalem, and also all the eastern churches, with various constructions on her trip out and her trip back."[59] In Jerusalem she would not have been viewed first and foremost as an exile from Constantinople but rather as the living face of imperial religious authority centered in the holy city.

This imperial piety was specifically linked with the rising tide of asceticism in the East, a religious endeavor that was notably open to female advancement.[60] In one story of Eudocia's journey to the holy land, her travels are inspired by the ascetic example of the aristocrat-turned-monk Melania. Melania's biographer has the empress address the holy woman: "I fulfill a double vow to the Lord, to venerate the holy places and to gaze upon my mother, for I have desired, while you yet serve the Lord in the flesh, to be worthy of your holiness."[61] Whether or not Eudocia actually praised Melania in so obsequious a fashion, the anecdote nonetheless draws attention to one way in which the Augustae were particularly apt representatives of imperial power in the holy land: as embodied links between imperial eminence and monastic virtue. Eudocia's sister-in-law Pulcheria attempted to Christianize the imperial house and court in Constantinople by closely directing her brother Theodosius's upbringing, and by herself making a public vow of virginity as a teenager.[62] Such overt attempts to intertwine imperial authority and religious distinction were

<hr />

[59]Socrates, *Historia ecclesiastica* 7.47 (GCS n.f. 1:394).

[60]Elizabeth A. Clark, "Ascetic Renunciation and Feminine Advancement: A Paradox of Late Ancient Christianity," in Clark, *Ascetic Piety*, 175–208; and, among other recent studies, Susanna Elm, *"Virgins of God": The Making of Asceticism in Late Antiquity* (Oxford: Clarendon Press, 1994); Gillian Cloke, *"This Female Man of God": Women and Spiritual Power in the Patristic Age, A.D. 350–450* (London: Routledge, 1995); and Teresa Shaw, *The Burden of the Flesh: Fasting and Sexuality in Early Christianity* (Minneapolis, Minn.: Fortress Press, 1998).

[61]Gerontius, *Vita Melaniae Iunioris* 58 (SC 90:242–44); Clark, "Claims on the Bones"; and idem, *The Life of Melania the Younger: Introduction, Translation, and Commentary* (Lewiston, N.Y.: Edwin Mellen Press, 1984), 140.

[62]On the asceticization of the court of Arcadius and Theodosius II see Holum, *Theodosian Empresses*, 92–97. Ancient sources disagree as to whether Pulcheria maintained this vow before or after her marriage to Theodosius's successor, Marcian: see Richard W. Burgess, "The Accession of Marcian in the Light of Chalcedonian Apologetic and Monophysite Polemic," *Byzantinische Zeitschrift* 86/87 (1993–94): 47–68.

fraught with difficulty in Constantinople, however: in a political capital matters of political import often overshadowed questions of pious dedication, and the alliance of the two was far from easy.[63] In Jerusalem, however, the flexibility of political power manifested through religious authority permitted the pilgrim empress Eudocia to pursue more effectively the embodiment of new imperial piety. Eudocia did not have to be an ascetic to Christianize her imperial majesty, but she was seen attending famous ascetics, and in this way worldly and imperial Christianity could draw on the spectacular religious authority of "world-renouncing" ascetics.

In addition to traditions linking Eudocia to Melania the Younger, other surviving hagiographic literature details Eudocia's imperial interactions with famous ascetics in and around Jerusalem. In the *Life of Peter the Iberian* Eudocia, inspired by rumors of holy land asceticism, makes a journey to the holy city "with imperial pomp."[64] Once there, she hears that her former foster son, the Georgian prince baptized as Peter, is living in a monastery, far from his childhood home at the court of Constantinople.[65] She presses for an interview with him, and when Peter reluctantly emerges to see her, she beams with pride: "Blessed are you, my son, for you have chosen goodness! Remember me in your holy prayers!" Peter abruptly cuts her off: "What power of speech [*parrēsia*] does a sinner have to pray?"[66] Eudocia, chastened, humbly replies with the only offer of support her former foster son will evidently accept: "Then may your sins be on my head, my son."[67] Peter retires to his cell, but soon after Eudocia insists on seeing him again. Peter, terrified of this worldly contact, takes the advice of a fellow ascetic, Zeno: "Run, save yourself!"[68] Peter flees to Gaza, where he eventually becomes bishop of Maiuma. In this brief tale

---

[63] See Holum, *Theodosian Empresses*, 79–146.

[64] John Rufus, *Vita Petri Iberi* 48.10. It is likely that this *vita* was originally composed in Greek but, like much non-Chalcedonian literature, survives only in Syriac and other non-Greek, Eastern languages: see Eduard Schwartz, *Johannes Rufus, ein monophysitischer Schriftsteller* (Heidelberg: Carl Winter's, 1912).

[65] John Rufus, *Vita Petri Iberi* 48.14–17; the text reiterates Eudocia's maternal affections for Peter: she was his "foster-mother," and in the imperial palace she was "a mother to him." See John Rufus, *Vita Petri Iberi* 16.8–12, where Theodosius and Eudocia come to love their young Georgian hostage "like a son."

[66] The Syriac for "power of speech" transliterates the Greek loanword.

[67] John Rufus, *Vita Petri Iberi* 48.25–49.

[68] John Rufus, *Vita Petri Iberi* 49.8–9.

of Eudocia's piety and Peter's intense desire to cut off all ties to the secular world there is a dramatic role-reversal: Eudocia goes from mother figure to suppliant, from empress receiving a foreign prince to pious traveler paying homage to a worthy ascetic.[69] This episode reveals the transformative interaction of imperial piety and Jerusalem asceticism.

In other hagiographic literature the presence of Augustae in the holy land affirmed the notions of aggressive appropriation and triumph found in many imperial Jerusalem monuments: as empresses in the holy land created a religious presence, they also demonstrated that the illustrious past must not only be acknowledged and built on but also mastered and triumphed over. I will return to the evolving stories of Helena's discovery of the True Cross and her increasingly embroidered imperial triumph over the historicized Jewish population of Jerusalem. Here it is worth noting how stories of Eudocia's interaction with the Syrian monk Barsoma, narrated in the monk's life, reiterate the imperial power of Christianity in the holy city, through representation of the empress's blunder and subsequent correction by the monk.[70] In the *Life* Barsoma demonstrates early on his tenacious hatred of the "Jews, pagans, and Samaritans" who fill the provinces of Palestine, Phoenicia, and Arabia and who mercilessly persecute the Christians.[71] He shows his fierce piety by swooping down into Palestine with a band of followers and burning synagogues there.[72] During one visit to Jerusalem, Barsoma reluctantly meets with the empress Eudocia and instructs her that the way of salvation is not to sit vigils and fast but rather to clothe and feed the poor.[73] Later, Eudocia is tricked by the Jews of Galilee into allowing them access

[69]My thanks to Cornelia Horn, whose work on the *Vita Petri Iberi,* and the relationship between Eudocia and Peter, has been most helpful.

[70]The *Life of Barsoma* is unfortunately only available in excerpts, published with summaries and French translations with the Syriac text: F. Nau, "Résumé de monographies syriaques: Barsauma; Abraham de la Haute-Montagne; Siméon de Kefar 'Abdin; Yaret l'Alexandrin; Jacques le Reclus; Romanus; Talia; Asia; Pantaléon; Candida," *Revue de l'Orient Chrétien* 18 (1913): 270–76, 379–89; 19 (1914): 113–34, 278–89. I distinguish the two journal volumes by Roman numerals I and II. See also F. Nau, "Deux épisodes de l'histoire juive sous Théodose II (423 et 438) d'après La Vie de Barsauma le Syrien," *Revue des Études Juives* 83 (1927): 184–206.

[71]Nau, "Résumé de monographies syriaques I," 274. Although the "pagans" are numerous, it is explicitly the "Jews and Samaritans who predominate and who persecute the Christians."

[72]Nau, "Résumé de monographies syriaques I," 382–85. The serial burning of synagogues is quickly followed by the burning of pagan temples in this section.

[73]Nau, "Résumé de monographies syriaques II," 115–17.

to the ruins of the Temple, and a riot ensues, during which the heavens (or Christian monks) rain down stones on the Jews on the Temple Mount. The Jews blame the crowd of monks and call in Roman guards. After it becomes clear to the Christian population that Eudocia is unnaturally partial to the Jews, they demand that the leader of the monks, Barsoma, come to Jerusalem. Barsoma arrives, has a miraculous standoff with the frightened Christian governor, and his monks are released, and Eudocia is left cowering.[74]

Barsoma's interactions with the empress are telling, not necessarily for their historical verisimilitude, but for how they configure the appropriate power of the empress with respect to the Christian capital of Jerusalem. As was the case in the *Life of Peter the Iberian,* the monk serves to enunciate the special bounds of imperial behavior in Christian Jerusalem: here, it is not for the empress to fast and sit vigils to prove her imperial sanctity; it is for her to clothe and feed the poor. Likewise, it is not for her to pass judgment "impartially," as she might in Constantinople, whether the complainant be Christian or Jewish or pagan;[75] it is for her to defend zealously the pious Christians in their own city and to uphold the divine sanction against the Jews. Imperial presence in the holy city of Jerusalem must serve to monumentalize, patronize, and make materially manifest the Christian triumph over the past. In the *Life of Barsoma,* as in other Christian texts, this conquered past is embodied by living Jews.

Eudocia Augusta patronized monasteries, gave lavishly to the holy city, built towers, and created shelters and hostels for pilgrims to the holy land.[76] Like her predecessor, Helena, Eudocia served to fashion symbolically and materially a particular imperial presence in Jerusalem, an imperial presence that emphasized triumph over and incorporation of the past into a masterful present. Like the absent emperors symbolized by their monuments in the holy city, the prominence of the Augustae highlights several factors in the creation of imperial piety from the Christian capital of Jerusalem: the emphasis on material representation as substitute for "original" presence (like monuments, the empress serves as corporeal

[74]Nau, "Résumé de monographies syriaques II," 120–25.

[75]Eudocia worsens her situation with the Jerusalemite Christians when she refuses to free them from prison for fear that the Jews will accuse her of "partiality" (Nau, "Résumé de monographies syriaques II," 122).

[76]Holum, *Theodosian Empresses,* 218–25.

"stand-in" for the emperor), the appropriation of religious authority through material piety (the stones of churches and the bodies of monks and pilgrims serving as comparable sites of pious benefaction), and the ambivalent and diffuse nature of authority as expressed in imperial Christianity. An emperor's power in Jerusalem was crafted preeminently through the physical display and the appropriation of the past, much as it would be in the capitals of Rome or Constantinople. In the Christian capital of Jerusalem, however, there would always additionally be something foreign about the past as it was imperially transformed; there would always (so the Christian feared) be Jews lurking in the shadows, waiting to sneak in and reassert their treacherous hold on the city, if the imperial presence does not prevent them. In Christian Jerusalem imperial power had to move through somewhat winding channels: the past in the holy city did not have only to be inherited or rebuilt, as in Rome or Constantinople; it had to be conquered.

"We Inhabitants of the Holy City": Monastic Jerusalem

Roman emperors utilized monumental building and the agency of the female members of their household to establish their own triumphant mastery of the holy city of Jerusalem. The ascetics who settled in and around Jerusalem did not construct their Christian space through overt triumph, however, but rather through more subtle gestures of erasure and appropriation. We have already seen how some monastic narratives (parts of the *Lives* of Melania, Peter, and Barsoma) could function to circumscribe and reinforce the triumphal piety of the imperial household through narrative representations of Empress Eudocia. Other textual strategies in the monastic texts of the period, in contrast to the aggressive triumphs of emperors, evoked a deserted landscape, ripe for ascetic settlement, graciously ceded to a new breed of Christian "natives" by long-faded ghosts. We might recall the monks and clergy who guided Egeria on her journey through the holy places. They had settled comfortably in the place of biblical predecessors, such as Moses and Elijah, and the way had evidently been cleared for them before their arrival: there were no traces of "impious inhabitants" whom they had to oust. The same narrative representation of emptied space reappears in much of the monastic literature of the fifth and sixth centuries, as Christians engaged in a sort of "anticonquest," by which they "secure[d] their innocence in the same moment as they assert[ed] their hegemony."[77] Several different traditions of monastic settlement emanate from the area around Jerusalem from the fourth through sixth centuries: the aristocratic ascetics of the Theodosian age, the anchoritic traditions attached (at least in literary terms) to Egyptian monasticism, and the extensive semianchoritic settlements in the Judaean desert outside the city.[78] In each of these monastic movements there is this sense of discovering a long-buried past, opening up and resettling empty yet significant spaces by divine authorization.

In the late fourth and early fifth centuries several different groups of aristocratic Roman ascetics left behind their opulent lives in Old Rome to settle within sight of the holy places of the Bible. Possibly these ascetics originally arrived with other western travelers of a religious bent, like Egeria, or the western noblewomen Silvia and Poemenia, driven by pious curiosity and enabled by leisure and wealth.[79] Certainly throughout the fifth century (as portions of the western empire destabilized), Jerusalem was viewed as a favorable destination for imperial elites, a site at which power and piety naturally coincided.[80] It would seem that in this period Jerusalem became a new center of gravity in the Christian Roman Empire, a place where pious imperial subjects could step into the stream of

[77]On "anti-conquest" see Mary Louise Pratt, *Imperial Eyes: Travel Writing and Transculturation* (London: Routledge, 1992), chaps. 3–4, cited here at 7.

[78]See the classic study of Derwas J. Chitty, *The Desert a City: An Introduction to the Study of Egyptian and Palestinian Monasticism Under the Christian Empire* (1966; repr., Crestwood: St. Vladimir's Seminary Press, 1995).

[79]Hunt, *Holy Land Pilgrimage*, 159–67. On Silvia (or Silvania) see Palladius, *Historia Lausiaca* 55.1 (text in *Palladio: La storia Lausiaca*, ed. G. J. M. Bartelink, intro. Christine Mohrmann, tr. Marino Barchiesi [Milan: Fondazione Lorenzo Valla, 1974], 250); and Paulinus of Nola, *ep.* 31.1 (CSEL 29:267–68); E. D. Hunt, "St. Silvia of Aquitaine: The Role of a Theodosian Pilgrim in the Society of East and West," *Journal of Theological Studies*, n.s., 23 (1972): 351–73; and idem, *Holy Land Pilgrimage*, 159–61. On Poemenia see Palladius, *Historia Lausiaca* 35.14–15 (Bartelink, *Palladio*, 176–78); and Paul Devos, "La 'servante de Dieu' Poemenia d'après Pallade, la tradition copte, et Jean Rufus," *Analecta Bollandiana* 87 (1969): 189–212.

[80]Most sources relate Melania the Younger's flight to Jerusalem to civic unrest in the western provinces: Palladius, *Historia Lausiaca* 54.7, 61.5 (Bartelink, *Palladio*, 248, 266); Gerontius, *Vita Melaniae Iunioris* 15–19 (SC 90:156–66); and see Clark, *Melania the Younger*, 102–9. Jerome speaks of receiving crowds of "once noble" refugees from Rome as beggars in "holy Bethlehem" (*Commentarius in Ezechielem* 3.praef. [CCL 75:91]). See Peter Brown, "The Patrons of Pelagius: The Roman Aristocracy Between East and West," in his *Religion and Society in the Age of Augustine* (London: Faber and Faber, 1972), 224.

sacred history and take position there, without fear of a recalcitrant past
or present struggling against them. One of the first of these noble ascetics
to settle permanently in Jerusalem was Melania (later known as "the
Elder"), who left Rome as a young widow with "all of her portable property . . . accompanied by various notable children and women."[81] She first
traveled to Alexandria so that she could visit the monks of the Egyptian
desert, who had already achieved celebrity status in the West.[82] She spent
some time visiting these monks and then accompanied several of them
into exile in Palestine in the mid-370s.[83] After a tussle with the local gov-
ernment, Melania founded a monastery on the Mount of Olives; she was
soon joined by Rufinus of Aquileia, and she remained there for almost
thirty years.[84] Palladius, who recounts Melania's travels in his *Lausiac History,* does not specify why the Roman noblewoman settled on the Mount
of Olives specifically, but he does note that Melania and Rufinus together
"welcomed those visiting Jerusalem on account of a vow, bishops and
monks and virgins, and they housed them at their own expense."[85] It
would seem that pilgrims and ascetics had already focused their reverence
on this site as one of the holy places of Jerusalem;[86] so Melania and her

---

[81]Palladius, *Historia Lausiaca* 46.1–3 (Bartelink, *Palladio,* 220–22); Francis X. Murphy,
"Melania the Elder: A Biographical Note," *Traditio* 5 (1947): 59–77.

[82]The circulation, and hasty translation, in the West of Athanasius's *Vita Antonii* ensured
instant fame for the monks of the Egyptian desert: see Jerome, *ep.* 3 (CSEL 54:12–18). Murphy,
"Melania," 66–67, assumes that Melania's primary reason for visiting the East was "to examine
the Egyptian system firsthand."

[83]See Rufinus of Aquileia, *Historia ecclesiastica* 11.3–4 (GCS n.f. 6:1003–8); and Murphy,
"Melania," 66–73, for a plausible reconstruction of the order of these events.

[84]Palladius, *Historia Lausiaca* 54–55 (Bartelink, *Palladio,* 244–52). Jerome, *ep.* 4.2.1 (CSEL
54:20), mentions Rufinus and Melania in Jerusalem. A decade or so later Jerome would gloss
over Melania's Egyptian sojourn in a letter written to Paula soon before their journey to Palestine: *ep.* 39.5.4–5 (CSEL 54:305) has Melania going straight from her dry-eyed stance at her
husband's graveside to a "ship setting sail for Jerusalem."

[85]Palladius, *Historia Lausiaca* 46.6 (Bartelink, *Palladio,* 224). What I have rendered "housed
at their own expense [*oikeiois analōmasin ōikodomēsan*]" could also be translated "edified at
their own expense" (as some translators suggest: see, e.g., Bartelink, *Palladio,* 225).

[86]Constantine had already built a church on the Mount of Olives, the "Eleona" church,
one of a triad that included the Holy Sepulcher and Nativity churches: Eusebius, *De laudibus
Constantini* 9.17 (PG 20:1372A–B). See also Peter Walker, *Holy City, Holy Places? Christian Attitudes to Jerusalem and the Holy Land in the Fourth Century* (Oxford: Clarendon Press, 1990),
173–98. Another church was supposedly built there by Poemenia in the fourth century. According to John Rufus, *Vita Petri Iberi* 30.13–18, Poemenia preceded Melania the Elder to the
Mount of Olives, leading Devos, " 'Servante de Dieu,'" 207–8, to conclude that she came in
the mid-370s. In general see Hagith S. Sivan, "Pilgrimage, Monasticism, and the Emergence of

companions founded a Christian settlement there, staking a claim in the heart of newly recovered Christian space. It is also notable (but not noted by Melania's admirers) that settlement on Mount Olivet placed Melania and her companions on the opposite side of the Temple Mount from the complex of the Holy Sepulcher, creating, in a sense, a bright Christian frame around the ruins of Jewish Jerusalem.[87]

If Melania the Elder's motives for settling on the Mount of Olives must remain somewhat speculative, Jerusalem's appeal for other prominent western ascetics is given more attention by her contemporary Jerome. Jerome came to Palestine with his friend and patroness Paula and her daughter Eustochium, from Rome, sometime in the latter half of the 380s.[88] In a letter written in Paula and Eustochium's voice to their friend Marcella in Rome, pleading with their spiritual "mother" to join them in the land of the Bible, Jerome describes a land rich with scriptural history but seemingly empty of inhabitants, ripe and waiting for their monastic settlement. Jerusalem holds Jerome's particular focus in this letter. Jerome anticipates (or perhaps repeats) comments that Marcella might make (based on choice New Testament verses) that Jerusalem was "cursed" and unfit for proper Christian habitation.[89] Jerome responds with a sweep of biblical history terminating in his and Paula's monastic venture:

From this peace Solomon, that is, "the peaceful one," was born there, and "his place was made in peace" (Ps 76.2), and he receives the names "king of kings" and "lord of lords" as a figure of Christ, under the etymology of the city's name. Why should we speak of David and all his progeny, who reigned in this city? As much as Judaea is exalted above all other provinces, so is this city exalted above all Judaea. To speak more succinctly, the glory of this province is derived from its capital city, and whatever fame the members have is always due to the head.[90]

Christian Palestine in the 4th Century," in Ousterhout, *Blessings of Pilgrimage*, 54–65.

[87]It is possible that this "framing" also explains, in part, Theodosius I's church at Gethsemane (down the hill from Olivet), sometime in the 390s.

[88]He writes a letter of farewell in 385 to Asella: "So pray that from Babylon I may look again at Jerusalem" (*ep.* 45.6.1 [CSEL 54:327]). Ferdinand Cavallera, *Saint Jérôme: Sa vie et son oeuvre*, 2 vols. (Louvain: Spicilegium Sacrum Lovaniense, 1922), 2:156, places his settlement in Bethlehem in 386, and his travels with Paula through Palestine and Egypt (see below) in late 385 to summer 386.

[89]Jerome, *ep.* 46.4–8 (CSEL 54:334–38).

[90]Jerome, *ep.* 46.3.4 (CSEL 54:332). Jerome draws on a common etymology of Solomon's

It seems the glorious Old Testament past of Judaea, and Jerusalem, persists even to this moment, imbuing its "inhabitants" with its glory. He also carefully recontextualizes the unsavory role Jerusalem played in the life of Jesus and even in the imperial history of Rome:

> At first blush you must acknowledge that it was not the place, but the people who sinned, since the capture of a city entails the slaying of its population. The city was destroyed so the people might be punished, and the Temple was overturned so that figurative offerings would be removed. As far as it pertains to the place, through the passing of time it has become much more majestic [multo augustior] than it was before.[91]

The suggestion is that the dirty slate was wiped clean (through the agency of Titus, presumably), its Jewish Temple destroyed, its inhabitants eradicated. The field has been left open for new inhabitants to rehabilitate the holy city that Jesus loved, now rendered "more majestic" for them. Jerome continues to catalogue these "new inhabitants," colonists from across the empire who are, he insists, absolutely fitting inhabitants of Jerusalem. People of Gaul, Britain, Armenia, Persia, India, Arabia, Egypt, Cappadocia, Syria, "all the swarms of the East," have arrived in Palestine "according to the Savior's words, 'Wherever the body is, there the eagles will be gathered together' (Luke 17.37); they all rush to these places and display to us the manifestation of diverse virtues. Dissonant voices, a single religion, almost as many singing choirs as there are different nations."[92] The image here is of bygone elimination and recent recolonization, invested with the transhistorical continuity of religious certitude. "It was not the place that sinned, but the people" might have served republican senators equally well as a slogan for the contested Roman colonization of the ruins of their defunct archrival Carthage, highlighting victorious recolonization and relegating the brutal triumph of conquest to a distant past.[93] Jerome's point to Marcella (and presumably other prominent

---

name as "peaceful [pacificus]" and likewise translates Salem (i.e., Jerusalem) in the psalm as "peace."

[91] Jerome, ep. 46.5.1–2 (CSEL 54:334).

[92] Jerome, ep. 46.10.1–2 (CSEL 54:339–40).

[93] See Cicero, De lege agraria 2.87–95 (LCL 466–70), an argument against colonization in Capua drawing heavily on parallels with colonization of Carthage, contains the warning: Carthaginienses fraudulenti [sunt] et mendaces non genere, sed natura loci (De lege agraria 2.95 [LCL 470]), the exact opposite of Jerome's claim of Jerusalem that non loci sed hominum

ascetic Christians in Rome) is that the true inhabitants of the holy city—Christians, specifically of a monastic vocation—have claimed their religious patrimony, long since rid of its disgraced former heirs and renovated for them alone.

I have already described how Jerome frequently, and even stubbornly, made reference to his own contact with Jewish "natives," who served him as living lexica of biblical wisdom. Yet in his descriptions of monastic settlement, both in the letter to Marcella and in other writings, the landscape is curiously empty of these knowledgeable natives. The image of Christian Jerusalem and its environs that Jerome portrays to the outside world is one that has been swept clean and prepared for a new Christian settlement, with lingering ghosts that mark the site's historical significance. This image is particularly sharp in Jerome's *Epitaphium Paulae*, a letter of solace written to Eustochium after the death of her mother, Paula (ca. 404). In this letter Jerome narrates Paula's travels from the port of Rome, through the islands of the Mediterranean, Syria and Phoenicia, Palestine, and into Egypt, ending with her settlement in secluded Bethlehem. The holy land through which Paula travels is thick with history but scarcely populated. Although she visits with live bishops and monks during her journey from Rome,[94] once she crosses down through Phoenicia, almost all of the people she "sees" are in fact long dead, heroes and villains of Palestinian history (biblical and Roman) who cede their place to Paula.[95] The one exception to this catalogue of ghosts is the proconsul of Palestine, a "friend of Paula's" who offers her use of his palace. She refuses, and presumably eschews his company as well, so that neither Paula (nor we, as readers) actually catch sight of him.[96] Throughout the holy

---

fuisse peccatum.

[94] Jerome, *ep.* 108.7.2–3 (CSEL 55:312–13).

[95] Jerome, *ep.* 108.8–14 (CSEL 55:313–25). Most of the characters she "sees" are biblical figures, but there are also historical and mythological personalities she (or Jerome) would have known from the histories of Josephus and later writers: Elijah, Paul, Josiah, the Philistines, Herod, Augustus, Cornelius, Philip and his daughters, Antipater (father of Herod the Great), Dorcas and Aeneas (from Acts), Joseph of Arimathea, Jonah, Andromeda, Cleopas, Solomon, Joshua, the Gibeonites, Helena of Adiabene, Hadrian, David, Rachel, the baby Jesus, the "slaughtered innocents," Herod (again), Mary and Joseph, Jacob, the Ethiopian eunuch, Sarah, Isaac, Abraham, Adam, Caleb, Othniel, the Moabites and Ammonites, Lazarus, Mary, Martha, Zacchaeus, Hiel, Elisha, Elijah (again), Eleazar, the Samaritan woman, Obadiah, John the Baptist, Sisera, Barak, the widow of Nain, Micah, and the Horites and Gittites.

[96] Jerome, *ep.* 108.9.2 (CSEL 55:315).

places, she sees nothing but biblical ghosts, imbuing the land at the same time with rich history and a sense of desertion. The multitude of ghosts bespeak a past now gone, to which Paula is both witness and heir.[97] Once she passes through the holy land, she continues on to Egypt and soon meets up with live Christians again.[98] But the live monks of Egypt do not draw Paula as strongly as do the ghostly visions of Palestine:

Forgetful of her sex and bodily weakness, she desired to stay with her girls among so many thousands of monks. And since they were all welcoming, she might have made the attempt, if the desire for the holy places had not exhibited a greater pull. . . . She returned with such speed you might have thought her a bird. Not long after, making up her mind to settle permanently in holy Bethlehem, she stayed for three years in confining accommodations, until she could construct cells and monasteries and establish for the many different pilgrims *en route* the sort of accommodations that Mary and Joseph had not found.[99]

Once settled in Bethlehem, Paula is firmly ensconced in scriptural history: she prefers for companions Mary and Joseph *redivivi* in the form of pious travelers, and not the thousands of monks of Egypt.[100] As is the case for Melania's earlier monastic settlement on the Mount of Olives, we are given no explicit reason for Paula to settle in Bethlehem, other than its obvious ties to a biblical past and its popularity with fourth-century pilgrims.[101] In the 380s and early 390s, before Jerome had occasion to start dissociating himself from his former friends in Jerusalem,[102] it seems that perhaps Jerome and Paula imagined their monastic settlement as an ex-

[97]See Blake Leyerle, "Landscape as Cartography in Early Christian Pilgrimage Narratives," *Journal of the American Academy of Religion* 64 (1996): 130–32; and Georgia Frank, *The Memory of the Eyes: Pilgrims to Living Saints in Christian Late Antiquity* (Berkeley: University of California Press, 2000), on "visuality" and biblical piety.

[98]Jerome, *ep.* 108.14.2 (CSEL 55:324).

[99]Jerome, *ep.* 108.14.3–4 (CSEL 55:325).

[100]See Bhabha, *Location of Culture,* 40–65; and cf. my discussion of Egeria in Chapter 4.

[101]Unfortunately, most of Jerome's correspondence from their first years in Bethlehem (assuming such existed) is lost. In a letter to Paula's son-in-law, Pammachius, after the death of her daughter, Paulina (ca. 398), he makes some mention of their (ascetically arduous) life in Bethlehem and his own intention to build a men's monastery to complement their women's monastery (*ep.* 66.13–14 [CSEL 54:663–65]).

[102]This dissociation resulted from the outbreak of the Origenist controversy, which pitted Jerome on the side of Epiphanius of Salamis and Theophilus of Alexandria against John of Jerusalem and Melania and Rufinus. See Hunt, *Holy Land Pilgrimage,* 168–79; Elizabeth A. Clark, *The Origenist Controversy: The Cultural Construction of an Early Christian Debate* (Princeton, N.J.: Princeton University Press, 1993), 16–42.

tension of the newly Christianized Jerusalem. Besides his extensive defense of Christian Jerusalem to Marcella, there survives also a letter to some Roman friends of Paula, in which Jerome presses them to join his and Paula's monastic endeavor in Palestine. In this letter Jerome uses the nearness of Jerusalem as a "selling point" for their pilgrimage to Bethlehem: "I exhort and entreat you, by the Lord's love, that you will bestow your countenance on us, and that by a visit to the holy places you will enrich us with such a gift. Surely, if our company displeases you, to pay reverence where the Lord's feet stood is a part of the faith, and to look on the seemingly fresh traces of his birth, and cross, and passion."[103] Jerome emphasizes the proximity of Bethlehem to Golgotha and the Holy Sepulcher ("his birth, his cross, his passion"), expanding Jerusalem's holy sphere a few miles up the road.[104] Thus the settlement of Christian Bethlehem, like that of the Mount of Olives, might have been viewed originally as the *re*settlement and *re*population of a depopulated, freshly Christianized holy city of Jerusalem.[105] Only later, once theological and social divisions pitted Jerome against Rufinus and Melania and John of Jerusalem, would he begin to emphasize the distance between the place of Jesus' birth and the place of his death;[106] but even then, it is entirely possible that the monks and pilgrims who continued to visit and settle in Bethlehem viewed their activity as the monastic colonization of the emptied spaces of sanctity attached to the holy city of Jerusalem.

Other ascetics made their home on the Mount of Olives, as well as in Bethlehem, drawn by a desire for the "holy places" and the reputations of the prominent monks who had settled there.[107] The activity of these aristocratic monastic colonizers in and around Jerusalem culminated with

[103]Jerome, *ep.* 47.2.2 (CSEL 54:346).

[104]Jerome would not have been the first to expand Christian Jerusalem in this manner: Cyril of Jerusalem also rather effectively claimed nearby holy sites as part of his Christian Jerusalem. Cf., e.g., Cyril of Jerusalem, *Catecheses* 14.23 and 16.4 (text in *Cyrilli Hiersolymum Archiepiscopi Opera*, ed. J. Rupp, 2 vols. [Munich: Stahl, 1860], here 2:140, 210); and the discussion in Walker, *Holy City,* 196–98.

[105]This might especially be the case if Melania, with Rufinus, had already staked out Jerusalem proper as their monastic "turf.

[106]See Jerome, *ep.* 58.2.3 (CSEL 54:529–30), for the famous claim: "Not to have seen Jerusalem, but to have lived well in Jerusalem is to be praised."

[107]See Clark, *Melania the Younger,* 116–17, 221–23 (notes); and Sylvester J. Saller, "L'epitafio di Eufemia al Getsemani," in *Ricerche archeologiche al Monte degli Ulivi,* ed. P. Virgilio and C. Corbo (Jerusalem: Studium Biblicum Franciscanum, 1965), 75–80.

the arrival of Melania the Elder's granddaughter and namesake. According to Palladius, Melania the Elder was instrumental in securing the ascetic vocation of her granddaughter, rushing from Palestine to Rome the
moment she heard rumor of Melania the Younger's desire to dedicate
herself to God.[108] In this version of the story Melania the Elder led her
granddaughter, along with other members of her family, from Rome toward Jerusalem, where she died soon after. Although it is unclear exactly
who is supposed to have accompanied her back to Palestine, and when,[109]
Palladius is clearly trying to suggest a monastic patrimony, from one
Melania to the next. By the time Melania the Younger's own companion
composed her hagiographic *vita*,[110] however, the name and memory of
Melania the Elder had vanished altogether: the *vita* makes it clear that the
younger Melania founded her own monasteries and did not merely build
on those of her grandmother.[111] Various explanations have been proposed
for this erasure from monastic memory and space on the Mount of Olives;[112] whatever Melania the Younger's original motives for establishing
her own monasteries and *martyria* and ignoring those of her grandmother, essentially blotting out her grandmother's ascetic fame on Olivet, Melania the Younger's ascetic settlement in Jerusalem demonstrates
the same processes of historical erasure and appropriation that had led
her aristocratic predecessors to settle in Jerusalem in the first place. The
past in Jerusalem was always alive and present and accessible, always po-
litely receding before new and more fitting inhabitants. Stepping into the
empty shoes of religious antecedents was not so aggressive an act of colonization as the triumphant construction of imperial Christian monuments executed by Constantine and his successors; nevertheless, it was an
act of demonstrable Christian authority, the power to step up and claim a
meaningful space that has been (somehow) vacated.

If Jerusalem emerged among aristocratic monks of the fifth century as

[108]Palladius, *Historia Lausiaca* 54.3 (Bartelink, *Palladio*, 246).

[109]Murphy, "Melania," 76–77, concludes that Melania the Elder died just prior to the sack
of Rome in 410.

[110]On the authorship and date of the *Vita Melaniae Iunioris* see Clark, *Melania the Younger*,
13–24; and Denys Gorce, *La vie de Sainte Mélanie*, SC 90 (Paris: Editions du Cerf, 1962), 54–
62.

[111]See Gerontius, *Vita Melania Iunioris* 41, 49, 57 (SC 90:204–6, 220–22, 240).

[112]See Clark, *Melania the Younger*, 141–52, 238–44 (notes).

a sort of congenial colonial outpost of Old Rome, a different stream of monastic hagiography configured Jerusalem, and its surrounding desert, as the sanctified ascetic outpost of Egyptian styles of monasticism. Jerome himself, once he took to constructing literary hagiographies to rival his Greek predecessor Athanasius,[113] placed his monastic heroes in a line of ascetic descent from Egyptian masters. Hilarion, born outside of Gaza, "a city of Palestine," is portrayed in Jerome's *Life of Hilarion* as the initiator of a new way of monastic life in the province of Palestine: "Indeed, there were not yet at that time monasteries in Palestine, nor had anyone known a monk in Syria before saint Hilarion. He was the first founder and teacher of this way of life and zeal in this province. Lord Jesus had old Antony in Egypt and he had young Hilarion in Palestine."[114] That "founder and teacher of this way of life [*fundator et eruditor huius conversationis*]" learned his monastic virtues while a student in Egypt, and he returned to the deserted land around Gaza to follow Antony's example.[115] Throughout the *vita* there is a sort of camaraderie between Antony and Hilarion, and it is understood that Hilarion has initiated in Palestine a way of monastic life modeled on his Egyptian predecessor. Like Antony's, Hilarion's example serves to populate a wilderness as "through all Palestine innumerable monasteries arose,"[116] and by Hilarion's sixty-third year (having begun his ascetic endeavor at the age of fifteen), he found himself "head of a large monastery" so full of monks and pious Christians seeking miracles "that the wilderness all around was filled with all sorts of people."[117] Jerome does not go so far as to cite Athanasius's famous slogan

---

[113]Paul B. Harvey Jr., "Saints and Satyrs: Jerome the Scholar at Work," *Athenaeum* 86 (1998): 35–56; Patricia Cox Miller, "Jerome's Centaur: A Hyper-Icon of the Desert," *Journal of Early Christian Studies* 4 (1996): 209–33; and Pierre Leclerc, "Antoine et Paul: Métamorphose d'un héros," in *Jérôme entre l'occident et l'orient*, ed. Y.-M. Duval (Paris: Etudes Augustiniennes, 1988), 257–65.

[114]Jerome, *Vita Hilarionis* 8.10–11. Numbering follows the critical text in *Vita di Martino, Vita di Ilarione, In Memoria di Paola*, ed. A. A. R. Bastiaensen and Jan W. Smit, intro. Christine Mohrmann, tr. (Italian) Luca Canali and Claudio Moreschini (Milan: Fondazione Lorenzo Valla, 1975), 90. See also *Vita Hilarionis* 2.1, 7.1, 13.6 (in which Hilarion and a demon converse in "pure Syriac"), 19.3, 33.1 (Bastiaensen, *Vita di Ilarione*, 74, 86, 104, 114, 142).

[115]Jerome, *Vita Hilarionis* 2.2–5 (Bastiaensen, *Vita di Ilarione*, 75–76). There is a certain pedagogical irony in Jerome's *vita*: Hilarion, the son of "idolaters [*idolis deditos*]," is sent to study grammar at Alexandria but instead studies monasticism from Antony in the desert, inverting a common secular ideal of "study abroad" in late antiquity.

[116]Jerome, *Vita Hilarionis* 15.3 (Bastiaensen, *Vita di Ilarione*, 106–8).

[117]Jerome, *Vita Hilarionis* 19.1 (Bastiaensen, *Vita di Ilarione*, 114).

and claim that the Palestinian desert "was made a city by monks,"[118] but the image is nonetheless similar: a once empty space is made into a miraculous center of holiness by monastic settlement, an outpost of sanctity. Although Jerome's *Life of Hilarion* shares with the stories of aristocratic monastic settlement the description of deserted spaces populated by holy men and women, it lacks the connection to historical *loca sancta* found in the settlements of Paula or the Melaniae: Hilarion settles in the desert of southern Palestine because it is his "hometown," not because he is drawn by a "desire for the holy places" like Paula's.[119] There are no ghosts among whom to settle, no subtle erasure relegated to the past, no absorption of the past into the present.

Later hagiography, produced in the sixth century, crafted a different narrative of monastic colonization, emphasizing the dramatic population of deserted spaces and appropriating the historical and religious significance of the holy city of Jerusalem. The most thorough hagiographic inscription of monastic settlement is the series of *vitae* written by Cyril of Scythopolis in the middle of the sixth century to commemorate the founders and builders of a series of coenobitic and semianchoritic monasteries (or *lauras*) in the Judaean desert east of Jerusalem.[120] Cyril's *Lives* narrate monastic settlement from roughly 400 to 550 and provide a theological as well as political framework for the sprawling settlements of monks outside the holy city.[121] The *Life of Euthymius* tells the story of an Armenian priest who resists moving up the clerical ladder (it is an "impediment to virtue") and "flees, going off to Jerusalem, desiring to in-

---

[118] See Athanasius, *Vita Antonii* 14.7 (SC 400:174).

[119] In fact, Jerome omits from the vita Hilarion's "one and only" visit to Jerusalem, which he mentions elsewhere: *ep.* 58.3.4 (CSEL 54:531).

[120] On Cyril of Scythopolis's *vitae* see John Binns, *Ascetics and Ambassadors of Christ: The Monasteries of Palestine, 314–631* (Oxford: Clarendon Press, 1994). Yizhar Hirschfeld, *The Judean Desert Monasteries of the Byzantine Period* (New Haven, Conn.: Yale University Press, 1992), provides archaeological data. Still useful is Chitty, *Desert a City*, 82–167.

[121] It is important to note that this is a decidedly pro-Chalcedonian, anti-Origenist hagiography, in contrast to the Monophysite (or anti-Chalcedonian) hagiography of a sixth-century Christian writer such as John Rufus: see Aryeh Kofsky, "Peter the Iberian: Pilgrimage, Monasticism, and Ecclesiastical Politics in Byzantine Palestine," *Liber Annuus* 47 (1997): 209–22; and Lorenzo Perrone, "Christian Holy Places and Pilgrimage in an Age of Dogmatic Conflicts: Popular Religion and Confessional Affiliation in Byzantine Palestine (Fifth to Seventh Centuries)," *Prôche-Orient Chrétien* 48 (1998): 5–37.

habit that desert."[122] He visits the holy sites of Jerusalem—"the holy cross, the holy Resurrection [church], and the other venerable places"[123]—and then settles near a *laura* (semianchoritic cluster of monastic cells) outside of Jerusalem.[124] From here Euthymius goes on to become the "shining star" of Palestinian monasticism,[125] founding monasteries, converting pagans, and becoming so emblematic of Palestinian *askēsis* that the empress Eudocia, on visiting that monastic superstar Simeon the Stylite, was reportedly told by that holy man, "I am exceedingly amazed that, having a spring nearby and ignoring it, you are so zealous to draw on the same water far away. Even now you have there the God-bearing Euthymius."[126] By midcentury, according to Cyril's *vita*, Euthymius has settled the wilderness outside of Jerusalem and become its emblematic holy "native."

The manner in which Euthymius (as well as his successor, Sabas) is said to have "gone native" in the Jerusalem wilderness is instructive in determining how monastic Jerusalem configured an identity that could masterfully appropriate the past without the overt shades of conquest evident in the triumphant munificence of emperors. Scholars often note that the great founders of Palestinian monasticism in Cyril's *vitae* all originated from outside the province of Palestine, in distinct contrast to their hagiographer. Robert Wilken has remarked, "Although Cyril of Scythopolis was a native of Palestine, all his heroes were natives of other countries. This feature of the work is no doubt deliberate."[127] No doubt:

---

[122]Cyril of Scythopolis, *Vita Euthymii* 5 (TU 49.2:13–14). Here, as throughout the *Vita Euthymii*, Cyril plays on the meaning of Euthymius's name as "desiring."

[123]Cyril of Scythopolis, *Vita Euthymii* 6 (TU 49.2:14).

[124]Cyril of Scythopolis, *Vita Euthymii* 6 (TU 49.2:14). The *laura* is at Pharan, presumably that founded in the early fourth century by Chariton; it is described in the anonymous *Vita Charitonis*, which was apparently written in response to Cyril's *vitae* (see Binns, *Ascetics and Ambassadors*, 46–47; and the introduction by Leah di Segni to her translation of the *Vita Charitonis* in *Ascetic Behavior in Greco-Roman Antiquity*, ed. Vincent L. Wimbush [Minneapolis, Minn.: Fortress Press, 1990], 393–96).

[125]Cyril of Scythopolis, *Vita Sabae* 7 (TU 49.2:90–91).

[126]Cyril of Scythopolis, *Vita Euthymii* 30 (TU 49.2:48).

[127]Wilken, *Land Called Holy*, 157. The subjects of the lives are from Armenia (Euthymius and John the Hesychast), Cappadocia (Sabas, Theodosius, and Theognius), Greece (Kyriakos), and Syria (Abraamius) (*Vitae Euthymii* 2, *Ioanni Hesychasti* 1, *Sabae* 1, *Theodosii* 1, *Theognii* 1, *Kyriaki* 1, *Abraamii* 1 [TU 49.2:8, 200, 86–87, 236, 241, 223, 243]). Where Schwartz's edition does not provide chapter numbers, I am following those of *Lives of the Monks of Palestine by Cyril of Scythopolis*, tr. R. M. Price (Kalamazoo, Mich.: Cistercian Studies, 1991).

and one of the effects of creating a cast of monastic settlers from everywhere *but* Palestine is to fashion a landscape devoid of "natives," lying
open and waiting for settlement and colonization from the outside.
Euthymius and those who follow him into the Judaean desert can *become*
natives, can settle outside the holy city and become "the great glory of
Palestine,"[128] partly because there is no one else there to claim such a
privilege. When Euthymius and Sabas settle in a new place in the desert,
they find either wild animals, demons, "Saracens," or nothing at all.[129]
There are no other "natives" whom they must supplant. Yet this fiction
of emptiness operates in tandem with a strong sense that the monks of
the Judaean desert are, in fact, taking on the roles of long-gone biblical
"natives." Euthymius, after visiting the holy places in Jerusalem and settling in the desert, goes into the "desert of Ziph, desiring to gaze upon
the caves in which David fled from Saul's presence."[130] Likewise,
Euthymius is described as having been granted the "gifts" of Moses,
Joshua, and Daniel,[131] a significant series of miraculous leaders who, in a
prior era, had served as victorious leaders of displaced Israelites. Euthymius, who travels from solitary cell to solitary cell throughout his life, is a
new leader of God's holy people, staking out the "promised land" of a
Christian empire in the manner of Moses.[132] Euthymius leads his new
Christian Israelites into a new promised land (which overlaps with the
"old" promised land). They are the new "tribes of Israel," a point driven
home when the empress Eudocia sees Euthymius's "monastic cells scattered over the desert"; at this sight she is alleged to have spontaneously
cited Numbers 24.5: "how beautiful are your houses, Jacob, and your
tents, Israel," the words uttered by the inspired prophet Balaam gazing
on the tribes of Israel before they crossed the Jordan.[133]

---

[128]Cyril of Scythopolis, *Vita Theodosii* 1 (TU 49.2:235).

[129]Wild animals: *Vita Euthymii* 8, *Vita Sabae* 33–34 (one of the numerous "lion" stories of
the *vitae*); demons: *Vita Euthymii* 12, *Vita Sabae* 27; Saracens: *Vita Euthymii* 10, 15, *Vita Sabae*
13–14; nothing at all: *Vita Euthymii* 14, *Vita Sabae* 15 (TU 49.2:24, 97–99, 15–16, 118–29, 22–23,
110–12, 18–21, 24–25, 96–97).

[130]Cyril of Scythopolis, *Vita Euthymii* 11 (TU 49.2:22), referring to 1 Sam 23.14.

[131]Cyril of Scythopolis, *Vita Euthymii* 13 (TU 49.2:23): he splits the seas, turns back the
Jordan, halts the sun, turns fire into dew (cf. Exod 14, Josh 3, 10.12–13, LXX Dan 3.50 [=
"Prayer of Azariah" 1.27]).

[132]Wilken, *Land Called Holy*, 159–61, points out that Euthymius's wanderings demarcate
the territory that would later be built up by his successor, Sabas.

[133]Cyril of Scythopolis, *Vita Euthymii* 35 (TU 49.2:53).

If Euthymius is the new Moses, leading his people to the promised land, then it is fair to cast Sabas as the new Joshua, building up the "cities" of the new kingdom of Israel.[134] Throughout the *Life of Sabas* a similar refrain recurs: his mission is to "build a city" in (or of) the desert, *polisthēnai tēn erēmon*.[135] Here the phrase is self-consciously modeled on Athanasius's *Life of Antony*, but the literal meaning has outgrown the earlier metaphor. With several dozen monasteries, and thousands of monks in the rough strip of land between Jerusalem and the Dead Sea, Sabas presided over something quite like a great holy city. Yet the city he has been sent to construct is not a new Christian *polis* but the holy city of Jerusalem itself. One of the first times Cyril uses the phrase "to build a city in the desert," it is in conjunction with Jerusalem: "he admitted the desire, pleasing to God, to take hold of the holy city and to seek solitude in the desert around it, for it was necessary that this city be built through him [*di' autou tautēn polisthēnai*] and that through him the prophecies of resounding Isaiah should be fulfilled."[136] The subject of *polisthēnai* is not terribly clear in this sentence (does *tautēn* refer to the "holy city" or the "desert around it"?),[137] nor does Cyril specify which prophecies of Isaiah Sabas is to fulfill through his "*polis*-building."[138] The editor of the Greek text suggests Isaiah 58.12: "Your ancient ruins shall be rebuilt; you shall

[134]Notably without the violence attendant on Joshua's conquest of Canaan: Sabas's is a bloodless conquest. On Sabas see Joseph Patrich, *Sabas, Leader of Palestinian Monasticism: A Comparative Study in Eastern Monasticism, Fourth Through Seventh Centuries* (Washington, D.C.: Dumbarton Oaks, 1995).

[135]The phrase recurs throughout the life: Cyril of Scythopolis, *Vita Sabae* 6, 15, 17, 19, 27, 50, 58 (TU 49.2:90, 98, 101, 104, 110, 141, 158).

[136]Cyril of Scythopolis, *Vita Sabae* 6 (TU 49.2:90).

[137]The grammatical difficulty is glossed over by the curious epigraph in Patrich's study of Sabas (see inside cover of Patrich, *Sabas*), where he cites this phrase but inserts the word *desert* so that it reads: "*edei gar di' autou tautēn* eremon *polisthēnai*," although the word *eremon* does not appear in the text or the critical apparatus.

[138]The middle form *polisthēnai* is difficult to render in English, since it can take a subject but already contains a subject (*polis*) in its root meaning. The English translator of the *vitae* consistently renders it "to colonize," although it is not clear that this is the verb used for the specific activity of creating a colony. In classical Greek *polizō* generally signifies "building" or "building a city" (s.v. Liddell-Scott-Jones, *A Greek-English Lexicon*, 9th ed. [Oxford: Clarendon Press, 1996]), whereas "colonize" is generally signified by forms of *oikizō* (s.v. Liddell-Scott-Jones, *Greek-English Lexicon*). The usage here (as in Athanasius) may also be drawing on the moralistic Christian understanding of *politeia*: see Michael J. Hollerich, *Eusebius of Caesarea's* Commentary on Isaiah: *Christian Exegesis in the Age of Constantine* (Oxford: Clarendon Press, 1999), 105–30.

raise up the foundations of many generations; you shall be called the re-
pairer of the breach, the restorer of streets to live in," which has the attraction of drawing on the language of urban development and of casting
the monks as rebuilders and resettlers of the promised land of Israel.[139]
Certainly the surface meaning seems to be that the desert will be filled
with monks, such that they will *seem* to be a city in and of themselves.
But this does not take into account the fact that in the *vitae* the monks
consider themselves to be inhabitants of one city: Jerusalem. Sabas himself is created archimandrite of all anchorites "under the holy city," that
is, under the jurisdiction of the bishop of Jerusalem.[140] Under Sabas's supervision the monks of the desert intervene in the ecclesiastical politics of
Jerusalem in the wake of the divisive Council of Chalcedon (451). Some
ten thousand monks arrive en masse in Jerusalem to bully the emperor's
nephew, Hypatius, and the *dux Palaestinae,* Anastasius.[141] When the emperor (also Anastasius) learns of this, he prepares to exile Sabas and his
coarchimandrite Theodosius, prompting "all the monks of the desert" to
write a petition to the emperor. In this petition the monks refer to themselves as "all the monks inhabiting the holy city."[142] Later, in the *Life of
Kyriakos,* the theological division of the Origenist controversy in the
monasteries of the desert is referred to as "the recent civil war in the holy
city."[143] At least by the time Cyril sits down to codify the lives of the
founders of these desert monasteries, they have not only taken up the
place of "new Israel" in the land of biblical promise, but they have attached that identity to the Christian capital of Jerusalem. Their appro-

---

[139]The English translator suggests, instead, Isa 41.18–20, 51.3, which speak of God creating a
"garden" in the wilderness and transforming dry land into wetlands. This seems less likely than
Schwartz's suggestion. See Wilken, *Land Called Holy,* 163–64, who also notes that (at least according to Jerome) Jews in the fourth and fifth centuries applied Isaiah 58.12 to their own
hopes of rebuilding a Jewish Jerusalem: Jerome, *Commentarius in Isaiam* 58.12 (CCL 73A:672–
73).

[140]Cyril of Scythopolis, *Vita Sabae* 30 (TU 49.2:115).

[141]Cyril of Scythopolis, *Vita Sabae* 56 (TU 49.2:151).

[142]Cyril of Scythopolis, *Vita Sabae* 57 (TU 49.2: 152–53), also "we dwellers of this holy
land" (*Vita Sabae* 57 [TU 49.2:156]). See also *Vita Sabae* 54 (TU 49.2:145), where Sabas pleads
at Anastasius's court specifically "on behalf of the holy city of God, Jerusalem" (*Vita Sabae* 51
[TU 49.2:143]).

[143]Cyril of Scythopolis, *Vita Kyriaki* 11 (TU 49.2:229).

priation of a rich past in an empty desert space is actualized around that holy city.[144]

Certainly the notion of Christians as "new Israel" was not new in the sixth century, but the novelty of Cyril's monks is that they grounded their "new Israel" in the topography of Roman Palestine. Their "heavenly Jerusalem" and "new Israel" are visible from their desert cells, located in the major see of Palestine.[145] By managing to dislodge the earthly Jerusalem into the portentously empty desert, the monks of Cyril's lives can accomplish two feats: they can claim a space without violently dislodging its prior inhabitants and thus arrogate to themselves unproblematically the status of "natives"; in addition, they can attach that new native, Christian identity to an ancient and venerable source of Christian authority by claiming they are the true "citizens of Jerusalem." The power they draw from this doubled act of settlement and resettlement is evident in the power (at least in Cyril's account) that they can draw from Jerusalem and wield all the way to the court at Constantinople.[146] They are at once settlers of an empty space, yet resettlers of the ancient Israelite capital. By subtly shifting the terrain of the "holy city" to a deserted site of ascetic self-mastery, they can retroactively erase their predecessors: they can colonize without conquest.

In all of these monastic stories, most of which focus on the city of Jerusalem, there is a certain ambivalence about the nature of Christian identity and self-mastery in the holy city. On the one hand, the space is configured as empty, remote, desolate, or deserted: it is a space apart from humanity and history, like the Egyptian desert, removed and thus safe for the radical alteration of self that is attendant on the late antique ascetic endeavor. On the other hand, the space is configured as full, marked, overspilling with a religious past that grants a particular and desired meaning to the monastic way of life in and around Jerusalem: the site of Paula's monasteries was determined by the ghostly tug of Mary and Joseph, not the lively sanctity of the "thousands" of Egyptian monks

[144]See Hirschfeld, *Judean Desert Monasteries*, 10; and Binns, *Ascetics and Ambassadors*, 80–98.

[145]Hirschfeld, *Judean Desert Monasteries*, 10, points out the desolate, isolated nature of the area of monastic settlement that Cyril inscribes as "empty" but also notes how close it was to major settlements.

[146]See, e.g., Cyril of Scythopolis, *Vita Sabae* 50–54 (TU 49.2:139–47).

she encountered. Monastic Jerusalem and its inhabitants emerge in a highly constructed space in which the past has been depopulated and re-settled by Christian colonists. The monks of Jerusalem have incorporated a rarefied sacred past into their sanctified ascetic present, creating identities grounded in an "uncanny repetition" of a past-in-present that can never be forgotten yet never perfected.[147] What we witness in the monastic endeavor, around the holy city, is an attempt to construe an imperial Christianity that has mastered the past victimlessly, an innocent yet still potent "anticonquest," quite a different strategy from the proud triumph of the emperors in Jerusalem. For other imperially minded Christians who did not come from the imperial court or a desert monastery, however, different and more complex strategies emerged in this period for eliciting a new Christian subjectivity from the spoils of the holy city of Jerusalem.

Invention of the Jew: Relics in the Christian Capital

Jerome, who so vividly depicted the scriptural ghosts that lured Paula to settle in Bethlehem, also described a charged moment at which one of those ghosts materialized fully into Christian perception. He evoked this moment in his ardent defense of the cult of relics against the Gallic detractor Vigilantius.[148] In response to Vigilantius's accusation that veneration of relics amounts to little more than paganism, Jerome retorts:

So are we sacrilegious when we enter the basilica of the apostles? Was Emperor Constantius sacrilegious, who transferred the holy remains of Andrew, Luke, and Timothy to Constantinople . . . ? Must he be considered sacrilegious, and now too Arcadius Augustus, who after so long a time has transferred the bones of blessed Samuel from Judaea to Thrace? Must all the bishops be judged not only sacrilegious but idiotic, who carried that most vile thing, piles of ashes in silk and a golden vessel? Are the peoples of all the churches stupid, who rushed out to the holy remains, and received the prophet with such joy as if they perceived him to be present and living, and the swarms of peoples joined together, from Palestine all the way to Chalcedon, and shouted Christ's praises in a single

[147]Bhabha, *Location of Culture*, 123–38.
[148]See David Hunter, "Vigilantius of Calagurris and Victricius of Rouen: Ascetics, Relics, and Clerics in Late Roman Gaul," *Journal of Early Christian Studies* 7 (1999): 401–30.

voice? Truly they were venerating Samuel and not Christ, whose priest [*levita*] and prophet Samuel was.[149]

Unlike the alluring ghosts of Paula's holy land travels who eventually drew her to settle in Bethlehem, Samuel's bones as they travel from Jerusalem to Constantinople are quite real, the ghost materialized and venerable, "present and living [*praesentem viventemque*]." Likewise the authority of the Christian emperor accompanies the venerated remains. The modulation between colonial discourses of conquest and erasure as forms of imperial appropriation has produced the prophet's ancient bones as a material focus of a triumphant Christian identity. For Vigilantius to condemn Jerome and Jerusalem he must also condemn the emperor and Constantinople; likewise, for the emperors in the capital to claim religious dominion to complement their political authority they must look to Jerusalem and acquire from there the relics of antiquity, like importing so much precious marble. The march of Samuel's bones is the triumphal procession of a Christian empire, and Jerusalem becomes simultaneously the site of imperial religious victory and a new epicenter of imperial piety, a quasi capital of the Christianized *imperium*.

From the fourth century onward Roman Palestine became the prime location for the production and dissemination of Christian relics, those bits of sanctity that could be uncovered through arcane knowledge or divine revelation: bones, clothes, books, sometimes dirt and water over which saints were believed to have passed.[150] The rapid and profligate dissemination of relics from the holy land to other provinces of the empire made materially manifest the charged networks of political and religious power resident in the Christian capital of Jerusalem.[151] Relics also demon-

---

[149]Jerome, *Contra Vigilantium* 5 (PL 23:343B–C). Jerome employs a sort of geographical metonymy here, saying "Judaea to Thrace" and "Palestine to Chalcedon," when he seems to mean *Jerusalem to Constantinople*. Contemporary Christian lore had Samuel originate a few miles north of Jerusalem, where it was likely that his *inventio* occurred: see Pierre Maraval, *Lieux saints et pèlerinages d'orient: Histoire et géographie des origines à la conquête arabe* (Paris: Editions du Cerf, 1985), 269–71, and nn. 141–42.

[150]See Hippolyte Delehaye, *Les origines du culte des martyrs* (Brussels: Société des Bollandistes, 1933), esp. 141–259; and the helpful section in Maraval, *Lieux saints*, 29–50; as well as Stemberger, *Jews and Christians*, 105–15.

[151]Peter Brown, *The Cult of the Saints: Its Rise and Function in Latin Christianity* (Chicago, Ill.: University of Chicago Press, 1981), focuses on western relic veneration. Hunt, *Holy Land Pilgrimage*, 128–54, points out that relic production was the special privilege of Palestine. An apt comparison might be the sale in the U.S. of French champagne and California sparkling

strate how intimately interwoven were the material and discursive practices of Christian empire building from the holy city: for a relic to retain
its cultural and economic value it had to be authenticated, most often
through elaborate telling and retelling of the story of its discovery (*inventio*).[152] It is in these tellings that we find inscribed the Palestinian Jew, the
fitful emblem of "old" Jerusalem who served to channel the power dynamics of the imperial Christian city. Günter Stemberger, in his survey
of archaeological and literary remains of the late ancient holy land, has
pointed out the predominance of Old Testament and Jewish figures in
Christian relic *inventiones* and suggests that "a number of questions arise
in this context: do these graves go back to Jewish tradition, are they
found because of Jewish information, are there clashes between Christians and Jews in the fight for the possession of such sites?"[153] These op-
tions—seamless linear progression from "old Israel" to "new Israel" or
fierce religious conflict between contentious "sister religions"—both
mask the political and social contexts in which Christians "invented" a
tractable Jewish past and, indeed, risk replicating the very processes of
conquest and appropriation that are embedded in the late antique discourses of relic invention.[154]

Consider again the image crafted by Jerome, of Arcadius bringing up
the bones of Samuel from Jerusalem to Constantinople, and how care-

---

white wine.

[152] A modern parallel might be the way in which the massive, multivolume *Description de
l'Égypte* authenticated the Orientalized desires of Napoleonic and imperial France, desires
made materially manifest by the "relic" of the *obélisque* displayed in the Place de la Concorde
in Paris: see Edward Said, *Orientalism* (New York: Vintage Books, 1979), 84–88. On authentication of touristic signs see Dean MacCannell, *The Tourist: A New Theory of the Leisure Class*
(New York: Schocken Books, 1976), 109–23, astutely applied to early Christian pilgrimage by
Leyerle, "Landscape as Cartography," 127–28.

[153] Stemberger, *Jews and Christians,* 105. The idea that Christians merely "took over" an ex-
isting cult of tomb veneration from Palestinian Jews comes from the problematic work of
Joachim Jeremias, *Heiligengräber in Jesu Umwelt (Mt. 23, 29; Lk. 11, 47): Eine Untersuchung zur
Volksreligion der Zeit Jesu* (Göttingen: Vandenhoeck & Ruprecht, 1958), which builds on the
titular gospel sayings to attempt to demonstrate a "cult of prophets" that preceded the Christian "cult of the saints." One of the primary sources for this argument, the so-called *Vitae
prophetarum,* has recently been shown to belong to a Christian, Byzantine milieu: see David
Satran, *Biblical Prophets in Byzantine Palestine: Reassessing the Lives of the Prophets* (Leiden: E. J.
Brill, 1995), 22–24, on Jeremias's use of this text and the subsequent assumptions made by
scholars of the holy land.

[154] The same masking of cultural imbalance may be found in certain historiographic treat-
ments of early pilgrimage as well: see above, Chapter 4, on the Bordeaux pilgrim.

fully yet ambiguously Jerome has invoked the language of imperial triumph.[155] As in classical Roman triumphs, we witness the imperial *triumphator*, Arcadius, his faithful army (the bishops), and the screaming throngs (*populi*, as Jerome appropriately calls them) cheering on his victory. We further witness their beloved prophet Samuel—yet here we might pause to consider: does Samuel march in triumph *with* Arcadius, as his star general? Or is he rather the foreign spoil, the defeated barbarian king, whom Arcadius brings home to New Rome in chains ("silk and golden vessel")? This doubled vision of Samuel as simultaneous spoil and spoiler signals the ambivalence of this inscription of Christian Empire. If imperial munificence in the holy city produced narratives of conquest, and monastic settlements around the holy city produced narratives of erasure and "anticonquest," the narratives of relic discoveries produce a subtle combination of these two strategies for establishing imperial Christian identity. In the circulation of relics that began to expand rapidly at the beginning of the fifth century, we see the ways in which the Jewish "other" might be conjured and absorbed by Christian Empire in the holy land; we also begin to envision the ways in which that figure once conjured simultaneously disrupted the discourses of Empire.[156]

The most famous, and consequently paradigmatic, holy land relic was the wood of the True Cross. Ritual and literary evidence survive from the second half of the fourth century describing Christian veneration of the True Cross; the most vivid is perhaps the anecdote that the pilgrim Egeria heard told in Jerusalem about another pilgrim who, in his zeal for a holy souvenir, "bit off and sneaked out a piece of the sacred wood."[157] Pieces of the wood traveled throughout the Christian Roman Empire

---

[155]Arcadius had celebrated in Constantinople a triumph over the barbarian general Gainas (a doubly ambiguous figure, a Gothic *magister militum*) in 400, six years before Jerome wrote *Against Vigilantius:* see McCormick, *Eternal Victory,* 49–51.

[156]Ora Limor, "Christian Sacred Space and the Jews," in *From Witness to Witchcraft: Jews and Judaism in Medieval Christian Thought,* ed. Jeremy Cohen (Wiesbaden: Harrassowitz Verlag, 1996), 55–77, treats many of the same relic *inventiones* (as well as stories from medieval Palestine) and concludes that "such legends serve a dual purpose. On the one hand they establish the authenticity of the traditions concerning the holy sites through the legitimation provided by the 'knowing Jew,' and, on the other hand, they perpetually recreate the authority of the Jew and his *Judaica Veritas*" (77). She understands the "knowing Jew" to be essential and authoritative in Christian traditions but does not, unfortunately, specify how Jews might possibly have exerted or expressed such "authority."

[157]*Itinerarium Egeriae* 37.2 (SC 296:286).

(presumably also through less furtive means),[158] demonstrating the ability of holy land relics to replicate themselves almost infinitely: as fragments were broken up, exchanged, and allotted to friends and family, these fragments rarely diminished the sanctity, quality, or even quantity of the original relic.[159]

As bits of the holy wood multiplied across the empire, so did the stories about how it came to be in Christian hands after three centuries of obscurity.[160] In the earliest stories, circulating in the 390s and early 400s, Helena, mother of the emperor Constantine, discovers the site, which has been covered over by pagan temples, thanks to a "heavenly sign."[161] In later versions of the story Helena makes her discovery by interrogating the "most learned of the Jews" of Jerusalem, who have craftily concealed the location since the time of Jesus.[162] The most elaborate narrative of the *inventio crucis* survives in a Syriac text that goes back to 500 C.E.[163] Recent scholarship suggests this legendary account of Helena's journey to Jerusa-

---

[158]Fragments of the True Cross are mentioned in the possession of Macrina, sister of Basil of Caesarea (see Gregory of Nyssa, *Vita Macrinae* 30 [SC 178:240–42]), Paulinus of Nola, Melania the Elder, Sulpicius Severus (see Paulinus of Nola, *ep.* 31.3–5 [CSEL 29:269–73]), Peter the Iberian (John Rufus, *Vita Petri Iberii* 23.21–24.3), and a host of other late ancient notables: see Hunt, *Holy Land,* 134 and notes.

[159]See Patricia Cox Miller, " 'Differential Networks': Relics and Other Fragments in Late Antiquity," *Journal of Early Christian Studies* 6 (1998): 113–38: "the so-called 'cult' of relics [is] . . . better described as an aesthetic in which division—the parceling-out of the bones, ashes, and other remains of the martyrs' bodies—was paradoxically also multiplication" (123). She cites here Paulinus of Nola, *ep.* 31.6 (CSEL 29:274), on the miraculous "lack of diminution" of the wood of the True Cross.

[160]Various attempts have been made by scholars to push the "real" *inventio crucis* back to the time of Helena: see Z. Rubin, "The Church of the Holy Sepulchre and the Conflict Between the Sees of Caesarea and Jerusalem," *Jerusalem Cathedra* 2 (1982): 79–105; followed by H. A. Drake, "Eusebius on the True Cross," *Journal of Ecclesiastical History* 36 (1985): 1–22; and Walker, *Holy City,* 245–80. Since these arguments rely on gaps and silences, they are essentially unprovable: see Cameron and Hall, *Eusebius, Life of Constantine,* 279–83.

[161]As in Rufinus, *Historia ecclesiastica* 10.7 (GCS n.f. 6:969–70), composed in the opening years of the fifth century. His story is similar to that of Ambrose, *De obitu Theodosii* 42–48 (CSEL 73:393–97), whose version is probably the oldest we have.

[162]The "learned Jews [*de Iudaeis peritissimos*]" appear in Paulinus of Nola, *ep.* 31.5 (CSEL 29:272). Sozomen, *Historia ecclesiastica* 2.1.4, writing in the 440s, states explicitly that it was not due to "some ancestral text belonging to a Jewish man" that Helena found the cross but to divine "signs and dreams" (GCS 50:48).

[163]The text of the "Judas Kyriakos" legend can be found in *The Finding of the True Cross: The Judas Kyriakos Legend in Syriac: Introduction, Text, and Translation,* ed. Han J. W. Drijvers and Jan Willem Drijvers (Louvain: Peeters, 1997), henceforth *Finding* (followed by pages of Syriac text and English translation); see also J. W. Drijvers, *Helena Augusta.*

lem and her determined recovery of this most sacred relic of the Passion had its origins in Jerusalem sometime in the fifth century.[164] It is a particularly rich and brutal story, in which Empress Helena brings her full power and piety to bear on a subject population in Jerusalem in order to find the object of her quest. This most anti-Jewish of the *inventio* legends became the most popular throughout the Middle Ages, translated into diverse vernacular languages and proliferating as profusely as the pieces of the True Cross themselves.[165]

According to this tale, on her arrival in Jerusalem Helena summons together all of the Jews remaining in the vicinity of the holy city (the text specifies "only 3,000"), berates them several times about their faithlessness to Christ, and demands from them "experts in the law" so she might interrogate them. The crowd is winnowed down twice in this manner (from three thousand to one thousand to five hundred), and the Jews cannot figure out what the empress wants from them.[166] Finally one of their number, appropriately named "Judas,"[167] proposes an answer: "I think that she is using us to make an inquiry about the wood on which our forefathers crucified Jesus. But make sure that if one of us knows it, he does not confess. If he does, all feasts of our forefathers will cease and the Law will also be abolished."[168] Judas here speaks as a resistant and loyal Jew, fearful for the annihilation of his people by the power of Jesus and seemingly unrepentant for the part Jews played in the Passion.

Judas's story becomes more complicated, however, when he reveals that his own family is descended from a group of Jews (including the protomartyr Stephen) who resisted the crucifiers of Jesus and, what's more, were crypto-Christians themselves. Judas's father on his deathbed had revealed their family's secret tradition, passed from father to son since the time of the Passion, and implored his son to follow in his own faith in Jesus as the Christ: "You, my son, do not revile him and do not

---

[164]On Jerusalem: Drijvers and Drijvers, *Finding,* 20–25. On the date: Drijvers and Drijvers, *Finding,* 20–22.

[165]See J. W. Drijvers, *Helena Augusta,* 165.

[166]Drijvers and Drijvers, *Finding,* 40 (Syr.), 58–60 (Eng.). I cite from the Petersburg/Leningrad Syriac MS, which the Drijvers assume to be the oldest extant version.

[167]Both as the representative "Jew" *(Yehudah)* and as the redeemer of Judas Iscariot's treachery (see Drijvers and Drijvers, *Finding,* 28–29).

[168]Drijvers and Drijvers, *Finding,* 40–42 (Syr.), 60 (Eng.).

despise those who believe in him; for you will have eternal life. If now, my son, in your days the Cross is searched for, show it."[169] As Judas relates all this to his fellow Jews, however, it is clear that his dying father was not particularly convincing: Judas does not *want* to tell the empress where the Cross is and so ensure the end of Jerusalem's Jews. Furthermore, he still identifies himself as one of those Jews whose "forefathers crucified Jesus."

Not until Helena threatens the remaining Jews with death by fire do they helpfully turn over Judas so he may reveal the location of the Cross. Judas still resists, however, stalling before the empress. Perhaps it is written down somewhere, he suggests. She demands to know where. He delays. She demands to be shown the location of Golgotha. He declares ignorance. The empress is fed up: " 'I swear by Christ, who was crucified, that I shall torture you with hunger and thirst until you tell me the truth.' And immediately she ordered him to be thrown into a dry well for seven days."[170] At the end of seven days Judas acquiesces, and the climactic revelation is achieved through the secret knowledge Judas received from his Hebrew ancestors in combination with his own pious prayers recited in Hebrew.[171] Judas is miraculously transformed by his own discovery into a faithful believer in Christ. He is placed in the care of the bishop of Jerusalem and, eventually, made into bishop himself under the name "Kyriakos."[172] His particular knowledge as a Jew of Jerusalem has ended in facilitating his own rejection of "Jewish ignorance" (as Judas later calls it)[173] and his transformation into the most pious and loyal of Christian bishops. His father's prophecy is brought to pass, as Helena "stirs up a persecution" against the remaining Jews and drives them out of "Jerusalem and from all of Judea."[174]

As Jan Willem Drijvers has pointed out in his thorough study of the legend and its significance, "The prominence of Judas is bound up with the message of the legend."[175] That message is in part one of imperial

[169] Drijvers and Drijvers, *Finding,* 42 (Syr.), 62 (Eng.).

[170] Drijvers and Drijvers, *Finding,* 44–46 (Syr.), 62–64 (Eng.).

[171] Drijvers and Drijvers, *Finding,* 46 (Syr.), 64 (Eng.).

[172] Drijvers and Drijvers, *Finding,* 48–50 (Syr.), 64–68 (Eng.).

[173] Drijvers and Drijvers, *Finding,* 50 (Syr.), 68 (Eng.).

[174] Drijvers and Drijvers, *Finding,* 52 (Syr.), 70 (Eng.).

[175] Drijvers, *Helena Augusta,* 177.

domination and cultural colonization, of conquest and succession that establishes a triumphant yet moderated imperial Christian identity. Judas, the local Jew, serves as a focal point for the construction of imperial Jerusalem and the powerful display of Christian dominion. Judas, as well as the host of confused and harangued Jews of Jerusalem, acts as the appropriate sign of authentication for the relic and as an appropriate object of the relic's imperial significance. Not only is the discovery made by the empress,[176] but it is made possible by her exertion of religious and political dominion over the "natives" of Jerusalem. Similarly, at the end of the story one of Helena's final acts is to have Judas Kyriakos find the nails of the cross so that they can be made into a bridle for Constantine's horse, arming the Roman emperor with Christian sanctity extracted from Jewish Jerusalem.[177]

Yet at the same time that Judas is the conquered object of imperial power and majesty (much like the "impious inhabitants" Eusebius conjured up just opposite his new Christian Jerusalem), Judas is also the new Bishop Kyriakos, willingly ceding his ancient Jewish secrets to his new Christian mistress. Judas Kyriakos is not simply overcome by a brute display of imperial might: he is also himself altered, absorbed into Christian subjectivity, transforming and transformed by the wood of the cross. The ambiguity of his identity—super-Jewish son of crypto-Christian Jews, resistant Jewish sage become pious Christian bishop—signals the constant interpenetrability of those very religiopolitical categories that seem so overdetermined in narratives of Christian triumph over Jews. Judas's religious identity is unstable from the outset and ultimately destabilizes the imperial Christian identity he is constructed to support. He is in many ways like Homi Bhabha's "colonial hybrid": "the articulation of the ambivalent space where the rite of power is enacted on the site of desire, making its objects at once disciplinary and disseminatory."[178] As both the object of imperial discipline and the agent of religious dissemination, Ju-

---

[176]Helena in these legends is generally entitled *Augusta*, emphasizing her close connection with the new Christian dynasty of Constantine; on connotations of her *imperium/basileia* see Holum, "Hadrian and St. Helena," 66–81 and above.

[177]Drijvers and Drijvers, *Finding*, 50–53 (Syr.), 70–71 (Eng.). This use of the nails is construed as a fulfillment of the prophecy of Zech 14.20, also noted in other, earlier versions of the legend (Ambrose and the Greek historians): see Drijvers, *Helena Augusta*, 112.

[178]Bhabha, *Location of Culture*, 113.

das, through the True Cross, symbolizes not only the result of Christian imperial power but its meandering processes. Judas the Jew is a "doubly inscribed figure [who faces] two ways without being two-faced."[179] The mutation of Judas from crafty "native" into pious bishop for that very reason alerts us that more than mere triumph is narrated by this text, more than a simple "replacement" of Jewish Jerusalem by Christian. The old city is not merely razed and built over; it is itself stratified, preserved, and incorporated into a new Christian landscape.

Another tale of relic discovery, from the beginning of the fifth century, makes similar use of the local, "doubly inscribed" Jew in order to authenticate religious dominion in the landscape of Christian Jerusalem. In 415 a priest named Lucianus from the suburbs of Jerusalem had visions that allegedly led him to discover the bones of Stephen, the first martyr.[180] Although he recorded his tale in Greek, we have extant two roughly contemporary Latin translations, designed to "travel" with the relics as pieces of Stephen made their way to various bishops across the Mediterranean.[181] Lucianus recounts how the first vision came to him one night as he slept in his customary place in the baptistery of the church, evidently keeping watch over the church vessels:

As if in a trance, and coming into semiconsciousness, I saw an old man with long white hair that was *hieroprepēs* (that is, worthy of a priest),[182] having an

---

[179]Bhabha, *Location of Culture*, 97.

[180]The critical edition of the two Latin texts is found in S. Vanderlinden, "*Revelatio Sancti Stephani* (BHL 7850–56)," *Revue des Études Byzantines* 6 (1946): 178–217. Lucianus, in both versions, says he is *presbyter de villa Caphargamala in territorio Hierosolymitano* (*Revelatio Sancti Stephani* 1.1 [Vanderlinden, "*Revelatio,*" 190–91]).

[181]The intimate relation of traveling bones and text is explained in the prefatory letter written by a certain Avitus: "So there may be no doubt, I have also sent to you [with the bones] the very letter and description, copied out in my own handwriting, of that holy priest to whom this revelation was made, which, insofar as I faithfully desired and sought out the full knowledge of the truth, I dictated in his same Greek language, but which I later translated into Latin" (*Epistula Aviti* 9 [Vanderlinden, "*Revelatio,*" 189]). All translations from the *Revelatio* are my own. Vanderlinden, "*Revelatio,*" 186, concludes that version A of the text is Avitus's translation, whereas the fuller and less lacunose version B comes from "la version officielle de la lettre de Lucien, faite par ordre de l'évêque Jean [de Jérusalem]."

[182]It is unclear what the term *hieroprepēn* signifies here: in biblical Greek it just means "reverend," although apparently Avitus (or whoever translated version A) wanted to emphasize the "priestly" root of the word and thus gives it in Latin also as *dignum sacerdotem* (the word does not appear at all in version B). Since Gamaliel's beard and clothes are mentioned elsewhere, I take it as likely that the term, at least in Lucianus's original Greek, referred to the specter's "old-man" hair (a variant in several MSS reads *geroprepēn,* that is, "fitting for an old man").

abundant beard, decked in a white robe in which were set golden gems that had the sign of the holy cross on them. Holding a golden wand in his hand, he came and stood to my right; and the golden wand pulsed and three times he called my name, saying, "Lucianus, Lucianus, Lucianus!"[183]

It turns out that this well-dressed and striking nocturnal visitor is none other than Gamaliel, "who reared the apostle Paul and taught him the law in Jerusalem."[184] Gamaliel's appearance is clearly meant to be both otherworldly—thus the glowing golden wand and shining, gilded garments—yet particularly Jewish: his abundant beard and his long, white "priestly" hair give his specter a certain aura of "the Old Law."

Like the Judas Kyriakos version of the *inventio crucis* legend, Lucianus's tale of revelation and relics is framed in a straightforwardly anti-Jewish manner.[185] Folded within the tale of discovery is Gamaliel's own story of Stephen's death at the hands of Jerusalem's Jews, Gamaliel's conversion as well as that of his friend (or nephew)[186] Nicodemus and his

---

Stemberger, *Jews and Christians,* 108, seems to think it indicates "priestly clothes" (in the German version, "Priesterkleidern"), which it might if *hieroprepēn* is taken as a noun modified by *longum* and not as an adjective modifying *canum* (along with *longum*). I have been unable to find any use of *hieroprepēs* as a noun.

[183]*Revelatio Sancti Stephani* (A) 2.3–5 (Vanderlinden, "*Revelatio,*" 192). Version B reads as follows:

> As if in a trance, becoming slowly aware, I saw a man of old age, tall in stature, dignified expression, an abundant beard, girded in a cloak in which the lower part was interwoven as if with golden crosses (and he held in his hand a golden wand), shod in boots gilded on the surface, walking around and facing me in silence. When I saw this, hesitating within myself I said, "Who do you think this is? Does he come from God's side or the adversary's?" For I was not unmindful of the Apostle's words when he said, "for even Satan transfigures himself into an angel of light" [2 Cor 11.4]. So when I saw him walking around I began to think to myself, "If this man is from God, he will call my name three times in succession; but if he addresses me only once, I shall not answer him." This one, doubting nothing, instead of walking around, came towards me, while the wand in his hand pulsed he shouted out my name three times, "Lucianus, Lucianus, Lucianus!"

Version B is generally more descriptive than Version A, which was probably compiled with more haste.

[184]*Revelatio Sancti Stephani* (A) 3.9; cf. Acts 22.3.

[185]Version B, which Vanderlinden postulated was designed for the Jerusalem area, is most explicit about this, placing the following exclamation in the mouth of Bishop John of Jerusalem: "If these things are as you say, dearest one, just as you saw . . . it is fitting for me to transfer thence blessed Stephen the first martyr and archdeacon of Christ, who first waged dominical war against the Jews [*qui primus adversus Iudaeos dominica bella bellavit*]" (*Revelatio Sancti Stephani* 6.34 [Vanderlinden, "*Revelatio,*" 209–11]).

[186]Version B adds the phrase *nepos meus.*

son Abibas,[187] and the order of their burial. Additional markers are scattered throughout the text that both intensify and ameliorate the Jewishness of Gamaliel and his crypt mates, similar to the manner in which his long beard and priestly robes are juxtaposed with cross-engraved gems. For instance, Gamaliel's son Abibas, who was baptized shortly after Gamaliel himself, is described as a *deuterōtēs tou nomou,* which has been translated into Latin as "a repeater of the Law," a *technicus terminus* attested in third- and fourth-century Christian texts that seems to signify the Aramaic term *tanna.*[188] Yet he is also interred with Gamaliel, Nicodemus, and Stephen because he was a "Christian neophyte"[189] and in fact is described as having remained "immaculate from his mother's womb" until death, an epithet surely more desirable for a fifth-century Christian ascetic than a first-century rabbi.[190] Place-names in the text are given by Gamaliel in the "local" dialect of Aramaic, translated for Lucianus's benefit into Greek.[191] When the bodies themselves are discovered in their respective coffins, an engraved marker indicates the names of the deceased in Hebrew words carved in Greek letters: "Celihel, which means God's crown [*stephanus Dei*], and Nasoam, which means Nicodemus, and Gamaliel."[192] The layering of identities is complex, producing strangeness and familiarity at once, integrating the alterity and even enmity of the

[187]Interestingly, some modern scholars render the name of Gamaliel's son as "Habib," the likely Hebrew or Aramaic original of the Grecized *Abibas* (see, e.g., Maraval, *Lieux saints,* 45; and Delehaye, *Origines,* 80), as if to reinscribe the Hebraic quality of the family of Gamaliel, replicating the confusion and multiplicity of identities within the text itself.

[188]See, e.g., Jerome, *Commentarius in Abacuc* 1.12.15 (CCL 76A:610), a roughly contemporary reference to "a wise man who is called a *deuterōmtēs* among them [i.e., the Jews]" (discussed in Chapter 3).

[189]The phrase is used in version B: Vanderlinden, "*Revelatio,*" 205. This is in contrast to Gamaliel's wife, Ethna, and their older son, Selemias, "who did not wish to be Christ's faithful" and were buried in Ethna's estate: *Revelatio Sancti Stephani* 3.15 (Vanderlinden, "*Revelatio,*" 200–201); version B adds that they were buried elsewhere because "they were not worthy of our company [*qui indigni habiti sunt societate nostra*]."

[190]*Revelatio Sancti Stephani* 4.24 (Vanderlinden, "*Revelatio,*" 204).

[191]For example, the northern part of Gamaliel's estate, where the remains are found, is called "in Syriac Dabatalia which means in Greek Andragathon" (*Revelatio Sancti Stephani* 7.36 [Vanderlinden, "*Revelatio,*" 210]). This emphasis on linguistic authenticity is compounded when Avitus (and the translator of version B) adds a further Latin gloss.

[192]*Revelatio Sancti Stephani* 7.43 (Vanderlinden, "*Revelatio,*" 213–14). The Hebrew words *kālil* and *nāṣaḥ ʿam* are literal translations of the Greek names *stephanos* and *nikodēmos* ("crown" and "the people conquers"). Note that *Gamaliel* is already sufficiently Hebrew not to require this sort of trilingualization.

past (embodied, once more, in Jews) into the Christian present. Gamaliel, like Judas Kyriakos, can represent at once the Jewish past that has been conquered and the Jewish past that has graciously ceded place and been absorbed into the Christian present.

This combination of foreignness and discovery—modulating the shrill triumph of munificent emperors and the perhaps too-muted settlement of monastics—is typical of colonialist discourses of appropriation, what Bhabha has called "the *productive* ambivalence of the object of colonial discourse—that 'otherness' which is at once an object of desire and derision, an articulation of difference contained within the fantasy of origin and identity."[193] The "fantasy" in the material construction of a Christian landscape through the discovery of relics appears in the collusion of the land's formerly "impious inhabitants," who can both explain and mediate the otherness of the past. Lucianus introduces himself at the beginning of the text as a priest "in the town of Caphargamala in the territory of Jerusalem."[194] The name of the town is manifestly foreign, neither Greek nor Latin; yet not until Gamaliel himself arrives do we discover that this is the name given to the land by Gamaliel himself, that it in fact means "Gamaliel's estate."[195] Thus the visions from Gamaliel directing Lucianus and the bishop of Jerusalem to his tomb function in an almost testatory fashion: he wills his own property to the church of Jerusalem, providing the Christians of the Jerusalem territory with the fantasy of colonial natives graciously ceding their land to imperial masters.

Soon after Lucianus's discovery, Stephen's bones traveled outward from Jerusalem, bearers of this new fantasy of imperial Christian domination stamped with the particular emphasis of Jerusalem.[196] The relics and

---

[193]Bhabha, *Location of Culture,* 67 (Bhabha's emphasis).

[194]*Revelatio Sancti Stephani* 1.1 (Vanderlinden, "*Revelatio,*" 190): *presbyter ecclesiae Dei quae est in villa Caphargamala in territorio Hierosolymorum.*

[195]*Revelatio Sancti Stephani* 3.11 (Vanderlinden, "*Revelatio,*" 196): *Caphargamala quod interpretatur villa Gamalielis.* Version B uses the more technical legal term *possessio: ad possessionem meam quam nomine meo appellavi Caphargamala* (Vanderlinden, "*Revelatio,*" 197).

[196]In both versions of the *revelatio* there is a final vision in which Lucianus is made to give the "greatest plow-ox" he finds in Caphargamala to Bishop John of Jerusalem, keeping for himself "the cart." In version B (what Vanderlinden takes to be the "official" Jerusalemite version) there is a telling explanation for this vision: "For I understood that saint Stephen himself was that great ox and that those carriages about which he spoke were the holy churches, and that Zion the first church itself was the greatest carriage" (*Revelatio Sancti Stephani* 6.32 [Vanderlinden, "*Revelatio,*" 207]).

their authenticating story carried with them the fantasy of dominion and capitulation, exemplified most stunningly by their *adventus* on the island of Minorca, where their presence and power resulted in the forced conversion of the Jews there.[197] Stephen's bones likewise served to mediate, and even complicate, rivalries within the imperial household of Theodosius II in Constantinople.[198] In the construction of this particular mode of imperial, religious authority Jerusalem could even claim primacy over Constantinople, just as the imperial identity of Constantinople could be invoked to defend the particular mode of religious dominion at work in Jerusalem.

The circulating narratives and bones of Saint Stephen and the True Cross provided imperial Christians with a new way of integrating the otherness of the past into the triumphant present, of more tightly linking the expressly imperial power of the court at Constantinople and the more subtle religious authority of the Christian capital of Jerusalem. The historian Sozomen, writing a few decades after Lucianus, produced two further *inventiones* in his *Church History,* both of which draw on the motifs of Lucianus's tale of *inventio* and incorporate the relics of the past into the imperial Christian present.[199] The first *inventio,* that of the minor prophets Micah and Habakkuk, comes into the historical narrative as Sozomen is describing the spiritual triumph of the church at the end of the fourth century. It was, he writes, a time in which "the church everywhere" was moved to follow the pious examples of their bishops and priests. The great piety of this age seemed confirmed when "Habakkuk, and not long after Micah, the first prophets, were brought to light."[200] The *inventor* is the "church administrator" of Eleutheropolis, Zebennos,

---

[197]See *Severus of Minorca: Letter on the Conversion of the Jews,* ed. Scott Bradbury (Oxford: Clarendon Press, 1996).

[198]As outlined by Clark, "Claims on the Bones"; and Holum, *Theodosian Empresses,* 103–4, 107–9, 189.

[199]On the "genre" of *inventiones* see Maraval, *Lieux saints,* 41–47. But it should be noted that many of his examples from which he attempts to draw " 'règles' d'une méthode d'invention" (43) come from after the dissemination of the text of Lucianus (in Latin and Greek) and must surely rely stylistically on this "best-seller" of relic stories. Sozomen was born in Palestine and perhaps incorporates "local" legends not found in his major source, the historian Socrates: see Glen Chesnut, *The First Christian Histories: Eusebius, Socrates, Sozomen, Theodoret, and Evagrius,* 2d ed. (Macon, Ga.: Mercer University Press, 1986), 200–202, on Sozomen's background and career at Constantinople.

[200]Sozomen, *Historia ecclesiastica* 7.29.1 (GCS 50:345).

who is guided to the bodies by "a divine vision of a dream." The tomb of
Micah is even described as a sort of local "tomb of the unknown holy
man": "those ignorant people [*agnooountes*] who live in the area call it
'Nephsameemana' in their native tongue [*tēi patriōi phōnēi*]," a title Sozomen plausibly translates from Aramaic into Greek as "tomb of the
faithful."[201] The element of the native-as-strange transformed into the na-
tive-as-familiar reappears through the linguistic registers of Aramaic and
Greek and the knowledgeable appropriation of the sacred past from "ignorant" locals by "knowing" locals, such as Zebennos or Sozomen.[202]

Once the bodies have been recovered and restored (after some thousand years) to Christian worship, Sozomen gives a sufficiently imperial
moral to the story. This anecdote of discovery and rightful appropriation
is understood to validate the entire enterprise of Christian Empire:
"These events, which occurred during that reign, suffice for the greater
glory [*eukleian*] of Christian teaching."[203] For Sozomen the discovery of
these ancient Jewish bones after centuries is a miraculous sign of favor
from the Christian God. That such a prize site could remain covered over
for so long, unrecognized by the (non-Christian?) locals, reinforces the
rightness and propriety of the new Christian natives. By retrieving the
"unknown prophets" from the hands of the (Jewish?) natives, Christian
identity is once again ineluctably entangled with "the other" through an
imperial discourse that "deterritorializes indigenous peoples, separating
them off from territories they may once have dominated, and in which
they continue to make their lives."[204] *Re*discovery, as narrated triumphantly by Sozomen, is impossible without the reminder of Jewish forgetfulness. Jews must remain present, if evanescent, to reiterate Christianity's "greater glory."

The motifs of local ignorance, divine approbation, and Christian in-

[201]Sozomen, *Historia ecclesiastica* 7.29.2–3 (GCS 50:345).

[202]The name *Zebennos* sounds more Aramaic than Greek, perhaps related to the verb *zaban*,
"to sell." The story may thus contrast the "good" Christian native bishop with the "bad," ignorant (presumably non-Christian) natives who do not recognize the grave.

[203]Sozomen, *Historia ecclesiastica* 7.29.3 (GCS 50:345).

[204]Pratt, *Imperial Eyes*, 135, says this of nineteenth-century tendencies to impose "landscape"
and archaeological "discovery" on territories such as Egypt and South America. See also 134:
"To revive indigenous history and culture as archeology is to revive them *as dead*. The gesture
simultaneously rescues them from European forgetfulness and reassigns them to a departed
age" (Pratt's emphasis).

heritance are reiterated in the last surviving chapter of Sozomen's history, which recounts the *inventio* of the bones of the prophet Zechariah.[205] The setting is a small village, Kaphar-Zachariah, "in the territory of Eleutheropolis, in Palestine." The *inventor* this time is not a priest or bishop but a tenant farmer named Kalemeros who, despite his unjust treatment of his fellow serfs, was visited by the prophet Zechariah in a dream and told where to dig (in a nearby garden) and what he would find (two coffins, a glass of water, and two harmless guardian snakes).[206] Once Kalemeros has followed these instructions, the prophet appeared to him again, "wearing a tunic, wrapped in a white robe," which leads Sozomen to suppose "that he was a priest."[207] Besides the well-preserved body of Zechariah, there was also a child's skeleton lying outside the coffin, at the prophet's feet, clad in royal garments.[208] Sozomen reports that "the wise men and priests" were confused about who the child was and why he should have been buried with the prophet. Whereas in the *inventio* of Stephen the crypt mates of the protomartyr were introduced by Gamaliel himself to the visionary priest Lucianus, here the answer comes from another "local" source of verification that is now in the hands of knowledgeable "local" Christians. A monk (appropriately named Zechariah) produces an apocryphal Hebrew text that tells of the untimely demise of the favorite son of King Joash one week after Joash had Zechariah put to death.[209] Thus a local farmer and an extracanonical (*ou tōn ekklēsiazomenōn*) Hebrew act

---

[205]In the preceding chapter Sozomen promised to relate the *inventiones* of Zechariah and Stephen (*Historia ecclesiastica* 9.16.4 [GCS 50:407]), but the extant history ends with a description of Zechariah's corpse. It is unclear whether Sozomen changed his mind, or never completed the history to his satisfaction, or ended up deliberately excising the ending to appease anti-Eudocia factions at the court of Constantinople, or perhaps even died before completing the history: see, in general, Chesnut, *First Christian Histories*, 203–4 and n. 20.

[206]Sozomen, *Historia ecclesiastica* 9.17.1–3 (GCS 50:407).

[207]Sozomen, *Historia ecclesiastica* 9.17.3 (GCS 50:407). The term *hiereus* used here may signify specifically an Old Testament priest; compare to Jerome's description of Samuel as *levita* above.

[208]Sozomen, *Historia ecclesiastica* 9.17.3 (GCS 50:407).

[209]Sozomen, *Historia ecclesiastica* 9.17.4 (GCS 50:408), based on 1 Chr 24.20–23: "King Joash did not remember the kindness that Jehoiada, Zechariah's father, had shown him, but killed his son. As he was dying, he said, 'May the Lord see and avenge!'" Of course, all of this depends on a common confusion between Zechariah son of Jehoiada in 1 Chronicles and the minor prophet, Zechariah son of Berechiah (or son of Iddo): cf. Luke 11.51 with Matt 23.35, and the similar confusion with the father of John the Baptist (also Zechariah) in the account of the Bordeaux pilgrim (see above, Chapter 4).

are the instruments of the Christian recovery of the bones of an Old Testament prophet, through the additional mediation of a local monk who
bears the name of that prophet: we need look no further for a demonstration of the ways in which Christian identity became intricately layered
with the shades of past and present, of appropriation and colonization, in
the "discovery" of ancient Jewish bones by fifth-century Christians. Like
Gamaliel, the Pharisee-turned-Christian, and Judas Kyriakos, the Jewish
scholar-turned-bishop, Kalemeros and the Hebrew text act as "local witnesses," at once the subject and object of Christian imperial power.[210]

Just as Samuel's bones burst forth triumphantly from Judaea to
Thrace, so, too, did the power of these *inventiones* that so prominently
featured Jewish characters. The dissemination of this new discourse of
power is evident from a narrative concerning Mary's robe that seems to
have circulated primarily in Constantinople.[211] This popular tale probably
originated in the late fifth or early sixth century[212] and recounts how two
noble generals, Galbius and Candidus, having recently returned to the
orthodox faith from the clutches of Arianism, made a fervent pilgrimage
from the court at Constantinople to Jerusalem.[213] Surprised en route by
sudden nightfall, they took shelter at the hostel of an "old Jewish woman
[*graus tis hebraia*]."[214] They discovered by chance a small back room, inside of which were "many sick people, men and women and children
stretched out with different and varied illness and tormented by unclean
spirits." They plotted to discover what was going on, and "having considered wisely [*sophōs*] they invited the Jewish woman to dine with them
so they might be able to figure out how to trick her as a lark and learn

[210]See Stemberger, *Jews and Christians,* 113.

[211]Greek text and French translation found in Antoine Wenger, *L'assomption de la T. S.
Vierge dans la tradition byzantine du VIe au Xe siècle: Études et documents* (Paris: Institut Fran-
çais d'Études Byzantines, 1955), 294–311. Most study has focused on seventh-century versions
of this narrative, revised in light of the Avar attacks on Constantinople in the 620s: see, e.g.,
Averil Cameron, "The Virgin's Robe: An Episode in the History of Early Seventh-Century
Constantinople," *Byzantion* 49 (1979): 42–56. I thank George Demacopoulos and Stephen
Shoemaker for directing me to this body of texts.

[212]See discussion in Wenger, *Assomption,* 111–36.

[213]*Inventio vestis Mariae* 2 (Wenger, *Assomption,* 294). Citations refer to the longer version,
which Wenger believes to be the earliest witness to the legend. Galbius and Candidus seem to
have been "persuaded" into the orthodox fold by the execution of some Arian relatives: *Inventio vestis Mariae* 1 (Wenger, *Assomption,* 294).

[214]*Inventio vestis Mariae* 2 (Wenger, *Assomption,* 294). She is also called a *Ioudaia gunē.*

from her what was in that back room and how those sick and weak people stretched out in it were being healed."

At first the woman refuses to eat with them, since "we Jews eat things you Christians don't"; but they insist that they are "honoring" her with their lofty company, and she acquiesces.[215] They proceed to get her very drunk on "Jewish wine [*hebraïkou oinou*]," and she reveals to them that she possesses Mary's last garment, given to the Jewish woman's ancestress (a servant) by the dying Virgin and passed down through the generations. It possesses the power to heal, and its fame has spread throughout Palestine.[216] We should note here, however, that the robe's fame has not spread to Christians in Palestine, from whom the pilgrim generals Galbius and Candidus might have learned of it, only to Palestine's Jewish inhabitants. It is, like the tomb of the "unknown holy man" in Sozomen's tale, a historical monument waiting to be "re/discovered" by more proper inheritors. The crafty noblemen beg permission to sleep in that back room, and during the night they take measurements of the box in which the garment is kept and have a duplicate box and robe made while they are in Jerusalem.[217] On their return they switch the boxes and sneak out before dawn with the sacred relic; the Jewish woman discovers what they have done only after the sick and dying in her hostel do not recuperate.[218] The robe has, apparently, been promoted from healing in the backwater of Jewish Palestine to protecting the elites of Constantinople. In this narrative, told and retold in New Rome, we see a combination of elements familiar from the Palestinian *inventiones:* the knowledgeable Jewish native who conceals Christian secrets that are retrieved by an imperial hand through trickery and force. Here, however, these elements are deployed in a new context: the prominent cult of the Virgin in Constan-

---

[215] *Inventio vestis Mariae* 3 (Wenger, *Assomption*, 296).

[216] *Inventio vestis Mariae* 4–6 (Wenger, *Assomption*, 296–98). Both the drunken ploy of the noble generals and the lowly status of the innkeeper's ancestor were "edited" out by subsequent narratives: see the discussion in Wenger, *Assomption*, 128–32.

[217] *Inventio vestis Mariae* 7–8 (Wenger, *Assomption*, 298).

[218] *Inventio vestis Mariae* 9–10 (Wenger, *Assomption*, 298–300). The sick as well as the Jewish innkeeper are the objects of deceit: "inside it (i.e., the box) they set the stretched-out veil they had fabricated, as an illusion and deceit [*phantasia kai apatē*] both of the Jewish woman and of the sick people sleeping there." On the discovery of the theft (which the Jewish woman attempts to conceal) see *Inventio vestis Mariae* 14 (Wenger, *Assomption*, 302).

tinople.[219] Furthermore, the tenor of the discourse of *inventio* has shifted subtly, conforming to the political might of Constantinople and not the religious hybridity of Jerusalem. The Jews in this story are utterly left behind—in fact, the Jews featured in the tale (an old Jewish woman and some ill Jewish locals) are presumably all but dead by the time Galbius and Candidus return to court at Constantinople. There is no mixture, no anxious intermingling of desire and disdain, no point at which "they" are inextricably bound into "us." The power of new Jerusalem's discourse of Jewish invention has itself been once more transformed into the banner of imperial power waving from the battlements of New Rome.

Christians in imperial Jerusalem built their religious and political authority on the bones of martyrs and on the fantasy of the cultural colonization of the ancient Jewish patrimony to which they had made themselves heirs. The stories attached to these relics, which authenticated their spiritual power, simultaneously underscored and naturalized the strangeness of these material and ideological acts of appropriation. Judas in the story of the True Cross and Gamaliel in the visions of the local priest Lucianus represented to the Byzantine Christian a new object of authority practiced by Christians in the fourth and fifth centuries. Jerusalem, with its shining new *martyria* and churches erected in face of the devastated Temple Mount, made palpable for the Christians of Empire this powerful paradox of otherness and sameness. The construction of the Christian city of Jerusalem by emperors, monks, and *inventiones* points to what theorists have called the hybrid nature of imperial discourse, the "process in which the single voice of colonial authority undermines the operation of colonial power by inscribing and disclosing the trace of the other."[220] In Christian Jerusalem the trace of the Jewish other must constantly be remastered and reconquered, and it paradoxically repeats the threat of its own resistance and power. This constant remastery, this continuous *process* of appropriation, served to keep those "traces of the other" alive and potent in the landscape of Christian Jerusalem. Those traces of the other, of the resistant Jews from a conquered past, also posed, therefore, a threat to the newly imperialized Christian self in its new capital city of Jerusalem.

[219]Vasiliki Limberis, *Divine Heiress: The Virgin Mary and the Creation of Christian Constantinople* (London: Routledge, 1994).
[220]Young, *Colonial Desire*, 23.

The Enemy Within Our Gates: Jews and Christian Conquest

Through imperial munificence, monastic settlement, and the "invention" of ancient relics, Christians created for themselves a religious identity capable of sustaining an imperial subjectivity focused on their holy capital of Jerusalem. I have outlined the necessity for incorporating the otherness of the past into this new imperial Christian subjectivity, the constant construction and absorption of an alterity that was often embodied in ghostly Jews or their venerated remains. I have also tried to suggest how this continuous representation and appropriation of a deeply other figure might serve to destabilize this imperial construction. The very processes of construction and appropriation that transformed the bones of ancient Jews into props for imperial Christian identity might, ironically and frighteningly, provide a space for Jews to subvert and resist the power of imperial Christianity. Could Judas Kyriakos revert to his former self? Could the placated shades of the Judaean desert reassert their claims to lands inhabited by the monks? Could the Christian city of Jerusalem throw down overnight the monuments of emperors and once more become the holy city of the Jews?

The awareness and fear of this resistance runs through Christian attempts to construct the Jew as eternally conquered and defeated. Just as Eusebius and Constantine constructed the Church of the Holy Sepulcher as the "new Jerusalem" triumphantly facing off the old one, so Christians throughout the fourth and fifth centuries rhetorically reinforced the bleak defeat made manifest in the empty space of the Jewish Temple. The Temple Mount lay bare, a desolate reminder of defeat to which Cyril of Jerusalem, in his catechetical lectures, could point the accusing finger: "Because of these words of Jesus, 'There will not be left here one stone upon another' (Matt 24.2) the Temple of the Jews just opposite us [*antikrus hēmōn*] is fallen."[221] Furthermore, Jews could be conjured up by Christian writers to suffer this defeat over and over. We can recall the rumored Jews of the Bordeaux pilgrim's account, filing in year after year, rending garments, moaning, and weeping over a pierced stone on the Temple Mount.[222] Jerome, commenting on some choice prophetic verses

---

[221]Cyril, *Catecheses* 10.11 (Rupp, *Cyrilli*, 1:276).
[222]*Itinerarium Burdigalense* 591.5–6 (CCL 175:16). See discussion in Chapter 4.

about tribulation and suffering,[223] is able to expand the defeat and humiliation of the Jews throughout their history, "whether from the Babylonian captivity or the most recent things they suffered from the Romans."[224] Jesus may have condemned Jerusalem for killing its prophets,[225] but those prophets have been vindicated by the defeats suffered by the descendants of those old, murderous inhabitants of the city. Their sorrowful history seems to replay itself in infinite registers, a "day of wrath" that dawns again and again:

Let us read Josephus, and the prophecy of Zephaniah, let us pay attention to their story: for this should not only be said concerning the [Babylonian] captivity, but even until the present day, these miserable farmhands [perfidi coloni] (as they became after the slaughter of these servants, even unto the most recent, the son of God) overcome with mourning, are prohibited from entering Jerusalem; and so that they might be allowed to weep over the ruin of their own city they pay a hefty price, and those who once shed Christ's blood now shed their own tears, and let not this weeping be to their credit![226]

All the miserable prophecies of destruction, Jerome insists, continue for the Jews to this day: "These things," Jerome announces coolly, "are said concerning the captivity of the Jews."[227] The warnings of Zephaniah, prophecies of destruction and demoralization, Jerome suggests, apply to the Jews not just in Babylonia, not just after the destruction of the Temple, but for now and always.[228]

Yet this constant defeat of the Jews, the annual reiteration of their divine punishment, only thinly covers over, and necessarily recalls and amplifies, Christian fears of the revival of their menacing otherness. Every

[223]Specifically Zeph 1.15–16: "The voice of the day of the Lord is bitter, there will be distress for the strong ones: that day is a day of wrath, a day of distress and anguish, a day of calamity and misery, a day of shadows and gloom, a day of cloud and whirlwind, a day of trumpet and noise over the fortified cities and over the lofty towers" (translation from Jerome's Latin version).

[224]Jerome, Commentarius in Sophoniam 1.642–64 (CCL 76A:672).

[225]Jerome refers here to Matt 23.34–37: Commentarius in Sophoniam 1.644–47 (CCL 76A:672–73).

[226]Jerome, Commentarius in Sophoniam 1.667–74 (CCL 76A:673).

[227]Jerome, Commentaries in Sophoniam 1.691–92 (CCL 76A:674).

[228]See Bhabha, Location of Culture, 50: "For the image—as point of identification—marks the site of an ambivalence. Its representation is always spatially split—it makes present something that is absent—and temporally deferred: it is the representation of a time that is always elsewhere, a repetition" (Bhabha's emphasis).

time the conquered Jew is conjured into the Christian imagination, so, too, is the menace that necessitated conquest. The interplay of conquest and resistance that emerges from this colonialist dialectic is likewise focused on the bare Temple Mount, on the threat of Jewish resurgence. This repetitive threat was made most palpable for Christians by the abortive attempt of the last pagan emperor, Julian, to permit the Jews to rebuild their Temple in Jerusalem.[229] Scholars generally assume that Julian's attempt to rejudaize Jerusalem was not only an attempt to revitalize ancient forms of religious cult but also to humiliate and demoralize Christians.[230] This was certainly how Christians understood it; church historians writing in the years that followed, however, were just as likely to place the blame for this anti-Christian plan on the Jews themselves. Rufinus, in his continuation of Eusebius's *Church History,* introduces the "miserable Jews" as "seduced by false hopes" and by the crafty Emperor Julian.[231] Soon after, however, the Jews show their true nature: "they began to insult" the Christians; "as if the age of their own kingdom had been restored to them, they threatened bitterly, showed their cruelty, in short behaving with great conceit and arrogance."[232] The historian Socrates similarly dismisses Julian early in his account to focus on the evil of the Jews. He describes Julian petulantly ordering the Jews to rebuild their Temple (since he can find no one else in the empire with his gory taste for animal sacrifice), and then promptly moving off the stage to wage his ill-fated campaign against the Persians. All the persistent malice rests with the Jews themselves: "The Jews, who had been desiring to seize the opportunity to build up their Temple once more in order to make sacrifices, became zealous for the task. They showed themselves to be fearful to the Christians, and they bragged amongst them, threatening to do to them the same things they themselves had suffered from the Romans long ago."[233] The Jews had merely been biding their time, and Julian's impiety was the

---

[229]See Julian, *ep.* 51, addressed to "the Jews of Jerusalem" (LCL 3:176–80). See the overview of Stemberger, *Jews and Christians,* 201–16, who helpfully canvasses the non-Christian sources on the subject; and Wilken, *Land Called Holy,* 139–40, who places Julian's offer in the context of fourth- and fifth-century Jewish messianism (126–48).

[230]See Julian, *ep.* 51 (397B) (LCL 3:178).

[231]Rufinus, *Historia ecclesiastica* 10.38 (GCS n.f. 6:997–98): *ut etiam infelices Iudaeos vanis spebus inlectos, ut ipse [sc. Iulianus] agitabatur, inluderet.*

[232]Rufinus, *Historia ecclesiastica* 10.38 (GCS n.f. 6:997–98).

[233]Socrates, *Historia ecclesiastica* 3.20.5 (GCS n.f. 1:215).

occasion for payback. The historian Sozomen, although making Julian markedly more villainous, nonetheless subordinates Julian's hatred to that of the Jews: "He did not act out of praise for their religion . . . but because the Jews have such hatred for them [that is, the Christians]."[234] The best way to hurt Christians, Julian supposedly reckoned, was to unleash the Jews on them. In a letter attributed to Cyril of Jerusalem that survives in Syriac, and may date from the late fourth century (if, indeed, it is not authentically Cyrillian),[235] the Jews take center stage alone in the catastrophic rebuilding project: Julian is not even mentioned.[236] The act of digging a new foundation for the Temple brings on catastrophic fires and earthquakes and ends with the Christians rioting and "driving out the demons of the city, and the Jews, and the whole city received the sign of baptism."[237] To Christian eyes the rebuilding of the Temple was a Jewish (and demonic) threat and the halting of this construction project a continuation of the catastrophe brought on Jerusalem's Jews by their Christ-killing.[238] In Christian historiography the Temple episode reiterated the threat of the Jews (who would do anything to reclaim the holy city from Christians), as well as their defeat (all attempts to rebuild the Temple ended in further conquest and humiliation).

The repetition of Jewish threat and Christian victory also reinforced notions of Christian imperial triumph, centered on the holy city. Julian, in terms of imperial Christianity, is nothing less than the anti-Constantine: Theodoret of Cyrrhus remarks that Julian "supplied as much [money] as possible, having commanded this, not operating out of munificence, but

---

[234] Sozomen, *Historia ecclesiastica* 5.22.2 (GCS 50:229).

[235] Sebastian Brock, "A Letter Attributed to Cyril of Jerusalem on the Rebuilding of the Temple," *Bulletin of the School of Oriental and African Studies* 40 (1977): 267–86 (Syriac text and English translation). See also idem, "The Rebuilding of the Temple Under Julian: A New Source," *Palestinian Exploration Quarterly* 108 (1976): 103–7. Philip Wainwright, "The Authenticity of the Recently Discovered Letter Attributed to Cyril of Jerusalem," *Vigiliae Christianae* 40 (1986): 286–93, defends the letter's attribution to Cyril; Wilken, *Land Called Holy*, 138–39, retains the dating to "around 400." On this debate see now Jan Willem Drijvers, "Cyril of Jerusalem on the Rebuilding of the Jewish Temple (A.D. 363)," in *Ultima Aetas: Time, Tense, and Transience in the Ancient World: Studies in Honour of Jan den Boeft*, ed. Caroline Kroon and Daan den Hengst (Amsterdam: VU University Press, 2000), 123–35. I refer to the author as [Cyril].

[236] [Cyril], *Epistula de templo* 1 (Brock, "Letter," 269) begins the letter by saying he is writing "concerning the Jews."

[237] [Cyril], *Epistula de templo* 6–7 (Brock, "Letter," 269–70 [Syr.] and 274–75 [Eng.]).

[238] See [Cyril], *Epistula de templo* 1 and 10 (Brock, "Letter," 269 and 271 [Syr.]).

battling against truth. He also sent a governor out who was worthy to exe-
cute his impious commands."[239] Whereas Constantine acted out of piety
and munificence to mark Christian triumph over and appropriation of the
past, Julian acted not from "munificence" but from hostility, in a vain and
impious attempt to use the conquered past to undo Christian victory.[240]
Throughout the fifth century, and into the sixth, this attempt on the part of
the Jews to reclaim their patrimony from the triumphant hands of the
Christians, with the collusion of the apostate emperor, became as thoroughly elaborated as the *inventiones crucis*.[241] The menace of the Jews and
their Temple became another narrative of conquest and appropriation to
be repeated by a triumphant Christian empire, one that brought the menace and fear of the colonized into sharper relief.

The degree to which Jerusalem became the material and ideological
focus of imperial Christian identity, as well as the degree to which Jews
were integral to that imperial Christian identity as the repeatedly conquered "enemy within," is most palpable in a later set of texts concerning
the fall of Jerusalem in the year 614 to Persian invaders. In the various
Christian literary representations of this massive defeat of imperial Christianity the Jews stand out as treacherous villains.[242] The most detailed account of the fall of Jerusalem from the period comes from a local monk,
Stratēgios.[243] One part of the narrative deals with the specific atrocities

[239]Theodoret, *Historia ecclesiastica* 3.20.3 (GCS 44:199).

[240]Stemberger, *Jews and Christians*, 206–7.

[241]See David Levenson, "Julian's Attempts to Rebuild the Temple: An Inventory of Ancient and Medieval Sources," in *Of Scribes and Scrolls: Studies on the Hebrew Bible, Intertestamental Judaism, and Christian Origins Presented to John Strugnell on the Occasion of his Sixtieth
Birthday*, ed. Harold W. Attridge, John J. Collins, and Thomas H. Tobin, S.J. (Lanham, Md.:
University Press of America, 1990), 261–79. I thank Stephen Shoemaker and Jan Willem Drijvers for bringing this survey of sources to my attention. See also Stemberger, *Jews and Christians*, 203–6 and notes. The *Life of Barṣoma*, with its conflict with Eudocia (see above), no
doubt draws on this same persistent fear/triumph dichotomy.

[242]Sophronius, who later became patriarch of Jerusalem, refers to the Jews of this period as
"friends of the Persians" in one of his recondite poems: *Anacreontica* 14.61 (text in *Sophronii
Anacreontica*, ed. M. Gigante [Rome: Gismondi, 1957], 105).

[243]The account survives in Georgian and Arabic recensions of a Greek original: G. Garitte,
La prise de Jérusalem par les Perses en 614, CSCO 202, Scriptores Iberici 11 (Georgian text),
CSCO 203, Scriptores Iberici 12 (Latin translation) (Louvain: CSCO, 1960); idem, *Expugna-
tionis Hierosolymae A.D. 614 Recensiones Arabicae*, CSCO 340 and 347, Scriptores Arabici 26
and 28 (Arabic texts), CSCO 341 and 348, Scriptores Arabici 27 and 29 (Latin translations)
(Louvain: CSCO, 1973–74), of which the Georgian versions are an earlier witness. See also
Alphonse Couret, "La prise de Jérusalem par les Perses en 614," *Revue de l'Orient Chrétien* 2

faced by the Christians following the fall of their holy city, not at the hands of the Persians but at the hands of the Jews. The Christians are sold into slavery, threatened with catastrophe if they do not convert to Judaism, tortured, burned alive, their churches and homes destroyed.[244] The Christians, glorying in this chance at martyrdom, naturally refuse any chance to save their bodies at the costs of their souls and make clear where the real conflict lies: they call out as one to the Jews that "the Persians are not the ones who kill us, but you are the ones who kill us!"[245] David Olster, in a study of anti-Jewish literature from the seventh and eighth centuries, has suggested that for Christians like Stratēgios the Persians were not the true enemies of the Christians but merely barbarian props: "The persecutor Antiochus [that is, Stratēgios] used was the Jews. The Christian stood in Christ's place, the Persians played the role of Pilate, and the Jews inherited the mantle of Judas."[246] Jews have maintained their position of absolute opposition to Christian subjectivity from that paradigmatic moment at which they called for Jesus' blood in first-century Jerusalem. Given the opportunity, in the Christian view of the world, the Jews will rise up and strike against their imperial Christian masters and make them suffer at every chance.

It is entirely unclear to what extent Jews did assist in the Persian sack of Jerusalem in 614, since our main sources are the obviously biased Christian laments and chronicles of the seventh century and later, which do not aspire to journalistic objectivity.[247] It is, of course, possible that

---

(1897): 143–64. On the identity of Stratēgios (who is often confused with another monk of Mar Saba, Antiochos, whose fragments of a similar but distinct account survive in PG 86:3222–23), see G. W. Bowersock, "Polytheism and Monotheism in Arabia and the Three Palestines," *Dumbarton Oaks Papers* 51 (1997): 9–10. Some modern studies refer mistakenly to "Antiochus Strategos," an "unfortunate hybrid [who] still stalks the literature on the seventh century" (Bowersock, "Polytheism and Monotheism," 9n33).

[244]Stratēgios, *Expugnatio Hierosolymae* 10 (CSCO 202:25–27 [Georgian], 340:18–19, 341:72–73 [Arabic]; CSCO 203:17–18, 341:112–13, 348:49 [Latin translations]).

[245]Stratēgios, *Expugnatio Hierosolymae* 10.8 (CSCO 202:27 [Georgian], 340:19, 341:72–73 [Arabic]; CSCO 203:18, 341:13, 348:49 [Latin]).

[246]David M. Olster, *Roman Defeat, Christian Response, and the Literary Construction of the Jew* (Philadelphia: University of Pennsylvania Press, 1994), 83.

[247]Averil Cameron, "The Jews in Seventh-Century Palestine," *Scripta Classica Israelica* 13 (1994): 75–93, remains highly skeptical. See also Brannon M. Wheeler, "Imagining the Sasanian Capture of Jerusalem: The 'Prophecy and Dream of Zerubbabel' and Antiochus Strategos' 'Capture of Jerusalem,'" *Orientalia Christiana Periodica* 57 (1991): 69–85, who anticipates Wilken, *Land Called Holy*, 202–15, in juxtaposing Christian and Jewish religious texts

Jews may have thrown open the gates of Christian Jerusalem to the Persians; it is also more or less unfalsifiable, so my point here is not to argue for the historicity or falsehood of this collusion between Jew and Persian in the attack on Christian Jerusalem but rather the reasons (beyond pure reportage) that Christians would have had for emphasizing such collusion.[248] It is, I suggest, the inevitable remainder of the colonial discourses used by imperial Christians in the material and intellectual construction of the Christian capital of Jerusalem. The colonialist fantasies of erasure, conquest, and appropriation cannot help but evoke their dreaded opposites: resistance, uprising, and colonial mimicry, those methods by which the objects of imperial authority reclaim some measure of power through those same cultural processes by which colonizer and colonized are dialectically constructed.[249] Christians, at the site of their imperial religious capital, constituted their authoritative selves through the mastery and appropriation of the historical otherness of, among others, the Jews. Yet by making this constant reiteration of Jewish presence so central to Christian identity—by placing Jewish colonial otherness in such intimate proximity to Christian imperial selfhood—Christians constantly invoked their own worst fear, the "return of the native," as it were. As Homi Bhabha has argued, the repetitious incorporation of the colonial other into the imperial self, the hybridity of colonialism, will always tend toward instability and chaos: "In the productivity of power, the boundaries of authority . . . are always besieged by 'the other scene' of fixations and phantoms."[250] The material and psychological fixations of imperial rule—the conquest of the past, the erasure of the present, the hybridization of self and other—will always leave open a space for resistance; in this sense it is perhaps not so naive for scholars to take the paranoid fantasies of Stratēgios and the other chroniclers of the fall of Jerusalem at face value, insofar as they narrate the ways in which the colonized *could* take on the

---

pertaining to this cataclysmic event.

[248]See, e.g., Stephen J. Shoemaker, " 'Let Us Go and Burn Her Body': The Image of the Jews in the Early Dormition Traditions," *Church History* 68 (1999): 783n41, 817–21.

[249]See the analysis of Homi Bhabha's concept of colonial "ambivalence" in Young, *Colonial Desire*, 160–63; and see Bhabha, *Location of culture*, 75: "This conflict of pleasure/unpleasure, mastery/defence, knowledge/disavowal, absence/presence, has a fundamental significance for colonial discourse."

[250]Bhabha, *Location of Culture*, 116.

savage and vengeful roles assigned to them by their colonizers. Whether or not Jews actually aided the Persian enemies of Christian Jerusalem (on which more below, in Chapter 6), there is a certain cultural truth embedded in these accounts that has been instantiated by the discourses of Christian Empire.[251] The very displacement and absorption of the past by which imperial Christianity operated in the holy city could narrate the failure of that religious *imperium* in only one, inescapable fashion. Rise brings fall, conquest brings rebellion, appropriation and erasure of the holy land Jews provokes their unrest: these are the fantasies and fears—and therefore, the ultimate realities—of Christian Empire.

The narratives of Jerusalem's fall demonstrate how the acts of erasure and appropriation most evident in Christian Jerusalem also make most discernible the instability of the imperial Christian discourses I have been describing, the points at which that subjected "other" retains its own measure of resistant power: "Erasing, to be sure, exhibits control; it demonstrates the power to destabilize. But in many instances erasure also witnesses the initiating power of the absent. Two forces, however unequal, are at play."[252] We see how the erasure of Jewish Jerusalem in the Madaba map, or the attempts of monks and emperors to absorb and master the historical otherness in the holy city, not only inscribe the power of Christians to remap their own world but also reiterate and reinforce the Jewish threat that was ostensibly constructed to be mastered. The construction of Christian imperial power ironically empowered Jewish resistance. To be sure, "power through being the spectacle of another's gaze is an ambiguous power,"[253] but it is a power, a meaningful form of individual and collective identity, nonetheless.

---

[251]See the discussion in Wheeler, "Imagining the Sasanian Capture," 84–85.

[252]Annabel Jane Wharton, "Erasure: Eliminating the Space of Late Ancient Judaism," in *From Dura to Sepphoris: Studies in Jewish Art and Society in Late Antiquity*, ed. Lee I. Levine and Zeev Weiss (Portsmouth, R.I.: JRA, 2000), 195.

[253]Anne McClintock, *Imperial Leather: Race, Gender, and Sexuality in the Colonial Contest* (London: Routledge, 1995), 157.

6 ☞ Conclusions: Reconsidering Jewish-Christian Relations

> It is not the colonialist Self or the colonized Other, but the disturbing distance in-between that constitutes the figure of colonial otherness.
>
> Homi K. Bhabha, "Interrogating Identity"

The question of whether Jews "really" assisted the Persians in the sack of Christian Jerusalem in the seventh century brings to the surface a historiographic debate that has been simmering in the study of ancient Jews and Christians in the past decades.[1] Simply put, historians interested in "Jewish-Christian relations" do not agree on whether to read early Christian literature as a species of rhetoric—which would deprive it of any reliable facticity—or as representation—which would signify that historians can safely use this material as evidence to reconstruct the ancient past.[2] This debate over rhetoric versus reality has come to signal, in recent decades, related questions of ethics in the study of ancient religious history. I would like to conclude my study by positioning its postcolonial readings in relation to this particular historiographic and ethical tug-of-war over "Jewish-Christian relations."

The question of "rhetoric versus reality" as applied to Christian writings on Jews from late antiquity can be traced back, in the modern period, to particular attitudes about religious, cultural, and historical "pro-

---

[1] See Elliott Horowitz, " 'The Vengeance of the Jews Was Stronger Than Their Avarice': Modern Historians and the Persian Conquest of Jerusalem in 614," *Jewish Social Studies* 4 (1998): 1–39.

[2] See Guy G. Stroumsa, "From Anti-Judaism to Antisemitism in Early Christianity?" in *Contra Iudaeos: Ancient and Medieval Polemics Between Christians and Jews,* ed. Ora Limor and Guy G. Stroumsa (Tübingen: J. C. B. Mohr [Paul Siebeck], 1996), 1–26.

gress" held by (predominantly) Christian historians at the turn of the twentieth century. The advent of "higher criticism" in the history of ancient religions served to validate certain supersessionist notions about the historical shift from what scholars termed *Spätjudentum*[3] to the early Christian movement.[4] This intersection of historical criticism and supersessionist history permeates the still influential works of Adolf von Harnack.[5] One of Harnack's earlier works was a philological and historical study of the *Altercatio Simonis Judaei et Theophili Christiani*, one of the few surviving examples of a "debate" genre that enjoyed some currency in late antiquity.[6] Harnack concluded that this text, and early

---

[3]According to Martin Jaffee, *Early Judaism* (Princeton, N.J.: Prentice-Hall, 1997), 22, and Anders Runesson, "Particularistic Judaism and Universalistic Christianity? Some Critical Remarks on Terminology and Theology," *Journal of Greco-Roman Christianity and Judaism* 1 (2001): 120, the term *Spätjudentum* was likely coined by German historian Wilhelm Bousset in his *Die Religion des Judentums in neutestamentlichen Zeitalter* (1903; repr., Berlin: Ruether and Reichard, 1906). See the critique of this term by Shaye J. D. Cohen, *From the Maccabees to the Mishnah* (Philadelphia, Pa.: Westminster Press, 1987), 19.

[4]Recent scholarship has begun to examine some of the intrinsic links between the rise of historical critical methods of scholarship in European and American universities and the emergence of particular notions of historical, theological, and cultural evolution. See, e.g., James Pasto, "Who Owns the Jewish Past: Judaism, Judaisms, and the Writing of Jewish History" (Ph.D. diss., Cornell University, 1999).

[5]For an analysis of this supersessionist "theological" model in Harnack, compared with post–World War II "parting of the ways" historiographic models, see Judith Lieu, " 'The Parting of the Ways': Theological Construct or Historical Reality?" *Journal for the Study of the New Testament* 56 (1994): 101–19. Lieu clearly prefers more recent historiography to Harnack's "history" (she places this term in quotation marks: see 102), although the essay as a whole argues for more fluid and localized "maps" of religious identity, which take diversity and multiplicity into strong account. On Harnack's continued influence in early Christian studies see L. Michael White, "Adolf Harnack and the 'Expansion' of Early Christianity: A Reappraisal of Social History," *Second Century* 5 (1985–86): 97–127.

[6]Adolf von Harnack, *Die Altercatio Simonis Judaei et Theophili Christiani nebst Untersuchungen über die antijüdische Polemik in der alten Kirche*, TU 1.3 (Leipzig: J. C. Hinrichs, 1883). The only other major extant example of this genre is Justin Martyr's *Dialogue with Trypho the Jew*, which is generally the centerpiece of discussions of historicity and "Jewish-Christian relations." We know of the existence of other dialogues from the first centuries (such as the "Dialogue of Jason and Papiscus") and the continuation of the genre well into the Byzantine period (see the rhetorical analysis of David M. Olster, *Roman Defeat, Christian Response, and the Literary Construction of the Jew* [Philadelphia: University of Pennsylvania Press, 1994], esp. 4–29, on the use of such "dialogues" in the history of Jewish-Christian "relations"). See also Stephen J. Shoemaker, " 'Let Us Go and Burn Her Body': The Image of the Jews in the Early Dormition Traditions,'" *Church History* 68 (1999): 775–823, who accuses Olster, despite his critique of Harnack, of "following Harnack closely in spirit" through his rhetorical reading of this literature (with a "deliberate disregard for the real social contact between Jews and Christians in the early Byzantine period" [784–85]).

Christian writings about Jews in general, had little or nothing to do with real Jewish-Christian interactions. Jews such as Simon were straw opponents, stereotyped figures against whom Christians could position themselves in order to justify their cultural and spiritual legitimacy to a gentile, pagan audience.[7]

This reading of such literature as a species of rhetorical device served the general supersessionist understanding of Judaism and Christianity in the first century. Judaism, Harnack and others posited, withdrew into its own exclusivism after the destruction of the Temple in 70 C.E.; it was the genius of early Christianity to take up the cause of "universal" spiritualism and become a true world religion. Harnack enshrined this viewpoint in his massively detailed history of the spread of Christianity:

The Jewish people, by their rejection of Jesus, disowned their calling and administered the death-blow to themselves; in their place came the new people of the Christians, who took over the entire tradition of Judaism. What was unserviceable in it was either reinterpreted, or allowed to drop away. . . . Yet gentile Christianity only brought to a conclusion a process which had begun long before in part of Judaism: the unbounding [Entschränkung] of the Jewish religion, and its transformation into a World Religion [Weltreligion].[8]

After their suicidal "death-blow" ancient Jews possessed nothing vital or interesting for Christians to interact with. By reading the literature of earliest Christianity as "rhetorical," Harnack thus disavowed any possibility of meaningful "Jewish-Christian relations."

Some of Harnack's contemporaries challenged the view of an ancient Judaism sapped of all vitality,[9] but his supersessionist historical vision

[7] See Harnack, Altercatio, 63–64, on this "scheinbare Polemik"; see also Shoemaker, " 'Let Us Go,'" 783–84.

[8] Adolf von Harnack, Die Mission und Ausbreitung des Christentums in den ersten drei Jahrhunderten, 2 vols., 3d. ed. (Leipzig: J. C. Hinrichs, 1915), 1:70–71. The English translation of the first edition (in which this paragraph remains more or less unaltered) is rather loose (see Adolf von Harnack, The Mission of Early Christianity, tr. J. Moffatt, 2 vols. [New York: G. P. Putnam, 1904–5], 1:81–82). See the critical evaluation of Shaye J. D. Cohen, "Adolph [sic] Harnack's 'The Mission and Expansion of Judaism': Christianity Succeeds Where Judaism Fails," in The Future of Early Christianity: Essays in Honor of Helmut Koester, ed. Birger A. Pearson with A. T. Kraabel, G. W. E. Nickelsburg, and Norman R. Petersen (Minneapolis, Minn.: Fortress Press, 1991), 163–69.

[9] In the pre–World War II period we can point to Jean Juster, Les Juifs dans l'Empire romain: Leur condition juridique, économique et sociale (Paris: Paul Geuthner, 1914); Wilhelm Bousset, Religion des Judentums; and A. Lukyn Williams, Adversus Judaeos: A Bird's-Eye View of

remained quite strong until World War II. As in so many areas of historical inquiry, the racialized violence of the Second World War must be viewed as a watershed of religious historiography, as John Gager thoughtfully pointed out:

The study of relations between Judaism and early Christianity, perhaps more than any other area of modern scholarship, has felt the impact of World War II and its aftermath. The experience of the Holocaust reintroduced with unprecedented urgency the question of Christianity's responsibility for anti-Semitism: not simply whether individual Christians had added fuel to modern European anti-Semitism, but whether Christianity itself was, in its essence and from its beginnings, the primary source of anti-Semitism in Western culture.[10]

A new note of historical responsibility was then sounded among historians of religion. In the light of the Holocaust scholars became sensitive to the ethical impact of their work beyond the academy. To vacate the spiritual vitality of ancient Jews might be to justify the violence perpetrated against them—then as well as now. A new sympathetic study of "Jewish-Christian relations" may be said to have emerged, in part, from the shadow of Nazi death camps.[11]

Possibly the most significant scholar of this new postwar view of "relations" was Marcel Simon; his work *Verus Israel: A Study of the Relations Between Christians and Jews in the Roman Empire (135–425)* was originally published in French in 1948 and has appeared in various versions up to the most recent English edition in the mid-1980s.[12] It is worth noting not

---

Christian Apologiae *until the Renaissance* (Cambridge, U.K.: Cambridge University Press, 1935). It is significant that each of these scholars (in the French, German, and British spheres, respectively) evince entirely different motives for his infusion of ancient Judaism with such liveliness: Juster is subtly apologetic (see vi–vii), Bousset presses the "syncretistic" agenda of the *Religionsgeschichtliche Schule* (see esp. 540–94), and Lukyn Williams is overtly missionizing (see xv–xvii).

[10]John Gager, *The Origins of Anti-Semitism: Attitudes Toward Judaism in Pagan and Christian Antiquity* (Oxford: Oxford University Press, 1985), 13.

[11]Equally significant in the decades following World War II was the issuing of the papal decretum *Nostra aetate* in 1965 (out of the second Vatican Council), which condemned anti-Semitic and anti-Jewish language in the Church and called for "fraternal dialogues [*fraternis colloquiis*]" between Catholics and Jews (as well as Buddhists, Hindus, and Muslims) (Latin text of the decretum found in the *Acta Apostolicae Sedis* 59 [1966]: 740–44).

[12]See Albert I. Baumgarten, "Marcel Simon's *Verus Israel* as a Contribution to Jewish History," *Harvard Theological Review* 92 (1999): 465–78, who points out that the original French version included a preface that directly acknowledged the postwar, post-Holocaust context of

only the ways in which Simon sought to revise previous scholarly discourse but also the assumptions and presuppositions that he let stand. Like Harnack, Simon accepted that the vitality (or feebleness) of ancient Jews related directly to the historicity (or falsity) of the texts depicting Jewish-Christian interaction. Simon reads the situation quite differently, however, and asks Harnack (posthumously): "Do men rage so persistently against a corpse?"[13] Simon's answer is "no," that there could not be so much rhetorical smoke without a real fire somewhere. He demonstrates in painstaking detail (as painstaking as Harnack's) the ways and degrees in which "relations" among Jews and Christians determined the levels of debate and conflict among them. He relies heavily on the early Christian writings about Jews that Harnack had dismissed. In the course of his study Simon reconstructs a robust and vital Judaism after the destruction of the Temple, a Judaism that demanded to be noticed by Christian contemporaries. Simon concludes: "The problem of Jewish-Christian relations in antiquity was not a fictive problem. The two religions confronted each other, in a conflict the principal aspects of which I have attempted to determine. Judaism, from one end to another of the period under consideration, did not cease to bother the Church."[14] Simon's revision of ancient Jewish-Christian "conflict" responded to a perceived need for a more fair and judicious evaluation of post-Temple Judaism, and it has remained highly influential.[15]

---

this study (although Simon is rather equivocal on the relation between "history" and theology here). The preface was not included in the English translation.

[13]Marcel Simon, *Verus Israel: A Study in the Relations Between Christians and Jews in the Roman Empire (135–425)*, tr. H. McKeating (Oxford: Oxford University Press, 1986), 140. Although I am citing from the 1986 English translation, the original French is equally colorful (if less gendered): "S'acharne-t-on avec une telle obstination sur un cadavre?" (Marcel Simon, *Verus Israel: Étude sur les relations entre Chrétiens et Juifs dans l'Empire Romain (135–425)* [Paris: Editions de Boccard, 1948], 171).

[14]Translation from the French: Simon, *Verus Israel*, 433. McKeating's English translation reads: "the problem of Jewish-Christian relations in the ancient world is a real one [n'est pas un faux problème]. The two religions did confront each other, in a conflict whose principal aspects I have attempted to delineate. From beginning to end of the period we have been considering, Judaism did not cease to trouble the Church" (English *Verus Israel*, 369).

[15]Simon himself remarked on the durability of his thesis in a postscript written in 1964: *Verus Israel*, 385, 390, 395, and 406 (references to the English translation) all note the validation or confirmation of various major theses of the original work. This postscript also broadly treats six issues: the vitality of Judaism; Jewish proselytism; the question of "anti-Semitism" in the early church; Jews in the Roman Empire; the identity of *minim*, or Jewish "heretics"; and the problem of "Jewish Christianity." All of these, incidentally, remain centrally debated subjects

The decades following the appearance of *Verus Israel* witnessed a re-
newed interest in the literature Harnack had once deemed historically
worthless and in its utility for "recovering" the vital relations of Jews and
Christians.[16] Archaeological evidence from the ancient Mediterranean
added an additional boost to the quest for plausible sites of Jewish and
Christian interaction, insofar as scholars could identify with much more
certainty those places in which Jews and Christians both lived and most
likely interacted.[17] But the nature of these interactions still relies heavily
on Christian literature.[18] There remained a certain consensus that, without the willingness to read Christian literature as a type of historical evidence, a reflection or record of real interactions, there would be little or
no way to judge how and on what terms Jews and Christians "related" at
all. Issues of historical ethics in this way became deeply intertwined with
the needs of historical reconstruction: reading Christian writings about
Jews as "real," as reflective of historical encounters, not only allowed
scholars a thicker description of ancient religious and cultural interactions but safeguarded a hale and hearty Judaism as well.

The debate over "rhetoric" and "reality" has been lately reopened, in
part motivated by the criticisms of Simon leveled by Miriam Taylor in a
1995 monograph.[19] Through her own particular postwar lens Taylor re-

---

in the history of ancient Judaism.

[16]Some studies of note operating from Simon's perspective are Nicholas De Lange, *Origen
and the Jews: Studies in Jewish-Christian Relations in Third-Century Palestine* (Cambridge, U.K.:
Cambridge University Press, 1976); S. G. Wilson, *Related Strangers: Jews and Christians, 70–
170 C.E.* (Minneapolis, Minn.: Fortress Press, 1995); William Horbury, *Jews and Christians in
Contact and Controversy* (Edinburgh: T. & T. Clark, 1998); and Shoemaker, " 'Let Us Go.'"

[17]See, e.g., the recent overview of Thomas Braun, "The Jews in the Late Roman Empire,"
Scripta Classica Israelica 27 (1998): 142–71, who surveys literary and archaeological evidence.
The assumption remains, however, that Jewish "vitality" leads inexorably to "relations." Certainly scholarship on late ancient Sardis—site of archaeological recovery and the recently discovered Paschal homily of the virulently anti-Jewish Melito—demonstrates the double-
pronged effort at historical reconstruction.

[18]This is also a result of the relative dearth of contemporary Jewish sources, although the
"countertextual" method of reconstructing "Jewish-Christian relations" in antiquity is often
still proposed: see Shoemaker, " 'Let Us Go,'" 787–88, who argues that "the surest way to
identify those instances seems to be [that] . . . we . . . critically assess the representations of
these Christian texts by comparing them with the polemics found in Jewish sources, scant
though they may be." Shoemaker attributes this strategy to medievalist David Berger (see
788n64) and pursues it in his *Church History* article.

[19]Miriam S. Taylor, *Anti-Judaism and Early Christian Identity: A Critique of the Scholarly
Consensus* (Leiden: E. J. Brill, 1995). The "scholarly consensus" throughout is generally repre-

turned to the idea that much of this literature is not real but rhetorical. Whereas, for Harnack, the rhetorical nature of these texts indicated the emptiness of ancient Judaism, for Taylor, reading these texts as rhetorical indicated the deeply symbolic and abiding nature of Christian anti-Judaism.[20] Historians such as Simon (whom she singled out in her work) in fact replayed this anti-Jewish tendency by reading the Christian literature as evidence of a lively and aggressive "conflict" between Jews and Christians. Despite noble intentions, Taylor claimed, the result of this reading is a sort of "they-asked-for-it" theory of anti-Semitism that places the blame for anti-Jewish language (and, implicitly, behavior) on the Jews themselves. Taylor's "critique" has repolarized the debate about Jewish-Christian relations. Articles and conference papers have been dedicated to answering her critique.[21] The current tenor of the debate is caught in something of a bind, seeking at once to recognize the brutality of early Christian "anti-Jewish" rhetoric without jettisoning some of our only sources for "Jewish-Christian relations." The plea has emerged not to throw the baby of history out with the bathwater of rhetoric.[22]

One of the benefits of colonial discourse analysis, through which I have attempted to reread Christian literature on Jews, is its refusal to separate rhetoric from reality in the way that is presupposed by both sides of this debate on "Jewish-Christian relations."[23] To separate "Christian rhetoric" from "Jewish reality" is to imagine that the Christians who enjoyed prestige and authority in the era after Constantine inhabited a different world than the Jews who were directly subject to that authority.

---

sented by Simon.

[20]Her arguments are similar to those of Rosemary Ruether, *Faith and Fratricide: The Theological Roots of Anti-Semitism* (New York: Seabury Press, 1974), although for ways in which Taylor distinguishes her arguments from Ruether's see Taylor, *Anti-Judaism*, 130–32.

[21]The most recent thorough response to Taylor's monograph is James Carleton Paget, "Anti-Judaism and Early Christian Identity," *Zeitschrift für Antikes Christentum* 1 (1997): 195–225, although Taylor makes almost perfunctory appearances in books and articles exploring "Jewish-Christian relations" in the vein of Marcel Simon: see, e.g., Judith Lieu, *Image and Reality: The Jews in the World of the Christians in the Second Century* (Edinburgh: T. & T. Clark, 1996), 213–15, and n. 72; and Horbury, *Jews and Christians*, 22–25 (generally unsympathetic).

[22]See, e.g., Carleton Paget, "Anti-Judaism," 224; and Shoemaker, "'Let Us Go,'" 786–88, who repeats the call for a "middle ground" (786).

[23]Additionally, in light of Stroumsa's argument that both sides of this debate miss the mark in some sense (see n. 2 of this chapter), I would suggest that his emphasis on a "market situation" among late ancient religions risks flattening the asymmetries of power relations in the Roman Empire in a way that postcolonial studies helps to avoid.

My understanding of Christian culture as *imperial* during this period should signal that the language of Christians was not incidental or without consequence: when imperial subjects speak authoritatively, we cannot dismiss it as "mere rhetoric." Nor, however, can we benignly condone imperial Christian language as "merely reflective" of "real" conflict between Jews and Christians, thereby flattening the imbalance of power that defines imperial existence. In the present understanding of human subjectivity and materiality, writes one postcolonial theorist, "no human utterance could be seen as innocent. . . . The place of language, culture and the individual in political and economic processes could no longer be seen as simply derivative or secondary."[24] Language is not a reflection of real cultural and political worlds; neither is language a merely rhetorical derivation of the real world. Language—or, to be more precise, the network of linguistic and material practices that we call discourse—is itself a site for the production of reality.

This interpretation of imperial Christian rhetoric as productive of new realities has been my central strategy throughout this study. Christian writings on Jews from the holy land of the later Roman Empire contributed to the creation of a world, a cultural universe in which Christian identity took on a new and authoritative role. In writings theological, academic, voyeuristic, polemical, hagiographic, and even historical, Christians enacted their own dominance through the idiom of the iconic Jew of the Christian holy land. This Jew could figure simultaneously as boon and threat, as beneficent absence or terrifying presence. Throughout the Christian literature of the fourth through sixth centuries, the figure of the Jew fittingly inscribed in the holy land aided in the production of the real exercise and internalization of Christian command: to be Christian meant, for the first time, to possess power. Power over the Jew, a theological ideal with deep roots in Christian doctrine, came to signify imperial power over a Christianized universe.

To those who might disclaim my reading as a thoroughly pessimistic understanding of power and religion that denies any form of strength or robustness to ancient Judaism—or that, indeed, it takes no account of "real Jews"—I would reiterate a point I have tried to emphasize throughout this study concerning the interplay of power and resistance. The nar-

---

[24]Ania Loomba, *Colonialism/Postcolonialism* (London: Routledge, 1998), 37.

ration and enactment of imperial religious power, giving it discursive life, signified not only that the power became real but that it also became contestable. To grant potency to Christian writings on Jews, to imbue them with reality while acknowledging their rhetorical form, is not to grant posthumously the Christians of Empire an unanswered victory. I have attempted to underscore, where appropriate, the ways in which colonialist discourses undermine themselves, despite the attempts of imperial power to mask their inherent instability. Indeed, by reading their rhetoric as reality, we cannot but imagine how it could be resisted: "the jagged testimony of colonial dislocation, its displacement of time and person, its defilement of culture and territory, refuses the ambition of any total theory of colonial oppression."[25] The inscription of totality invokes the fear of fragmentation, and the naturalization of power only thinly veils power's disruption. We should not imagine the very real effects of imperial rhetoric without also imagining the always potential resilience of colonial opposition. There cannot but be "real Jews" in this mix of imperial Christian discourses; they are called forth by the Christians themselves, who must then repeatedly face what they have conjured up. This is the cultural truth I have suggested emerges from the shockingly brutal accounts of Jewish violence against Christians in the seventh-century fall of Christian Jerusalem.

When I call for the integration of rhetoric and reality, do I confess that the "real" relations of Jews and Christians in the ancient world are lost to us? Can we never know if Jews *really* opened up the gates of Jerusalem to Persian invaders and took cruel revenge on the Christian inhabitants of the city? Can we never know *why* Jews in their synagogue in Nazareth were unable, or unwilling, to move their own furniture while Christians dragged it around? Can we never know just exactly how Jerome and his Jewish consultants behaved toward one another? Perhaps we cannot, with any falsifiable certainty. But in order to understand the motivations and operations of "Jewish-Christian relations" in a manner historically *and* ethically meaningful, we can perhaps agree with Gayatri Chakravorty Spivak: "what I find useful is the sustained and developing work on the *mechanics* of the constitution of the Other; we can use it to much greater analytic and interventionist advantage than the invocations of the *authen-*

[25]Homi K. Bhabha, *The Location of Culture* (London: Routledge, 1994), 41.

ticity of the Other."[26] Although scholars who have invested the recovery of real Jews from the rhetoric of Christian literature with historical inquiry and ethical integrity may find the abandonment of "the Other's authenticity" a difficult pill to swallow, I hope to have suggested the benefits of investigating the mechanics of that other's construction, the ways in which we begin to comprehend the significant interplays and consequences of politics and culture, of religion and identity.

[26]Gayatri Spivak, "Can the Subaltern Speak?" originally in *Marxism and the Interpretation of Culture,* ed. C. Nelson and L. Grossberg (Basingstoke: Macmillan, 1988), 271–313; cited here from *Colonial Discourse and Postcolonial Theory: A Reader,* ed. Patrick Williams and Laura Chrisman (New York: Columbia University Press, 1994), 66–111, at 90 (Spivak's emphasis).

Bibliography

A list of abbreviations is found on p. ix. Unless otherwise noted in references, translations from ancient and modern foreign languages are my own. English translations, when easily accessible, are listed in the bibliography for the reader's convenience.

Primary Sources

Ambrose. *De obitu Theodosii*. Text in *Sancti Ambrosii Opera*. Ed. O. Faller. CSEL 73. Vienna: Tempsky, 1955, 371–406.

Ammianus Marcellinus. *Res gestae*. Text and translation in *Ammianus Marcellinus*. 3 vols. Ed. J. C. Rolfe. LCL. Cambridge, Mass.: Harvard University Press, 1963–64.

Anonymi narratio de aedificatione templi sancti Sophiae. Text in *Scriptores originum constantinopolitanarum*. 2 vols. Ed. Theodor Preger. Leipzig: Teubner, 1901–7, 1:74–108.

Athanasius. *Vita Antonii*. Text and French translation in *Vie d'Antoine*. Ed. G. J. M. Bartelink. SC 400. Paris: Editions du Cerf, 1994.

Augustine. *Confessiones*. Text in *Augustinus, Opera I.1*. Ed. L. Verheijen. CCL 27. Turnhout: Brepols, 1971.

———. *De doctrina christiana*. Text in *Augustinus, Opera IV.1*. Ed. Joseph Martin. CCL 32. Turnhout: Brepols, 1962, 1–167.

———. *Epistulae*. Text in *Sancti Aureli Augustini Hipponiensis Episcopi Epistulae*. Ed. A. Goldbacher. CSEL 34.1–2, 44, 57–58. Vienna: Tempsky, 1895–1923.

Cassius Dio. *Historia Romana*. Text and translation in *Dio's Roman History*. 9 vols. Ed. Ernest Cary. LCL. Cambridge, Mass.: Harvard University Press, 1914–27.

Cicero. *Brutus*. Text and translation in *Brutus. Orator*. Ed. G. L. Hendrickson. LCL. Cambridge, Mass.: Harvard University Press, 1939.

———. *In Caecilio*. Text and translation in *The Verrine Orations*. 2 vols. Ed. L.

H. G. Greenwood. LCL. New York: Putnam; Cambridge, Mass.: Harvard University Press, 1928–35.

———. *De lege agraria.* Text and translation in *The Speeches of Cicero.* Ed. John Henry Freese. LCL. New York: Putnam, 1930.

———. *De optimo genere oratorum.* Text and translation in *De inventione. De optimo genere oratorum. Topica.* Ed. H. M. Hubbell. LCL. Cambridge, Mass.: Harvard University Press, 1949.

———. *De oratore.* Text and translation in *De Oratore.* 2 vols. Ed. H. Rackham. LCL. Cambridge, Mass.: Harvard University Press, 1942.

Codex Theodosianus. Text in *Theodosiani Libri XVI.* 2 vols. Ed. Theodor Mommsen. Berlin: Weidmann, 1934.

Cosmas Indicopleustēs. *Topographia christiana.* Text and French translation in *Topographie chrétienne.* 3 vols. Ed. Wanda Wolska-Conus. SC 141, 159, 197. Paris: Editions du Cerf, 1968–73.

Cyril of Jerusalem. *Catecheses.* Text in *Cyrilli Hiersolymum Archiepiscopi Opera.* 2 vols. Ed. J. Rupp. Munich: Stahl, 1860, 1:28–2:343. Translation in *The Work of Saint Cyril of Jerusalem.* 2 vols. Ed. Leo P. McCauley, S.J., and Anthony A. Stephenson. FC 61, 64. Washington, D.C.: Catholic University of America Press, 1969–70.

———. *Epistula ad Constantium de cruce.* Text in *Cyrilli Hiersolymum Archiepiscopi Opera.* 2 vols. Ed. J. Rupp. Munich: Stahl, 1860, 2:434–41.

———. *Procatechesis.* Text in *Cyrilli Hiersolymum Archiepiscopi Opera.* 2 vols. Ed. J. Rupp. Munich: Stahl, 1860, 1:2–27.

———. [sp.] *Epistula de Templo.* Text and translation in Brock, "Letter Attributed to Cyril of Jerusalem" (q.v. sub *Secondary Sources*).

Cyril of Scythopolis. *Vitae Monachorum.* Text in *Kyrillos von Skythopolis.* Ed. Eduard Schwartz. TU 49.2. Leipzig: J. C. Hinrichs, 1939. Translation in R. M. Price. *Lives of the Monks of Palestine by Cyril of Scythopolis.* Cistercian Studies 114. Kalamazoo, Mich.: Cistercian Studies, 1991.

———. *Vita Abraamii:* TU 49.2:273–80; Price, *Lives,* 273–80.

———. *Vita Euthymii:* TU 49.2:6–83; Price, *Lives,* 1–83.

———. *Vita Ioanii Hesychasti:* TU 49.2:201–22; Price, *Lives,* 220–42.

———. *Vita Kyriaki:* TU 49.2:222–35; Price, *Lives,* 245–59.

———. *Vita Sabae:* TU 49.2:85–200; Price, *Lives,* 93–209.

———. *Vita Theodosii:* TU 49.2:235–41; Price, *Lives,* 262–67.

———. *Vita Theognii:* TU 49.2:241–43; Price, *Lives,* 269–71.

Epiphanius. *Ancoratus.* Text in *Epiphanius Werke.* Vol. 1. Ed. Karl Holl. GCS 25 (1–149). Leipzig: J. C. Hinrichs, 1915.

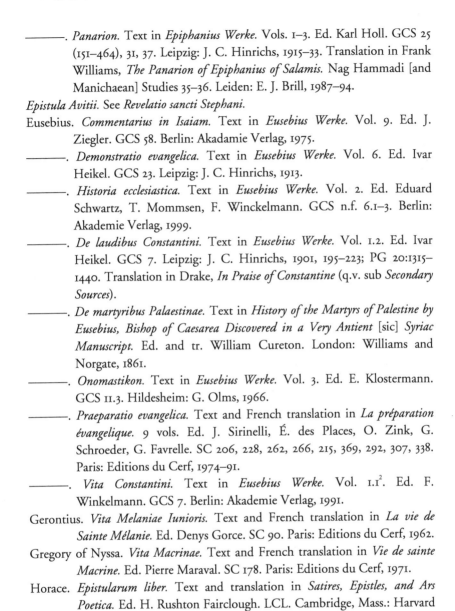

————. *Panarion.* Text in *Epiphanius Werke.* Vols. 1–3. Ed. Karl Holl. GCS 25 (151–464), 31, 37. Leipzig: J. C. Hinrichs, 1915–33. Translation in Frank Williams, *The Panarion of Epiphanius of Salamis.* Nag Hammadi [and Manichaean] Studies 35–36. Leiden: E. J. Brill, 1987–94.

Epistula Avitii. See *Revelatio sancti Stephani.*

Eusebius. *Commentarius in Isaiam.* Text in *Eusebius Werke.* Vol. 9. Ed. J. Ziegler. GCS 58. Berlin: Akadamie Verlag, 1975.

————. *Demonstratio evangelica.* Text in *Eusebius Werke.* Vol. 6. Ed. Ivar Heikel. GCS 23. Leipzig: J. C. Hinrichs, 1913.

————. *Historia ecclesiastica.* Text in *Eusebius Werke.* Vol. 2. Ed. Eduard Schwartz, T. Mommsen, F. Winckelmann. GCS n.f. 6.1–3. Berlin: Akademie Verlag, 1999.

————. *De laudibus Constantini.* Text in *Eusebius Werke.* Vol. 1.2. Ed. Ivar Heikel. GCS 7. Leipzig: J. C. Hinrichs, 1901, 195–223; PG 20:1315–1440. Translation in Drake, *In Praise of Constantine* (q.v. sub *Secondary Sources*).

————. *De martyribus Palaestinae.* Text in *History of the Martyrs of Palestine by Eusebius, Bishop of Caesarea Discovered in a Very Antient* [sic] *Syriac Manuscript.* Ed. and tr. William Cureton. London: Williams and Norgate, 1861.

————. *Onomastikon.* Text in *Eusebius Werke.* Vol. 3. Ed. E. Klostermann. GCS 11.3. Hildesheim: G. Olms, 1966.

————. *Praeparatio evangelica.* Text and French translation in *La préparation évangelique.* 9 vols. Ed. J. Sirinelli, É. des Places, O. Zink, G. Schroeder, G. Favrelle. SC 206, 228, 262, 266, 215, 369, 292, 307, 338. Paris: Editions du Cerf, 1974–91.

————. *Vita Constantini.* Text in *Eusebius Werke.* Vol. 1.1^2. Ed. F. Winkelmann. GCS 7. Berlin: Akademie Verlag, 1991.

Gerontius. *Vita Melaniae Iunioris.* Text and French translation in *La vie de Sainte Mélanie.* Ed. Denys Gorce. SC 90. Paris: Editions du Cerf, 1962.

Gregory of Nyssa. *Vita Macrinae.* Text and French translation in *Vie de sainte Macrine.* Ed. Pierre Maraval. SC 178. Paris: Editions du Cerf, 1971.

Horace. *Epistularum liber.* Text and translation in *Satires, Epistles, and Ars Poetica.* Ed. H. Rushton Fairclough. LCL. Cambridge, Mass.: Harvard University Press, 1929.

Infancy Gospel of Thomas. Text and translation in *The Infancy Gospels of James and Thomas.* Ed. Ronald Hock. Santa Rosa, Calif.: Polebridge Press, 1995.

Inventio crucis. Text and translation in *The Finding of the True Cross: The Judas*

Kyriakos Legend in Syriac: Introduction, Text, and Translation. Ed. Han J. W. Drijvers and Jan Willem Drijvers. CSCO 565, Subsidia 93. Louvain: Peeters, 1997.

Inventio vestis Mariae. Text and French translation in Wenger, *Assomption* (q.v. sub *Secondary Sources*).

Itinerarium Antonini Placentini. Text in *Itineraria et alia geographica.* Ed. P. Geyer. CCL 175. Turnhout: Brepols, 1965, 129–53. English translation in Wilkinson, *Jerusalem Pilgrims Before the Crusades* (q.v. sub *Secondary Sources*).

Itinerarium Burdigalense. Text in *Itineraria et alia geographica.* Ed. P. Geyer and O. Cuntz. CCL 175. Turnhout: Brepols, 1965, 1–26. English translation in Wilkinson, *Egeria's Travels to the Holy Land* (q.v. sub *Secondary Sources*).

Itinerarium Egeriae. Text and French translation in *Égérie, Journal de voyage.* Ed. Pierre Maraval. SC 296. Paris: Editions du Cerf, 1982, 121–319. English translation in Wilkinson, *Egeria's Travels to the Holy Land* (q.v. sub *Secondary Sources*).

Itineraria Romana. Text in *Itineraria Romana.* 2 vols. Ed. Otto Cuntz and Joseph Schnetz. 1929. Repr., Lipsius and Stuttgart: Teubner, 1990.

Jerome. *Apologia contra Rufinum.* Text and French translation in *Apologie contre Rufin.* Ed. Pierre Lardet. SC 303. Paris: Editions du Cerf, 1983.

———. *Commentarius in Abacuc.* Text in *Opera Exegetica.* Part 6a. Ed. M. Adriaen. CCL 76A. Turnhout: Brepols, 1970, 579–654.

———. *Commentarius in Abdiam.* Text in *Opera Exegetica.* Part 6. Ed. M. Adriaen. CCL 76. Turnhout: Brepols, 1969, 349–75.

———. *Commentarius in Amos.* Text in *Opera Exegetica.* Part 6a. Ed. M. Adriaen. CCL 76A. Turnhout: Brepols, 1970, 211–348.

———. *Commentarius in Danielem.* Text in *Opera Exegetica.* Part 5. Ed. F. Gloire. CCL 75A. Turnhout: Brepols, 1964.

———. *Commentarius in Ecclesiasten.* Text in *Opera Exegetica.* Part 1. Ed. M. Adriaen. CCL 72. Turnhout: Brepols, 1959, 249–361.

———. *Commentarius in Epistolam ad Ephesios.* PL 26:468–590.

———. *Commentarius in Epistolam ad Galatas.* PL 26:331–468.

———. *Commentarius in Epistolam ad Titum.* PL 26:589–636.

———. *Commentarius in Ezechielem.* Text in *Opera Exegetica.* Part 4. Ed. F. Gloire. CCL 75. Turnhout: Brepols, 1964.

———. *Commentarius in Hieremiam.* Text in *Opera Exegetica.* Part 3. Ed. S. Reiter. CCL 74. Turnhout: Brepols, 1960.

———. *Commentarius in Ioelem.* Text in *Opera Exegetica.* Part 6. Ed. M. Adriaen. CCL 76. Turnhout: Brepols, 1969, 159–209.

————. *Commentarius in Ionam.* Text in *Opera Exegetica.* Part 6. Ed. M. Adriaen. CCL 76. Turnhout: Brepols, 1969, 377–419.

————. *Commentarius in Isaiam.* Text in *Opera Exegetica.* Parts 2 and 2a. Ed. M. Adriaen. CCL 73–73A. Turnhout: Brepols, 1963.

————. *Commentarius in Malachiam.* Text in *Opera Exegetica.* Part 6a. Ed. M. Adriaen. CCL 76A. Turnhout: Brepols, 1970, 901–42.

————. *Commentarius in Naum.* Text in *Opera Exegetica.* Part 6a. Ed. M. Adriaen. CCL 76A. Turnhout: Brepols, 1970, 525–78.

————. *Commentarius in Sophoniam.* Text in *Opera Exegetica.* Part 6a. Ed. M. Adriaen. CCL 76A. Turnhout: Brepols, 1970, 655–711.

————. *Commentarius in Zachariam.* Text in *Opera Exegetica.* Part 6a. Ed. M. Adriaen. CCL 76A. Turnhout: Brepols, 1970, 747–900.

————. *Contra Vigilantium.* PL 23:353–68.

————. *Epistulae.* Text in *Sancti Hieronymii Eusebii Epistulae.* Ed. I. Hilberg and M. Kamptner. CSEL 54, 55, 56. Vienna: Verlag der Österreichischen Akademie der Wissenschaften, 1996.

————. *Hebraicae quaestiones in libro Geneseos.* Text in *Opera Exegetica.* Part 1. Ed. P. de Lagard. CCL 72. Turnhout: Brepols, 1959, 1–56.

————. *Liber interpretationis hebraicorum nominum.* Text in *Opera Exegetica.* Part 1. Ed. P. de Lagard. CCL 72. Turnhout: Brepols, 1959, 57–161.

————. *Onomasticon Eusebii.* See Eusebius, *Onomastikon.*

————. *Praefationes in libris veteris testamenti.* Vulgate: Text in *Biblia sacra iuxta Vulgatam versionem.* 2 vols. Ed. R. Weber et al. Stuttgart: Würtembergische Bibelanstalt, 1964. Septuagint: PL 28–29.

————. *Tractatus de psalmis.* Text in *Opera Homiletica.* Part 1. Ed. G. Morin. CCL 78. Turnhout: Brepols, 1958, 3–447.

————. *De viris inlustribus.* Text in *Hieronymi Liber de Viris Inlustribus.* Ed. E. C. Richardson. TU 14.1. Leipzig: J. C. Hinrichs, 1896.

————. *Vita Hilarionis.* Text and Italian translation in *Vita di Martino, Vita di Ilarione, In Memoria di Paola.* Ed. A. A. R. Bastiaensen and Jan W. Smit, intro. Christine Mohrmann, tr. Luca Canali and Claudio Moreschini. Vite dei Santi 4. Milan: Fondazione Lorenzo Valla, 1975, 69–143.

John Rufus. *Vita Petri Iberi.* Text and German translation in Richard Raabe, *Petrus der Iberer: Ein Charakterbild zur Kirchen- und Sittengeschichte des fünften Jahrhunderts.* Leipzig: J. C. Hinrichs, 1895.

Julian. *Epistulae.* Text and translation in *The Works of the Emperor Julian.* Vol. 3. Ed. William Cave Wright. LCL. New York: Putnam, 1923.

Julius Africanus. *Epistula ad Origenem.* Text and French translation in *Origène: Sur les écritures; Philocalie, 1–20; Lettre à Africanus sur l'histoire de Suzanne.* Ed. Nicholas De Lange. SC 302. Paris: Editions du Cerf, 1983, 514–21.

Justin Martyr. *Apologia.* Text and French translation in *Saint Justin, Apologies: Introduction, texte critique, traduction, commentaire et index.* Ed. André Wartelle. Paris: Études Augustiniennes, 1987.

Leviticus Rabbah. Text in *Midrash Wayyikra Rabbah, a Critical Edition Based on Mss. and Genizah Fragments with Variants and Notes.* 5 vols. Ed. Mordecai Margulies. Jerusalem: Keren Yehudah Leb, 1953–60.

Life of Barsoma (see Nau, "Résumé des monographies syriaques," sub *Secondary Sources*).

"Nostra Aetate." *Acta Apostolicae Sedis* 59 (1966): 740–44.

Origen. *Commentariorum series in Matthaeum.* PG 13:1599–1800.

———. *Commentarius in Matthaeum.* Text and French translation in *Commentaire sur l'Évangile selon Matthieu.* Ed. R. Girod. SC 162. Paris: Editions du Cerf, 1970. Text in *Origenes Werke.* Vol. 10. GCS 38. Ed. E. Benz and E. Klostermann. Leipzig: J. C. Hinrichs, 1935.

———. *Commentarius in psalmo 37.* Text and French translation in *Homélies sur les Psaumes 36 à 38.* Ed. Emanuela Prinzivalli, Henri Crouzel, and Luc Brésard. SC 411. Paris: Editions du Cerf, 1995, 258–327.

———. *Contra Celsum.* Text and French translation in *Contre Celse.* 5 vols. Ed. Marcel Borret. SC 132, 136, 147, 150, 227. Paris: Editions du Cerf, 1967–76.

———. *Epistula ad Africanum.* Text and French translation in *Origène: Sur les écritures; Philocalie, 1–20; Lettre à Africanus sur l'histoire de Suzanne.* Ed. Nicholas De Lange. SC 302. Paris: Editions du Cerf, 1983, 522–73.

———. *Exhortatio ad martyrium.* Text in *Origenes Werke.* Vol. 1. Ed. P. Koetschau. GCS 2. Leipzig: J. C. Hinrichs, 1899.

———. *Homiliae in Ezechielem.* Text and French translation in *Homélies sur Ézéchiel.* Ed. Marcel Borret. SC 352. Paris: Editions du Cerf, 1989.

———. *Homiliae in Ieremiam.* Text and French translation in *Homélies sur Jérémie.* 2 vols. Ed. Pierre Husson and Pierre Nautin. SC 238. Paris: Editions du Cerf, 1976–77.

———. *De principiis.* Text and French translation in *Traité des principes.* 5 vols. Ed. Henri Crouzel and M. Simonetti. SC 252, 253, 268, 269, 312. Paris: Editions du Cerf, 1978–84.

———. *Selecta in Genesim.* PG 12:91–146.

———. *Selecta in Psalmo 1.* PG 12:1075–1100.

Origo Constantini. Text in *Origo Constantini, Anonymus Valesianus,* part 1, *Text und Kommentar.* Ed. Ingemar König. Trier Historische Forschungen 11. Trier: Verlag Trierer Historische Forshungen, 1987.

Palladius. *Historia Lausiaca.* Text and Italian translation in *Palladio: La storia Lausiaca.* Ed. G. J. M. Bartelink, intro. Christine Mohrmann, tr. Marino Barchiesi. Vite dei Santi 2. Milan: Fondazione Lorenzo Valla, 1974.

Paulinus of Nola. *Epistulae.* Text in *Sancti Pontii Meropii Paulini Nolani Opera.* 2nd ed. Vol. 1. Ed. William Hartel and Margit Kamptner. CSEL 29. Vienna: Verlag der Österreichischen Akademie der Wissenschaften, 1999.

Pausanias. *Graeciae descriptio.* Text and translation in *Pausanias' Description of Greece.* 5 vols. Ed. W. H. S. Jones. LCL. New York: Putnam, 1918–35.

Peter the Deacon. *Liber de locis sanctis.* Text in *Itineraria et alia geographica.* Ed. R. Weber. CCL 175. Turnhout: Brepols, 1965, 91–103.

Procopius. *Aedificia.* Text and translation in *Procopius.* Vol. 7. Ed. H. B. Dewing. LCL. Cambridge, Mass.: Harvard University Press, 1940.

Protoevangelium Iacobi. See Émile Stycker, sub *Secondary Sources.*

Revelatio sancti Stephani. Text in S. Vanderlinden. *"Revelatio Sancti Stephani* (BHL 7850–56)." *Revue des Études Byzantines* 6 (1946): 178–217.

Rufinus. *Apologia contra Hieronymum.* Text in *Opera.* Ed. M. Simonetti. CCL 20. Turnhout: Brepols, 1961, 37–123.

———. *Historia ecclesiastica.* See Eusebius, *Historia ecclesiastica.*

———. *Praefationes in libros Origenis Periarchon.* Text in *Opera.* Ed. P. Koetschau. CCL 20. Turnhout: Brepols, 1961, 245–48.

Socrates. *Historia ecclesiastica.* Text in *Kirchengeschichte.* Ed. G. C. Hansen. GCS n.f. 1. Berlin: Akademie Verlag, 1995.

Sophronius. *Anacreontica.* Text in *Sophronii Anacreontica.* Ed. M. Gigante. Rome: Gismondi, 1957.

Sozomen. *Historia ecclesiastica.* Text in *Kirchengeschichte Sozomenus.* Ed. Joseph Bidez. GCS 50. Berlin: Akademie Verlag, 1957.

Stratēgios. *Expugnatio Hierosolymae.* Texts and translations: G. Garrite. *La prise de Jérusalem par les Perses en 614.* CSCO 202, Scriptores Iberici 11 (Georgian text); CSCO 203, Scriptores Iberici 12 (Latin translation). Louvain: CSCO, 1960. Idem. *Expugnationis Hiersolymae A.D. 614 Recensiones Arabicae.* CSCO 340 and 347, Scriptores Arabaci 26 and 28 (Arabic texts). CSCO 341 and 348, Scriptores Arabaci 27 and 29 (Latin translations). Louvain: CSCO, 1973–74.

Suetonius. *De vita Caesarum.* Text and translation in *Suetonius.* 2 vols. Ed. J. C.

Rolfe. LCL. New York: Macmillan, 1914.

Symmachus. *Epistulae*. Text in *Symmaque: Lettres*. Ed. J.-P. Callu. Paris: Société Édition Belles Lettres, 1972–95.

Tacitus. *Historia*. Text and translation in *Tacitus: The Histories*. 4 vols. Ed. John Jackson. LCL. Cambridge, Mass.: Harvard University Press, 1925–37.

Talmud Bavli. Text in *Talmud Bavli*. 20 vols. Vilna: Almanah & Romm, 1880–92 (repr., N.p.: Jerusalem, 1980). Translation in *The Babylonian Talmud*. 34 vols. Ed. I. Epstein et al. London: Soncino Press, 1935–52.

Talmud Yerushalmi. Text in *Talmud Yerushalmi*. 7 vols. Vilna: Romm, 1922 (repr., N.p.: Jerusalem, 1970).

Tertullian. *Adversus Marcionem*. Text in *Opera Catholica, Adversus Marcionem*. Ed. Aem. Kroymann. CCL 1. Turnhout: Brepols, 1954, 441–726.

———. *De carne Christi*. Text in *Opera Montanistica*. Ed. Aem. Kroymann. CCL 2. Turnhout: Brepols, 1954, 873–917.

———. *De resurrectione mortuorum*. Text in *Opera Montanistica*. Ed. J. G. P. Borleffs. CCL 2. Turnhout: Brepols, 1954, 921–1012.

Theodoret. *Historia ecclesiastica*. Text in *Kirchengeschichte*. Ed. Léon Parmentier. GCS 44 (19). Berlin: Akademie Verlag, 1954.

Valerius Bergidensis. *Epistula de beatissima Egeria*. Text and French translation in *Égérie, Journal de voyage*. Ed. Manuel C. Díaz y Díaz. SC 296. Paris: Editions du Cerf, 1982, 336–49.

Vita Charitonis. Text in G. Garitte. "La vie prémétaphrastique de s. Chariton." *Bulletin de l'Institut Historique Belge de Rome* 21 (1941): 5–46. Translation in Leah di Segni. "Life of Chariton." In *Ascetic Behavior in Greco-Roman Antiquity*. Ed. Vincent L. Wimbush. Studies in Antiquity and Christianity. Minneapolis, Minn.: Fortress Press, 1990, 393–421.

Vita Epiphanii. PG 41:23–114.

Zosimus. *Nova historia*. Text in *Histoire Nouvelle de Zosime*. Ed. François Paschoud. Paris: Editions "Les Belles Lettres," 1971.

Secondary Sources

Adkin, Neil. "A Note on Jerome's Knowledge of Hebrew." *Euphrosyne* 23 (1995): 243–45.

Adler, William. "Eusebius' *Chronicle* and Its Legacy." In Attridge and Hata, *Eusebius* (q.v.), 467–91.

Aijaz, Ahmad. *In Theory: Classes, Nations, Literatures*. Verso: London, 1992.

Alcock, Susan E. *Graecia Capta: The Landscapes of Roman Greece.* Cambridge, U.K.: Cambridge University Press, 1993.

Alexander, Philip S. "Jerusalem as the *Omphalos* of the World: On the History of a Geographical Concept." In Levine, *Jerusalem* (q.v.), 104–19.

Anderson, Benedict. *Imagined Communities: Reflections on the Origin and Spread of Nationalism.* Rev. ed. London: Verso, 1991.

Arafat, K. W. *Pausanias' Greece: Ancient Artists and Roman Rulers.* Cambridge, U.K.: Cambridge University Press, 1996.

Armstrong, Gregory. "Imperial Church Building in the Holy Land in the Fourth Century." *Biblical Archaeologist* 30, no. 3 (1976): 90–102.

Attridge, Harold, and Gohei Hata, eds. *Eusebius, Christianity, and Judaism.* Detroit, Mich.: Wayne State University Press, 1992.

Aviam, Mordechai. "Christian Galilee in the Byzantine Period." In Meyers, *Galilee* (q.v.), 281–300.

Avi-Yonah, Michael. *The Jews of Palestine.* New York: Schocken, 1976.

———. *The Madaba Mosaic Map with Introduction and Commentary.* Jerusalem: Israel Exploration Society, 1954.

Baker, Alan R. H., and Gideon Biger, eds. *Ideology and Landscape in Historical Perspective: Essays on the Meanings of Some Places in the Past.* Cambridge Studies in Historical Geography. Cambridge, U.K.: Cambridge University Press, 1992.

Bammel, C. P. "Die Hexapla des Origenes: Die *Hebraica Veritas* im Streit der Meinungen." *Augustinianum* 28 (1988): 125–49.

Bardy, Gustave. "Saint Jérôme et ses maîtres hébreux." *Revue Bénedictine* 46 (1934): 145–64.

———. "Les traditions juives dans l'oeuvre d'Origène." *Revue Biblique* 34 (1925): 217–52.

Barnes, T. D. *Athanasius and Constantius: Theology and Politics in the Constantinian Empire.* Cambridge, Mass.: Harvard University Press, 1993.

———. "The Composition of Eusebius' *Onomasticon*." *Journal of Theological Studies,* n.s., 26 (1975): 412–14.

———. *Constantine and Eusebius.* Cambridge, Mass.: Harvard University Press, 1981.

———. *The New Empire of Diocletian and Constantine.* Cambridge, Mass.: Harvard University Press, 1982.

Barr, James. "St. Jerome and the Sounds of Hebrew." *Journal of Semitic Studies* 12 (1967): 1–36.

Baumgarten, Albert I. "Marcel Simon's *Verus Israel* as a Contribution to Jewish

History." *Harvard Theological Review* 92 (1999): 465–78.

Baur, Ferdinand Christian. "Die Christuspartei in der korinthischen Gemeinde, der Gegensatz des petrinischen und paulinischen Christentums in der ältesten Kirche, der Apostel Paulus in Rome." *Tübinger Zeitschrift für Theologie* 5, no. 4 (1831): 61–206.

Bell, Catherine. *Ritual Theory, Ritual Practice.* New York: Oxford University Press, 1992.

Bhabha, Homi K. *The Location of Culture.* London: Routledge, 1994.

Binns, John. *Ascetics and Ambassadors of Christ: The Monasteries of Palestine, 314–631.* Oxford Early Christian Studies. Oxford: Clarendon Press, 1994.

Blowers, Paul. "Origen, the Rabbis, and the Bible: Towards a Picture of Judaism and Christianity in Third-Century Caesarea." In Kannengeisser and Petersen, *Origen of Alexandria* (q.v.), 96–116.

Blumenkranz, Bernhard. "Augustin et les Juifs, Augustin et le judaïsme." *Recherches Augustiniennes* 1 (1958): 225–41.

———. *Die Judenpredigt Augustins: Ein Beitrag zur Geschicthe der jüdisch-christlichen Beziehungen in den ersten Jahrhunderten.* Basler Beiträge zur Geschichtswissenschaft 25. Basel: Helbing & Lichtenhahn, 1946.

Boatwright, M. T. *Hadrian and the City of Rome.* Princeton, N.J.: Princeton University Press, 1987.

Bousset, Wilhelm. *Die Religion des Judentums in neutestamentlichen Zeitalter.* Berlin: Ruether and Reichard, 1906.

Bowersock, G. W. "Polytheism and Monotheism in Arabia and the Three Palestines." *Dumbarton Oaks Papers* 51 (1997): 1–10.

Bowman, Glenn. " 'Mapping History's Redemption': Eschatology and Topography in the *Itinerarium Burdigalense.*" In Levine, *Jerusalem* (q.v.), 163–87.

Boyarin, Daniel. *Border Lines: Hybrids, Heretics, and the Partition of Judaeo-Christianity.* Divinations. Philadelphia: University of Pennsylvania Press, 2004.

Bradbury, Scott, ed. *Severus of Minorca: Letter on the Conversion of the Jews.* Oxford Early Christian Texts. Oxford: Clarendon Press, 1996.

Brakke, David. " 'Outside the Places, Within the Truth': Athanasius of Alexandria and the Localization of the Holy." In *Pilgrimage and Holy Space in Late Antique Egypt,* ed. David Frankfurter, 445–81. Religions in the Graeco-Roman World 134. Leiden: Brill, 1998.

Braun, Thomas. "The Jews in the Late Roman Empire." *Scripta Classica Israelica* 27 (1998): 142–71.

Braun, Willi, and Russell T. McCutcheon, eds. *Guide to the Study of Religion.*

London: Cassell, 2000.

Brock, Sebastian. "A Letter Attributed to Cyril of Jerusalem on the Rebuilding of the Temple." *Bulletin of the School of Oriental and African Studies* 40 (1977): 267–86.

———. "The Rebuilding of the Temple Under Julian: A New Source." *Palestinian Exploration Quarterly* 108 (1976): 103–7.

Brooks, Roger. "Straw Dogs and Scholarly Ecumenism: The Appropriate Jewish Background to the Study of Origen." In Kannengeisser and Petersen, *Origen of Alexandria* (q.v.), 63–95.

Brown, Dennis. *Vir Trilinguis: A Study in the Biblical Exegesis of Saint Jerome.* Kampen: Pharos, 1992.

Brown, Peter. *Augustine of Hippo.* Berkeley: University of California Press, 1967.

———. *The Cult of the Saints: Its Rise and Function in Latin Christianity.* Haskell Lectures on History of Religions, n.s., 2. Chicago, Ill.: University of Chicago Press, 1981.

———. "The Patrons of Pelagius: The Roman Aristocracy Between East and West." In *Religion and Society in the Age of Augustine,* by Peter Brown, 208–26. London: Faber and Faber, 1972.

———. *Power and Persuasion in Late Antiquity: Towards a Christian Empire.* The Curti Lectures 1988. Madison: University of Wisconsin Press, 1992.

———. *Society and the Holy in Late Antiquity.* Berkeley: University of California Press, 1982.

Brox, N. "Das 'irdische Jerusalem' in der altchristlichen Theologie." *Kairos,* n.s., 28 (1986): 152–73.

Brubaker, Leslie. "Memories of Helena: Patterns in Female Imperial Matronage in the Fourth and Fifth Centuries." In *Women, Men, and Eunuchs: Gender in Byzantium,* ed. Liz James, 52–75. London: Routledge, 1997.

Burgess, Richard W. "The Accession of Marcian in the Light of Chalcedonian Apologetic and Monophysite Polemic." *Byzantinische Zeitschrift* 86/87 (1993–94): 47–68.

Burrus, Virginia. "The Heretical Woman as Symbol in Alexander, Athanasius, Epiphanius, and Jerome." *Harvard Theological Review* 84 (1991): 229–48.

Cameron, Alan. "The Roman Friends of Ammianus." *Journal of Roman Studies* 54 (1964): 15–28.

Cameron, Averil. *Christianity and the Rhetoric of Empire: The Development of Christian Discourse.* Sather Classical Lectures 55. Berkeley: University of California Press, 1991.

―――. "Constantinus Christianus?" *Journal of Roman Studies* 73 (1983): 184–90.

―――. "Eusebius' *Vita Constantini* and the Construction of Constantine." In *Portraits: Biographical Representation in the Greek and Latin Literature of the Roman Empire,* ed. M. J. Edwards and Simon Swain, 145–74. Oxford: Clarendon Press, 1997.

―――. "The Jews in Seventh-Century Palestine." *Scripta Classica Israelica* 13 (1994): 75–93.

―――. *The Later Roman Empire, A.D. 284–430.* Cambridge, Mass.: Harvard University Press, 1993.

―――. "Redrawing the Map: Early Christian Territory After Foucault." *Journal of Roman Studies* 76 (1986): 266–71.

―――. "The Virgin's Robe: An Episode in the History of Early Seventh-Century Constantinople." *Byzantion* 49 (1979): 42–56.

Cameron, Averil, and Stuart G. Hall. *Eusebius, Life of Constantine, Translated with Introduction and Commentary.* Clarendon Ancient History Series. Oxford: Clarendon Press, 1999.

Campbell, Mary. *The Witness and the Other World: Exotic European Travel Writing, 400–1600.* Ithaca, N.Y.: Cornell University Press, 1988.

Cansdale, Lena. "Cosmas Indicopleustes: Merchant and Traveller." In Engemann, *Akten* (q.v.), 609–16.

Cardman, Francine. "Fourth-Century Jerusalem: Religious Geography and Christian Tradition." In *Schools of Thought in the Christian Tradition,* ed. Patrick Henry, 49–64. Philadelphia, Pa.: Fortress Press, 1984.

―――. "The Rhetoric of Holy Places: Palestine in the Fourth Century." *Studia Patristica* 17, no. 1 (1982): 18–25.

Carleton Paget, James. "Anti-Judaism and Early Christian Identity." *Zeitschrift für Antikes Christentum* 1 (1997): 195–225.

Casson, Lionel. *Travel in the Ancient World.* London: George Allen & Unwin, 1974.

Cavallera, Ferdinand. *Saint Jérôme: Sa vie et son oeuvre.* 2 vols. Études et Documents 1–2. Louvain: Spicilegium Sacrum Lovaniense, 1922.

Chadwick, Henry. *Priscillian of Avila: The Occult and the Charismatic in the Early Church.* Oxford: Clarendon Press, 1976.

Chesnut, Glenn F. "A Century of Patristic Studies, 1888–1988." In *A Century of Church History: The Legacy of Philip Schaff,* ed. Henry W. Bowden, 36–77. Carbondale: Southern Illinois University Press, 1988.

―――. *The First Christian Histories: Eusebius, Socrates, Sozomen, Theodoret, and Evagrius.* 2d ed. Macon, Ga.: Mercer University Press, 1986.

Chidester, David. "Colonialism." In Braun and McCutcheon, *Guide to the Study of Religion* (q.v.), 423–37.

———. *Savage Systems: Colonialism and Comparative Religion in Southern Africa.* Charlottesville: University of Virginia Press, 1996.

Chitty, Derwas J. *The Desert a City: An Introduction to the Study of Egyptian and Palestinian Monasticism Under the Christian Empire.* Crestwood, N.Y.: St. Vladimir's Seminary Press, 1995.

Chrisman, Laura. "The Imperial Unconscious? Representations of Imperial Discourse." *Critical Quarterly* 32, no. 3 (1990): 38–58. Repr. in Williams and Chrisman, *Colonial Discourse* (q.v.), 498–516.

Clark, Elizabeth A. *Ascetic Piety and Women's Faith: Essays on Late Ancient Christianity.* Studies in Women and Religion 20. Lewiston, N.Y.: Edwin Mellen Press, 1986.

———. "Ascetic Renunciation and Feminine Advancement: A Paradox of Late Ancient Christianity." In E. Clark, *Ascetic Piety* (q.v.), 175–208.

———. "Claims on the Bones of Saint Stephen: The Partisans of Melania and Eudocia." In E. Clark, *Ascetic Piety* (q.v.), 95–123.

———. "Foucault, the Fathers, and Sex." *Journal of the American Academy of Religion* 56 (1988): 619–41.

———. "Ideology, History, and the Construction of 'Woman' in Late Ancient Christianity." *Journal of Early Christian Studies* 2 (1994): 155–84.

———. *Jerome, Chrysostom, and Friends: Essays and Translations.* Studies in Women and Religion 1. New York: Edwin Mellen Press, 1979.

———. *The Life of Melania the Younger: Introduction, Translation, and Commentary.* Studies in Women and Religion 14. Lewiston, N.Y.: Edwin Mellen Press, 1984.

———. *The Origenist Controversy: The Cultural Construction of an Early Christian Debate.* Princeton, N.J.: Princeton University Press, 1992.

———. *Reading Renunciation: Asceticism and Scripture in Early Christianity.* Princeton, N.J.: Princeton University Press, 1999.

———. "The State and Future of Historical Theology: Patristic Studies." In E. Clark, *Ascetic Piety* (q.v.), 3–19.

Clark, Gillian. " 'Let Every Soul Be Subject': The Fathers and the Empire." In *Images of Empire,* ed. Loveday Alexander, 251–75. Journal for the Study of the Old Testament Supplement 122. Sheffield: Sheffield Academic Press, 1991.

Cloke, Gillian. *"This Female Man of God": Women and Spiritual Power in the Patristic Age, A.D. 350–450.* London: Routledge, 1995.

Cohen, Bernard S. *Colonialism and Its Forms of Knowledge: The British in India.*

Princeton, N.J.: Princeton University Press, 1996.

Cohen, Jeffrey J., ed. *The Postcolonial Middle Ages.* The New Middle Ages. New York: Saint Martin's, 2000.

Cohen, Jeremy. *Living Letters of the Law: Ideas of the Jew in Medieval Christianity.* Berkeley: University of California Press, 1999.

Cohen, Shaye J. D. "Adolph Harnack's 'The Mission and Expansion of Judaism': Christianity Succeeds Where Judaism Fails." In *The Future of Early Christianity: Essays in Honor of Helmut Koester,* ed. Birger A. Pearson with A. T. Kraabel, G. W. E. Nickelsburg, and Norman R. Petersen, 163–69. Minneapolis, Minn.: Fortress Press, 1991.

———. *From the Maccabees to the Mishnah.* Library of Early Christianity. Philadelphia, Pa.: Westminster Press, 1987.

Cohn, Erich W. "Second Thoughts About the Perforated Stone on the Haram of Jerusalem." *Palestine Exploration Quarterly* 114 (1982): 143–46.

Courcelle, Pierre. *Late Latin Writers and Their Greek Sources.* Tr. Harry E. Wedeck. Cambridge, Mass.: Harvard University Press, 1969.

Couret, Alphonse. "La prise de Jérusalem par les Perses en 614." *Revue de l'Orient Chrétien* 2 (1897): 143–64.

Crawford, M. H. "Greek Intellectuals and the Roman Aristocracy in the First Century B.C." In *Imperialism in the Ancient World,* ed. P. D. A. Garnsey and C. R. Whittaker, 193–207 and 330–39 (notes). Cambridge University Research Seminar in Ancient History. Cambridge, U.K.: Cambridge University Press, 1978.

Croke, Brian. "The Origins of the Christian World Chronicle." In *History and Historians in Late Antiquity,* ed. Brian Croke and Alanna Emmet, 116–31. Sydney: Pergamon Press, 1983.

Dagron, Gilbert. *Naissance d'une capitale: Constantinople et ses institutions de 330 à 451.* Bibliothèque Byzantine, Études 7. Paris: Presses Universitaires de France, 1974.

Dauphin, Claudine. *La Palestine byzantine: Peuplement et populations.* 3 vols. British Archaeological Reports International Series 726. Oxford: Archaeopress, 1998.

de Bruyn, Theodore S. "Ambivalence Within a 'Totalizing Discourse': Augustine's Sermons on the Sack of Rome." *Journal of Early Christian Studies* 1 (1993): 405–21.

Dechow, Jon F. *Dogma and Mysticism in Early Christianity: Epiphanius of Cyprus and the Legacy of Origen.* North American Patristics Society Monograph Series 13. Macon, Ga.: Mercer University Press, 1988.

De Lange, N. R. M. *Origen and the Jews: Studies in Jewish-Christian Relations in*

Third-Century Palestine. University of Cambridge Oriental Publications 25. Cambridge, U.K.: Cambridge University Press, 1976.

Delehaye, Hippolyte. *Les origines du culte des martyrs.* Subsidia Hagiographica 20. Brussels: Société des Bollandistes, 1933.

Devos, P. "La date du voyage d'Égérie." *Analecta Bollandiana* 85 (1967): 165–94.

———. " 'Lecto ergo ipso loco': A propos d'un passage d'Égérie (*Itinerarium* III,6)." In *Zetesis: Album amicorum,* 646–54. Antwerp: Nederlandsche Boekhandel, 1973.

———. "La 'servante de Dieu' Poemenia d'après Pallade, la tradition copte, et Jean Rufus." *Analecta Bollandiana* 87 (1969): 189–212.

Dissanakyake, Wimal, and Carmen Wickramagamge. *Self and Colonial Desire: Travel Writings of V. S. Naipaul.* Studies of World Literature in English 2. New York: Peter Lang, 1993.

Donceel-Voûte, Pauline. "La carte de Madaba: Cosmographie, Anachronisme, et Propagande." *Revue Biblique* 95 (1988): 519–42.

Donner, Herbert. *The Mosaic Map of Madaba: An Introductory Guide.* Palaestina Antiqua 7. Kampen: Kok Pharos, 1992.

———. *Pilgerfahrt ins Heilige Land: Die ältesten Berichte christlicher Palästinapilger (4.-7. Jahrhundert).* Stuttgart: Verlag Katholisches Bibelwerk, 1979.

Douglass, Laurie. "A New Look at the *Itinerarium Burdigalense.*" *Journal of Early Christian Studies* 4 (1996): 313–33.

Doval, Alexis. *Cyril of Jerusalem, Mystagogue: The Authorship of the Mystagogic Catecheses.* Patristic Monograph Series 17. Washington, D.C.: Catholic University Press, 2001.

———. "The Date of Cyril of Jerusalem's Catecheses." *Journal of Theological Studies,* n.s., 48 (1997): 129–32.

Drake, H. A. *Constantine and the Bishops: The Politics of Intolerance.* Baltimore, Md.: Johns Hopkins University Press, 2000.

———. "Eusebius on the True Cross." *Journal of Ecclesiastical History* 36 (1985): 1–22.

———. *In Praise of Constantine: A Historical Study and New Translation of Eusebius' Tricennial Orations.* University of California Publications: Classical Studies 15. Berkeley: University of California Press, 1976.

Drijvers, Han J. W., and Jan Willem Drijvers, eds. *The Finding of the True Cross: The Judas Kyriakos Legend in Syriac: Introduction, Text, and Translation.* CSCO 565, Subsidia 93. Louvain: Peeters, 1997.

Drijvers, Jan Willem. "Cyril of Jerusalem on the Rebuilding of the Jewish Temple (A.D. 363)." In *Ultima Aetas: Time, Tense, and Transience in the*

Ancient World: Studies in Honour of Jan den Boeft, ed. Caroline Kroon and Daan den Hengst, 123–35. Amsterdam: VU University Press, 2000.

———. "Helena Augusta: Exemplary Christian Empress." *Studia Patristica* 24 (1993): 85–90.

———. *Helena Augusta: The Mother of Constantine the Great and the Legend of Her Finding of the True Cross.* Brill's Studies in Intellectual History 27. Leiden: E. J. Brill, 1992.

———. "Promoting Jerusalem: Cyril and the True Cross." In *Portraits of Spiritual Authority: Religious Power in Early Christianity, Byzantium, and the Christian Orient,* ed. Jan W. Drijvers and John W. Watt, 79–95. Religions in the Graeco-Roman World 137. Leiden: Brill, 1999.

Droge, Arthur J. "The Apologetic Dimensions of the *Ecclesiastical History.*" In Attridge and Hata, *Eusebius* (q.v.), 492–509.

Dummer, J. "Ein naturwissenschaftliches Handbuch als Quelle für Epiphanius von Constantia." *Klio* 55 (1973): 289–99.

Duval, Noël. "Essai sur la signification des vignettes topographiques." In Piccirillo and Alliata, *Madaba Map Centenary* (q.v.), 134–46.

Duval, Y.-M. "Saint Augustin et le Commentaire sur Jonas de Saint Jérôme." *Revue des Études Augustiniennes* 12 (1966): 9–40.

Eagleton, Terry. *Ideology: An Introduction.* London: Verso, 1991.

Elm, Susanna. "Perceptions of Jerusalem Pilgrimage as Reflected in Two Early Sources on Female Pilgrimage (3rd and 4th Centuries A.D.)." *Studia Patristica* 20 (1987): 219–23.

———. *"Virgins of God": The Making of Asceticism in Late Antiquity.* Oxford Classical Studies. Oxford: Clarendon Press, 1994.

Elsner, Jaś. *Art and the Roman Viewer.* Cambridge, U.K.: Cambridge University Press, 1995.

———. "Describing Self in the Language of Other: Pseudo(?) Lucian at the Temple of Hierapolis." In Goldhill, *Being Greek Under Rome* (q.v.), 123–53.

———. "The *Itinerarium Burdigalense:* Politics and Salvation in the Geography of Constantine's Empire." *Journal of Roman Studies* 90 (2000): 181–95.

Elsner, Jaś, and Joan-Pau Rubiés, eds. *Voyages and Visions: Towards a Cultural History of Travel.* London: Reaktion Books, 1999.

Engemann, Josef, ed. *Akten des XII. internationalen Kongresses für Christliche Archäologie (Bonn 22.-28. September 1991).* Jahrbuch für Antike und Christentum 20, no. 1/Studi di Antichità Cristiana 52. Münster: Aschendorffsche Verlag; Vatican City: Pontifical Institute of Christian Archaeology, 1995.

Ernout, A. "Les mots grecs dans la Peregrinatio Aetheriae." *Emaerita* 20 (1952): 298–307.

Feldman, Emanuel. "The Rabbinic Lament." *Jewish Quarterly Review* 63 (1972): 51–75.

Feldman, Louis. "Origen's *Contra Celsum* and Josephus' *Contra Apionem:* The Issue of Jewish Origins." *Vigiliae Christianae* 44 (1990): 105–35.

Finn, Thomas. *From Death to Rebirth: Ritual and Conversion in Antiquity.* New York: Paulist Press, 1997.

Foucault, Michel. *The History of Sexuality.* Vol. 1, *An Introduction.* Tr. Robert Hurley. New York: Pantheon, 1978.

Frank, Georgia. *The Memory of the Eyes: Pilgrims to Living Saints in Christian Late Antiquity.* Transformation of the Classical Heritage 30. Berkeley: University of California Press, 2000.

Frede, Michael. "Eusebius' Apologetic Writings." In *Apologetics in the Roman Empire: Pagans, Jews, and Christians,* ed. Mark Edwards, Martin Goodman, and Simon Price, 223–50. Oxford: Oxford University Press, 1999.

Fredriksen, Paula. "Augustine and Israel: *Interpretatio ad litteram,* Jews and Judaism in Augustine's Theology of History." *Studia Patristica* 38 (2001): 119–35.

———. *Augustine and the Jews.* New York: Doubleday, 2004.

———. "*Excaecati Occulta Justitia Dei:* Augustine on Jews and Judaism." *Journal of Early Christian Studies* 3 (1995): 299–324.

———. "*Secundum Carnem:* History and Israel in the Theology of St. Augustine." In *The Limits of Ancient Christianity: Essays on Late Antique Thought and Culture in Honor of R. A. Markus,* ed. William Klingshirn and Mark Vessey, 26–41. Ann Arbor: University of Michigan Press, 1999.

French, Dorothea R. "Mapping Sacred Centers: Pilgrimage and the Creation of Christian Topographies in Roman Palestine." In Engemann, *Akten* (q.v.), 792–97.

Fürst, Alfons. *Augustins Briefwechsel mit Hieronymus.* Jahrbuch für Antike und Christentum Ergänzungsband 29. Münster: Aschendorffsche Verlagsbuchhandlung, 1999.

———. "Kürbis oder Efeu? Zur Übersetzung von Jona 4:6 in der Septuaginta und bei Hieronymus." *Biblische Notizen* 72 (1994): 12–19.

Gager, John. *The Origins of Anti-Semitism: Attitudes Toward Judaism in Pagan and Christian Antiquity.* Oxford: Oxford University Press, 1985.

Gibbon, Edward. *The History of the Decline and Fall of the Roman Empire.* 1781.

Ed. David Womersley. London: Penguin, 1994.

Ginzberg, Louis. "Die Haggada bei den Kirchenvätern, VI.: Der Kommentar des Hieronymus zu Jesaja." In *Jewish Studies in Memory of George A. Kohut,* ed. Salo Baron and Alexander Marx, 279–314. New York: Alexander Kohut Memorial Foundation, 1935.

Goldhill, Simon, ed. *Being Greek Under Rome: Cultural Identity, the Second Sophistic, and the Development of Empire.* Cambridge, U.K.: Cambridge University Press, 2001.

Goranson, Stephen. "The Joseph of Tiberias Episode in Epiphanius: Studies in Jewish and Christian Relations." Ph.D. diss., Duke University, 1990.

———. "Joseph of Tiberias Revisited: Orthodoxies and Heresies in Fourth-Century Galilee." In Meyers, *Galilee* (q.v.), 335–43.

Graves, Robert. *Count Belisarius.* London: Penguin, 1954.

Groh, Dennis. "Jews and Christians in Late Roman Palestine: Towards a New Chronology." *Biblical Archaeologist* 51 (1988): 80–96.

———. "The *Onomasticon* of Eusebius and the Rise of Christian Palestine." *Studia Patristica* 18 (1983): 23–31.

Grützmacher, Georg. *Hieronymus: Eine biographische Studie zur alten Kirchengeschichte.* 3 vols. Studien zur Geschichte der Theologie und der Kirche 6.3, 10.1, 10.2. 1901–8. Repr. Darmstadt: Scientia Verlag, 1969.

Guha, Ranajit. "On Some Aspects of the Historiography of Colonial India." *Subaltern Studies* 1 (1982): 1–8.

———, ed. *A Subaltern Studies Reader, 1986–1995.* Minneapolis: University of Minnesota Press, 1997.

Habas (Rubin), E. "The Jewish Origins of Julius Africanus." *Journal of Jewish Studies* 45 (1994): 86–91.

Habicht, Christian. *Pausanias' Guide to Ancient Greece.* Sather Classical Lectures 50. Berkeley: University of California Press, 1985.

Hagendahl, Harald. "Jerome and the Latin Classics." *Vigiliae Christianae* 28 (1974): 216–27.

———. *Latin Fathers and the Classics: A Study on the Apologists, Jerome, and Other Christian Writers.* Studia Graeca et Latina Gothoburgenses 6. Göteborg/Stockholm: Almqvist and Wiksell, 1958.

Hall, Linda Jones. "Berytus, 'Mother of Laws': Studies in the Social History of Beirut from the Third to Sixth Centuries A.D." Ph.D. diss., Ohio State University, 1996.

Harnack, Adolf von. *Die Altercatio Simonis Judaei et Theophili Christiani nebst Untersuchungen über die antijüdische Polemik in der alten Kirche.* TU 1.3. Leipzig: J. C. Hinrichs, 1883.

————. *Die Mission und Ausbreitung des Christentums in den ersten drei Jahrhunderten.* 2 vols. 3d ed. Leipzig: J. C. Hinrichs, 1915. English translation of first edition: *The Mission of Early Christianity.* 2 vols. Tr. J. Moffatt. New York: G. P. Putnam, 1904–5.

Harries, Jill. "Introduction: Background to the Code." In Harries and Wood, *Theodosian Code* (q.v.), 1–16.

Harries, Jill, and Ian Wood, eds. *The Theodosian Code.* Ithaca, N.Y.: Cornell University Press, 1993.

Harrison, M. *A Temple for Byzantium: The Discovery and Excavation of Anicia Juliana's Palace-Church in Istanbul.* Austin: University of Texas Press, 1989.

Harvey, Graham. *The True Israel: Uses of the Names Jew, Hebrew, and Israel in Ancient Jewish and Early Christian Literature.* Arbeiten zur Geschichte des Antiken Judentums und des Urchristentums 35. Leiden: E. J. Brill, 1996.

Harvey, Paul B., Jr. "Saints and Satyrs: Jerome the Scholar at Work." *Athenaeum* 86 (1998): 35–56.

Harvey, Susan Ashbrook. "Olfactory Knowing: Signs of Smell in the *vitae* of Simeon Stylites." In *After Bardaisan: Studies on Continuity and Change in Syriac Christianity in Honour of Professor Han J. W. Drijvers,* ed. G. J. Reinink and A. C. Klugkist, 23–34. Orientalia Lovaniensia Analecta 89. Leuven: Peeters, 1999.

————. "St. Ephrem on the Scent of Salvation." *Journal of Theological Studies,* n.s., 49 (1998): 109–28.

————. "The Stylite's Liturgy: Ritual and Religious Identity in Late Antiquity." *Journal of Early Christian Studies* 6 (1998): 523–39.

Haverling, Gerd. "Symmachus and Greek Literature." In *Greek and Latin Studies in Memory of Cajus Fabricius,* ed. Sven-Tage Teodorsson, 188–205. Studia Graeca et Latina Gothoburgensia 54. Göteborg: Acta Univers-itatis Gothoburgensis, 1990.

Hennings, Ralph. *Der Briefwechsel zwischen Augustinus und Hieronymus und ihr Streit um den Kanon des Alten Testaments und die Auslegung von Gal. 2,11–14.* Supplements to Vigiliae Christianae 21. Leiden: E. J. Brill, 1994.

————. "Rabbinisches und antijüdisches bei Hieronymus Ep 121,10." In *Christliche Exegese zwischen Nicaea und Chalcedon,* ed. J. van Oort and U. Wickert, 49–71. Kampen: Kok Pharos, 1992.

Hirschfeld, Yizhar. *The Judean Desert Monasteries of the Byzantine Period.* New Haven, Conn.: Yale University Press, 1992.

Hirshman, Marc. *A Rivalry of Genius: Jewish and Christian Biblical Interpretation in Late Antiquity.* Tr. Batya Stein. SUNY Series in Judaica: Hermeneutics, Mysticism, and Religion. Albany: SUNY Press, 1996.

Hollerich, Michael J. *Eusebius of Caesarea's* Commentary on Isaiah: *Christian Exegesis in the Age of Constantine.* Oxford Early Christian Studies. Oxford: Clarendon Press, 1999.

Holum, Kenneth G. "Hadrian and St. Helena: Imperial Travel and the Origins of Christian Holy Land Pilgrimage." In Ousterhout, *Blessings of Pilgrimage* (q.v.), 66–81.

———. *Theodosian Empresses: Women and Imperial Dominion in Late Antiquity.* Transformation of the Classical Heritage 3. Berkeley: University of California Press, 1982.

Honoré, Tony. *Law in the Crisis of Empire, 379–455 A.D.: The Theodosian Dynasty and Its Quaestors.* Oxford: Clarendon Press, 1998.

Horbury, William. *Jews and Christians in Contact and Controversy.* Edinburgh: T. & T. Clark, 1998.

Horowitz, Elliott. " 'The Vengeance of the Jews Was Stronger Than Their Avarice': Modern Historians and the Persian Conquest of Jerusalem in 614." *Jewish Social Studies* 4 (1998): 1–39.

Hunt, E. D. "Constantine and Jerusalem." *Journal of Ecclesiastical History* 48 (1997): 405–24.

———. "The Date of the *Itinerarium Egeriae.*" *Studia Patristica* 38 (2001): 410–16.

———. *Holy Land Pilgrimage in the Later Roman Empire, A.D. 312–460.* Oxford: Clarendon Press, 1982.

———. "The Itinerary of Egeria: Reliving the Bible in Fourth-Century Palestine." In *The Holy Land, Holy Lands, and Christian History,* ed. R. N. Swanson, 34–54. Studies in Church History 36. Suffolk: Boydell Press, 2000.

———. "Saint Silvia of Aquitaine: The Role of a Theodosian Pilgrim in the Society of East and West." *Journal of Theological Studies,* n.s., 23 (1972): 351–73.

———. "Theodosius I and the Holy Land." *Studia Patristica* 29 (1997): 52–57.

———. "Travel, Tourism, and Piety in the Roman Empire: A Context for the Beginnings of Christian Pilgrims." *Echos du Monde Classique* 28 (1984): 391–417.

———. "Were There Christian Pilgrims Before Constantine?" In *Pilgrimage Explored,* ed. J. Stopford, 25–40. Suffolk: York Medieval Press, 1999.

Hunter, David. "Vigilantius of Calagurris and Victricius of Rouen: Ascetics,

Relics, and Clerics in Late Roman Gaul." *Journal of Early Christian Studies* 7 (1999): 401–30.

Irshai, Oded. "Cyril of Jerusalem: The Apparition of the Cross and the Jews." In Limor and Stroumsa, *Contra Iudaeos* (q.v.), 86–104.

Isaac, Benjamin. "Eusebius and the Geography of Roman Provinces." In *The Near East Under Roman Rule: Selected Papers,* by Benjamin Isaac, 284–309. Leiden: Brill, 1998.

Jacobs, Andrew S. "Visible Ghosts and Invisible Demons: The Place of Jews in Early Christian *Terra Sancta.*" In Meyers, *Galilee* (q.v.), 359–76.

Jaffee, Martin. *Early Judaism.* Princeton, N.J.: Prentice-Hall, 1997.

Janson, Tore. *Latin Prose Prefaces: Studies in Literary Conventions.* Studia Latina Stockholmiensia 13. Stockholm: Almquist & Wiksell, 1964.

Jay, Pierre. "La datation des premières traductions de l'Ancien Testament sur l'hébreu par saint Jérôme." *Revue des Études Augustiniennes* 28 (1982): 208–12.

———. *L'exégèse de Saint Jérôme d'après son "Commentaire sur Isaïe."* Paris: Études Augustiniennes, 1985.

Jeremias, Joachim. *Heiligengräber in Jesu Umwelt (Mt. 23, 29; Lk. 11, 47): Eine Untersuchung zur Volksreligion der Zeit Jesu.* Göttingen: Vandenhoeck & Ruprecht, 1958.

Johnson, Maxwell E. "Reconciling Cyril and Egeria on the Catechetical Process in Fourth-Century Jerusalem." In *Essays in Eastern Initiation,* ed. Paul Bradshaw, 18–30. Nottingham: Grove Books, 1988.

Jones, A. H. M. *The Later Roman Empire, 284–602: A Social, Economic, and Administrative Survey.* 2 vols. Norman: University of Oklahoma Press, 1964.

Jones, A. H. M., and T. C. Skeat. "Notes on the Genuineness of the Constantinian Documents in Eusebius' *Life of Constantine.*" *Journal of Ecclesiastical History* 5 (1954): 196–200.

Jones, Tom B. *In the Twilight of Antiquity: The R. S. Hoyt Memorial Lectures (1973).* Minneapolis: University of Minnesota Press, 1978.

Juster, Jean. *Les Juifs dans l'Empire romain: Leur condition juridique, économique et sociale.* Paris: Paul Geuthner, 1914.

Kaimio, Jorma. *The Romans and the Greek Language.* Commentationes Humanarum Litterarum 64. Helsinki: Societas Scientiarum Fennica, 1979.

Kamesar, Adam. "The Evaluation of the Narrative Aggada in Greek and Latin Patristic Literature." *Journal of Theological Studies,* n.s., 45 (1994): 37–71.

————. *Jerome, Greek Scholarship, and the Hebrew Bible: A Study of the* Quaestiones Hebraicae in Genesim. Oxford Classical Monographs. Oxford: Clarendon Press, 1993.

Kannengeisser, Charles, and William L. Petersen, eds. *Origen of Alexandria: His World and Legacy.* Christianity and Judaism in Antiquity 1. Notre Dame, Ind.: University of Notre Dame Press, 1988.

Kaster, Robert. *Guardians of Language: The Grammarian and Society in Late Antiquity.* Transformation of the Classical Heritage 11. Berkeley: University of California Press, 1988.

Kedar-Kopfstein, Benjamin. "Jewish Traditions in the Writings of Jerome." In *The Aramaic Bible: Targums and Their Historical Context,* ed. D. R. G. Beattie and M. J. McNamara, 420–30. Journal for the Study of the Old Testament Supplement 166. Sheffield: Sheffield Academic Press, 1994.

Kelly, J. N. D. *Early Christian Creeds.* 3d ed. New York: D. McKay, 1972.

————. *Jerome: His Life, Writings, and Controversies.* London: Duckworth, 1975.

Kelly, Joan. "The Doubled Vision of Feminist Theory." *Feminist Studies* 5 (1979): 216–27. Repr. in idem, *Women, History, and Theory: The Essays of Joan Kelly,* 51–64. Women in Culture and Society. Chicago, Ill.: University of Chicago Press, 1984.

Kimelman, Reuven. "Rabbi Yohanan and Origen on the Song of Songs: A Third-Century Jewish-Christian Debate." *Harvard Theological Review* 73 (1980): 567–95.

Klijn, A. F. J., and G. J. Reinink. *Patristic Evidence for Jewish-Christian Sects.* Supplements to Novum Testamentum 36. Leiden: E. J. Brill, 1973.

Koch, Glenn Alan. "A Critical Investigation of Epiphanius' Knowledge of the Ebionites: A Translation and Critical Discussion of *Panarion* 30." Ph.D. diss., University of Pennsylvania, 1976.

Koester, Craig. "The Origin and Significance of the Flight to Pella Tradition." *Catholic Biblical Quarterly* 51 (1989): 90–106.

Kofsky, Aryeh. "Eusebius of Caesarea and the Christian-Jewish Polemic." In Limor and Stroumsa, *Contra Iudaeos* (q.v.), 59–84.

————. "Peter the Iberian: Pilgrimage, Monasticism, and Ecclesiastical Politics in Byzantine Palestine." *Liber Annuus* 47 (1997): 209–22.

Kötting, Bernhard. *Peregrinatio Religiosa: Wallfahrten in der Antike und das Pilgerwesen in der alten Kirche.* Forschungen zur Volkskunde 33/34/35. Münster: Regensberg, 1950.

Krautheimer, Richard. *Three Christian Capitals: Topography and Politics.* Berkeley: University of California Press, 1983.

Lamberigts, M. "Augustine as Translator of Greek Texts." In *Philohistôr: Miscellanea in honorem Caroli Laga septuagenarii*, ed. A. Schoors and P. van Deun, 151–61. Orientalia Lovaniensia Analecta 60. Leuven: University Press, 1994.

Lapin, Hayim. "Jewish and Christian Academics in Roman Palestine: Some Preliminary Observations." In *Caesarea Maritima: A Retrospective After Two Millennia*, ed. Avner Raban and Kenneth G. Holum, 496–512. Documenta et Monumenta Orientis Antiqua 21. Leiden: E. J. Brill, 1996.

Lardet, Pierre. *L'apologie de Jérôme contre Rufin: Un commentaire.* Supplements to Vigiliae Christianae 15. Leiden: E. J. Brill, 1993.

Lease, Gary. "Ideology." In Braun and McCutcheon, *Guide to the Study of Religion* (q.v.), 438–47.

Le Boulluec, Alain. *La notion d'hérésie dans la littérature grecque (IIe–IIIe siècles).* 2 vols. Paris: Études Augustiniennes, 1985.

Leclerc, Pierre. "Antoine et Paul: Métamorphose d'un héros." In *Jérôme entre l'occident et l'orient*, ed. Y.-M. Duval, 257–65. Paris: Etudes Augustiniennes, 1988.

Lederman, Yohanan. "Les évêques juifs de Jérusalem." *Revue Biblique* 104 (1997): 211–22.

Levenson, David. "Julian's Attempts to Rebuild the Temple: An Inventory of Ancient and Medieval Sources." In *Of Scribes and Scrolls: Studies on the Hebrew Bible, Intertestamental Judaism, and Christian Origins Presented to John Strugnell on the Occasion of his Sixtieth Birthday*, ed. Harold W. Attridge, John J. Collins, and Thomas H. Tobin, S.J., 261–79. College Theology Society Resources in Religion 5. Lanham, Md.: University Press of America, 1990.

Levi, Annalina. *Itineraria picta: Contributo allo studio della Tabula Peutingeriana.* Rome: Brettschneider, 1967.

Levine, Lee I., ed. *Jerusalem: Its Sanctity and Centrality to Judaism, Christianity, and Islam.* New York: Continuum, 1999.

Leyerle, Blake. "Landscape as Cartography in Early Christian Pilgrimage Narrative." *Journal of the American Academy of Religion* 64 (1996): 119–43.

———. "Pilgrims to the Land: Early Christian Perceptions of the Galilee." In Meyers, *Galilee* (q.v.), 348–53.

Liddell, Henry George, Robert Scott, Henry Stuart Jones. *A Greek-English Lexicon.* 9th ed. Oxford: Clarendon Press, 1996.

Lieu, Judith. "Epiphanius on the Scribes and Pharisees (*Pan.* 15.1–16.4)." *Journal of Theological Studies,* n.s., 39 (1988): 509–24.

———. *Image and Reality: The Jews in the World of the Christians in the Second Century.* Edinburgh: T. & T. Clark, 1996.

———. " 'The Parting of the Ways': Theological Construct or Historical Reality?" *Journal for the Study of the New Testament* 56 (1994): 101–19.

Lim, Richard. "Christian Triumph and Controversy." In *Late Antiquity: A Guide to the Postclassical World,* ed. G. W. Bowersock, Peter Brown, and Oleg Grabar, 196–218. Cambridge, Mass.: Belknap Press of Harvard University Press, 1999.

———. *Public Disputation, Power, and Social Order in Late Antiquity.* Transformation of the Classical Heritage 23. Berkeley: University of California Press, 1995.

Limberis, Vasiliki. *Divine Heiress: The Virgin Mary and the Creation of Christian Constantinople.* London: Routledge, 1994.

Limor, Ora. "Christian Sacred Space and the Jews." In *From Witness to Witchcraft: Jews and Judaism in Medieval Christian Thought,* ed. Jeremy Cohen, 55–77. Wolfenbüteler Mittelalter-Studien 11. Wiesbaden: Harrassowitz Verlag, 1996.

Limor, Ora, and G. G. Stroumsa, eds. *Contra Iudaeos: Ancient and Medieval Polemics Between Christians and Jews.* Texts and Studies in Medieval and Early Modern Judaism 10. Tübingen: J. C. B. Mohr (Paul Siebeck), 1996.

Loomba, Ania. *Colonialism/Postcolonialism.* The New Critical Idiom. London: Routledge, 1998.

Lorenz, Rudolf. *Arius Judaizans? Untersuchung zur dogmengeschichtlichen Einordnung des Arius.* Forschungen zur Kirchen- und Dogmengeschichte 31. Göttingen: Vandenhoek & Ruprecht, 1980.

Lukyn Williams, A. *Adversus Judaeos: A Bird's-Eye View of Christian Apologiae Until the Renaissance.* Cambridge, U.K.: Cambridge University Press, 1935.

MacCannell, Dean. *Empty Meeting Grounds: The Tourist Papers.* London: Routledge, 1992.

———. *The Tourist: A New Theory of the Leisure Class.* New York: Schocken Books, 1976.

MacCormack, Sabine. *Art and Ceremony in Late Antiquity.* Transformation of the Classical Heritage 1. Berkeley: University of California Press, 1981.

———. "Loca Sancta: The Organization of Sacred Topography in Late Antiquity." In Ousterhout, *Blessings of Pilgrimage* (q.v.), 7–40.

MacKenzie, John. *Orientalism: History, Theory, and the Arts.* Manchester: Manchester University Press, 1995.

Mango, Cyril. *Le développement urbain de Constantinople, IVe–VIIe siècles.* Paris: Diffusion de Boccard, 1990.

Ma'oz, Zvi. "Comments on Jewish and Christian Communities in Byzantine Galilee." *Palestine Exploration Quarterly* 117 (1988): 59–68.

Maraval, Pierre. *Lieux saints et pèlerinages d'Orient: Histoire et géographie des origines à la conquête arabe.* Paris: Editions du Cerf, 1985.

————. "Une querelle sur les pèlerinages author d'un texte patristique (Grégoire de Nysse, *Lettre* 2)." *Revue d'Histoire et de Philosophie Religieuses* 66 (1982): 131–46.

Markus, Robert. *The End of Ancient Christianity.* Cambridge, U.K.: Cambridge University Press, 1990.

————. "How on Earth Could Places Become Holy? Origins of the Christian Idea of Holy Places." *Journal of Early Christian Studies* 2 (1994): 257–71.

Matthews, John. *Western Aristocracies and Imperial Court, A.D. 364–425.* Clarendon: Oxford, 1975. Repr., Clarendon: Oxford, 1990.

McClintock, Anne. *Imperial Leather: Race, Gender, and Sexuality in the Colonial Contest.* London: Routledge, 1995.

McCormick, Michael. *Eternal Victory: Triumphal Rulership in Late Antiquity, Byzantium, and the Early Medieval West.* Past and Present Publications. Cambridge, U.K.: Cambridge University Press, 1986.

McLellan, David. *Ideology.* 2d ed. Minneapolis: University of Minnesota Press, 1995.

McNeil, Brian. "Jesus and the Alphabet." *Journal of Theological Studies,* n.s., 27 (1976): 126–28.

Meyers, Eric M. "Early Judaism and Christianity in the Light of Archaeology." *Biblical Archaeologist* 51 (1988): 69–79.

————, ed. *Galilee Through the Centuries: Confluence of Cultures.* Duke Judaic Studies 1. Winona Lake, Ind.: Eisenbrauns, 1999.

————, ed. *Oxford Encyclopedia of Archaeology in the Near East.* Oxford: Oxford University Press, 1997.

Milani, Celestina. *Itinerarium Antonini Placentini: Un viaggio in Terra Santa del 560–570 d.C.* Scienze Filologiche e Letteratura 7. Milan: Università Cattolica del Sacro Cuore, 1977.

Miles, Margaret. "Santa Maria Maggiore's Fifth-Century Mosaics: Triumphal Christianity and the Jews." *Harvard Theological Review* 86 (1993): 155–75.

Miller, Patricia Cox. "The Blazing Body: Ascetic Desire in Jerome's Letter to Eustochium." *Journal of Early Christian Studies* 1 (1993): 21–45.

———. " 'Differential Networks': Relics and Other Fragments in Late Antiquity." *Journal of Early Christian Studies* 6 (1998): 113–38.

———. "Jerome's Centaur: A Hyper-Icon of the Desert." *Journal of Early Christian Studies* 4 (1996): 209–33.

Mimouni, Simon C. *Le judéo-christianisme ancien: Essais historiques.* Patrimoines. Paris: Editions du Cerf, 1998.

———. "Pour une définition nouvelle du judéo-christianisme ancien." *New Testament Studies* 38 (1992): 161–86.

Mitchell, Timothy. *Colonising Egypt.* Cambridge Middle East Library. Cambridge, U.K.: Cambridge University Press, 1988.

Moore-Gilbert, Bart. "Postcolonial Cultural Studies and Imperial Historiography: Problems of Interdisciplinarity." *Interventions* 1 (1999): 397–411.

———. *Postcolonial Theory: Contexts, Practices, Politics.* London: Verso, 1997.

Mosshammer, Alden A. *The* Chronicle *of Eusebius and Greek Chronographic Tradition.* Lewisburg, Pa.: Bucknell University Press, 1979.

Mulzer, Martin. "Mit der Bibel in der Hand? Egeria und ihr 'Codex.'" *Zeitschrift der deutsches Palästina-Vereins* 112 (1996): 156–64.

Murphy, Francis X. "Melania the Elder: A Biographical Note." *Traditio* 5 (1947): 59–77.

Nau, F. "Deux épisodes de l'histoire juive sous Théodose II (423 et 438) d'après La Vie de Barsauma le Syrien." *Revue des Études Juives* 83 (1927): 184–206.

———. "Résumé de monographies syriaques: Barsauma; Abraham de la Haute-Montagne; Siméon de Kefar 'Abdin; Yaret l'Alexandrin; Jacques le Reclus; Romanus; Talia; Asia; Pantaléon; Candida." *Revue de l'Orient Chrétien* 18 (1913): 270–76, 379–89; 19 (1914): 113–34, 278–89.

Nautin, Pierre. "Le premier échange épistolaire entre Jérôme et Damase: Lettres réelles ou fictives?" *Freiburger Zeitschrift für Philosophie und Theologie* 30 (1983): 331–47.

Newman, Hillel I. "Jerome's Judaizers." *Journal of Early Christian Studies* 9 (2001): 421–52.

Nugent, B. P. "Jerome's Prologues to His Commentaries on the Prophets." Ph.D. diss., University of Texas at Austin, 1992.

Olster, David M. *Roman Defeat, Christian Response, and the Literary Construction of the Jew.* Middle Ages Series. Philadelphia: University of Pennsylvania Press, 1994.

Opelt, Ilona. *Hieronymus Streitschriften*. Heidelberg: Carl Winter-Univers-
    itätsverlag, 1973.
———. "San Giraolamo e i suoi maestri ebrei." *Augustinianum* 28 (1988): 327–
    38.
Ousterhout, Robert, ed. *The Blessings of Pilgrimage*. Illinois Byzantine Studies 1.
    Urbana: University of Illinois Press, 1990.
Palmer, Andrew. "Egeria the Voyager, or the Technology of Remote Sensing in
    Late Antiquity." In *Travel Fact and Travel Fiction: Studies on Fiction,
    Literary Tradition, Scholarly Discovery, and Observation in Travel
    Writing*, ed. Zweder von Martels, 39–53. Brill Studies in Intellectual
    History 55. Leiden: Brill, 1994.
Parkes, J. *The Conflict of the Church and the Synagogue*. London: Soncino Press,
    1934.
Pasto, James. "Islam's 'Strange Secret Sharer': Orientalism, Judaism, and the
    Jewish Question." *Comparative Studies in Society and History* 40 (1998):
    437–74.
———. "When the End Is the Beginning? or When the Biblical Past Is the
    Political Present: Some Thoughts on Ancient Israel, 'Post-Exilic
    Judaism,' and the Politics of Biblical Scholarship." *Scandinavian
    Journal of the Old Testament* 12 (1998): 157–202.
———. "Who Owns the Jewish Past: Judaism, Judaisms, and the Writing of
    Jewish History." Ph.D. diss., Cornell University, 1999.
Patrich, Joseph. *Sabas, Leader of Palestinian Monasticism: A Comparative Study
    in Eastern Monasticism, Fourth Through Seventh Centuries*. Dumbarton
    Oaks Studies 32. Washington, D.C.: Dumbarton Oaks, 1995.
Perkins, Judith. *The Suffering Self: Pain and Narrative Representation in the Early
    Christian Era*. London: Routledge, 1995.
Perrone, Lorenzo. "Christian Holy Places and Pilgrimage in an Age of Dogmatic
    Conflicts: Popular Religion and Confessional Affiliation in Byzantine
    Palestine (Fifth to Seventh Centuries)." *Prôche-Orient Chrétien* 48
    (1998): 5–37.
———. " 'The Mystery of Judaea' (Jerome, *ep.* 46): The Holy City of Jerusalem
    Between History and Symbol in Early Christian Thought." In Levine,
    Jerusalem (q.v.), 221–39.
Peterson, Erik. *Der Monotheismus als politisches Problem: Ein Beitrag zur
    Geschichte der politische Theologie im Imperium Romanum*. Leipzig:
    Jakob Hegner, 1935.
Piccirillo, Michele, and Eugenio Alliata, eds. *The Madaba Map Centenary: Trav-
    elling Through the Byzantine Umayyad Period*. Proceedings of the Inter-

national Conference Held in Amman, 7–9 April 1997. Studia Biblica Franciscanum, Collectio Maior, 40. Jerusalem: Studium Biblicum Franciscanum, 1998.

Pourkier, Aline. *L'hérésiologie chez Épiphane de Salamine*. Christianisme Antique 4. Paris: Beauchesne, 1992.

Prakash, Gyan. "Subaltern Studies as Postcolonial Criticism." *American Historical Review* 99 (1994): 1475–90.

Pratt, Mary Louise. *Imperial Eyes: Travel Writing and Transculturation*. London: Routledge, 1992.

Pullan, Wendy. "The Representation of the Late Antique City in the Madaba Map: The Meaning of the Cardo in the Jerusalem Vignette." In Piccirillo and Alliata, *Madaba Map Centenary* (q.v.), 165–69.

Rawson, Elizabeth. *Intellectual Life in the Late Roman Republic*. Baltimore, Md.: Johns Hopkins University Press, 1985.

Rebenich, Stefan. *Hieronymus und sein Kreis: Prosopographische und sozial-geschichtliche Untersuchungen*. Historia Einzelschriften 72. Stuttgart: Franz Steiner Verlag, 1992.

———. "Jerome: The 'Vir Trilinguis' and the 'Hebraica Veritas.' " *Vigiliae Christianae* 47 (1993): 50–77.

Rivers, Joseph T., III, "Pattern and Process in Early Christian Pilgrimage." Ph.D. diss., Duke University, 1983.

Robinson, Bernard P. "Jonah's Qiqayon Plant." *Zeitschrift für die Alttestamentliche Wissenschaft* 97 (1985): 390–403.

Roll, Israel. "Roads and Transportation in the Holy Land in the Early Christian and Byzantine Times." In Engemann, *Akten* (q.v.), 1166–70.

———. "The Roman Road System in Judaea." *Jerusalem Cathedra* 3 (1986): 136–61.

Rubin, Z. "The Church of the Holy Sepulchre and the Conflict Between the Sees of Caesarea and Jerusalem." *Jerusalem Cathedra* 2 (1982): 79–105.

Ruether, Rosemary. *Faith and Fratricide: The Theological Roots of Anti-Semitism*. New York: Seabury Press, 1974.

Runesson, Anders. "Particularistic Judaism and Universalistic Christianity? Some Critical Remarks on Terminology and Theology." *Journal of Greco-Roman Christianity and Judaism* 1 (2001): 120–44.

Ryan, Simon. "Inscribing the Emptiness: Cartography, Exploration, and the Construction of Australia." In *De-Scribing Empire: Post-Colonialism and Textuality*, ed. Chris Tiffin and Alan Lawson, 115–30. London: Routledge, 1994.

Safrai, Ze'ev. *The Missing Century: Palestine in the Fifth Century: Growth and*

Decline. Palaestina Antiqua 9. Leuven: Peeters, 1998.

Said, Edward. *Culture and Imperialism*. New York: Alfred A. Knopf, 1993.

———. *Orientalism*. New York: Pantheon, 1978. Repr., New York: Pantheon, 1991.

———. "The Text, the World, the Critic." In *Textual Strategies: Perspectives in Post-Structuralist Criticism*, ed. Josué V. Harari, 161–89. Ithaca, N.Y.: Cornell University Press, 1979.

———. *The World, the Text, and the Critic*. Cambridge, Mass.: Harvard University Press, 1983.

Saller, Sylvester J. "L'epitafio di Eufemia al Getsemani." In *Ricerche archeologiche al Monte degli Ulivi*, ed. P. Virgilio and C. Corbo, 75–80. Studium Biblicum Franciscanum 16. Jerusalem: Studium Biblicum Franciscanum, 1965.

Salzmann, Michele Renée. *The Making of a Christian Aristocracy: Social and Religious Change in the Western Roman Empire*. Cambridge, Mass.: Harvard University Press, 2002.

Satran, David. *Biblical Prophets in Byzantine Palestine: Reassessing the Lives of the Prophets*. Studia in Veteris Testamenti Pseudepigrapha 11. Leiden: E. J. Brill, 1995.

Schliemann, Heinrich. *Mykenae: Bericht über meine Forschungen und Entdeckungen in Mykenae und Tiryns*. 1878. Repr., Darmstadt: Wissenschaftliche Buchgesellschaft, 1964.

Schmidt, Catherine. "The Guided Tour: Insulated Adventure." *Urban Life* 7 (1979): 441–68.

Schmidt, Johann Ernst Christian. *Bibliothek für Kritik und Exegese des Neuen Testaments und ältesten Christengeschichte*. 2 vols. Hadamar: Neue Gelehrtenbuchhandlung, 1797–1803.

Schur, Nathan. *History of the Samaritans*. Beiträge zur Erforschung des Alten Testaments und des Antiken Judentums 18. Frankfurt am Main: Peter Land, 1992.

Schwartz, Eduard. *Johannes Rufus, ein monophysitischer Schriftsteller*. Sitzungberichte, Heidelberg. Philosoph-Historische Klasse 16. Heidelberg: Carl Winter's, 1912.

Schwartz, Seth. *Imperialism and Jewish Society, 200 B.C.E. to 640 C.E.* Jews, Christians, and Muslims from the Ancient to the Modern World. Princeton, N.J.: Princeton University Press, 2001.

Shahid, Irfan. "The Madaba Mosaic Map Revisited: Some New Observations on Its Purpose and Meaning." In Piccirillo and Alliata, *Madaba Map Centenary* (q.v.), 147–54.

Shaw, Teresa. *The Burden of the Flesh: Fasting and Sexuality in Early Christianity.*
    Minneapolis, Minn.: Fortress Press, 1998.

Shoemaker, Stephen J. " 'Let Us Go and Burn Her Body': The Image of the
    Jews in the Early Dormition Traditions." *Church History* 68 (1999):
    775–823.

Simon, Marcel. *Verus Israel: A Study in the Relations Between Christians and Jews
    in the Roman Empire (135–425).* Tr. H. McKeating. Oxford: Oxford
    University Press, 1986. Original French version: *Verus Israel: Étude sur
    les relations entre Chrétiens et Juifs dans l'Empire Romain (135–425).*
    Bibliothèques des Écoles Françaises d'Athènes et de Rome. Paris:
    Editions de Boccard, 1948.

Sivan, Hagith. "Pilgrimage, Monasticism, and the Emergence of Christian
    Palestine in the 4th Century." In Ousterhout, *Blessings of Pilgrimage*
    (q.v.), 54–65.

———. "Who Was Egeria? Piety and Pilgrimage in the Age of Gratian."
    Harvard Theological Review 81 (1988): 59–72.

Smith, Jonathan Z. *To Take Place: Toward Theory in Ritual.* Chicago Studies in
    the History of Judaism. Chicago, Ill.: University of Chicago Press,
    1987.

———. "What a Difference a Difference Makes." In *"To See Ourselves as Others
    See Us": Christians, Jews, "Others" in Late Antiquity,* ed. Jacob Neusner
    and Ernest Frerichs, 3–48. Chico, Calif.: Scholars Press, 1985.

Spitzer, Leo. "The Epic Style of the Pilgrim Aetheria." *Comparative Literature* 1
    (1949): 225–58.

Spivak, Gayatri Chakravorty. "Can the Subaltern Speak?" In *Marxism and the
    Interpretation of Culture,* ed. C. Nelson and L. Grossberg, 271–313.
    Basingstoke: Macmillan, 1988. Repr. in Williams and Chrisman,
    Colonial Discourse (q.v.), 66–111.

———. *A Critique of Postcolonial Reason: Toward a History of the Vanishing
    Present.* Cambridge, Mass.: Harvard University Press, 1999.

———. *The Spivak Reader: Selected Works of Gayatri Chakravorty Spivak.* Ed.
    Donna Landry and Gerald MacLean. New York: Routledge, 1996.

Spurr, David. *The Rhetoric of Empire: Colonial Discourse in Journalism, Travel
    Writing, and Imperial Administration.* Post-Contemporary
    Interventions. Durham, N.C.: Duke University Press, 1993.

Stark, Rodney. *The Rise of Christianity: A Sociologist Reconsiders History.*
    Princeton, N.J.: Princeton University Press, 1996.

Steininger, Christine. *Die ideale christliche Frau,* virgo-vidua-nupta: *Eine Studie
    zum Bild der idealen christlichen Frau bei Hieronymus und Pelagius.* St.

Otillien: EOS Verlag, 1997.

Stemberger, Günter. "Hieronymus und die Juden seiner Zeit." In *Begegnungen zwischen Christentum und Judentum in Antike und Mittelalter: Festschrift für Heinz Schrechenberg*, ed. Dietrich-Alex Koch and Hermann Lichtenberger, 347–64. Schriften des Institutum Judaicum Delitzschianum 1. Göttingen: Vandenhoeck & Ruprecht, 1993.

———. *Jews and Christians in the Holy Land: Palestine in the Fourth Century.* Tr. Ruth Tuschling. Edinburgh: T. & T. Clark, 2000.

Stern, Ephraim, ed. *The New Encyclopedia of Archaeological Excavations in the Holy Land.* Jerusalem: Israel Exploration Society, 1993.

Strack, H. L., and G. Stemberger. *Introduction to the Talmud and Midrash.* Tr. Markus Bockmuehl. Edinburgh: T. & T. Clark, 1991.

Stroumsa, G. G. "From Anti-Judaism to Antisemitism in Early Christianity?" In Limor and Stroumsa, *Contra Iudaeos* (q.v.), 1–26.

———. "'Vetus Israel': Les juifs dans la littérature hiérosolymitaine d'époque byzantine." *Revue de l'Histoire des Religions* 125 (1988): 115–31.

Stycker, Émile. "Une ancienne version latine du protévangile de Jacques." *Analecta Bollandiana* 83 (1965): 351–410.

———. *La forme la plus ancienne du Protévangile de Jacques.* Subsidia hagiographa 33. Brussels: Société de Bollandistes, 1961.

Swain, Simon. *Hellenism and Empire: Language, Classicism, and Power in the Greek World, A.D. 50–250.* Oxford: Clarendon Press, 1996.

Taylor, Joan E. *Christians and the Holy Places: The Myth of Jewish-Christian Origins.* Oxford: Clarendon Press, 1993.

———. "The Phenomenon of Early Jewish-Christianity: Reality or Scholarly Invention?" *Vigiliae Christianae* 44 (1990): 313–34.

Taylor, Miriam S. *Anti-Judaism and Early Christian Identity: A Critique of the Scholarly Consensus.* Studia Post-Biblica 46. Leiden: E. J. Brill, 1995.

Thomsen, Peter. "Palästina nach den Onomasticon Eusebius." *Zeitschrift des deutschen Palästina-Vereins* 26 (1903): 97–142, 145–88.

Thornton, T. C. G. "The Stories of Joseph of Tiberias." *Vigiliae Christianae* 44 (1990): 54–63.

Tsafrir, Yoram. "The Holy City of Jerusalem in the Madaba Map." In Piccirillo and Alliata, *Madaba Map Centenary* (q.v.), 155–63.

Turner, Victor, and Edith Turner. *Image and Pilgrimage in Christian Culture: Anthropological Perspectives.* New York: Columbia University Press, 1978.

Ulrich, Jörg. *Euseb von Caesarea und die Juden: Studien zur Rolle der Juden in der Theologie des Eusebius von Caesarea.* Patristische Texte und Studien 49.

Berlin: Walter de Gruyter, 1999.

Urbach, E. E. "The Homiletical Interpretation of the Sages and the Expositions of Origen on Canticles, and the Jewish Christian Disputation." *Scripta Hierosolymitana* 22 (1971): 247–75.

Vessey, Mark. "Conference and Confession: Literary Pragmatics in Augustine's *'Apologia contra Hieronymum.'*" *Journal of Early Christian Studies* 1 (1993): 175–213.

———. "The Demise of the Christian Writer and the Remaking of 'Late Antiquity': From H.-I. Marrou's Saint Augustine (1938) to Peter Brown's Holy Man (1983)." *Journal of Early Christian Studies* 6 (1998): 337–411.

———. "Jerome's Origen: The Making of a Christian Literary Persona." *Studia Patristica* 28 (1993): 135–45.

Vincent, Hugues, and F.-M. Abel. *Jérusalem: Recherches de topographie, d'archéologie et d'histoire.* Vol. 2, *Jérusalem nouvelle.* Paris: Gabalda, 1912–26.

Wainwright, Philip. "The Authenticity of the Recently Discovered Letter Attributed to Cyril of Jerusalem." *Vigiliae Christianae* 40 (1986): 286–93.

Walker, P. W. L. *Holy City, Holy Places? Christian Attitudes to Jerusalem and the Holy Land in the Fourth Century.* Oxford Early Christian Studies. Oxford: Clarendon Press, 1990.

Ward, Eileen F. "Mourning Customs in 1, 2 Samuel." *Journal of Jewish Studies* 23 (1972): 1–27, 146–66.

Warmington, B. H. "The Sources of Some Constantinian Documents in Eusebius' *Ecclesiastical History* and *Life of Constantine.*" *Studia Patristica* 18, no. 1 (1986): 93–98.

Wehnert, Jürgen. "Die Auswanderung der Jerusalemer Christen nach Pella— historisches Faktum oder theologische Konstruktion?" *Zeitschrift für Kirchengeschichte* 102 (1991): 231–55.

Weingarten, Susan. "Was the Pilgrim from Bordeaux a Woman? A Reply to Laurie Douglass." *Journal of Early Christian Studies* 7 (1999): 291–97.

Wenger, Antoine. *L'assomption de la T. S. Vierge dans la tradition byzantine du VIe au Xe siècle: Études et documents.* Archives de l'Orient Chrétien 5. Paris: Institut Français d'Études Byzantines, 1955.

Wharton, Annabel Jane. "The Baptistery of the Holy Sepulcher in Jerusalem and the Politics of Sacred Landscape." *Dumbarton Oaks Papers* 46 (1992): 313–25.

———. "Erasure: Eliminating the Space of Late Ancient Judaism." In *From

Dura to Sepphoris: Studies in Jewish Art and Society in Late Antiquity, ed. Lee I. Levine and Zeev Weiss, 195–214. Journal of Roman Archaeology Supplementary Series 40. Portsmouth: JRA, 2000.

———. *Refiguring the Post Classical City: Dura Europos, Jerash, Jerusalem and Ravenna.* Cambridge, U.K.: Cambridge University Press, 1995.

Wheeler, Brannon M. "Imagining the Sasanian Capture of Jerusalem: The 'Prophecy and Dream of Zerubabel' and Antiochus Strategos' 'Capture of Jerusalem.' " *Orientalia Christiana Periodica* 57 (1991): 69–85.

White, L. Michael. "Adolf Harnack and the 'Expansion' of Early Christianity: A Reappraisal of Social History." *Second Century* 5 (1985–86): 97–127.

Wiesen, David S. *St. Jerome as a Satirist: A Study in Christian Latin Thought and Letters.* Cornell Studies in Classical Philology 34. Ithaca, N.Y.: Cornell University Press, 1964.

Wilde, Oscar. "The Decay of Lying." 1889. Repr. in *The Artist as Critic: Critical Writings of Oscar Wilde,* ed. Richard Ellmann, 290–320. New York: Random House, 1968.

Wilken, Robert. "Heiliges Land." In *Theologische Realenzyklopädie.* Vol. 14. Berlin: Walter de Gruyter, 1985.

———. *The Land Called Holy: Palestine in Christian History and Thought.* New Haven, Conn.: Yale University Press, 1992.

Wilkinson, John. "Christian Pilgrims in Jerusalem During the Byzantine Period." *Palestine Exploration Quarterly* 108 (1976): 75–101.

———. *Egeria's Travels to the Holy Land.* Warminster: Aris & Phillips, 1981.

———. *Jerusalem Pilgrims Before the Crusades.* Warminster: Aris & Phillips, 1977.

———. "Jewish Holy Places and the Origins of Christian Pilgrimage." In Ousterhout, *Blessings of Pilgrimage* (q.v.), 41–53.

Williams, Megan Hale. "Jerome's Biblical Criticism and the Making of Christian Scholarship." Ph.D. diss., Princeton University, 2002.

Williams, Patrick, and Laura Chrisman, eds. *Colonial Discourse and Post-Colonial Theory: A Reader.* New York: Columbia University Press, 1994.

Wilson, S. G. *Related Strangers: Jews and Christians, 70–170 C.E.* Minneapolis, Minn.: Fortress Press, 1995.

Winkelmann, F. *Euseb von Kaisareia: Der Vater der Kirchengeschichte.* Biographien zur Kirchengeschichte. Berlin: Verlags-Anstalt Union, 1991.

Wolfe, Patrick. "History and Imperialism: A Century of Theory, from Marx to Postcolonialism." *American Historical Review* 102 (1997): 388–420.

Wolska, Wanda. *La Topographie Chrétienne de Cosmas Indicopleustès: Théologie et science au VIe siècle.* Etudes Byzantines 3. Paris: Presses Universitaires, 1962.

Woolf, Greg. "Becoming Roman, Staying Greek: Culture, Identity, and the Civilizing Process in the Roman East." *Proceedings of the Cambridge Philological Society* 40 (1994): 116–43.

Wright, John. "Origen in the Scholar's Den: A Rationale for the Hexapla." In Kannengeisser and Petersen, *Origen of Alexandria* (q.v.), 48–62.

Yarnold, Edward. *Cyril of Jerusalem.* The Early Church Fathers. London: Routledge, 2000.

Young, Frances M. "Did Epiphanius Know What He Meant by 'Heresy'?" *Studia Patristica* 17, no. 1 (1982): 199–205.

Young, Robert. *Colonial Desire: Hybridity in Theory, Culture, and Race.* London: Routledge, 1995.

———. *Postcolonialism: An Historical Introduction.* London: Blackwell, 2001.

———. *White Mythologies: Writing History and the West.* London: Routledge, 1990.

Zanker, Paul. *The Power of Images in the Age of Augustus.* Tr. Alan Shapiro. Jerome Lectures 16. Ann Arbor: University of Michigan Press, 1988.

Index